Copyright © 2012 by William B. Lee

ISBN-13: 978-1-60427-062-4

Printed and bound in the U.S.A. Printed on acid-free paper.

10 9 8 7 6 5 4 3 2 1

Library of Congress Cataloging-in-Publication Data

Lee, William B., 1941-
    Creating entrepreneurial supply chains : a guide for innovation and growth
/ by William B. Lee.
        p. cm.
    Includes bibliographical references and index.
    ISBN 978-1-60427-062-4 (hbk. : alk. paper)
    1. Business logistics. 2. Entrepreneurship. I. Title.
    HD38.5.L4373 2012
    658.7—dc23

2011043690

Direct all inquiries to J. Ross Publishing, Inc., 5765 N. Andrews Way, Fort Lauderdale, FL 33309.

Phone: (954) 727-9333
Fax: (561) 892-0700
Web: www.jrosspub.com

Creating Entrepreneurial Supply Chains

A Guide for Innovation and Growth

William B. Lee, Ph.D.

Dedication

I am most richly blessed with a wonderful family to whom I dedicate this book:
Jane, my lovely and gracious wife;
My daughter, Karen, son-in-law, Ric, and grandsons, Barclay and Philip;
My son, Richard, and granddaughter, Abigail;
I love you all, and thank you for being such a great family.

—W. B. Lee

TABLE OF CONTENTS

FOREWORD

The entrepreneurial supply chain is a new concept. I have not seen anyone else write on the subject, and yet it is a powerful idea whose time has come. The notion that the elements of supply chains—from suppliers' suppliers to customers' customers—can be used in an entrepreneurial manner is a commanding thought. Dr. Lee is one of the most knowledgeable, innovative, and eloquent individuals in the field of operations and supply chain management. In a word, "He knows his stuff!"

Most people think of entrepreneurship in terms of start-up businesses, but Dr. Lee takes the thought much further into large companies with what has become known as "corporate entrepreneurship." He shows how sizeable companies such as Cisco, 3M, CEMEX, Corning, Sysco, and others have developed entrepreneurial supply chains.

A unique feature of this book is the use of case studies. As a university professor, I understand the value of cases as vehicles for learning, and there is a case at the end of each chapter featuring Baker Hughes, an actual $20+B (sales) company. These cases supplement Bill's own powerful ideas in a particularly effective manner.

This book explores entrepreneurial supply chains from a variety of angles. First, supply chains and entrepreneurship are introduced and weaved together. He shows why and how this makes sense. Next, he discusses the *why* of entrepreneurial supply chains, including the practical and legal forms of entrepreneurial supply chains.

Then, how and where opportunities are likely to appear, and how to recognize them, are discussed. The author considers the entire end-to-end supply chains (from suppliers' suppliers to customers' customers) in the search of opportunities and needs for entrepreneurial activities.

His discussion of entrepreneurial supply chain risks is one of the most powerful chapters in the book, which could easily apply to almost any enterprise. Due diligence and the business planning process is one way that he proposes to mitigate the risks of the ventures, and the how-to-do-it discussion is especially poignant for going forward with entrepreneurial supply chain undertakings.

The final chapter deals with "Reaping the Payoff," and shows how companies gain the benefits of their efforts. There is a case study of Sysco, the large food-service distribution company, to illustrate these ideas.

Finally, Appendix A deals with "Visioning Entrepreneurial Supply Chains." It is a how-to-do-it guide to generating a vision of the venture. Appendix B presents a sample business plan for an entrepreneurial supply chain enterprise in a unique way. He presents a funeral home as an entrepreneurial supply chain endeavor, something most of us likely have not thought about. Appendix C shows how to build education and training programs for entrepreneurial supply chains. Appendix D contains a glossary of terms, including terms for entrepreneurism, project management, and supply chains.

I sincerely recommend this book from a real leader in the fields of operations and supply chain management.

F. Robert Jacobs, PhD
Chase Faculty Fellow and Professor of Operations and
Supply Chain Management
Kelley School of Business
Indiana University

PREFACE

The term, *entrepreneurial supply chains*, is not in common use today. That is unfortunate, because it has a powerful meaning that can help most companies increase both innovation and growth in their businesses. The Preface opens with some useful definitions.

Entrepreneur, entrepreneurial. The terms, *entrepreneur* and *entrepreneurial*, are listed in most dictionaries. The definitions generally refer to an individual or small group of individuals who begin a business in a start-up mode. These individuals begin with innovative ideas which they believe hold the opportunity for profit and growth. They organize their resources, obtain other resources, and begin the venture. The entrepreneurs and their investors bear the risks and potential profit of the business enterprise. One dictionary[1] provides the following definition.

> *Entrepreneur. n. A person who undertakes an enterprise or business with the chance of profit or loss.*

One of the reasons that start-ups are so important is that *every large company today originally began as a start-up enterprise.* One of the classic stories of entrepreneurship is of HP (Hewlett-Packard) which was started by Stanford University classmates, Bill Hewlett and Dave Packard, in a one-car garage in Palo Alto, CA. Today, HP claims to be the world's largest information technology company with more than 300,000 employees, 2010 net revenues of $126 billion (up 10% from 2009), and 2010 GAAP operating profit of $11.5 billion (up 13% from 2009). This 2010 performance was in spite of being in the middle of one of the world's worst recessions. Bill and Dave were entrepreneurs in the true sense of the word, and their company has carried on the tradition. Entrepreneurship usually refers to start-up enterprises, but that need not always be the case.

There is more to entrepreneurship than just start-ups. Also in use are the terms, *intrapreneur* and *corporate entrepreneurism*. These terms refer to entrepreneurial activity that takes place within a larger company. Some companies are famous for their corporate entrepreneurism—case studies of companies such as Baker Hughes, 3M, and CEMEX are cited throughout the book, and key points are drawn from the cases.

Also included in the definitions are undertakings such as partnerships, joint ventures, alliances, and other organizational forms of entrepreneurial ventures.

All the way through the book, *entrepreneur* and *entrepreneurial* are used as all-inclusive terms.

Innovation.   This word is used in the book's subtitle because it is intimately linked with the concept of entrepreneurship. Entrepreneurial innovation means that new methods, ideas, processes, and products are brought into play in creative, imaginative, and novel ways to generate new value for the firm. The authors of one of the best books on innovation[2] define it as follows.

> *Innovation is the process of creating and delivering new customer value in the marketplace.*

Supply Chain.   The supply chain typically deals with providing products as needed, perhaps in a replenishment mode for a manufactured product as needed by consumers.

> *The supply chain begins with customers' customers and ends with suppliers' suppliers. The supply chain represents the linkage among all elements of material flow, information flow, and cash flow. It also includes the management of all activities involved with planning, sourcing, making, delivery, and returning of products. Supply chains occur in different types of companies, such as manufacturing, distribution, retail, energy, and even banks and insurance companies. Any organization that has a flow of material or products, information, cash, and so forth, can qualify as a supply chain organization.*

An Aside: I have a friend who is director of supply chain management for a unit of a state government that is responsible for incarceration of youthful offenders. He talks about purchasing, resupplying, and maintaining "everything from vehicles to toilet paper." Even an organization that one would not normally think of as having a supply chain has a very extensive one with annual spend of many millions of dollars.

Please see the website of the Supply Chain Council in which they use *plan, source, make, deliver*, and *return* as the five key elements in their SCOR® (Supply Chain Operations Reference) model. More will be said on SCOR later in the book. SCOR provides an influential framework for understanding of supply chains and, by extension, of *entrepreneurial* supply chains.

Many people consider the term *supply chain* to be a misnomer for essentially two reasons. First, the term *supply* many times causes people to think automatically of suppliers and hence to think only of one side of the linkage—the supply side. Some have proposed the term *demand chain* to illustrate the primacy of the demand (or customer) linkages. Others have proposed the term *value chain* to emphasize the flow of value in the linkages. Although the term *supply chain* is too restrictive, it nevertheless is the accepted terminology, and this book continues with it while at the same time acknowledging its limitations.

Second, the term *chain* many times causes people to think automatically of a linear series of links in the relationships. The saying, "A chain is only as strong as its weakest link," is commonly used. However, the problem with the word *chain* is that it implies a one-to-one linear relationship, when the real metaphor is more like a web with multiple-to-multiple relationships along the supply chain. Again, while the word, chain, is too restrictive, it will continue to be used because it is accepted practice.

Entrepreneurial Supply Chains. Crafting a definition is not easy, because *entrepreneurial supply chains* require mind-set shifts. The traditional view of supply chains is focused mainly on cost, quality, and delivery. Anyone who looks at the metrics that are used to judge typical supply chain operations can see these three as dominant. However, consider an entrepreneurial supply chain as being concerned mainly with innovation and growth *in addition to* cost, quality, and delivery. Simply put, cost, quality, and delivery are necessary but not sufficient success factors for entrepreneurial supply chains.

Please recognize, again, that there are various organizational forms of entrepreneurial supply chains. This includes start-ups, corporate entrepreneurship, alliances, joint ventures, partnerships, and others. The definition for this book includes all these forms of ventures.

> *An entrepreneurial supply chain connects customers' customers with suppliers' suppliers and incorporates innovative entrepreneurial activities. Entrepreneurial activities should recognize and respond to opportunities and needs that appear from time to time along the supply chains and that call for entrepreneurial responses.*

Entrepreneurial supply chains reach out from the business in both directions—to both suppliers and customers. Entrepreneurial and innovative ideas thus can enhance the growth objectives of natural partners in the supply chains.

Where This Is Going

Many supply chains need a major transformation to make them more entrepreneurial. This book recognizes the increased need for entrepreneurship within many companies, focusing on unexplored opportunities for growth and innovation. Entrepreneurial and innovative ideas can enhance the growth objectives of natural partners in the supply chains. This book shows how entrepreneurial supply chains can enhance the value of the business regardless of its form.

Exploring why and how entrepreneurial supply chains drive innovation and growth takes readers through the entire process of opportunity identification, due diligence, writing the business plan, managing risks, integrating the entrepreneurial supply chain venture, and reaping the payoff. Appendices include visioning the entrepreneurial supply chain, a sample business plan, a sample education and training plan, and a glossary of terms.

This book presents a "how to do it" process to create entrepreneurial supply chains, including:

- How to understand what's wrong with the existing situation prior to embarking on an entrepreneurial supply chain venture. What is the venture intended to accomplish?
- How to develop a five- to ten-year vision of what entrepreneurial supply chains mean to the organization. What would the benefits be?
- How to work out a going-forward plan to create entrepreneurial supply chains. What steps need to be accomplished, in what sequence, when, and by whom?
- How to assess the risks of the venture. What can stop or delay success?
- How to perform due diligence and develop the business plan. What are the critical issues requiring an investigation of the proposed venture prior to moving ahead, and what business arrangements are necessary to ensure success?

Embedded in the book is relevant research from numerous sources, with significant sources referenced at the end of each chapter. Some of the subjects cited are:

- Entrepreneurship, corporate entrepreneurship, intrapreneurship, innovation, and supply chains.
- Identifying high-potential opportunities.
- Managing risk in entrepreneurial ventures.
- Keys to successful relationships between customers and suppliers throughout the supply chains.
- Managing change so as to improve the venture's chances of success.

Case studies of real companies provide a significant feature of the book. A continuing case study on Baker Hughes Incorporated provides a thread throughout all chapters in sections identified as "How Baker Hughes Does It." Baker Hughes is a large global equipment and services provider to the oil and gas industry that is in the process of remaking its supply chains. At the end of each chapter, these sections explain how Baker Hughes accomplished the subject of the chapter.

Each chapter also includes at least one summary of a business school case study that provides an opportunity for further study and reflection. These case studies include Tennant Company, Taylor Fresh Foods, Corning Incorporated, Cisco Systems, Valhalla Partners, 3M Corporation, Sysco Corporation, Service Corporation International, and Goldman Sachs. The different cases are intended to make different learning points. A few companies are not generally considered as companies with supply chains. For example, Goldman Sachs is important for its people-development approaches, and the Valhalla Partners case is important because of its unique approach to due diligence.

Differentiation from Other Books on Supply Chains

There are several noteworthy approaches that strongly differentiate this book from others in the field.

- *Direct links of supply chains to entrepreneurship are provided.* In other books supply chains are not tied to entrepreneurship as strongly as in this book in spite of the importance of the subject. Supply chain personnel are in a unique position to identify needs and opportunities for entrepreneurial ventures, ranging from customers' customers to suppliers' suppliers. Writings on supply chains generally do not mention entrepreneurship, innovation, or growth—three key terms for this book.

- *Innovation is shown to be both an important prerequisite and a significant outcome of entrepreneurial supply chains.* Innovation is the process of inventing or introducing something new—a new idea, invention, or way of doing something. The creation and delivery of new customer value in the marketplace also provides the basis for a sustainable return to the entrepreneurial supply chain venture.

- *Growth is the natural outcome of innovative and entrepreneurial supply chains.* Companies are strongly focused on growth, and many people say that "not to grow is to die" when referring to the life cycles of companies. Surprisingly, however, entrepreneurship, innovation, and growth generally are not connected in the literature.

- *Real-world cases demonstrate the premises of the book.* Every chapter includes at least one case study that is relevant to the subject of the chapter.

- *One company, Baker Hughes Incorporated, is a continuous case study throughout the book.* Every chapter has a section called "How Baker Hughes Does It," which takes the subject of the chapter and ties it directly to this real company.

- *Learning objectives and a set of questions to assist the reader appear in every chapter.* These features assist readers and instructors who may be using the book in an academic course or an executive education program.

- *Extensive references are provided for further research and study.* References in each chapter are from mainstream sources that are easily accessible. Publications such as the *Harvard Business Review* and *MIT Sloan Management Review* are aimed at senior leaders and referenced frequently; academic sources such as the *Journal of Operations Management* are cited, too. In addition, practitioner-oriented publications such as the *Supply Chain Management Review* and a number of books are also cited. The case studies are all available from www.harvardbusinessonline.com.

- *An extensive glossary is provided in Appendix D.* The meanings of these terms are all available in other sources, but they are gathered here in one place for the reader's convenience.

What to Expect in the Chapters and Appendices

- *Chapter 1—Introduction to Supply Chains and Entrepreneurship* focuses on what entrepreneurial supply chains are and why they are important. It also includes background on entrepreneurship, entrepreneurial trends, and entrepreneurial thinking.

- *Chapter 2—Why "Entrepreneurial" Supply Chains* includes various practical and legal forms of entrepreneurial relationships, including alliances, consortia, dealers, joint ventures, and partnerships. It explains the different ways these can be used in a practical sense.

- *Chapter 3—Utilizing Customers and Suppliers as Sources of Ideas and Opportunities* shows that identifying entrepreneurial opportunities can be a difficult process. Industry analyses can be used to frame the opportunity and find a way to delve deeply into multilevel supply chains for ideas and opportunities.

- *Chapter 4—How We Know We Have Opportunities* focuses on an analytical process to identify a set of entrepreneurial opportunities.

- *Chapter 5—Managing the Risks of Entrepreneurial Supply Chains* shows that the risks of entrepreneurial ventures can be significant, from macro to micro. Various risk-analysis, risk-mitigation, and risk-management approaches are applicable to entrepreneurial supply chains.

- *Chapter 6—Due Diligence and the Business Plan* takes the reader through the process of due diligence regardless of the type of entrepreneurial supply chain venture under consideration.

- *Chapter 7—Implementing Entrepreneurial Supply Chains* develops a formal change management program. Turning a non-entrepreneurial company into an entrepreneurial one can be a major exercise in managing large-scale change. This chapter presents the essence of such a program.

- *Chapter 8—Reaping the Payoff* includes important topics such as reaping the payoff through continuous improvement, closed or open innovation, and effective entrepreneurial supply chain strategy. An interesting history of management thought is included with a synopsis of the entrepreneurial career of Commodore Cornelius Vanderbilt, the richest man in the world during his lifetime and a forerunner of entrepreneurial supply chains.

- *Appendix A—Visioning Entrepreneurial Supply Chains* shows how to begin to communicate a clear vision for entrepreneurial supply chains. An outline with ideas for a retreat to develop a vision for entrepreneurial supply chains is provided.

- *Appendix B—Sample Business Plan for an Entrepreneurial Supply Chain Opportunity* presents a sample business plan for a start-up entrepreneurial opportunity as a spin-off from a larger company.

- *Appendix C—Sample Education and Training Programs for Entrepreneurial Supply Chains* explains the concept of an entrepreneurial supply chain academy along with action learning projects.
- *Appendix D—Glossary* provides definitions for key terms that are useful with entrepreneurial supply chains.

References

1. The Oxford American Dictionary and Thesaurus with Language Guide. 2003. Oxford University Press, New York and Oxford.
2. Carlson, Curtis R. and William W. Wilmot. 2006. *Innovation: The Five Disciplines for Creating What Customers Want*, Crown Business, New York. p. 6.

ACKNOWLEDGMENTS

First and foremost, in my acknowledgments for this book, I have learned a great deal from my wife, Jane. She has been a wonderful supporter, friend, and companion for over 45 years.

I also acknowledge Al Napier, my friend of many years, who has been an inspiration for this book. Both Al and his wife, Liz, are good friends of Jane and me. He is a Professor of Management and Entrepreneurship in the Jesse H. Jones Graduate School of Business at Rice University, Houston, TX. Al and I collaborated on some early work that led to this book, but he had more important things to do than write a book with me! I am grateful for his insight. He contributed some substantial ideas for Chapter 5 and Appendix B. I have reproduced some of those with his permission.

Another acknowledgment goes to Mike Katzorke, also a friend of many years and coauthor of the book *Leading Effective Supply Chain Transformations: A Guide to Sustainable World-Class Capability and Results* (J. Ross Publishing, 2010). Mike hired me as a supply chain consultant when he was at AlliedSignal, again after he moved to Cessna Aircraft, and again at Smiths Aerospace. In addition to having a client/consultant relationship over many years, we have become good friends as have our wives, Jane and Julie. I am grateful for the friendship of Mike and Julie.

One feature of this book is the continuing case study on Baker Hughes, a large, well-respected equipment and services supplier to the oil and gas industry. I especially appreciate the support of Gary Flaharty, Vice President of Investor Relations, and Art Soucy, Vice President of Supply Chain. I have known Gary for many years, so I called him before starting the book to ask about doing an extensive case study. Gary checked it out within the company, obtained permission, and introduced me to Art, who was my guide and primary source of information. Also involved in these discussions were Maria Claudia Borras, David Emerson, Jan Kees van Gaalen, Dale Kunneman, Scott Schmidt, Mike Sumruld, and Jim Vounassis. I especially appreciate Katy Gonzales, Art's very capable administrative assistant, who kept those meetings straight for me and got me to where I was supposed to be at the time I was supposed to be there. Katy, you are terrific! Thank you to everyone at Baker Hughes who helped with this book.

I have many other people to acknowledge, but not enough space to do so except to say to all readers—"Thank you very much, I am grateful!"

ABOUT THE AUTHOR

 **William (Bill) B. Lee,** PhD, was Professor of Management Practice for a number of years in the Jesse H. Jones Graduate School of Business at Rice University in Houston, TX. Dr. Lee also held positions at Rice as Associate Dean of Executive Education and Director of Energy Programs. He spent 10 years on the faculty of the College of Business Administration at the University of Houston, and was chair of the Department of Systems and Operations Management while there.

Dr. Lee earned a PhD in Business Administration from the University of North Carolina at Chapel Hill, an MBA from Rollins College, and a BSEE from Vanderbilt University. He has had careers in academia and industry, consulting, and teaching in over 50 countries. In the years prior to preparing this publication, he consulted and taught in various venues in the United States, Germany, India, China, and Saudi Arabia. He was a keynote speaker at the Shanghai Economic Forum in 2008.

Dr. Lee is the author of over 75 books, articles, and academic presentations. His research and teaching interests are in global supply chain management, primarily for large, complex companies. He coauthored a book entitled *Leading Effective Supply Chain Transformations: A Guide to Sustainable World-Class Capability and Results* with Michael R. Katzorke (J. Ross Publishing, 2010), and is an active educator, consultant, and author.

He and his wife, Jane, live and work in Houston and on Galveston Island, Texas. He can be contacted at wbleephd@ymail.com.

Web
Added
Value™

This book has free material available for download from the
Web Added Value™ resource center at **www.jrosspub.com**

At J. Ross Publishing we are committed to providing today's professional with practical, hands-on tools that enhance the learning experience and give readers an opportunity to apply what they have learned. That is why we offer free ancillary materials available for download on this book and all participating Web Added Value™ publications. These online resources may include interactive versions of material that appears in the book or supplemental templates, worksheets, models, plans, case studies, proposals, spreadsheets and assessment tools, among other things. Whenever you see the WAV™ symbol in any of our publications it means bonus materials accompany the book and are available from the Web Added Value™ Download Resource Center at www.jrosspub.com.

Downloads for *Creating Entrepreneurial Supply Chains: A Guide for Innovation and Growth* consist of answers to end-of-chapter questions and the following presentations for use in educational courses:

- Building Blocks for Excellence in Entrepreneurial Supply Chains
- Entrepreneurial Supply Chains Executive Workshop
- Strategic Issues for Entrepreneurial Supply Chains

CHAPTER 1

INTRODUCTION TO SUPPLY CHAINS AND ENTREPRENEURSHIP

LEARNING OBJECTIVES

1. Be able to articulate a broad understanding of supply chains and supply chain management.
2. Understand why companies have multiple supply chains, a supply network, or a value web, and why different expressions are used with slightly different meanings.
3. Comprehend the meaning of entrepreneurial supply chains and why they are useful for companies.
4. Understand how you know when you are thinking entrepreneurially, and what to do with entrepreneurial thinking when you get it.

"Investment must be rational. If you can't understand it, don't do it."
—Warren Buffett

"Be who you are and say what you mean.
Those who matter don't mind, and those who mind don't matter."
—Dr. Seuss

Warren Buffett's quote is one of the best ones on investing, and by extension, on entrepreneurship. Simply put, entrepreneurial supply chain activities *must make sense*. If we cannot understand why we're considering an entrepreneurial venture, why we're doing something, or how we can explain it, then we should not do it. It's as simple as that.

> **KEY IDEA**
>
> If the U.S. Postal Service had originally been more entrepreneurial and innovative, competitors FedEx, UPS, and other delivery services may never have come into existence.

Dr. Seuss's quote is also relevant. Some who read the book will disagree with some of what the author has to say. But, this book can be viewed as an opportunity to hear someone else's viewpoint.

Supply chains and supply networks, demand chains and demand networks, value chains and value networks, and the list goes on. This list goes on and on, too: entrepreneurs, entrepreneurship, intrapreneuring, corporate entrepreneurship, entrepreneurial, etc. So it goes with terms and terminology about where we are and where we are going. Can terminology help to point the way?

Not to clog this book with buzzwords, but:

> *At the end of the day, it's important to achieve a win-win solution. Be sure to think outside the box to demonstrate thought leadership. And harness key learning to change the game on that mission-critical project.*[1]

Huh?

This book will be clear and straightforward, trying not to get hung up on terminology, nor using too many clichés or buzzwords.

This is not a book on "what supply chains are" or "how to manage supply chains." It also is not a book on "entrepreneurship." There are enough books on those subjects already. However, there appears to be no other book dedicated to the subject of *entrepreneurial supply chains.* That's a pity, except that means there is a huge need for this one!

This book recognizes the state of many companies' supply chains that are in dire need of transformation to make them more entrepreneurial and more innovative. The book recognizes the lack of entrepreneurship within too many companies. It focuses on supply chains that present unexplored opportunities for competitive advantage. It also discusses how supply chains can be used to enable and encourage entrepreneurial activity. The book's subtitle, *A Guide to Innovation and Growth*, tells almost as much as the main title: companies' entrepreneurial supply chains can drive innovation and growth, and vice-versa.

Why do companies find it so hard to grow? If you want some evidence, just go to *Fortune* magazine's annual list of the world's largest companies. Compare the latest list with the list of 20 years ago—they're not the same! Many companies that were on the list then are not on the list now, or they are much further down the list. New companies have arisen. Why? Well, hopefully you can find some of the answers in this book as you struggle with supply chain issues of entrepreneurship, innovation, and growth.

A LITTLE HISTORY OF MANAGEMENT THOUGHT

So, where did supply chain management come from, and how did it get to its present state? Supply chain management has been around for millennia, but not by that name, of course. Let's examine a little bit of history as a way of setting the stage for the present.

Many of today's ideas about supply chains can be traced back to the ancient Egyptians and the pyramids. The pyramids were massive supply chain undertakings, especially in the era of 3000–2000 B.C. Quarrying large pieces of stone, shaping the stone, transporting it to the location of the pyramid, constructing the pyramid, and so forth, took enormous skill and massive resources. The best known Egyptian pyramids are those found at Giza, on the outskirts of Cairo. Several of the Giza pyramids are counted among the largest structures ever built. The great pyramid of Cheops, for example, covers 13 acres, contains about 2,300,000 stone blocks, and is estimated to have taken over 100,000 men more than 20 years to construct[2]—quite a supply chain project.

An Aside: Claude George was a professor in the Business School of the University of North Carolina at Chapel Hill. Professor George taught a required course in this subject for doctoral students, which I feel was one of the most valuable courses I ever took. Serious students of management have a lot to learn about supply chain management by studying its history.

According to Mark Lehner (2010),[2] the earliest known Egyptian pyramid is the Pyramid of Djoser, which was built during the third dynasty, about 2600–2500 B.C. This pyramid and its surrounding complex were designed by the architect Imhotep, and generally are considered to be the world's oldest monumental structures constructed of dressed masonry. According to Professor Claude George (1968),[3] the ancient Egyptians also added to our knowledge of supply chains in other ways. Circa 4000 B.C., they recognized the need for planning, organizing, and controlling. Around 2600 B.C., they developed the concept of decentralization in organizations. The concept of centralized organizations was developed about 1000 years later.

A whole book on the history of supply chains could follow, but you get the point. Supply chains have been around for awhile! Instead, this chapter will provide an introduction and an overview of supply chains and entrepreneurship.

SUPPLY CHAINS AND SUPPLY CHAIN MANAGEMENT EXPLAINED?

What are supply chains, and what is supply chain management? The Council of Supply Chain Management Professionals (CSCMP)[4] defines *supply chain management* as follows:

> *Supply chain management encompasses the planning and management of all activities involved in sourcing and procurement, conversion, logistics and all management activities. Importantly, it also includes coordination and collaboration with channel partners, which can be suppliers, intermediaries, third party service providers, and customers.*

KEY IDEA
How can rice production in India affect wheat output in the U.S., the shipping industry in Norway, and rubber production in South America? Source: T. Rowe Price television ads in late 2010 and early 2011, discussing global supply chains as investment opportunities.

In essence, supply chain management (SCM) integrates supply and demand within and across organizations. SCM is an integrating function with primary responsibility for linking major business functions and business processes within and across companies into a cohesive and high-performing business model. It includes all of the product flow activities including suppliers and suppliers' suppliers, manufacturing operations, and distribution to customers and customers' customers—from the original source of raw materials to the ultimate user as well as return/recycle of the product. It drives coordination of processes and activities with and across marketing, sales, product design, finance, information technology, and other functional activities.

You already know a lot about supply chain management if you are reading this book, and some familiar material is included intentionally. The simple reason to use a very broad description of supply chain management is not to get hung up on narrow definitions about what's in and what's not in the supply chain.

The Value Chain

Today's notions of supply chains are derived at least in part from Michael Porter's[5] concept of the *value chain*. An adaptation of his generic value chain is shown in Figure 1.1. Porter (1985) defines the value chain as follows:

> *A value chain is a collection of activities performed to design, produce, and market, deliver, and support its product [which] can be represented using a value chain. . . . A firm's value chain . . . [is] a reflection of its history, its strategy . . . and the underlying economics of the activities themselves.*

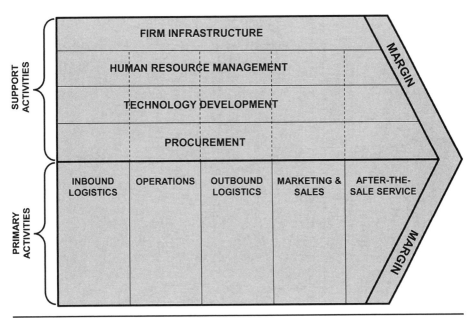

Figure 1.1   The Generic Value Chain. Adapted from: Porter, Michael E., *Competitive Advantage: Creating and Sustaining Superior Performance*, The Free Press, 1985.

Porter distinguishes the firm value chain, business unit value chain, channel value chain, buyer value chain, and supplier value chain, as shown in Figure 1.2. Later, his structure will lead us into how an entrepreneurial supply chain works.

Porter's framework is designed primarily for established companies and not generally for start-up entrepreneurial companies. However, recognize that even the smallest start-ups will have to perform most or all of the activities described, even though they typically will not have an organizational structure for them.

Porter focuses on the business unit level of the firm and distinguishes between primary activities and support activities. The five *primary activities* include those which are generally attributed to companies with products: inbound logistics, operations, outbound logistics, marketing and sales, and after-the-sale service. This is the product life cycle, which is easy for most people to visualize. It is generally thought of applying to manufacturing companies, but it also could apply to wholesale, distribution, or retail firms.

Each primary activity can be disaggregated into a number of discrete entities that may be unique to the firm or its industry. Clearly, every company configures

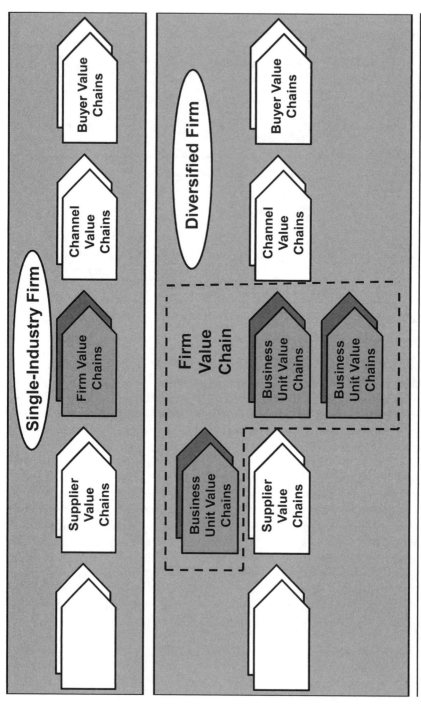

Figure 1.2 The Value System. Adapted from: Porter, Michael E., *Competitive Advantage: Creating and Sustaining Superior Performance*, The Free Press, 1985.

its activities differently. Each primary activity typically presents opportunities for entrepreneurial supply chain ventures, for example:

- *Inbound logistics* involves obtaining the product inputs from suppliers and the physical process of getting them from the supplier to where the operation is being conducted. Some companies obtain their inputs from a relatively few suppliers, while others use many suppliers. Some companies use trucking for their inbound transportation, while others use rail or ocean freight. Some companies use only domestic suppliers, while others use global sourcing. They are all different.
- *Operations* usually are defined as conversions. These could be physical conversions in the case of manufacturing companies or conversions of time and/or location in the case of distribution companies. Some companies have product designs that use few components, while others use many components. Some companies outsource most of their manufacturing, while others outsource little, if any. Some companies use a few large facilities, while others use more and smaller facilities. Some companies manufacture globally, while others keep their operations domestic. Again, they are all different.
- *Outbound logistics* are associated with physically moving the products from the operations locations to the customers' locations. This could include physically assembling a customer's order, scheduling a carrier, and offloading the products at the customer's location. Some companies ship directly from manufacturing plants to customers, while others use distribution centers to store inventory and get it closer to the customers. Some companies ship via air freight, while others use trucking. Some companies use third-party logistics providers, while others operate their own trucking fleets. Some companies, such as IKEA, have their customers physically take the products home from the retail store and even have them assemble the products. They are all different.
- *Marketing and Sales* usually include developing and implementing a strategy for marketing and selling the products along with the marketing activities of setting the price, promoting the product, packaging and branding, forecasting sales in different target markets, actually selling the product, and so forth. Some companies have their own sales force, while others use manufacturers' representatives that sell their products as well as products of other companies. Some companies aggressively use trade shows to exhibit their products, while others promote their products over the Internet. They are all different.
- *Service* is after-the-sale support of the product, and is considered part of the supply chains. This could include providing maintenance, repair, and operations (MRO) support, along with training of customers' personnel and providing a reliable service parts supply. In fact, the service parts

supply chain is an important and distinct activity in many companies. For example, this is a big deal in aircraft manufacturers such as Cessna, Lear, and Boeing. An aircraft on the ground (AOG) is an occasion for "pulling out all the stops" to get service parts and maintenance personnel to repair the aircraft as correctly and quickly as possible. They recognize that AOGs can be very costly to their customers, keeping customers' airplanes up and running is a very high priority for them. Some companies outsource service while others provide their own service and see it as an important component of their business. Service is different among industries and companies.

An Aside: Many companies are missing a big entrepreneurial supply chain bet by not focusing on after-the-sale service. This can be a very profitable niche. Good service can provide a strong competitive advantage for a company that does it well. Consider, for example, manufacturers of home appliances such as dishwashers, washing machines, clothes dryers, and so forth. Have you ever tried to get one repaired? First, you certainly cannot take it into a repair place. Second, getting someone to commit to come to your home within a reasonable time is sometimes impossible, depending on where you live. ("You'll be here in two weeks. Well, how do I dry my clothes in the meantime?") Third, even when they promise to come on a given day, they will not say they will arrive at a certain time. ("You'll be here sometime between 8:00 and 1:00 maybe? Do I have to take a day off from work just to stay home and wait for you? Is your time more valuable than mine—I am the customer, you know.") Fourth, "What do you mean you don't have the part in your truck? Do I have to go through this all over again so that you can come back later?" And on and on. It should not be too hard to manage this, should it?

Porter also describes four *support activities*: firm infrastructure, human resource management, technology development, and procurement. These frequently are described as *overhead activities*. Unfortunately, the word "overhead" has negative connotations as something that weighs down the organization, is bureaucratic, or costs too much. Porter prefers (as does your author) using the term "support activities" to imply activities that keep the organization running effectively and efficiently.

Porter points out that support activities can be a powerful source of competitive advantage. In a large company such as Wal-Mart, for example, information technology (IT) is critical to success. IT captures store-level, point-of-sale data on products, customers, purchases, and so forth, down to the time of day at which purchases are made. Thus, they can provide Procter & Gamble (P&G) with data on how many boxes of Pampers are sold in any store at particular times and days of the week. For P&G, this is very important data for their marketing and product resupply purposes.

An Aside: In Sam Walton's autobiography,[6] he discussed information technology and distribution. The book was published in 1992, but the basic ideas are valid today, albeit whether or not the numbers are current. He said, "I think it's fair to say that our distribution system is the envy of everyone in our industry . . . the cost savings alone would make the investment worthwhile. Our costs run less than 3 percent to ship goods to our stores, while it probably costs our competitors between 4½ to 5 percent . . ."

Interestingly, Walton also said that they would never sell anything that was not "made in America." Wow! They have really gotten away from that one, haven't they? In any case, Walton's autobiography has a lot of worthwhile ideas and is a good read.

As with primary activities, Porter disaggregates support activities into their value-adding components:

- *Firm infrastructure* is a catch-all category of activities such as general management, accounting and finance, government and regulatory affairs, and legal. Sometimes there may be confusion about which level in the corporate hierarchy an activity should be performed. For example, general accounting may be performed at the business unit or facility level, while other, specialized accounting (such as taxes) may be performed at the corporate level. Financing activities likely will take place at the corporate level, and it is fair to say that most legal work takes place at the corporate level; however, these certainly are not universal. Companies may all be different.
- *Human resource (HR) management* typically is responsible for recruiting, selecting, hiring, training and developing, evaluating, compensating, providing benefits, and other activities for all personnel, from front-line employees to the CEO and chair of the board. HR functions typically occur at different levels of the organization. The overall compensation plan and the benefits programs typically are handled at the corporate level. Whereas, recruiting, selecting, training, and so forth of first-line personnel are usually handled at the local level.
- *Technology development* usually is focused on both products and processes. Porter points out that the traditional research and development (R&D) is too narrow of a term for these purposes, although it would be included as an activity under the broader term of technology development. IT devel-

opment would be included in this category, although the actual operation of IT likely would be included as part of firm infrastructure.

- *Procurement* includes the acts of determining short- and long-term needs for purchased inputs, sourcing of suppliers, and development and management of suppliers. Actual operation of the purchasing function (placing purchase orders, receiving the inputs, and so forth) likely would be included in the operations portion of the firm's primary activities.

Porter implies that *everything* the firm does should be considered as either a primary or supporting activity. The labels are somewhat arbitrary and should be chosen to provide the best insights into the business. Furthermore, all linkages both internally and externally should be captured in the value chain definition.

A few thoughts about value chains are important to mention:

- Companies will define their value chain structure and activities in different ways, and the same function can be performed in different ways.
- Improving support activities frequently can make a significant difference in how the primary activities perform. For example, improving the sourcing activity within procurement likely will improve the finished product, either in cost or quality.
- The value chain really is a value web or a value network because of multiple linkages both inside and outside the firm.
- Most companies have multiple value chains. For example, different product lines likely will have different value chains, and the differences between product value chains and MRO value chains will likely be quite different as well.
- Opportunities for entrepreneurial supply chains abound within and among these activities.

Supply Chain Operations Reference (SCOR®) Model

The Supply Chain Council (www.supply-chain.org) was formed in the mid-1990s, building on Porter's value chain which was proposed about ten years earlier. The work of the Supply Chain Council is more pragmatic than Porter's work. It also has been implemented more widely; however, Porter's conceptualization provides the underlying theoretical basis for the supply chain operations reference (SCOR) model.

As shown in Figure 1.3, the SCOR model is adapted from the Supply Chain Council. It perhaps is the best known supply chain model. It is slightly modified in the figure to emphasize some points, but basically it consists of five elements: Plan, Source, Make, Deliver, and Return.

In this representation of the SCOR model, "Our Company" sits in the middle with its own Plan, Source, Make, Deliver, and Return activities. Upstream, "Our Suppliers" have the same five activities. Downstream, "Our Customers" also have

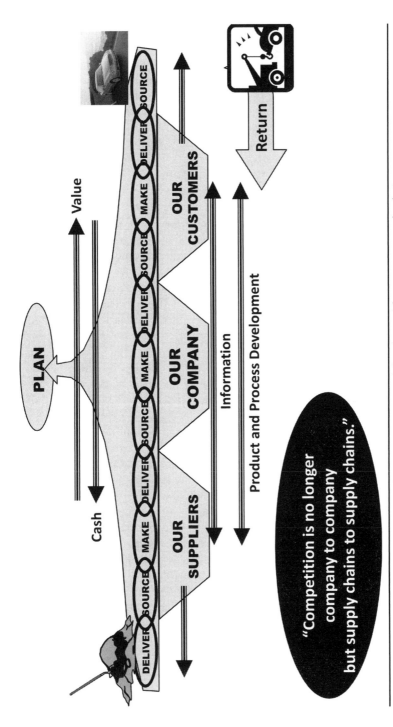

Figure 1.3 Supply Chain Operations Reference (SCOR) Model. Adapted from: www.supply-chain.org

the same five activities. We can extend these to whatever level of complexity is appropriate for any given situation.

The notation in the figure, "Competition is no longer company to company but supply chains to supply chains" is a relevant assertion that captures the essence of what is happening in today's competitive environment. Companies frequently produce products that are essentially identical to those from other companies. Companies also frequently sell to the same customers and purchase from the same suppliers. So, how can one company maintain its competitive advantage over others? One way is by how well they manage their supply chains. The SCOR model is one tool in this management process. Also, the SCOR model provides a framework for identifying entrepreneurial supply chain opportunities.

The Source, Make, and Deliver activities drive value from left to right across the supply chain, with the lowest level value being at the ultimate supplier (digging ore or coal out of the ground, drilling for oil and gas, or growing plants and animals). The highest level value is at the ultimate customer (the automobile in this representation).

As value increases from left to right in Figure 1.3, cash moves from right to left. Thus, the faster the product inventory moves through the supply chain, the faster the cash also moves. As will be seen, the speed of cash flow is an important supply chain performance metric.

The Plan is portrayed as encompassing the ultimate supplier (shown as digging ore out of the ground) to the ultimate customer with the product being recycled (shown as an automobile being towed away). Practically speaking, of course, it doesn't work exactly this way—the planning activity at best includes one or two supply chain levels from Our Company.

Information moves both ways through the supply chain and spans the entire chain. Demand information moves from right to left, and supply information moves from left to right. Cash flow information moves both ways, with invoices moving from left to right, and actual cash moving from right to left.

Product and process development encompasses the entire chain, usually within one company, but increasingly, these are collaborative relationships among adjacent entities in the chain. This will lead to a further discussion of entrepreneurial and innovative supply chains on a deeper level in subsequent chapters.

SCOR is a multi-level model that provides a structure and a language for communicating about supply chain issues and among supply chain players. Level 1, depicted in Figure 1.3, is the top level of the model. Level 2 can be configured based on a particular company's situation, such as the following.

1. *Plan*: Plan the supply chain, plan source, plan make, plan deliver, and plan return.
2. *Source*: Source stocked product, source make-to-order product, and source engineer-to-order product.

3. *Make*: Make make-to-stock product, make make-to-order product, and make engineer-to-order product.
4. *Deliver*: Deliver stocked product, deliver make-to-order product, and deliver engineer-to-order product.
5. *Source Return*: Source defective product to return, source MRO product to return, and source excess product to return.
6. *Deliver Return*: Deliver defective product to return, deliver MRO product to return, and deliver excess product to return.

Level 3 of the SCOR model defines the process flow, inputs and outputs, source of inputs, and destination of outputs for each Level 2 process element. For example, Deliver Stocked Product can be a Level 2 process element. Level 3 of the model will define how this element works. It defines the process flow to deliver stocked product, the inputs and outputs of the process, the source of the inputs, and the destinations of the outputs. Level 3 could include, for example, receive order, select carrier, route shipments, consolidate orders, receive product at customer's site, and so forth.

Level 4 of SCOR is where the actual implementation occurs for the supply chain management practices. Level 4 disaggregates Level 3 to the task level. For example, receive order disaggregates into tasks such as enter order, verify order, check credit, and so forth.

Level 5 of SCOR disaggregates Level 4 tasks into individual activities, such as accessing credit screens, reviewing outstanding credit, and contacting accounting.

Members of the Supply Chain Council gain access to the entire SCOR model: best practices, databases, case studies, and a myriad of other useful information for those interested in the study of supply chain management.

Multiple Supply Chains or Supply Networks or Value Webs?

Until now, a single supply chain has been discussed, but that's really not the way it is. Companies rarely have a single supply chain. People often have misconceptions and talk as if they have or want a single supply chain for their entrepreneurial venture. As such, there is often a tendency to think in terms of designing a single supply chain strategy, a single group of processes for that single supply chain, and perhaps a single supply chain organization. This type of thinking applies to incoming supply chains from suppliers as well as outgoing supply chains to customers. Just as a business often serves multiple markets with different key success factors and associated strategies, the business normally is supported by multiple supply chains requiring differing strategies and processes for optimal results. Sometimes this situation even calls for different supply chain organizations.

A company that sells final products to its customers also may sell service or MRO aftermarket parts, and perhaps, services. The company may have a supply chain organization for the finished product and another for its service or MRO aftermarket business. See Figure 1.4 for a view of multiple supply chains with aftermarkets. There are several opportunities for entrepreneurial ventures in examples in this figure.

Let's consider the original equipment manufacturing (OEM) business and the maintaining organization as the primary businesses in the supply chain. Think about everything else in the figure as a possible entrepreneurial venture: as a start-up enterprise, an acquisition, a corporate entrepreneurship project, a joint venture, an alliance, or any form of organization. (Organizational forms are discussed in Chapter 2.) Entrepreneurial opportunities can be present in OEM parts suppliers, parts suppliers, the OEM aftermarket business, the OEM parts distribution businesses, and the non-OEM aftermarket suppliers. Increasingly, companies may outsource their purchasing, inventory control, maintenance and other functions.

Entrepreneurial endeavors such as these can make sense when there are strong reasons for multiple supply chains. As an example, Marshall Fisher (1997)[7] published an outstanding article that addressed the question of multiple supply chains. Over the years, Fisher's article has been a thought provoker for many supply chain professionals and executives. Succinctly and effectively, Fisher made the case that the key success factors for a product or service determine the strategies and business processes that must drive the supply chains. Taking that thought to the next level, before supply chains are defined to support the products or

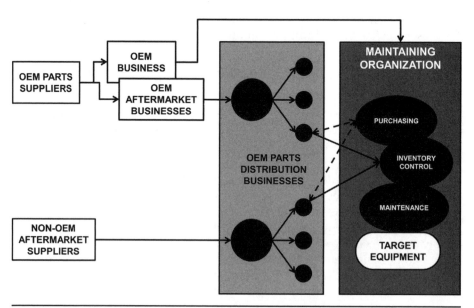

Figure 1.4   Multiple Supply Chains with Aftermarkets.

services, the *nature* of the demand in those products or services markets needs clear understanding by the designers.

Fisher suggested that, by their nature, products can be described as basic (or commodity or functional) products or innovative (or differentiated) products. Basic (functional) products are described as satisfying basic needs, high cost or price competitive, and therefore, requiring highly efficient supply chains to support them in that competitive environment. These products are sometimes referred to as "nuts, bolts, and screws." Additionally, the products from one manufacturer do not differ significantly from others.

Innovative products, on the other hand, typically have new and differentiated aspects. (For example, fast changing technology or fashion goods usually are considered to be innovative and/or differentiated products.) Innovative products require a high level of market responsiveness due to somewhat unpredictable demand and relatively short product life cycles. A high level of market responsiveness necessitates a highly flexible supply chain to support the needed responsiveness. Also, their shorter product life cycles need appropriate supply chains.

Fisher made the general point that different products and services require different supply chains. Although Fisher's points are extremely important, supply chains are more complicated than what he presented. What if a business has products and services with differing key success factors requiring differing supply chain process strategies to support them? Should these requirements be served from a single supply chain process?

In businesses that serve multiple markets, the potential for conflict in priorities is real, if not a certainty. A conflict in priorities can, of course, be highly detrimental to an enterprise's competitive success in serving each of its markets well. Associated long-term financial results also can be degraded. So, supply chain planning and design for successfully competing in multiple markets needs to be at least equaled by deployment execution. Simply, although the business wants elements of the enterprise to focus on specific markets, the business also needs these elements to work with the others to optimize overall business performance and success, not just optimizing individual pieces with a resulting sub-optimization of the entire enterprise. These multiple-market scenarios are approached with visioning (see Appendix A, Visioning Entrepreneurial Supply Chains) for multiple supply chains that address the problem of serving multiple businesses from the supply chain organization(s).

Why We Want an Entrepreneurial Supply Chain?

Entrepreneurial supply chains involve asking questions, such as: Why do we want supply chains to be entrepreneurial? What are our goals? What kinds of strategies do we need to put into place? Can we actually implement an entrepreneurial supply chain? What do we have when we get it? Does anyone really care?

In answer to these questions, growth and innovation may be two of our goals. We can say that we want a supply chain to contribute to the company's growth or to add to its innovation capability. Michael Treacy (2003),[8] who writes on corporate growth, asserts:

> . . . *big chunks of Corporate America, along with their counterparts in Asia and Europe, have fallen victim to no-growth paralysis—a broad, profound, systemic illness worsened by constant denial. It represents a serious threat to the health of the business community here and around the world.*

An Aside: In *Leading Effective Supply Chain Transformations* (J. Ross Publishing, 2010), that I coauthored with Michael Katzorke, the thesis was that supply chains are in dire need of transformation to make them more responsive to the marketplace. That book presented a process for transforming supply chains. This book takes those ideas further with a focus on entrepreneurship and innovation.

Treacy and others cite growth as key to business life or death, and a primary measure of business success. It is similar to saying "if we are not growing, we are dying." We even have sayings, such as the "no-growth economy," the "deindustrialization of America," and "an economy of hamburger flippers at McDonald's." Many of these phrases refer directly to supply chains—the loss of manufacturing facilities and jobs in America.

There are relationships here, in the correlation, if not causation, of phenomenon such as "deindustrialization" and the need for entrepreneurial supply chains. Additional steps along the road toward innovative and entrepreneurial supply chains are given in this book. Notice that there is some consistency, and supply chains are in dire need of transformation, both to improve their operations, and to become more innovative and entrepreneurial.

ENTREPRENEURSHIP AND CORPORATE ENTREPRENEURSHIP

While supply chains generally are not considered in the context of entrepreneurship, they present a unique opportunity to enhance the value of the business. Entrepreneurial and innovative ideas thus can be linked to natural partners in the total chain from the ultimate supplier to the ultimate customer.

Entrepreneurship and innovation are sometimes spoken in the same breadth. However, entrepreneurship is not innovation, and innovation is not entrepreneurship, although there is a strong connection between the terms.

Drucker (1985)[9] links the two terms. He says:

Innovation and entrepreneurship are discussed under three main headings: the Practice of Innovation; the Practice of Entrepreneurship; and Entrepreneurship Strategies. Each of these is an "aspect" of innovation and entrepreneurship rather than a stage.

> ### KEY IDEA
>
> *Innovation* can be defined as a new way of doing things. *Entrepreneurship* can be defined as the act of assembling resources, without regard to resources controlled, including innovations, finance, and business acumen in an effort to enhance economic value. This approach to entrepreneurship may result in new organizations or may be part of revitalizing mature organizations in response to a perceived opportunity or necessity.

The most obvious form of entrepreneurship is that of starting a new business; however, in recent years, the term has been extended to include other forms of entrepreneurial activity. For example, entrepreneurship within a firm or large organization may be referred to as intrapreneurship or corporate entrepreneurship. *Corporate entrepreneurship* can be defined as "the process by which teams within an established company conceive, foster, launch, and manage a new business that is distinct from the parent company but leverages the parent's assets, market position, capabilities, or other resources."[10]

Entrepreneurial ventures may include start-ups and various forms of corporate entrepreneurship. They may include many forms of ownership and organization: mergers and acquisitions, joint ventures, partnerships, coalitions, consortia, licensing, franchising, various forms of collaboration, and so forth. Also, entrepreneurship may include shrinking the organization through spin-offs or selling pieces of the business, which for some reason no longer fit the company's needs. Such spin-offs may significantly enhance the value of the enterprise, which of course is the objective of entrepreneurial ventures.

As an example of spin-offs adding value to the firm, John Deere, the world's largest maker of farm equipment and a major supplier of construction equipment, got through the 2008–2009 recession in good shape, in part because of spin-offs of weaker members of their entrepreneurial supply chain:

> *Deere's farm-equipment unit still comprises 90 percent of its sales. Even here, Deere's gotten tough, cancelling franchise contracts with smaller dealers . . . encouraging them to partner with higher-volume dealership chains.*[11]

This, of course, is an example of reconfiguring the supply chains for entrepreneurial purposes.

Where Did Ideas of Entrepreneurship Originate?

Joseph Schumpeter (1883–1950)[12] frequently is recognized as an intellectual father of entrepreneurship. To him, an entrepreneur is a person who is willing and able to convert a new "innovative" idea into a successful business, perhaps creating an *innovative*, successful business. He used the phrase "creative destruction" to define what happens when the old ways of doing business are destroyed and replaced by new ways.

For Schumpeter, innovation could result in new businesses and new industries. It also could result in new combinations of currently existing technologies. Schumpeter cites as an example the combination of a steam engine and buggy-making technologies to produce an innovation, the car, or as it was known at the time, the "horseless carriage." Of course, this obviously was a transformational innovation, but it did not require the development of a new technology, merely the application of existing technologies in a new manner. However, new technologies may have been required, perhaps, say, in the power train that linked the engine with the wheels.

Theodore Levitt (1960) published a well-known article[13] entitled "Marketing Myopia." He introduced the famous question, "What business are you really in?" and with it the claim that, had railroad executives seen themselves in the transportation business rather than the railroad business, they could have continued to grow. But they were not risk takers in the sense of looking for entrepreneurial opportunities that differed from traditional railroads.

To Drucker, entrepreneurship is about taking risk. The behavior of the entrepreneur reflects a person willing to put his or her career and financial security on the line to take risks in the name of an idea, spending both time and capital on an uncertain venture.

Another of the bases for entrepreneurship is the work of the 2009 Nobel Prize in Economics co-winner, Oliver Williamson, of the University of California at Berkeley. Some of his original work and theories were published in *The Economist* (October 17, 2009, 92). In that article, Williamson discussed transactions that would make them more or less entrepreneurial in nature. Thus transactions could be tested against decisions by companies to integrate parts of their supply chain. This theory has held up remarkably well in practice. One of Williamson's better known examples is that when an electricity generator can choose to buy from many nearby coal mines that produce coal of a particular quality, it tends to buy its coal on an open market. But if there is only one nearby mine that can be relied upon as a supplier, the electricity generator tends to own it. A transaction that could be done on the market moves into the firm, and the coal mine becomes an integrated segment of the company. This is an example of the essence of entrepreneurial supply chains.

Williamson's points can be said of companies' supply chains on both the supplier and customer sides. There is a history of discussing this as the "make versus buy" decisions, but that usually has been in terms of a rather simplistic situation without any real strategic view behind it. With the concept of *entrepreneurial supply chains*, a more complex set of ideas is introduced.

Innovation is an idea at the core of entrepreneurial supply chains; it is a new way of doing something. It may refer to incremental or radical changes in thinking, products, processes, and/or organizations. Something new generally must be substantially different to be innovative. In business, it is usually thought that the change must increase value of some sort: value to the business, customer, or organization. The goal of innovation is *positive change*, to make something better. Innovation leading to increased value is the fundamental source of increasing wealth in an economy and increasing value in a business. Entrepreneurial supply chains likely are very innovative.

The *entrepreneurial supply chain* idea is akin to vertical integration, but it is more than that. It is not just vertical integration—it has an entrepreneurial focus, which may be *horizontal* integration if that makes sense in specific contexts.

The idea also may include various forms of integration, from outright mergers and acquisitions to joint ventures and other cooperative and collaborative arrangements between two or more parties. Entrepreneurial supply chains do not have to involve ownership, although that is what many people think when they consider entrepreneurship. A collaborative arrangement (for technology, for example) can be just as entrepreneurial as an ownership arrangement, and can yield profitable benefits to all parties.

ENTREPRENEURIAL GIANTS IN THE BUSINESS ENVIRONMENT

Various notions of entrepreneurship have been around for many years. Harvard Business School published a case note[14] by Nancy F. Koehn (2002) that illustrates how six entrepreneurs translated their own insights and inspirations into enduring businesses. The six entrepreneurs are discussed briefly in the following paragraphs. Each began with a supply chain of some sort, as Koehn notes:

- Josiah Wedgwood (1730–1795) developed widespread consumer interest in china in eighteenth-century Britain. Wedgwood started his own china firm in 1759, which ultimately became known as the "Queen's Ware" china. He was an innovator of new designs and ways of making china, notably a way of measuring kiln temperatures accurately. The company is still in business today, known as Waterford Wedgwood, after it was bought by Waterford in 1986. However, in 2009 it was placed in receivership from which it was purchased, and went on to celebrate 250 years of being in business.

    Wedgwood employs over 2,000 people and distributes to 90 countries. It is still one of the world's best known brands. It started as an entrepreneurial venture with a unique supply chain.

- Henry Heinz (1844–1919) expanded markets in food processing, but he started with his own supply chain. At age 8, young Henry was canvassing the neighborhood with a basket under each arm selling vegetables from the family garden door-to-door. By age 9, he was growing, grinding, bottling, and selling his own brand of horseradish sauce. In 1869, Heinz founded what later was to become the H. J. Heinz Company, still known by that name today. As of 2010, Heinz is a $10B global company employing about 32,500 people.
- Marshall Field (1834–1906) worked to develop mass retailing, originally in Chicago as Marshall Field department stores, later to be purchased in 2005 by Macy's, which shut down the Marshall Field brand. As a retailer, Field recognized that he was at the end of the supply chain that began in locations far from Chicago. Among his many innovations, he is credited with opening the first European buying office in Manchester, England, in order to obtain British goods for his store. This, of course, gave him control of at least part of his supply chain. The quotes, "Give the lady what she wants" and "The customer is always right" are attributed to Field, according to the company website.
- Estee Lauder (1906 or 1908–2004) created new markets in prestige cosmetics. Lauder was the only woman on *Time* magazine's 1998 list of the 20 most influential business geniuses of the twentieth century. She began by working in her father's hardware store, where she gained an understanding of entrepreneurship and what it takes to be a successful retailer, according to the corporation's website (2010). She understood very well the retail end of the supply chain.
- Howard Schultz (b. 1953) built consumer connections with coffee through his company, Starbucks. As of 2009, the company had 16,706 stores (8,850 company-operated and 7,856 licensed stores), operating in more than 50 countries, with more than 30 blends plus handcrafted beverages, merchandise, fresh food, and consumer products. Starbucks emphasizes its effort to be a "responsible company" with ethical sourcing, environmental stewardship, and community involvement. Practically from its beginning, Starbucks has been known as an innovative, entrepreneurial company. In addition, there are multiple business school cases written about Starbucks.[15] The company has (apparently) successfully locked in strategic and high quality suppliers over the years. These consistent, quality supply chains could provide Starbucks with a competitive advantage over their competitors. Further, its supply chain allows Starbucks to more accurately predict upcoming supply shortages due to the fact that their raw material (coffee beans) is a commodity grown in developing countries that are subject to political instability, and is a commodity subject to the unpredictability of

the weather. The first Starbucks opened in 1971 in Seattle's historic Pike Place Market. According to the corporate website, the story is that Howard Schultz first walked into a Starbucks store in 1981 and joined the company a year later. In 1983, Schultz traveled to Italy and became captivated with Italian coffee bars and the romance of the coffee experience. He had a vision to bring the Italian coffeehouse tradition back to the United States as a place for conversation and a sense of community. From the beginning, Starbucks set out to be a different kind of company, although they did not necessarily use the words "an innovative, entrepreneurial company" at the time.

- Michael Dell (b. 1965) enhanced the markets in personal computers and in the process built a substantial company. Dell certainly was a supply chain innovation leader. Dell delivers innovative technology and services. As a leading technology company, Dell offers a broad range of products, including mobility products, desktop PCs, software, peripherals, servers, networking, storage, and so forth. Dell's services include a broad range of configurable IT and business related services, including infrastructure technology, consulting, and business process services. Dell was founded in 1984 by Michael Dell on a simple concept: by selling computer systems directly to customers, Dell can best understand their needs and efficiently provide the most effective computing solutions to meet those needs. As reported, at the end of fiscal 2010, Dell had approximately 96,000 employees with about 36,600 located in the United States. Revenues for fiscal 2010 were about $53B.

EVOLUTION OF SUPPLY CHAINS AND SUPPLY CHAIN THINKING

Supply chain management has seen transformations in the past. Let's start over two hundred years ago to look at some transformations and people who made them. Remember Eli Whitney, Frederick W. Taylor, or Henry Ford? Many people will recall them, at least vaguely, but of course not personally!

Eli Whitney probably is most famous for his invention of the cotton gin in 1793. For our purposes, however, consider that he generally is credited (with some dispute) with inventing the concept of the *interchangeability of parts*. At age 14, Whitney operated a profitable nail manufacturing operation in his father's workshop during the American Revolutionary War. Whitney, who had never made a gun in his life, later obtained a contract in January 1798 to deliver 10,000–15,000 muskets in 1800.

Few of us remember Taylor, though, in part because he was around about a hundred years ago. However, Taylor had a major transformative impact on *the works*, as manufacturing was called then, in his search for ways of improving industrial efficiency. Taylor generally is acknowledged as the founder of scientific management with his ideas of the "one best way" to perform work. An early predecessor of what today is called supply chain management. Taylor was an innovator who is widely credited with improving industrial efficiency. But he also was an entrepreneur, working with a number of companies to grow their business.

Taylor's scientific management consisted of four principles:

1. Replace rule-of-thumb work methods with methods based on a scientific study of the tasks, using techniques such as time-and-motion studies.
2. Scientifically select, train, and develop each employee, rather than passively leaving them to train themselves.
3. Provide detailed instruction and supervision of each worker in the performance of that person's discrete task.
4. Divide work nearly equally between managers and workers, so that the managers apply scientific management principles to planning the work, and the workers actually perform the tasks.

The ideas of Whitney and Taylor were keys to Henry Ford's implementation of the assembly line in the early 1900s. Not only did Taylor show how to determine the one best way to perform work, but he also was a proponent of the standardization of parts. Ford used both of these concepts in the design of his automotive assembly line. Furthermore, Ford was an advocate of an integrated supply chain. For his Model T automobile, he mined the ore, turned the ore into steel, shaped and machined the steel into parts, grew the rubber for the tires, and assembled the automobile in his own factory. Ford founded the Ford Motor Company, which is still one of the world's largest enterprises today. This was the first great modern integrated industrial enterprise (supply chain), if the Egyptians and the pyramids are not counted.

Whitney, Taylor, and Ford were all innovators and entrepreneurs along the supply chain.

ENTREPRENEURIAL THINKING

Entrepreneurial thinking is difficult to describe, which makes it also difficult to implement. One reason it is difficult to describe is that companies frequently fail to establish a clear set of objectives about what will make the effort worthwhile. In other words, what do you do with entrepreneurial thinking when you get it?

Entrepreneurialism is not making incremental changes or improvements. It means taking a hard look at the business and its "as-is" situation, and setting demanding goals about how much it takes in additional profits to really make a difference in the business. For example, say you agree that a 10% increase in after-tax profits is a suitably demanding goal. Then, everything else being the same, the entrepreneurial venture would have to yield a 10% increase in total company revenues within a relatively short time period. What would it take to get everyone in the company aligned around the necessary actions to achieve this goal?

When the company does some framing of the entrepreneurial objectives, it should construct and maintain an assumptions register and an opportunities register. The *assumptions register* keeps track of the assumptions behind the company's entrepreneurial thinking, such as:

- Assume that an annual 10% after-tax profit increase from new supply chain ventures is the minimum acceptable objective.
- Assume that any new supply chain venture will increase (or, at least, not dilute) the company's gross margins.
- Assume that any new supply chain venture will be synergistic with the existing business.

An *opportunities register* keeps track of a pipeline of new supply chain venture opportunities. The opportunities register keeps the following types of information:

- Name and description of the opportunity
- Key milestones and dates from the opportunity work plan
- Key data on the opportunity
- Probability estimates on the key information

As previously stated, entrepreneurial thinking does not come easily. There are always difficulties, as shown in Figure 1.5, which illustrates some of the barriers to entrepreneurial thinking, along with some of the ways companies have attacked the barriers.

One way to approach entrepreneurial thinking is to consider a five-step process, with relevant questions to ask at each step, as follows:

1. *As-Is situation*: What is the current situation with our supply chains?
   - How entrepreneurial are the current supply chains?
   - What are the current strengths, weaknesses, opportunities, and threats with the supply chains?
2. *To-Be vision*: What is the vision for the business in the five- to ten-year time frame?
   - What are the customers' and stakeholders' required results for entrepreneurial supply chains, along with innovation and growth objectives?
   - How can a look into the future be described?
3. *Path forward*: How do we reach the vision?
   - What are the gaps between the as-is and the to-be situations?
   - How do we close the gaps?
   - How do we prioritize the actions?
   - What are the detailed plans?

Barriers to Entrepreneurial Thinking	Overcoming the Barriers
Insufficient entrepreneurial zeal	Create a compelling business case for entrepreneurship, innovation, and growth. Empower the organization. Give authority to accountable individuals and teams. Measure progress.
Unsatisfactory strategic focus on innovation and growth	Ensure that corporate strategies focus on innovation and growth. Develop a clear statement of strategies and tactical priorities around innovation and growth, which the organization can embrace.
Lack of leadership attention to innovation and growth	Develop entrepreneurial leadership skills through opportunities to lead projects and drive key entrepreneurial business initiatives. Ensure that senior leaders send strong signals through their actions that innovation and growth are important.
Inadequate commitment to innovation and growth	Increase participation by establishing and utilizing entrepreneurial project teams. Involve key people in creating the entrepreneurial imperative.
Lack of education and training in entrepreneurship, innovation, and growth	Develop, update, and refine process- and mindset-focused education and training programs. Identify, design, and implement external education and training on innovation and growth.
Insufficient results orientation	Develop consensus around the organization's current (as-is) approaches to entrepreneurship as well as the future (to-be) vision. Ensure an adequate focus on innovation and growth.

Figure 1.5　Barriers to Entrepreneurial Thinking.

4. *Risks*: What could stop or delay success of the plan?
   - How can we analyze the risks?
   - How can we plan to mitigate the risks?
5. *Drumbeat*: How can we ensure timely execution of the plan?
   - How can we implement a disciplined rhythm of execution of the plan?
   - How can we ensure follow-up engagement with the plan?

THINKING ABOUT ENTREPRENEURIAL SUPPLY CHAINS

Five ways of thinking about entrepreneurial supply chains, are as follows:

1. Customer-focused thinking
2. Competitor-focused thinking
3. Supplier-focused thinking
4. Innovation-focused thinking
5. Internal process-focused thinking

Yes, but how do we do it? There are numerous approaches to linking customers, competitors, suppliers, innovations, and internal processes with action items. Think of a matrix with these five ways of thinking linked with potential ways of creating entrepreneurial supply chains, as outlined below. In the outline, some ideas are presented about how to go about creating an entrepreneurial supply chain, which are expanded in the next chapter:

1. *Start-ups*—New ventures of some sort.
2. *Acquisitions*—One company purchases another that has a market position, unique technology, or other attribute(s) of interest. These can be for vertical, horizontal, strategic, or financial purposes.
3. *Alliances*—Agreements to cooperate in some way.
4. *Coalitions*—Similar to alliances, but generally with less structure, less formality, and less long-lasting.
5. *Collaboration*—Usually even less formal or long-lasting than coalitions.
6. *Consortia*—Associations among business firms that are formed for specific purposes.
7. *Franchises*—Authorizations granted for the purpose of doing business in a particular way, in a particular geography, and so forth.
8. *Joint ventures*—Almost always formal legal arrangements for a particular purpose.
9. *Licenses*—Permits from one company to use or sell the products of another.
10. *Mergers*—Legal combination of two companies into one.
11. *Outsourcing*—Decisions by one company typically to purchase services from another, such as manufacturing, accounting, or another service. This generally is not looked upon as an entrepreneurial venture, but it easily can be considered as such by either the outsourcing company or the company providing the outsourcing services.
12. *Partnerships*—Usually formal arrangements between companies for a specific purpose.
13. *Reverse supply chains*—Focus on the capture and use of used products and materials.
14. *Divesting, exiting, and harvesting*—Usually voluntary withdrawals from a business or part of a business. Start-ups frequently have well-defined strategies for exiting the business, usually by selling it to another.

These issues concerning entrepreneurial supply chains are introduced in order to stimulate thinking about how entrepreneurial supply chains may be represented.

INTRODUCTION TO ENTREPRENEURIAL SUPPLY CHAIN CASES

Examples of innovative and entrepreneurial companies appear throughout the book. They are different types of companies in different industries, but they have some things in common: innovative and entrepreneurial thinking. The following five examples will be cited from time to time: Cisco Systems, Dell, National Oilwell Varco (NOV), Sysco, and Valero Energy Corporation.

Cisco Systems, Inc.

Cisco has long been known as a supply chain leader. According to its corporate website, the company was founded in 1984 and currently claims approximately 66,000 employees. Cisco fits this book as a case study. It views its internal innovation, acquisition strategy, and partner approaches as differentiators in the market. Like many companies, the ability to innovate has become a key to success, particularly for technology companies. Cisco's acquisition strategy is to look for acquisitions that capitalize on new technologies and new business models. Its seven acquisitions in 2009 fit the definition of adding to Cisco's supply chain; for example, their acquisitions included software, hardware, and application-specific companies. They include cable, security, mobility, collaboration, data centers, and consumer-focused companies.

Cisco's partner strategy looks for best-in-class companies, with long-term partnerships that are mutually beneficial and consider its partners to be an extension of Cisco. Again, these partnerships fit the definition of entrepreneurial supply chain ventures.

Dell Corporation

Dell Corporation was founded by Michael Dell in his dormitory room at the University of Texas in 1984 with the simple concept of selling computers directly to consumers. Dell enhanced the markets in personal computers and in the process, built a substantial company and supply chain leader. He envisioned that Dell could best understand customer needs and efficiently provide effective computing solutions to meet those needs.

Today, Dell Corporation delivers innovative technology and services. As a leading technology company, Dell offers a range of products, including mobile, desktop PCs, software, peripherals, servers, networking, and storage. Dell services also include a range of configurable IT and business related services, including infrastructure technology, consulting, and business process services. At the end of fiscal 2010, Dell had approximately 96,000 employees with about 36,600 located in the United States. Revenues for fiscal 2010 were about $53B.

Over time, Dell expanded its business model to include a broader portfolio of products and services, and has added new distribution channels, such as retail, system integrators, value-added resellers, and distributors, which allow Dell to reach even more end users around the world. To optimize its global supply chain to best serve its global customer base, Dell transitioned a portion of its production capabilities to contract manufacturers.

Dell discusses its business strategy which contains numerous references to its supply chains in its FY2010 Form 10-K. It cites three primary components to its strategy: improve core business; shift the portfolio to higher margin and recurring revenue offerings; and balance liquidity, profitability, and growth. It also cites "selective acquisitions" as part of its overall growth strategy.

Dell now is offering financing to small businesses to purchase its products.[16] Dell has offered new financing arrangements to small businesses including interest-free deals. It thus enhances its supply chain connections with certain customer segments.

Dell has improved its competitiveness through cost savings initiatives, which are focused on improving design, supply chain, logistics, and operating expenses to adjust to the changing dynamics of the industry. They are seeking to simplify their product offerings to eliminate complexity that does not generate customer value, while continuing to focus on product leadership. Dell seeks to employ a collaborative approach to product design and development in which its engineers, with direct customer input, design innovative solutions and work with a global network of technology companies to architect new system designs, influence the direction of future development, and integrate new technologies into its products.

Third parties manufacture some of the products sold under the Dell brand. Dell has expanded its use of contract manufacturers and manufacturing outsourcing relationships to achieve goals of generating cost efficiencies, delivering products faster, better serving customers in certain segments and geographical areas, and delivering a world-class supply chain. Throughout its history, Dell has been known as having entrepreneurial supply chains.

National Oilwell Varco

National Oilwell Varco (NOV) was named to *Fortune*'s list of the World's Most Admired Companies in 2010.[17] NOV traces its history back to 1841. With more than 700 manufacturing, sales, and service centers worldwide, NOV is one of the largest suppliers of equipment to the global energy industry.

NOV provides major mechanical components for land and offshore drilling rigs, complete land drilling and well servicing rigs, tubular inspection and internal tubular coatings, drill string equipment, extensive lifting and handling equipment, and a broad selection of down hole drilling motors, bits, and tools. The company also provides supply chain services through its network of distribution service centers located near major drilling and production activities worldwide. NOV is widely recognized as one of the most innovative and entrepreneurial companies in the global energy industry.

Sysco

Sysco describes itself on its corporate website as "a leader in selling, marketing, and distributing food products to restaurants, healthcare, and educational facilities, lodging establishments, and other customers who prepare meals away from home." Its family of products also includes equipment and supplies for the food-service and hospitality industries.

Since its initial public offering in 1970, when sales were $115 million, Sysco has grown to $37 billion in sales for fiscal year 2008. Sysco operates from over 170 locations with over 50,000 employees throughout North America, serving more than 400,000 customers. In 2010, *Fortune* (March 22, 2010) listed Sysco as one of the "Most Admired" companies, ranking Sysco #1 in its industry, Wholesalers: Food and Grocery. Sysco is included in this book because it has a long history of being an innovative and entrepreneurial company with its supply chain.

Valero Energy Corporation

Valero Energy Corporation is a *Fortune* 500 company based in San Antonio and is North America's largest independent petroleum refiner and marketer. As of 2010, Valero supplied fuel and products from 15 refineries and 9 ethanol plants, stretching from California to Canada to the Caribbean. According to Valero, well-positioned pipelines and terminals allow the organization to deliver fuels more "quickly, responsibly, and efficiently" than any other refiner on the continent. Valero's diversified product slate supports dozens of industries, from health care and plastics to transportation, beauty products, and manufacturing.

On Jan. 1, 1980, Valero was born as the corporate successor of LoVaca Gathering Company, a natural-gas gathering subsidiary of the Coastal States Gas Corporation. The company's formation was far from a smooth one. LoVaca and Coastal had contracts to supply natural gas to utilities around Texas. Due to the natural-gas shortage in the 1970s, LoVaca was unable to honor its contracts. After more than six years of litigation, a $1.6 billion settlement was reached, which included the formation of Valero as a new company separate from Coastal. At the time, it was the largest corporate spinoff in U.S. history.

HOW BAKER HUGHES DOES IT

Baker Hughes Incorporated serves as a continuing case study in this book. Every chapter has a short section on Baker Hughes, an entrepreneurial, innovative, and growing company providing reservoir consulting, drilling, formation evaluation, pressure pumping, completion and production products and services to the worldwide oil and gas industry. These sections will be titled with some variation on "How Baker Hughes Does It," and will discuss how Baker Hughes implements the subject of the chapter. The intention is to illustrate how one real company puts into practice the ideas, concepts, tools, and techniques of entrepreneurial supply chains. However, Art Soucy, Vice President, Supply Chain, at Baker Hughes cautioned the author as follows when we were beginning discussions about material for the book:

> *Please recognize, Bill, that this is a work-in-process. We're nowhere near finished. We don't have all the answers, and we don't even have all the questions. We know that we want to have supply chains that are more entrepreneurial and more innovative. Those are our goals and that is our journey.*

Baker Hughes says the following about itself on its website (2010; 2011):

> *For more than a century, innovation has been part of our DNA . . . Baker Hughes creates value from oil and gas reservoirs with high-performance drilling, evaluation, completions and production technology and services, integrated operations and reservoir consulting . . . for the global oil and gas industry.*

Baker Hughes in its present form was created in 1987 with the merger of Baker International and Hughes Tool Company, both of which began at the start of the twentieth century. R. C. Baker and Howard Hughes, Sr., began their respective companies with innovations in the early 1900s that helped to develop the early petroleum industry. Baker's major innovations were in the completions area of the industry. Hughes invented the first roller cutter bit that dramatically improved the drilling process. The companies have continued being innovative and entrepreneurial in the intervening years. The combination of Baker International and Hughes Tool Company was complementary.

Baker Hughes is headquartered in Houston, TX, and generally is recognized as one of the leading companies in the global oil and gas services industry. For Baker Hughes, in FY2010, year-ended December 31 sales were in excess of $14.4B with a net income of $819M, with results from the BJ Services merger only included since April 28, 2010. Baker Hughes operates in over 80 countries with approximately 53,100 employees. It considers its primary competitors across most of its products and services to be Schlumberger (FY2010 sales in excess of $27B), Halliburton (FY2009 sales in excess of $14B), and Weatherford (FY2009 sales in excess of $8B). They also compete on a more limited basis with other companies such as National Oilwell Varco, Champion Technologies, NALCO Holding, and Newpark Resources.

In 2009, Baker Hughes reorganized itself. The primary driver was recognition of a change in the market toward the national oil companies (NOCs). While NOCs are far from homogeneous, they require go-to-market strategies that differ from company to company. The organization of the company changed from a portfolio of operating divisions organized by product lines with certain functions performed at the enterprise level. The new organization is more of a matrix that has a geographically organized operations structure; a product-line structure for technology innovation, engineering and product development, and marketing; and an enterprise-wide organization for other functions such as supply chain.

There had been a settlement with the United States Department of Justice and Securities and Exchange Commission over alleged violations of the Foreign Corrupt Practices Act from 1999–2002. The FCPA settlement actually delayed Baker Hughes' reorganization. This settlement was a watershed event for Baker Hughes, and served as a wake-up call for the company. As a result of the settlement, among other things, the company's reorganization tightened financial systems controls that resulted in more process-oriented operations. For example, one significant action was that the company largely replaced its third-party agent structure around the world with its own people. As one vice president told the author, "We're a much stronger company now." Baker Hughes takes its compliance responsibilities very seriously, and one can see strong statements to that effect on its website. But it is not just website public relations. Having seen the company "up close and personal" for several months, the author can testify to this seriousness of purpose.

Throughout its history, Baker Hughes considered itself to be an entrepreneurial company. It has acquired and integrated numerous oilfield companies including Brown Oil Tools, CTC, EDECO, and Elder Oil Tools (completions); Milchem and Newpark (drilling fluids); EXLOG (mud logging); Eastman Christensen and Drilex (directional drilling and diamond drill bits); Teleco (measurement while drilling); Tri-State and Wilson (fishing tools and services); Centrilift (artificial lift); Aquaness, Chemlink, and Petrolite (specialty chemicals); Western Atlas (seismic exploration and well logging); and others. The company acquired BJ Services in 2010, an acquisition that made a significant impact on the company and its products and services.

Innovation and growth relating to Baker Hughes' acquisitions and new business ventures is supported by a network of technology centers, centers of excellence, and education centers. These are located in key hydrocarbon-producing areas of the world. They include the Center for Technology Innovation (Houston, Texas), Celle (Germany) Technology Center, Houston Technology Center, Russian Science Center, Dhahran (Saudi Arabia) Technology Center, Rio de Janeiro (Brazil) Technology Center, Western Hemisphere Education Center (Houston), Eastern Hemisphere Education Center (Dubai), and elsewhere.

Baker Hughes continues to receive recognition for its technological innovation. In October 2010, the company captured four awards at the prestigious 9th Annual World Oil Awards dinner. Baker Hughes also had six other technologies named as finalists in the competition. At the 2011 Offshore Technology Conference (a leading industry conference), Baker Hughes' technologies received the Hart's E & P Meritorious Engineering Awards (MEA) for having outstanding new technologies in 4 of 12 MEA categories, more than any other oilfield service company. These are important recognitions by the company's peers in the oil industry, and show the company's focus on technological innovation.

As is true of almost all case studies, information was prepared as the basis for discussion rather than to illustrate effective or ineffective handling of any particular situation. One last comment: the basic information for these sections comes from discussions with a number of Baker Hughes executives, the corporate website, and internal documents to which the author was given access. Information that may be considered proprietary to the company was omitted or disguised. Baker Hughes was asked to scrutinize these sections to ensure that they were accurate and that information that properly should remain within the company was not inadvertently given away. However, the information is honest and not a "puff piece," nor are there "gotcha" opportunities to cast criticism. Most readers will understand and appreciate the need for caution and delicate handling of proprietary information.

A CASE NOTE FOR FURTHER STUDY

"A Note on the Value of Information in an Entrepreneurial Venture" by Paul W. Marshall

At the end of every chapter is a case note for further study. If the book is being used in an academic course or executive education course, supplemental cases and notes are useful for the instructor to provide further reading, study, and discussion with the participants. If the book is being used for a company project, these case notes can be used for additional reading and learning. The cases are available at www.harvardbusinessonline.com. These cases were prepared as the basis for discussion rather than to illustrate either effective or ineffective handling of any particular situation. For this chapter, readers should obtain a copy of "A Note on the Value of Information in an Entrepreneurial Venture" by Paul W. Marshall.[18]

Entrepreneurial ventures have an uncertainty about their outcome. The typical method of entrepreneurial funding is to invest in stages or rounds. Between each round of investing, it is possible to collect information about market and technical conditions and on management's ability to make progress against planned objectives. Based on this information, existing and new investors can decide whether to make the next round of financial commitments or to abandon the venture.

Simplified visual reference to multistage funding is available in Figure 1.6. At the beginning of the note, Professor Marshall cited Benjamin Franklin's celebrated quote: "Nothing is certain but death and taxes." This certainly is true for the outcomes of funding for entrepreneurial ventures.

Clearly, as Figure 1.6 illustrates, there are two rounds of funding along with the value of information. The case makes the point that the value of information is determined by three factors.

1. The economics of the underlying venture (the size of the payoff if the venture succeeds and the amount of money that must be invested);
2. The degree of uncertainty in the venture (the probability of the venture being successful); and
3. The accuracy of the information being obtained (assumed to be perfect in this example).

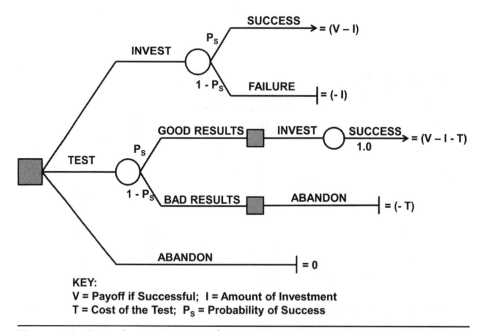

Figure 1.6 Example Decision Tree for an Entrepreneurial Venture. Adapted from: Marshall, Paul W., "A Note on the Value of Information in an Entrepreneurial Venture," Harvard Business School, Case # 9-802-143, Rev. December 16, 2002. (See www.harvard businessonline.com to obtain a copy.)

This case uses a decision analysis (decision tree) framework to structure the information-gathering and funding process for a new venture. It is advised for the reader to understand this framework and analysis approach before going much further.

The decision tree illustrates three alternatives: invest all the money now, invest enough to gain information, or abandon the project. Investing all the money now results in either success or failure, each with a payoff, either positive or negative. Investing enough to gain information yields either good results or bad results, which lead the decision maker to either invest more or abandon the project. The decision tree is built in this manner with enough specificity to frame a useful decision.

The ultimate result from this decision analysis is a determination of the value of information in the project.

For use in academic courses or executive/professional education, the instructor should consider using this note to begin the course. It provides a good and simple introduction to the decision processes in entrepreneurial ventures, regardless of the type of venture.

A FINAL WORD ON INTRODUCTION TO SUPPLY CHAINS AND ENTREPRENEURSHIP

This chapter has introduced the concepts of entrepreneurial supply chains and how they link with innovation and growth. These concepts help with the following:

- Setting strategic *direction* for the entrepreneurial business and its associated supply chains;
- Establishing the *objectives* to deliver results from the entrepreneurial supply chains;
- Identifying the *initiatives* required to meet those objectives and deploying them down through the organization;

> **KEY IDEA**
>
> Place an emphasis on what works in practice rather than on abstract theory.

- Creating *measures* to track progress toward the objectives;
- Identifying *resources* to complete the initiatives and aligning responsibility among accountable individuals and groups; and
- Specifying *behaviors* that are required to implement the entrepreneurial business strategy.

ASSURANCE OF LEARNING QUESTIONS

The following questions will help you to check yourself on the chapter content:

1. Look at *Fortune*'s latest list of the largest companies and compare it with the list of 20 years ago. Look at the companies that are no longer on the list, then do some research to determine what happened. Some may have been acquired, some may have gone out of business, and others may have dropped in size so that they no longer qualify. What can you learn from this?
2. In your own words, explain how a supply chain can lead to innovation and growth in a company.
3. Choose a company in which you are interested and visit their website. Go through the information presented and determine to what extent they have entrepreneurial supply chains. Compare that company with the introductions of the companies in this chapter (Cisco, Dell, National Oilwell, Varco, Sysco, Valero, and Baker Hughes), which are used throughout the book.
4. Explain what you think the author means by this statement: "The *entrepreneurial supply chain* idea is akin to vertical integration, but it is more than that."

The author's suggestions for answers to some of the review questions throughout the book can be found in the Web materials for this book available from the WAV Download Resource Center at www.jrosspub.com/wav.

REFERENCES

1. Cutter, Chip. January 18, 2010. "'Right Size' Corporate Jargon?" Houston Chronicle. B8.
2. Lehner, Mark. *The Complete Pyramids: Solving the Ancient Mysteries*. London, Thames & Hudson, 2008.
3. George, Claude S., Jr. *The History of Management Thought*. Englewood Cliffs, N.J.: Prentice-Hall, Inc. 1968. xiii.
4. Council of Supply Chain Management Professionals (CSCMP). January 2010. http://www.cscmp.org/aboutcscmp/definitions.org
5. Porter, Michael E. *Competitive Advantage: Creating and Sustaining Superior Performance*. New York, The Free Press, 1985.
6. Walton, Sam, with John Huey. *Made in America: My Story*. New York, Bantam Books, 1992. 265.
7. Fisher, Marshall L. March-April 1997. "What Is the Right Supply Chain for Your Product?" Harvard Business Review.
8. Treacy, Michael. *Double-Digit Growth: How Great Companies Achieve It—No Matter What*. New York: Portfolio, 2003. 2–3.
9. Drucker, Peter F. *Innovation and Entrepreneurship*. New York, Collins Business, 1985. vii.

10. Wolcott, Robert C., and Michael J. Lippitz. Fall 2007. "The Four Models of Corporate Entrepreneurship." *MIT Sloan Management Review*, 49(1), 75.
11. Kingsbury, Kathleen. March 23, 2010. "Deere's Harvest," *Time*. 12–14.
12. Schumpeter, Joseph A. *Capitalism, Socialism, and Democracy, Second Edition*, New York. Harper and Brothers. 1947.
13. Levitt, Theodore. (July 2004). "Marketing Myopia." *Harvard Business Review/ HBR Classic*.
14. Koehn, Nancy F. "Entrepreneurial History: A Conceptual Overview." Harvard Business School Note #5-801-368, Rev. October 15, 2002.
15. See the following as an example: Honack, Richard. "Growing Big While Staying Small: Starbucks Harvests International Growth," Kellogg School of Management, Case #KEL447, 2009; Lee, Hau. "Starbucks Corporation: Building a Sustainable Supply Chain," Stanford Graduate School of Business, Case #GS-54, May 2007; Moon, Youngme, and John Quelch, "Starbucks: Delivering Customer Service," Harvard Business School, Case #9-504-016, July 10, 2006.
16. Scheck, Justin. (March 30, 2010). "Dell Lending Spurs Small-Business Sales." *The Wall Street Journal*.
17. "World's Most Admired Companies." (March 22, 2010). *Fortune*. 121–136.
18. Marshall, Paul W. (December 16, 2002). "A Note on the Value of Information in an Entrepreneurial Venture." Harvard Business School, Case #9-802-143.

CHAPTER 2

WHY "ENTREPRENEURIAL" SUPPLY CHAINS

LEARNING OBJECTIVES

1. Why it is hard to be entrepreneurial in the supply chain.
2. How entrepreneurial supply chains create value in the enterprise.
3. Compare and contrast the various practical and legal forms of entrepreneurial relationships.
4. The role of innovation in entrepreneurial supply chains.

"We mean to have less of government in business as well as more business in government."

—President Warren G. Harding
Address to Congress, April 12, 1921

Things sure have changed since President Harding's time! Today we need, more than ever, an entrepreneurial spirit in business in the United States as well as around the world. Contrary to what some people may think, the foundation of the free enterprise system is not government, it is entrepreneurship. However, entrepreneurship needs a free-enterprise government to thrive, and a free-enterprise government cannot endure without entrepreneurial ventures.

Why do entrepreneurial supply chains matter? First, supply chains matter because entrepreneurship matters. Second, supply chains matter because they represent a very good way to implement entrepreneurial activities. Now, the attention turns to various, practical ways of how value is created in entrepreneurial supply chains and, thus, ways in which entrepreneurial supply chains can be established.

Supply chains are often characterized merely as *cost centers* without much credit being given to their potential as generators of innovation and growth. A cost center mindset limits the possibilities of one of the most powerful competitive weapons that companies have.

Supply chains are the only part of the company with the charter to reach out on both the demand side and supply side. The outgoing supply chains reach customers and customers' customers. Incoming supply chains originate with suppliers and suppliers' suppliers. Thus, supply chains are well positioned to be the entrepreneurial drivers of the company. Entrepreneurial supply chains can look for innovation and revenue opportunities wherever they may be found: upstream on the supply side, downstream on the demand side, or with competitors in the middle.

> **KEY IDEA**
>
> Supply chains should *not* be simply cost centers.

Opportunities for entrepreneurial focus are shown in Figure 2.1: Our Company sits in the middle, along with Our Current Suppliers and Our Current Customers. Both suppliers and customers could present entrepreneurial opportunities for growth and/or innovation for multiple reasons. Either suppliers or customers may have innovative technology. They may be purchased on an entrepreneurial basis, or there may be opportunities for joint ventures

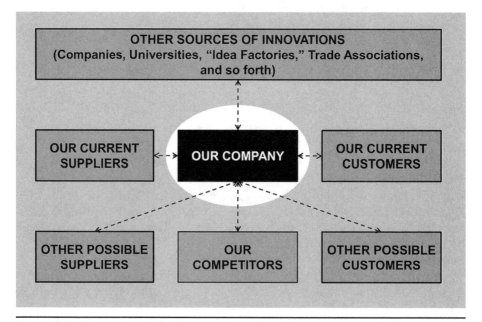

Figure 2.1   Opportunities for Entrepreneurial Focus.

and other combinations. Across the bottom of the figure are Other Possible Suppliers, Our Competitors, and Other Possible Customers—which also present entrepreneurial opportunities for growth and innovation. Like "Our Suppliers" and "Our Customers", these enterprises may have technology, may be purchased, or may contain opportunities for joint ventures and other combinations. In addition, "Other Sources of Innovations" could be possible in other companies, universities, "idea factories," and trade associations, which do not fit into the classifications of suppliers (current and possible), customers (current and possible), or competitors (current and possible). These other sources can also present entrepreneurial opportunities.

An Aside: When a large company has well in excess of 50% in its defined market share in the dominant segment of its industry, significant growth in that segment is difficult except as customers grow. However, there are several adjacent segments of the industry that present growth opportunities, particularly for a company that can offer innovative products and services. Growth in adjacent segments, while not easy, can be experienced through the ideas portrayed in Figure 2.1.

Companies typically stick close to their core business when looking for growth opportunities. They may look to augment market share through changing their pricing, varying their product mix, introducing new variants of their products, making incremental customer-facing improvements, or expanding into new geographical areas. For example, O'Sullivan (2010)[1] offered some ways to reinvigorate growth in a business after poor economic times. She cited four ideas:

1. *Cultivate what you have.* In one example, Darden Restaurants renovated some of their existing Red Lobster restaurants instead of "making bigger bets."

2. *Pick your spots.* An interviewee stated that the company was "investing . . . in innovation . . . and upgrading . . . experimenting with new marketing efforts." But the company paid for that spending by "delayed infrastructure investments in its offices."

3. *Meet the customer halfway.* The first step in moving from cost cutting to growth is to "talk to your customers about their needs . . . [which may] have changed during the recession." In other examples, Coach, the well-known handbags and accessories brand, bought its Chinese distributor; Siemens explored new industries and technologies.

4. *Go shopping.* Acquisitions can be small and strategic, like a technology or a product, customer, or geographic segment. The CFO of Darden Restaurants stated that any acquisitions are likely to be horizontal (such as other restaurant chains), but not vertical (such as a food supplier or restaurant technology provider).

As this article shows, many potential avenues exist to create entrepreneurial supply chains by observing what others have done and then adapting their ideas to one's own situation.

WHY IT IS HARD TO BE ENTREPRENEURIAL IN THE SUPPLY CHAIN

The cost center mindset that confines supply chains obviously goes a long way toward keeping them from being entrepreneurial. Those of us who have had supply chain management responsibilities are familiar with the push for short-term performance, and how this push sometimes overwhelms everything else. Metrics such as on-time delivery, perfect order fulfillment, and inventory turnover can easily become the be-all, end-all of performance management.

Metrics are important, particularly to the customers whose businesses depend on their suppliers delivering orders on-time and in-full. However, readers should understand how short-term metrics can inhibit an entrepreneurial mindset in the supply chain.

> **KEY IDEA**
>
> Short-term metrics inhibit entrepreneurial mindsets in the supply chain.

Similarly, many supply chain organizations lack long-term incentives. This helps to keep these organizations in a perpetual focus on short-term performance. The supply chain is not often asked to make long-term, strategic decisions. When asked to do that, as often as not, the question is where to locate a new distribution center, whether to send manufacturing offshore, or whether to outsource a key element of the supply chain.

Unfortunately, opportunities for mistakes and errors are high in supply chains, as are opportunities for unforeseen problems outside of the control of the company. The result is that the total organization tends to view supply chains as tactical, problem-prone organizations, rather than as strategic elements of the company.

THE PROCESS TO CREATE NEW VENTURES WITHIN EXISTING ORGANIZATIONS— CORPORATE ENTREPRENEURSHIP

The failure rate of new ventures is very high. Many estimates are available from various research studies. Some of these estimates are that up to 90% of new ventures that are brought to market do not succeed. Ventures that do best in creating customer value will use some of the ideas that underlie the success rates of new ventures. Figure 2.2 shows potential results from new ventures that exhibit four sets of characteristics:

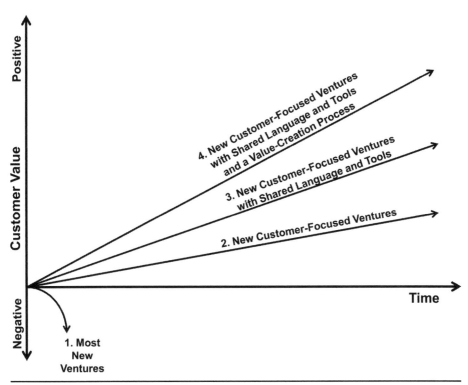

Figure 2.2 Ventures That Do Best in Creating Customer Value. Adapted from: Carlson, Curtis R. and William W. Wilmot, *Innovation: The Five Disciplines for Creating What Customers Want*, Crown Business, 2006, p. 4.

1. *Most ventures fail within a short period of time.* Companies typically fail because customers don't want their products or services—the venture did not understand its customers and their needs or, for whatever reason, did not deliver against those needs. Of course, they can fail for many other reasons, such as lack of financing, technology, poor location, and unforeseen events. Conversations that the author has had with various venture capitalists suggest that lack of a good marketing plan is a fatal flaw for many companies. Whatever the reason(s), new ventures fail frequently.

2. *New customer-focused ventures (ventures that understand their customers and their needs) usually do not fail.* They of course are unlikely to grow in a straight-line fashion as shown in the exhibit; nevertheless, they have a tendency to grow (albeit, slowly) over time. The level of understanding the customers perhaps creates a primary fault line between success and failure of new ventures.

3. *Customer-focused ventures that have a shared language and a set of tools for understanding customer value tend to do even better.* While understanding the customers is necessary, it is not sufficient by itself for outstanding success. Shared tools can include an entrepreneurial supply chain visioning process (Appendix A); an outline of a sample business plan (Appendix B); and a sample education and training program (Appendix C). A shared language can begin with a glossary (Appendix D). These are just a few possibilities for shared tools.

4. *Customer-focused ventures that, in addition, have a defined systematic value-creation process tend to do the best.* This approach is presented throughout this book.

So, is there a way to enhance the chances of success in start-ups? The answer is *maybe*! Most start-ups fail because they are making products for which there is no market. The so-called *lean start-up* approach focuses on quickly finding out what the market is, and whether the product and business model fit the market. Thus, advocates of this approach emphasize starting out small and getting products and services to the market quickly. The *lean start-up* idea has created much attention in Silicon Valley, a hotbed of entrepreneurial start-ups.

Lean start-ups emphasize some of the same ideas, concepts, tools, and techniques as does the Japanese approach to lean manufacturing—eliminate waste, defined as anything that doesn't produce value for the customer. For example, lean start-ups deliberately seek a minimal amount of funding under the theory that a lack of funds forces the company to get to market quickly and with a minimum of waste, including time. Early and constant focus on the customer is the heart and soul of lean start-ups, and is an element of a systematic value-creation process.

Systematic Value-Creation Process

What is a systematic value-creation process, particularly for corporate entrepreneurship? One simple explanation from Ashton et al. (2003) is as follows:[2]

- *Protect* what you have (determine why you're successful and decide what's most worth protecting), and make that your first priority;
- *Penetrate* existing customers and market segments further (focus on your strengths) by offering enhanced products and services;
- *Extend* your business with new products and services for existing customers, or for new customers for existing products and services; and
- *Reach out* with entrepreneurial ventures beyond the current business, such as starting of new businesses, mergers and acquisitions, joint ventures, licensing, and other activities.

Creating value can be the basis for a formal, systematic process. For example, "protecting what you have" can begin with performing a strengths, weaknesses, opportunities, and threats (SWOT) analysis on each business unit or segment of the business. SWOT has been around for years, and still is one of the most useful tools for defining how the business competes. Strengths and weaknesses describe the distinctive internal competences and limitations of the firm in terms of concerns such as products, services, management talent, and reputation. Strengths are the decisive factors that must be protected. Opportunities and threats refer to external considerations such as the industries in which the firm operate, and its customers, competitors, suppliers, and financing.

Also, "protecting what you have" may include understanding the difference between qualifiers and winners for your business. What qualifies you to do business with your customers? *Qualifiers* are the criteria that a company must meet for a customer to even consider it as a possible supplier. *Winners*, simply put, are what wins business from customers.

Furthermore, qualifiers and winners may differ from one company to another, and for different channels or markets. Qualifiers may be the products that a company offers in the marketplace—does a company offer the products that potential customers want? Companies sometimes look for International Standards Organization (ISO) certification in certain areas as required to qualify potential suppliers. Product technology also frequently composes a qualification to do business with a particular customer. Winners, for example, easily can include the company's technology that clearly outperforms the competition's technology. Winners also can be just-in-time delivery, or any number of other short-term metrics.

Different situations require different actions to protect the existing business from the competition. A little later in this chapter, practical and legal forms for entrepreneurial ventures are considered that are intended to protect what you have, as well as penetrate new customers or markets.

The Innovation Process

Systematic value creation requires innovation, and innovation requires a process. Innovative companies consistently demonstrate that investments in their innovative capabilities dependably yield superior results. But, what kinds of results are meaningful? Three kinds come to mind: the cost of achieving innovation; the amount of innovation accomplished; and the time to realize the benefits from innovation, which frequently is measured as the time to market.

Innovation does not just happen! Chesbrough and Garman[3] (2009) present a useful set of ideas about how to manage innovation. Even though

> **KEY IDEA**
>
> "At the heart of entrepreneurship is innovation—the effort to create purposeful, focused change in a business."
> —*Peter Drucker*

their article is written for "lean times," as they say in their title, it is equally valid for companies, anytime. Chesbrough and Garman's Inside-Out Process, shown in Figure 2.3, presents ideas about how to move different innovation projects forward. Some strategic innovation projects may move forward by retaining them within the company (middle arrow in Figure 2.3). This works if the company is an active innovator, continually engaging with its customers, suppliers, collaborators, academic experts, and others. Further, this approach is enhanced if the company has a track record of moving innovations successfully into the marketplace and achieving profitability targets.

However, what should drive outsourcing of innovation? What about situations when the company lacks expertise or resources, or what about when technical hurdles are significant and beyond the capabilities of the company? Innovation projects may be moved forward by opening them up to investment and development by outside firms (top arrow in Figure 2.3).

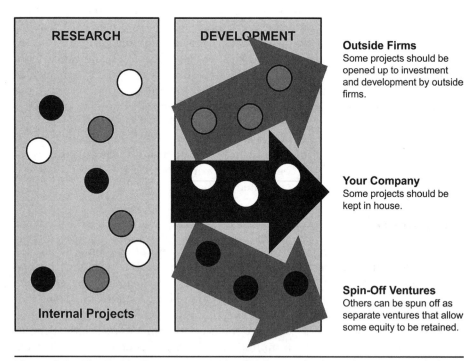

Figure 2.3 The Inside-Out Process. Adapted from: Chesbrough, Henry W. and Andrew R. Garman, "How Open Innovation Can Help You Cope in Lean Times," *Harvard Business Review*, Vol. 87, No. 12, December 2009, p. 71.

When should companies give the innovation job to outside *experts?* And, how much outsourcing is too little or too much? Outsourcing works best with non-strategic projects for which the company may not have appropriate expertise or resources to pursue. It also can be the correct course of action if the company does not have a track record in developing this type of innovation. When outside firms are used to carry out internal projects, the company may be able to reduce its costs without sacrificing innovation and growth opportunities for those projects.

Chesbrough and Garman's third approach to moving innovations forward is the spin-off (bottom arrow in Figure 2.3). These opportunities might be spun off as separate ventures that allow some equity to be retained in the company. They suggest launching it as an independent business and perhaps becoming its first customer. This approach might work if the innovation does not fit with the company's expertise or path forward as an enterprise.

The Competitive Advantage of an Entrepreneurial Context

These three approaches can serve as an introduction to a more extensive set of paths forward for entrepreneurial innovations, as discussed in the next section. First, it is important to consider the competitive advantage of having an entrepreneurial context within which to work.

A *context for corporate entrepreneurship* is a formal framework and process for how the organization manages its entrepreneurial ventures. The context could also be called a "mind-set for corporate entrepreneurship." Peter Drucker (1985) called this entrepreneurial context "systematic entrepreneurship."[4] He cited McDonald's Corporation as an example:

> By applying management concepts and management techniques, standardizing the "product," designing process and tools, and basing training on analysis of the work to be done, and then setting the standards it required, McDonald's both drastically upgraded the yield from resources, and created a new market and a new customer.

McDonald's took these ideas, concepts, tools, and techniques, and replicated them thousands of times around the world.

Similarly, in a wider context there is a competitive advantage of a company having a context for corporate entrepreneurship by creating new businesses from within existing businesses. Teams within an established company conceive, develop, launch, lead, and improve a new business. These new ventures are distinct from the parent company, and yet they leverage the parent company's resources, capabilities, capital, and perhaps its management, customers, suppliers, and technologies.

In regard to building businesses from within organizations, Wolcott and Lippitz[5] discuss four processes. Each process approach provides certain benefits—and raises specific challenges. They put forward two dimensions (resources and organizational ownership) under the control of management that differentiate how companies can approach corporate entrepreneurship. This results in a two-by-two matrix with four models as shown in Figure 2.4.

The first dimension (horizontal in Figure 2.4) is *organizational ownership*—who within the company has primary ownership for the creation of new businesses? Is that ownership diffused across the organization or is that ownership focused on a designated group? The second dimension (vertical in Figure 2.4) is the *resource authority*—who within the company has the funding authority to support the creation of new businesses? Is the resource authority within a dedicated group with a corporate pool of money? Alternatively, are projects funded in an ad hoc manner, perhaps through business-unit budgets?

Together, according to Wolcott and Lippitz, the organizational ownership and resource authority dimensions generate a two-by-two matrix with four models that define a context for corporate entrepreneurship:

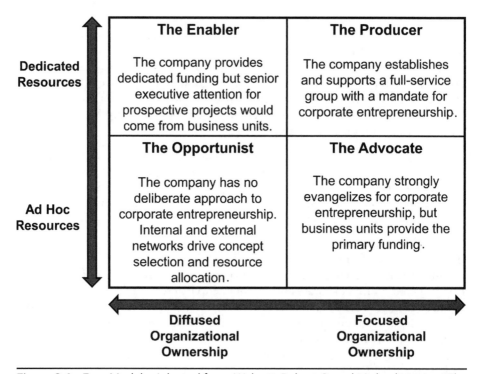

Figure 2.4   Four Models. Adapted from: Wolcott, Robert C. and Michael Lippitz, "The Four Models of Corporate Entrepreneurship," *MIT Sloan Management Review*, Vol. 49, No. 1, Fall 2007, pp. 75–82.

- *The Enabler*, a dedicated resource authority and diffused organizational ownership. There is a pot of money at the corporate level into which business units can tap. The basic premise is that employees will be willing to develop new ventures if they are given adequate resources and if there is no formal organizational ownership group. Successful companies using this model provide clear criteria for selecting opportunities to pursue, guidelines for resource allocation, clear decision-making processes, and active support from senior management. Since the organizational ownership is diffused, this means that employees need to have entrepreneurial capabilities—they are recruited, trained, and developed with those capabilities in mind.
- *The Producer*, a dedicated resource authority and focused organizational ownership. There is a pot of money at the corporate level along with corporate ownership of the entrepreneurial effort. The basic premise here is that corporate entrepreneurship can be effectively pursued if both resource authority and organizational ownership are dedicated and focused. This model aims to protect and develop entrepreneurial ventures with both resources and organizational support. The Producer model is more highly structured than the Enabler model.
- *The Advocate*, a focused organizational ownership and ad hoc resource authority. There are no corporate-level resources, but there is corporate-level ownership of the entrepreneurial efforts. The basic premise here is that corporate entrepreneurship can best be advanced if the organizational ownership is assigned to a definite group, while the resources come from the business units who will benefit from the venture. Focused organizational ownership would have the capability to move entrepreneurial ventures forward with the support and protection of the corporate enterprise. This ensures that the ventures fit within the overall corporate strategy.
- *The Opportunist*, a diffused organizational ownership and ad hoc resource authority. There is no corporate-level sponsorship or resources. The basic premise here is that corporate entrepreneurship proceeds (if at all) based on the efforts of project champions who create new businesses, perhaps in spite of the organization. There is no purposeful approach to corporate entrepreneurship—it "just happens" based on good ideas pushed by dedicated people who generate their own funding and their own organizational support.

The importance of having a context for corporate entrepreneurship cannot be overemphasized—it doesn't just happen, it must be managed and it needs a definite strategy. Corporate entrepreneurship is driven by innovation, and companies that can generate their own growth (organically and not by acquisition) are going to be at a premium. Corporate entrepreneurship thus needs processes to make them effective.

OBJECTIVES OF ENTREPRENEURIAL SUPPLY CHAIN VENTURES

Many studies have been conducted to determine the objectives of entrepreneurial ventures—some of which are applicable to supply chains and some are not. Dushnitsky,[6] while not writing specifically about supply chains, provides a survey of the relevant information on the subject. The following was extracted from his summary of some of those objectives. Please note that he was writing about corporate venture capital, which is slightly different from corporate entrepreneurship. The author believes that he has been faithful to the research in the abstraction of those objectives that apply to entrepreneurial supply chains.

In Dushnitsky's structure, one of the main players is the parent corporation, which conducts a corporate entrepreneurship program, e.g., Cisco, Dell. The parent corporation may have an internal group or department, or even a separate subsidiary to carry out corporate entrepreneurship as outlined in the structure by Wolcott and Lippitz. *Corporate development* is a common term used by the parent company to describe its ventures. The parent company invests in *entrepreneurial ventures*, which can be start-ups, mergers, acquisitions, or joint ventures. When such ventures mature, they may be folded into a business unit, used to form a new business unit, set up as a subsidiary, or transitioned into another organizational structure, as discussed later in this chapter. He makes the point that the definitions do not include investments by financial firms aimed solely at diversifying their financial portfolios as well as investments by independent venture capital funds.

Dushnitsky observes that established corporations are second only to independent venture capital funds in the amount of monies invested in entrepreneurial ventures. This opinion seems reasonable.

The overwhelming primary objective of investments in entrepreneurial supply chains seems to be "return on investment." Caution sould be stressed in interpreting this conclusion and while financial returns are necessary, they are not necessarily sufficient to stimulate many entrepreneurial investments.

In addition to financial considerations, many companies point to the importance of various strategic objectives, saying that they need both financial *and* strategic objectives to make a given investment worthwhile. Many studies have identified strategic benefits, some of which are the following possibilities:

- Provide exposure to new technology;
- Find potential mergers, acquisitions, and other combinations;
- Accelerate entry into new markets;
- Enhance demand;

- Supply capability to manufacture new products;
- Create potential to market new products;
- Acquire new knowledge;
- Develop potential to improve business processes, frequently manufacturing;
- Enhance exposure to international business opportunities;
- Provide opportunity to license others' technologies or products;
- Enhance the prospect of marketing others' technologies or products internationally;
- Expand the parent firm's contacts beyond its current network; and
- Develop new business relationships.

Notice that these objectives are not ranked. Most research that identifies objectives does some rank ordering of them within their own study. Ranking across studies is not the purpose; rather it is to suggest why companies might want to engage in corporate supply chain entrepreneurship.

Dushnitsky also discusses structures for how companies approach and govern entrepreneurial ventures, as shown in Figure 2.5. These range from tight to loose structures between the parent company and the entrepreneurial ventures. *Tight structures* are typically direct investments by the parent company in the entrepreneurial ventures. The parent company, for example, if it has a current business unit in the target area of the entrepreneurial venture, may make a direct investment and operate the new venture in conjunction with the current business unit. At the other end of the spectrum are loose structures, such as dedicated venturing funds and joint ventures, within the parent company that invest in the entrepreneurial entities.

Wholly-owned subsidiaries are separate organizational arrangements set up for the sole purpose of pursuing entrepreneurial ventures. These typically operate somewhere between tight and loose structures.

PRACTICAL AND LEGAL FORMS OF ENTREPRENEURIAL RELATIONSHIPS

Contrary to popular belief, entrepreneurial ventures may or may not require ownership. The primary purpose of entrepreneurial ventures is to create value—usually, but not always, value for the shareholders (or *stakeholders*, a more inclusive term). But how is shareholder or stakeholder value created? It's not necessarily by ownership, per se.

Usually, stakeholder value is created by implementing a competitive strategy that has value as its primary objective. But how should we define this elusive thing called *value*?

Many times we speak of *fair market value* as the appropriate definition. But what is that? Porter's term, *value chain*, is more-or-less, but not quite, synonymous with the supply chain. This is how value is delivered, from the ultimate

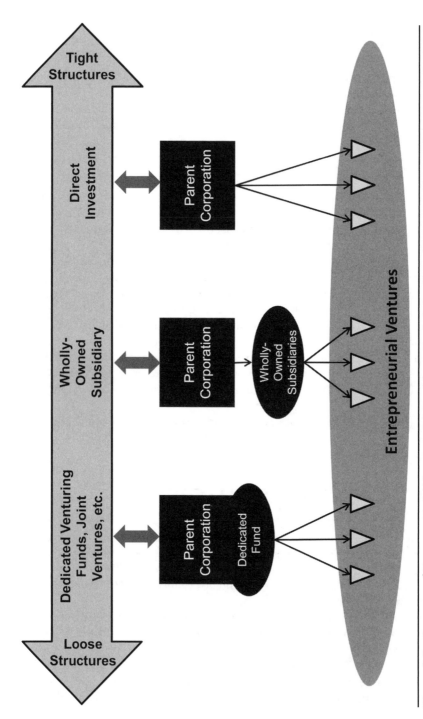

Figure 2.5 Structure of Entrepreneurial Ventures. Adapted from: Dushnitsky, Gary, "Corporate Venture Capital: Past Evidence and Future Directions," Chapter 15, p. 408, in *The Oxford Handbook of Entrepreneurship*, Edited by Mark Casson, Bernard Yeung, Anuradha Basu, and Nigel Wadeson, 2006, Oxford University Press.

supplier (say, those who dig the ore out of the ground, drill for oil and gas, or grow plants and animals) to the ultimate customer (say, buyers of the finished automobile or gasoline that fuels the automobile or food at the grocery store). The fair market value is established, at each link along the chain, between the seller and the buyer.

Following up on Porter's concept of the value chain, it was mentioned that the term *value chain* did not really catch on, as did the much simpler to understand (but less correct) term, *supply chain*. The concept of the value chain really is fundamentally different from supply chain.

Every business operates a value delivery chain, regardless of whether it is simple or complex, or whether it involves actual physical products or services. A successful business must have a clear vision of that chain along with the entities that are part of the chain and how each entity delivers value.

We often speak of companies delivering a *value proposition*. Essentially, a value proposition is the entire set of resulting experiences that some customers get from the business interaction. These experiences can be described in any number of ways, as positive or negative.

Fair market value frequently is spoken of as a value proposition in the following terms: Fair market value is the cash (or cash equivalent) price at which title to goods or services would change between a willing seller and a willing buyer when neither is acting under duress and both have realistic knowledge of the pertinent information. But how do we generate fair market value in the supply chain, especially when it is entrepreneurial? There are a number of ways of delivering value, and the following discussion involves some of them.

Some people feel that private equity firms are the most sophisticated discerners of the monetary value of companies. Others would argue that this is a very one-dimensional view of value. Suppose a private equity firm looked at the value of the venture? Pozen[7] addressed this issue along five dimensions, and suggests that these are the types of questions they would ask:

1. *Is there too much cash on the balance sheet?* Private equity firms like to minimize idle cash, whereas public firms tend to build up cash under the assumption that it makes their balance sheets look stronger. They also feel that cash is a safety cushion in the event of a downturn in the business, or that it is available to fund mergers, acquisitions, or other initiatives. Private equity firms have other uses for cash and may prefer to deploy it elsewhere. These firms look at the cash for their own purposes and not for the benefit of the business—thus they are not hesitant to strip the cash out of a healthy business to the extent that it struggles to have enough cash to do what it feels the need to do for its own benefit.

2. *Is the capital structure optimal?* Public firms tend to strive for a low debt-to-equity ratio, whereas private equity firms are notorious for loading up

a company with debt. Pozen observes that the optimal debt-to-equity likely is somewhere between the two preferences.

3. *Does the operating plan significantly increase shareholder value?* Private equity firms generally seek to improve significantly the operating performance of companies, which is an appropriate strategy.

4. *Is executive compensation tied closely enough to shareholder value?* Private equity firms tend to offer equity incentives to a much smaller group of executives as opposed to larger numbers in public companies. Rewarding a larger, as opposed to a smaller, number of executives with equity works under the theory that equity linkages motivate everyone in the company and the greater the number of motivated individuals in an organization, the better.

5. *Do directors devote enough time and have enough incentive to increase shareholder value?* Boards of companies controlled by private equity firms tend to be smaller than those of public companies. This may make sense from their standpoint, given that private equity firms want to maintain closer control over their portfolio of companies. However, both public and private firms should have broader input to their boards of directors, which argues for somewhat larger groups.

Entrepreneurial supply chain companies need to consider these arguments, because they likely will need to consider aspects of both sides of these questions.

Next, what approaches do we have with which to proceed with entrepreneurial supply chain companies? Let's consider a few.

Start-Ups

Start-ups are new ventures of some sort. We frequently think of entrepreneurial ventures as start-ups. Someone comes up with an idea for a new product or service, offers it to the marketplace, and becomes successful with it—or unsuccessful!

Two examples of entrepreneurial supply chains that have been around awhile are Hewlett-Packard and Amazon.com. However, there are thousands of start-ups in the United States annually; these are two of the most successful that almost everyone recognizes instantly. The entrepreneurs built supply chains that were entirely new. The Amazon and Hewlett-Packard start-ups really were entrepreneurial supply chains.

One visionary concept is of Mr. Hewlett and Mr. Packard in 1939, starting up an electronics company, literally in a garage, resulting in today's Hewlett-Packard (HP) with FY2010 sales of $126B, and over 300,000 employees operating in more than 170 countries around the world. According to its corporate website, as of August 2011, HP claimed to have the world's largest personal computer supply chain, including tens of thousands of resellers and retailers around the world.

Over the past few years, HP has continued to invest for growth in innovative technology and acquisitions. The HP *2009 Annual Report* states that since 2004 the company has invested more than $17B in research and development and over $20B in acquisitions. The 2010 announcement of HP's intention to acquire 3Com Corporation is an example of their continuing focus on the entrepreneurial supply chain, as it has been broadly defined in this book. 3Com had technology that complemented HP's existing offerings and expanded HP's presence in the networking segment of the industry. HP previously acquired EDS to expand their offerings in services, another important segment in their growing supply chain presence in downstream businesses.

For their upstream supply chain, HP has a fairly standard set of arrangements. Like others in their industry, HP utilizes a number of outsourced manufacturers so as to gain cost efficiencies and reduce time to market for certain products. HP builds products to stock, builds to order, and configures products to order. Most of their suppliers are multiple sourced, but some are single sourced, not significantly different from others in the same industry.

HP, of course, operates globally in terms of demand, supply, workforce, and technology. According to their Form 10-K, HP believes these global operations help the company respond to changing global demand, among other things, by providing stability to the company's supply chains.

Amazon.com also is a prime example of an entrepreneurial supply chain company. As of April 2010, Amazon.com stated on its corporate website that "We seek to be Earth's most customer-centric company for three primary customer sets: consumer customers, seller customers, and developer customers." Amazon.com was founded by Jeff Bezos in 1994, and launched online in 1995. It started as an online bookstore, but soon significantly diversified to other product lines (horizontal ventures), using the same infrastructure and business model for additional products.

One of the most informative sources of information on Amazon is its Form 10-K. As of January 29, 2010, Amazon.com describes itself as an on-line retail business. As such, the principal competitive factors in its businesses include selection of products along with their price and convenience, including fast and reliable fulfillment as one key component. They operate under a variety of business arrangements, including numerous seller programs and other commercial agreements, strategic alliances, and business relationships.

While it has been successful, Amazon.com is not without risks, also described in their Form 10-K. It clearly states that continued expansion into new products, services, technologies, and geographic regions subjects them to additional risks. Since Amazon has a highly seasonal business model, it may experience significant fluctuations in its operating results. Also, its business is dependent on its supply chain performance, including successfully operating its fulfillment centers.

Amazon's 2009 net sales were approximately $24.5B with net income of about $902m. 2009 inventory turnover was about 12 times. It generally expects to collect from their customers before paying their suppliers (a powerful tool for profitability, once accomplished). As of December 31, 2009, Amazon reported 24,300 full- and part-time employees; however, employment fluctuates considerably with its business.

Thomas L. Friedman (2010), columnist for *The New York Times*, wrote[8] about a start-up called EndoStim, which was developing a proprietary medical device to treat acid reflux. Friedman was writing neither about the company's product nor whether it would succeed in the marketplace. Rather, he was making a point about the role of entrepreneurship in the economy, which bears repeating. As Friedman described it, EndoStim is a "very lean start-up" which takes advantage of current technologies—teleconferencing, e-mail, the Internet—to "access the best expertise and low-cost, high-quality manufacturing anywhere." The venture money, core innovation, and key management are located in the United States, but management comes from all over the world—Australia, Chile, Cuba, India, Israel, South Africa, and Uruguay. He observes that "global supply chains have become scale-free, able to serve the small as well as the large, the garage inventor and Sony. . . . we still have risk takers . . . who know what world they're living in—and are just doing it."

Stories written by high-profile individuals like Friedman help validate the opinions in this book.

However, Friedman is not totally accurate, according to Andy Grove, former Chairman and CEO of Intel. Grove stated the following.[9]

> *Friedman is wrong. Start-ups are a wonderful thing, but they cannot by themselves increase . . . employment. Equally important is what comes [next] . . . as technology goes from start-up to mass production. This is the phase where companies scale up. . . . Scaling is hard work but necessary to make innovation matter.*

KEY IDEA

"Scaling up is hard work, but necessary to make innovation matter."—*Andy Grove*

Grove's powerful comments fit into the thesis of this book, making the point that as entrepreneurs in Silicon Valley came up with an invention, investors gave them money to build their businesses. Grove also talked about when, in 1968, two well-known technologists and their investor friends anted up $3 million to start a company—Intel—to make memory chips for the computer industry. We all know the success of Intel. He goes on to cite Tandem Computers, Sun Microsystems, Cisco, Netscape, and others that went through the same process.

Acquisitions

Acquisitions occur when one company purchases another company or part of another company. Usually, but not always, the acquiring company is the larger or more powerful company. The acquired company usually goes out of existence by being incorporated into the acquiring company.

Sometimes, an acquisition works differently. For example, when AlliedSignal purchased Honeywell, it changed the corporate name to Honeywell. The press reports indicated that the name change was chosen because Honeywell was a more technological name, and AlliedSignal wanted that cachet.

Another example was reported by Worthen, Tuna, and Scheck (2009)[10] about Oracle Corporation buying Sun Microsystems to increase its vertical integration in the industry. This gave Oracle more than software in its portfolio of products—an entrepreneurial supply chain move. However, Sun was still in business under its own name, and Oracle did not change its name to Sun.

> **KEY IDEA**
>
> Mergers and acquisitions frequently are discussed together, but are very different.

While the Oracle/Sun deal was presented as a vertical acquisition, it could have been described as an *adjacent-market acquisition*—one in which Oracle used its expertise in software to (hopefully) succeed in the adjacent markets of computer work stations, where Sun was well positioned.

Several types of acquisitions exist that are relevant to entrepreneurial supply chains. Most, but not all, are done to provide growth to the acquiring company:

- *Vertical acquisitions*—a manufacturing company purchases a supplier, or a supplier purchases a manufacturing company. This is likely the most common form of entrepreneurial supply chains, or at least the type many people think of most often.
- *Horizontal acquisitions*—a distribution company operating in the Southeast United States purchases another similar distribution company operating in the Northeast. Or, based on information from its corporation website in 2010, consider a company such as Consolidated Graphics, a leading company in the commercial printing industry with an entrepreneurial spirit relative to its supply chain. Having seen consolidation at work in other industries, the founder set out to bring individual printers together into a strong, national company with tremendous resources, capabilities, and buying power. Companies such as Consolidated Graphics frequently are referred to as *roll-up* companies that acquire smaller companies and then "roll them up" into a larger and more powerful company. We generally recognize these as horizontal acquisitions because the acquired companies are similar to the companies already in the collection.
- *Strategic acquisitions*—a company might have a strategic or disruptive technology and is acquired by another primarily to obtain that technology. These could be either vertical or horizontal acquisitions, but they are done predominately for strategic reasons.

- *Financial acquisitions*—not surprisingly, financial acquisitions are done primarily for financial reasons, such as to increase return on investment. However, growth also may be an objective. Financial transactions can be made for vertical or horizontal or strategic reasons in addition to financial ones.

Alliances

Alliances typically are agreements to cooperate in some ways between two or more companies. Usually, there is an affinity among the alliance members. Prominent supply chain alliances include those among airlines, in which the participating airlines gain advantages (such as coordinated scheduling) without the difficulties of mergers or acquisitions. Some of the three largest airline alliances are *OneWorld* (American Airlines, British Airways, Japan Airlines, and others), *Sky Team* (Delta, Air France, KLM, and others), and *Star Alliance* (Singapore Airlines, United, and others).

Unfortunately, the term *alliance* can have many meanings, but they fall short of full acquisitions or mergers. Instead, they are more like formal relationships than simple purchasing transactions. Alliances may include equity transactions or not, whereas acquisitions and mergers almost always include equity.

Hughes and Weiss[11] remark that the number of corporate alliances increases by about 25% a year, and account for nearly a third of many companies' revenue and value—yet the failure rate is around 60–70%. Many people with experience in alliances stress the importance of trust and communication, and the ability to resolve the inevitable disagreements that arise in such arrangements.

Organizations tend to use alliances where uncertainty is high, entering an unfamiliar market or developing a new technology with which the company has little experience or capability. Such uncertainty may preclude doing an acquisition or merger, or some other more binding arrangement.

Dyer, Kale, and Singh[12] point out, correctly, that, "alliances and acquisitions are alternative strategies; that is, the decision to do one usually implies not doing the other. If companies actually factored that into their decisions, they would make better deals."

Breakouts

An interesting entrepreneurial supply chain growth strategy is used by some companies, and it goes by several different terms, *breakout* being one of them. The Sysco case study mentions the term *foldout venture* (see Chapter 8). Breakouts are common with distribution companies.

If a suitable acquisition candidate was not available in a certain geographic area that Sysco had been serving from other locations some distance away, they would employ the foldout approach. In 1995, Sysco determined that once a sales level of about \$100–125M had been attained in an area, the market would support a stand-alone operating company with its own distribution center. The business in that area would be split off from existing operating entities, and a new foldout company would be established. The advantages of this approach for Sysco were numerous, including putting operating companies physically closer to their customers and reducing overall transportation costs.

Sysco is the only company that the author knows for sure has systematically applied this concept, but other retailers, equipment manufacturers, wholesalers, and distributors could provide more examples. Companies such as W. W. Grainger and Graybar Electric on the *Fortune 500* list of "Wholesalers: Diversified" would be likely foldout candidates, as could the following in different sectors:

> *Beverages: Coca-Cola Enterprises, Dr. Pepper, Snapple Group*
> *Construction and Farm Machinery: Caterpillar, John Deere, Terex*
> *Food and Drug Stores: CVS Caremark, Kroger, Walgreen's, Safeway*
> *General Merchandisers: Wal-Mart, Target, Sears Holdings, Macy's*
> *Wholesale Electronics and Office Equipment: Ingram Micro, Arrow Electronics*
> *Wholesale Food and Grocery: CHS, Core-Mark Holdings, Sysco*
> *Wholesale Health Care: McKesson, Cardinal Health*

All of these types of companies have geographically dispersed operations and would be candidates for a breakout strategy.

A theoretical breakout example is given in Figure 2.6, showing a regional distribution center created in Bakersfield, CA. According to the city's website (May 2011), Bakersfield is a city of about 325,000 in its incorporated area and the 59th largest city in the United States. Previously, Bakersfield was served by operating companies and their regional distribution centers, mostly from Los Angeles, San Francisco, and Las Vegas—each of which had a portion of the business in Bakersfield and its surrounding area. Los Angeles is about 100 miles from Bakersfield, San Francisco is about 250 miles, and Las Vegas is about 225 miles. All three of these locations had developed their own business in the Bakersfield area, and were even competing with each other somewhat.

To create the breakout, the company would have split off the Bakersfield-area business that was being served by the other three distribution centers. An operating company could then be established in Bakersfield, which had the critical mass and the entrepreneurial orientation to generate a higher growth rate in that area. Their customers thus could receive better service and more attention from their new, local breakout operating company, with its own regional distribution center, than any of the other three could provide. For the Los Angeles, San Francisco, and Las Vegas units, the breakout would reduce their geographic territory, but also allow them to focus better on their remaining customers and to grow new ones. It is easy to see how efficiencies, such as in transportation costs, would be enhanced in all four areas.

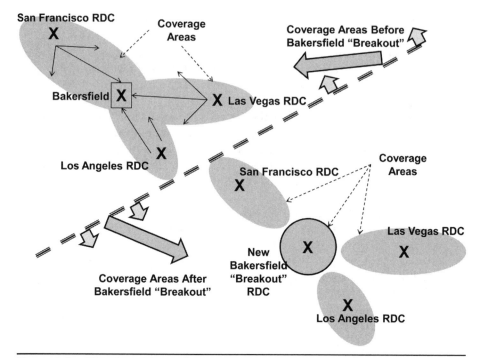

Figure 2.6   "Breakout" Example.

Coalitions

Coalitions are similar to alliances, but generally are thought of as less formal and not as long-lasting. They can be viewed as temporary alliances to pursue a particular set of actions, say, a coalition of companies to influence legislative or governmental actions.

Sometimes, however, coalitions may be long term in nature. Porter[13] puts forth the following definition:

> *Coalitions are formal, long-term alliances between firms that link aspects of their businesses, but fall short of a merger. They include joint ventures, licensing agreements, supply agreements, marketing agreements, and a variety of other arrangements.*

Porter links coalitions with his value chain, which disaggregates a firm into discrete activities performed to build value from suppliers (and, perhaps, suppliers' suppliers) to customers (and, perhaps, customers' customers). Each activity along the value chain can be part of a coalition that enhances or extends the total value of the chain. This will be discussed frequently as we progress through the book.

It is fair to say that an exact meaning of the term *coalition* really does not exist—it is used in many different contexts, with different meanings—and Porter's is only one definition.

Collaboration

Dictionary definitions of *collaboration* generally mention "working together." Working together is exactly what is meant by a collaborative supply chain, that is, a supply chain in which everyone works together in a cooperative fashion to achieve a common set of objectives.

Supply chain collaboration is a hot topic among supply chain executives. Ireland and Crum[14] illustrate this point with the following:

> *Companies are increasingly looking beyond their individual enterprises . . . [and] are developing a supply chain transformation strategy, with supply chain collaboration as a foundation of the strategy.*

Collaborations tend to be thought of perhaps as even less formal or long-lasting than coalitions. Ideas about supply chain collaboration have been around for many years, but have not been outlined in a categorization such as in this book. Only in the last few years have there been systematic studies of supply chain collaboration, which is usually broadly defined.

Supply chain collaboration applies internally to a company's own supply chain, and extends externally in both directions from suppliers and suppliers' suppliers to customers and customers' customers. When the company collaborates with its suppliers and customers, together they can build mutual confidence, develop better rapport, and increase innovation to everyone's benefit.

Furthermore, as discussed previously, the company can collaborate with its competitors, say, in opening up new markets or developing new technologies. For example, in the aftermath of the 1989 Exxon Valdez oil spill in Alaska, the oil transportation industry developed a collaborative arrangement to pool their efforts to provide oil-spill expertise and clean-up capability for that critical and hazardous route.

Internal collaboration forms an underpinning upon which all other collaboration rests. Without the capability of collaborating well internally, it is difficult for a company to collaborate effectively with outsiders. Before companies begin to collaborate with other companies, they should develop their own internal collaboration culture.

Consortia

A consortium is an association among business firms that is formed for a specific purpose. It differs from joint ventures and other collaboration entities in the sense that consortia frequently include competitors.

In supply chain circles, one of the best known consortia is the Supply Chain Council, which states the following on its website:

Supply Chain Council (SCC), a global nonprofit organization, focuses on helping our members make dramatic and rapid improvements across all supply chain processes. Members may access our SCOR frameworks, benchmarking, training, certification, research, and networking.

SCC was formed in 1996 with 69 companies, and currently has several hundred organizations as members. SCC has a number of competitive member companies who have agreed to work together to advance the supply chain field. One major advance has been the Supply Chain Operations Reference (SCOR) Model, which provides information on so-called "standard" supply chain processes. SCOR 9.0 was released in 2008.

Some advantages of the SCC and other consortia are as follows.

- Help members make better informed decisions in the area of focus.
- Provide non-competitive and cooperative opportunities for discussions about the area of focus.
- Develop models (like the SCOR model, for example) against which member companies can benchmark and improve themselves.
- Conduct conferences at which new ideas, concepts, tools, and techniques can be presented and discussed.

There are many other examples of consortia, such as the National Center for Manufacturing Sciences (NCMS). NCMS cites three reasons to work with them:

1. Targeted knowledge transfer
2. Industry-leading time to market
3. Cross-discipline collaboration

NCMS claims over 100 member companies, including organizations such as Boeing, Caterpillar, Ford, Georgia Tech, Honeywell, Penn State, Purdue, Raytheon, Toyota, and others.

Dealers

Perhaps the most commonly known use of the term *dealer* is a "car dealer." A car dealer usually has a contract (an entrepreneurial supply chain contract) with an automobile manufacturer to sell that company's cars at the retail level. Thus, your local Ford, General Motors, or Toyota automobile dealers are part of the manufacturers' entrepreneurial supply chains, even though the manufacturers have no equity interest in the dealers. New car dealers also usually sell parts and provide service. New car dealers usually are franchised enterprises.

Automobile dealers, however, do not have to sell new cars—they can be used car dealers and simply buy and sell previously owned vehicles. Of course, other types of dealers exist, such as antique dealers who buy and sell antiques, and art dealers who specialize in various forms of art.

Franchises

A franchise is an authorization granted (say, by McDonald's or Burger King) to an individual, group, or company to do business in a certain way and to sell the franchisor's (the seller of the franchise) products and/or services in a certain way. Usually, the franchisee (the buyer of the franchise) must adhere to certain restrictions on the way that business is conducted.

Franchisors' business models develop initially in many different ways. McDonald's perhaps is the most well-known franchisor in the world, having opened the first store in 1955 in Des Plaines, IL. Its corporate website describes how founder Ray Kroc organized his business, as follows:

> . . . *[The business was] built on taking care of the customer, providing a clean, family environment, and serving hot, fresh product, fast. The attention was in the details, making sure nothing was left to chance.*

McDonald's franchisees agree to use the firm's successful business model.

Franchising offers good opportunities for entrepreneurial supply chain endeavors. Businesses that work best in the franchising model tend to have a good profitability record and an easily duplicated business model. They typically can be called horizontally diversified supply chains.

Joint Ventures

A joint venture (frequently called a JV) is almost always a formal legal arrangement whereby two or more entities combine their resources, usually including equity, to pursue a particular objective. However, the term *JV* refers to the purpose of the entity and not to its legal form. Therefore, a joint venture may be a corporation, a partnership, or other legal structure, depending on a number of legal and financial considerations.

> **KEY IDEA**
>
> The *term joint venture* (JV) does not refer to a legal form. A JV may be a partnership, corporation, or other form of legal entity.

For example, a local company in Saudi Arabia might join with a giant multinational company on a manufacturing venture. The local company may have the local contacts, knowledge of the local business climate and culture, legal legitimization, and local management. But the local company may lack the technical and other expertise that is required. JVs between multinationals and local partners are common in various parts of the world. These frequently provide opportunities for entrepreneurial supply chain ventures on the part of both the larger company and the local company.

JVs between more-or-less equal partners, however, are becoming more common. One example is the Saudi Arabia Basic Industries Corporation (SABIC). As of May 2010, information on its corporate website mentioned that SABIC is one of the world's leading manufacturers of chemicals, fertilizers, plastics, and metals. SABIC makes use of the abundant hydrocarbon raw material feedstock to be found in the Kingdom of Saudi Arabia. Plus, it has expanded aggressively around the world, sometimes by itself and sometimes with joint ventures and other forms of partnerships. Many of the world's largest companies have been in these types of relationships with SABIC. SABIC has acquired Huntsman Corporation and General Electric's plastics business in recent years in large entrepreneurial supply chain ventures.

An Aside: Full Disclosure: I have consulted extensively with SABIC and have taught in SABIC's corporate supply chain and operations management education activities.

Basically, the JV forms a new business. Studies of JVs over the years have shown that they frequently form an entrepreneurial supply chain entity. In many cases, these are between firms in buyer-seller roles. Sometimes, JVs substitute somewhat for a company's internal research and development activity. High-tech and pharmaceutical companies seem to be particularly active with technology-based JVs.

Licensing

A license is a permit from one company to use or sell the products of another. One company may license its technology to another for use in a particular application or a particular geographic area. Intellectual property licenses are among the most common.

Licensing is used frequently in entrepreneurial supply chains. If an entrepreneur wants to establish a start-up business, rather than develop its own brand or its own technology, it may license a brand or technology from another company.

In pharmaceutical industries, licensing is common for small niche companies with a unique technology that license the technology to the large companies.

Mergers

A merger is a legal combination of two companies into one. Usually, but not always, a merger is between two more-or-less equal companies. Even if the merger is not a true merger of equals, it may be presented that way publically. One famous example in recent years is the "merger" between Daimler-Benz and Chrysler. In reality, it was an "acquisition" by Daimler-Benz of Chrysler to form DaimlerChrysler.

Exxon and Mobil "merged" to form ExxonMobil, but Exxon really "acquired" Mobil. A few years ago, the author was seated on a plane next to a Mobil vice president. This was just after the announcement, but before the consummation of the transaction. Asked what he would be doing after the "merger," the vice president remarked that he would still be doing exploration work, but that he would no longer be a vice president. Asked why, he smiled and said, "Because it's ExxonMobil and not MobilExxon."

KEY IDEA
Merger and acquisition terminology is like "putting lipstick on a pig!"

Another famous and interesting "merger" several years ago was between AlliedSignal and Honeywell, cited earlier. Actually, AlliedSignal bought Honeywell and then changed its name to Honeywell. In a more recent example, Southwestern Bell acquired AT&T, and then changed its name to AT&T.

A combination likely will be called a *merger* when both companies agree that joining together is in the best interest of both companies. But when the deal is unfriendly, that is, when one company does not want to be acquired, it is almost always regarded as an acquisition. Whether a purchase is considered a merger or an acquisition frequently depends on whether the purchase is friendly or hostile. Hostile takeovers almost always are presented as acquisitions, whereas friendly combinations almost always are presented as mergers. It's all in the perception and the "eye of the beholder"!

Outsourcing

Outsourcing can significantly affect companies' supply chains. Furthermore, outsourcing can be considered as an entrepreneurial venture, especially when it is used to enhance stakeholder value.

Handley and Benton (2009)[15] published a study of outsourcing as it affects how companies manage their global supply chains. They said that "there is hardly a more salient question faced by industrial leaders than which aspects of our value chain should we perform internal to our organization and which aspects should we source externally?" When they say *source externally*, they could have just as easily referred to enhancing entrepreneurial supply chains instead of referring to outsourcing.

In the past, this topic typically was studied as the "make-or-buy" question, and more recently as the "outsourcing" question. Handley and Benton called it "reshaping of existing firm boundaries." Now, we are studying it somewhat differently as the "entrepreneurial supply chain" question. These three questions are in the same genre, albeit more complex, as we move from make or buy to outsourcing, and to entrepreneurship.

Handley and Benton discuss previous research and report mixed results from outsourcing, with some reports as follows:

- 64% of the companies studied reported that they had brought outsourcing back in-house.
- 20–25% of outsourcing relationships were reported as failing within two years, with half failing within five years.
- Only 34% of companies were reported as being satisfied with the provider's innovative contributions.
- 75% were reported being ill-prepared for the outsourcing initiative.

This, and other research, suggest there is a significant gap between expectations and reality in the business of outsourcing.

Ihlwan (2010) published an interesting article[16] in *Bloomberg BusinessWeek*, comparing Sony's and Samsung's approaches to outsourcing the manufacturing of television sets. Simply put, Sony believed in hiring others to do its manufacturing in order to cut costs. Samsung's president, however, was quoted as saying, "Giving up manufacturing is tantamount to abandoning your brand"—sound like a strategic rationale?

Here are some issues to consider when deciding whether to outsource:

- *Start with a strategic rationale to either outsource or not to outsource.* Why should it be done, or not? What are the benefits and risks of outsourcing?
- *Evaluate your own existing core competencies and those you would like to have in the future.* Sony apparently no longer believed that its core competencies included manufacturing, whereas Samsung did. This is a key distinction.
- *Pay particular attention to the role of innovation.* Research and development has become a hot new area for outsourcing in order to cut R&D costs and to get products to market faster. However, caution is urged. There are real questions about whether this trend has gone too far. More companies are bringing R&D back inside the company because of the critical nature of much innovation. This seems to be true for companies in which innovation is (or should be) an important core competency.
- *Consider how the outsourcing relationships can be compared with other forms of entrepreneurial ventures.* With entrepreneurial ventures, companies look at much more than the incremental costs of the product. They look at all aspects of the venture, including strategy, governance, investment requirements, and core competencies. All too often, the outsourcing company simply looks at the incremental costs of the product and not at the allied aspects of the business.

PARTNERSHIPS

In a general sense, an entrepreneurial supply chain *partnership* is a business arrangement wherein two or more parties agree to cooperate in some sort of a venture to advance their mutual interests. Agreement is key. There needs to be agreement on the objectives of the partnership, the areas and levels of responsibilities, governance of the venture, financial issues, definitions of conflicts of interests, and other items.

In a legal sense, there can be general partners and limited partners. General partners have responsibility and authority to manage the venture. Limited partners give up a role in management in return for limitations on their liabilities. There also can be silent partners who provide capital, but whose identity is not publicly disclosed. Legal and taxation issues of partnerships are beyond the scope of this discussion.

Partnerships usually entail some formal arrangement between companies. For example, an aircraft manufacturer forms a partnership with an engine manufacturer. The aircraft company may agree to give the engine partner preferential access to its aircraft and even to its early product technology development activities. In return, the engine manufacturer may agree to provide certain technology, lead times, and prices that other aircraft manufacturers do not get.

Companies often talk about having strategic partnerships with a few partners, but not many. Often, these are for products or services that require strong technology capabilities and for which there are few suppliers. Strategic partnerships, to make them successful, need significant investment and attention on both sides of the relationship. Strategic partnerships, in this context, are strong business agreements frequently with legal arrangements that specify the details of the partnership.

Reverse Supply Chains

Reverse supply chains focus on the capture and use of used products and materials. Recall Figure 1.3, the Supply Chain Operations Reference (SCOR) Model and the "return" attribute of the SCOR model from the Supply Chain Council. The return feature generally is considered to have two elements: 1) remanufacturing or reconditioning, usually of high-value items; and 2) recycling or waste disposal of low-value items.

Some companies have turned reverse supply chains into entrepreneurial ventures, such as Dell. The following is a quote from Dell's corporate website in May, 2010:

> If your electronic equipment is less than three years old, you may be eligible for a Dell Gift Card through our Dell Exchange program. It is a great way to keep your electronics current and your discards out of a landfill.

Furthermore, as part of this entrepreneurial supply chain venture, Dell sells refurbished Dell products with certain guarantees.

Many other companies, Waste Management among them, have built thriving businesses on the reverse supply chain concept. As of May 2010, Waste Management even advertises on its website for acquisition opportunities:

> *Waste Management is interested in growing through strategic acquisitions. Throughout our history, we have acquired hundreds of companies and our acquisition team is continually evaluating new opportunities. We have the experience to quickly evaluate a company, close a transaction and integrate the acquired business into Waste Management.*

Waste Management makes both horizontal and vertical acquisitions, and is well-known for the total number of its entrepreneurial acquisitions. Clearly, this is a company in which its primary business is the reverse supply chain.

Divesting, Exiting, and Harvesting Strategies

In the use of terminology here, the use of the words *divesting, exiting,* and *harvesting* mean voluntary withdrawals but not failures of the business. *Voluntary withdrawal* occurs when the firm is sold, merged, or closed by its owners. Involuntary exit may occur when the firm fails, is purchased, perhaps goes into bankruptcy, or is taken over by its creditors.

When should the equity holders of an entrepreneurial supply chain venture exit the enterprise? Traditionally, the answer to this has been when the value of the exit or "harvest" strategy is greater than the value of continuing in the business. For example, say the net present value of the discounted anticipated cash flow for continuing in the business is $10m; whereas, a buyer for the business surfaces and offers $12m. If the equity holders are profit-maximizing decision-makers, they likely will take the $12m.

Frequently, when equity holders exit the business, it is the result of a well thought out exit strategy. Say the objective is to build the business to a certain level of sales and earnings; when that is accomplished, the business is sold.

SOURCES OF VALUE CREATION

Regardless of how the entrepreneurial supply chain venture is organized (operationally, financially, or legally), it is in business to create value for its stakeholders. The following are some of the ways in which such value can be created.

Operating synergy is one of the first sources of value creation that is mentioned about many ventures, particularly mergers and acquisitions. Almost any merger or acquisition that is announced as pending or consummated has the objective of operating synergy prominently discussed. But, as mentioned in the sidebar on page 63, some of this may be "lipstick on a pig" because it is so commonly highlighted, almost like it's expected. It would be too clearly noticeable if it was not mentioned. Who knows, sometimes it may even be true!

Think of four possibilities for value creation through operating synergy. *Operating synergy* is:

1. Higher returns from changes in or execution of the company's strategy, perhaps by a larger company;
2. Higher returns from consolidation of competition in which two or more competitors are brought together, such as the airline merger (or, was it an acquisition?) between Delta and Northwest, and total industry capacity was reduced as a result;
3. Savings from greater efficiency in the supply chain (procurement, production, and distribution); and
4. Savings from elimination of duplicate costs, usually some management positions such as going from two CEOs to one and from two CFOs to one, and so forth, as well as overhead or support costs such as combining two sets of accounting and human resources functions.

Let's take these one at a time.

Higher returns from changes in or execution of the company's strategy has several components, but let's start with one of the standard metrics, return on invested capital (ROIC). This, of course, is a ratio—return divided by invested capital. This also frequently is measured as *return on assets* or *return on equity* in which the denominator is either total assets or total equity.

Return is earnings (broadly speaking, revenue minus costs). It's fair to say that companies pay significantly more attention to maximizing "return" than they do to minimizing invested capital, assets, or equity. While cash flow is not "return," it is used frequently as a surrogate measure and thus also is a key attention grabber.

Operating synergy focuses on the numerator, return, *and* the denominator (invested capital, assets, or equity). Strategy determines cash flow and net income; the same assets operated with a better strategy can have a higher return. Management is the key to changes in or execution of strategy.

> **KEY IDEA**
>
> Success comes when the numerator (return) is growing at a higher sustained rate than the denominator (invested capital, assets, or equity).

Higher returns from consolidation of competition means that fewer players are competing in the industry. Airline mergers (acquisitions?) almost always in recent years have cited the elimination of competition as a primary objective. Fewer flights allow for higher fares.

Savings from greater efficiency in the supply chains (procurement, production, and distribution) can mean a number of things for operating synergy, such as more efficiency in procurement can result from greater consolidation of suppliers. A larger company likely can consolidate the supply base from, say, both companies prior to a merger or acquisition, and concentrate the buying on the better suppliers. Focusing on using only the better suppliers necessarily will reduce the total number of suppliers. More efficiency in production possibly might result from consolidation of factories. And, more efficiency in distribution could result from fewer, better located, and more efficient distribution centers.

Savings from elimination of duplicate costs almost always occurs from support costs such as finance and accounting, human resources, legal, and other areas. This, again, often is cited as justification for mergers and acquisitions.

HOW BAKER HUGHES LOOKS AT ENTREPRENEURIAL SUPPLY CHAINS

Companies cite many reasons for new ventures. For example, Baker Hughes is one of the largest equipment and services companies (mostly, but not exclusively) serving the upstream (exploration and production) areas of the global oil and gas industry. The company has grown through a wide variety of combinations over the years.

Baker Hughes' supply chain organization is responsible for procurement and manufacturing of their products, as well as for both inbound and outbound logistics and distribution. They have manufacturing operations in various countries, including but not limited to the United States (Texas, Oklahoma, Louisiana), Canada, the United Kingdom (Scotland, England), Germany, South America (Venezuela, Argentina), the Middle East (UAE, Saudi Arabia), and the Asia Pacific region (Thailand, China, Singapore). Product development, technology, marketing, and delivery take place through primarily a product-line organization. Sales and field operations take place through a geographic organization.

In a press release dated April 28, 2010, Baker Hughes' Chairman, President, and Chief Executive Officer, Chad C. Deaton, said the following about value creation from a recently announced *merger* (please see terminology discussion earlier in this chapter!) with BJ Services:

> *We have filled an important gap in the products and services we offer. BJ Services strengthens the combined company's integrated services offerings and will complement the products and services offered by Baker Hughes. The combined company is better positioned to compete and win around the world.*

Baker Hughes has a long history of entrepreneurial supply chain start-ups, mergers, acquisitions, and other ventures. Baker Hughes began in its present form in 1987 with the merger of Baker International and Hughes Tool Company, but the legacy companies are over 100 years old. Baker Hughes has acquired and integrated numerous oil field companies and is one of the more successful enterprises with an entrepreneurial supply chain culture.

The Baker Hughes Empowerment Process, shown in Figure 2.7, illustrates conceptually how Baker Hughes empowers its product lines, supply chains, and regions to be entrepreneurial. This is portrayed as a three-dimensional matrix in which the cells of the matrix specify high-value opportunities when they are identified from all three dimensions. For example, the cell identified in the middle of the matrix could be for an idea that is pushed by the drilling and evaluation manufacturing infrastructure activities for the Asia/Pacific region.

Ideas generated from all three dimensions (product lines, regions, and supply chain components) figuratively go into a "fuzzy front end" funnel that contains various criteria, such as:

1. *Product-line ideas.* These would be ideas that originate largely from the various product-line organizations as defined by Baker Hughes, such as drilling and evaluation, completions and production, pressure pumping, and so forth. These could be any number of types of ideas:
   a. *Line-extension ideas.* These could be ideas for slight variations of existing products (e.g., make it slightly longer, shorter, wider, more powerful, and so on). Admittedly, it is unfair to speak in this manner about

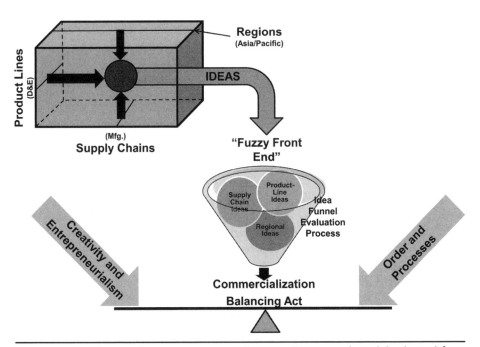

Figure 2.7 Baker Hughes Empowerment Process. Conceptual model adapted from discussions with executives of Baker Hughes. Used with permission.

a high-technology company such as Baker Hughes, but it is not unlike Double Stuff Oreos as a line extension of original Oreos! (The author likes Oreos!) Usually, line extensions might meet slightly different needs of a particular segment of customers.

b. *Adjacent ideas.* These could be ideas for products that meet the needs of, say, adjacent customers or markets, or they could be adjacent products or technologies such as other products that could be used together with a product that is already in the company's portfolio. A lower-cost pump, for example, could be considered as an adjacent product. Perhaps it could be associated with a new entrepreneurial venture, say, in a low-manufacturing-cost country.

c. *Gap-filling ideas.* These could be ideas for products to fill gaps in Baker Hughes' product portfolios. The company has numerous product lines in which gaps could exist to serve particular customer segments. A product-line organization could recommend that the company develop or acquire gap-closing products for these customers.

2. *Supply chain ideas.* These would be ideas that originate from various supply chain entities to address the following:

a. *Manufacturing ideas.* New manufacturing plants or new processes could be needed to enhance the entrepreneurial supply chain activities for particular products and/or particular areas of the world.

b. *Make-versus-buy ideas.* A product or component perhaps could be better, cheaper, or faster if it was made instead of bought, or vice versa. These issues occur frequently in a global company such as Baker Hughes.

c. *Know-how ideas.* The company has extensive experience in numerous activities and processes, but from time to time will need to obtain additional know-how, say, for manufacturing processes or for a new product. This could be accomplished by acquisition of a company with that know-how, or by start-up of a particular know-how capability.

d. *Lower-cost ideas.* Sometimes a particular region needs the company's products, but at a lower cost than the company normally can produce. This could drive an entrepreneurial supply chain venture to achieve the lower cost, say, with a joint venture in China or India.

3. *Regional ideas.* These would be ideas that originate from the various regions of the world in which the company operates and as shown on their website: North America (46% of the FY2010 revenue); Europe, Africa, Russia Caspian (21%); Middle East, Asia Pacific (16%); and Latin America (11%). These may be any number of types of ideas, such as:

a. *Infrastructure-filling ideas*. These could be ideas to fill infrastructure needs such as a new distribution center that could enhance entrepreneurial supply chain activities in a particular region.
b. *Partner ideas*. These could be relationship needs such as joint ventures, partnerships, or alliances—any of which could enhance entrepreneurial supply chains in a region.
c. *New-business ideas*. A particular region might have a need for Baker Hughes to open repair businesses to serve customers in specific areas. A region also might, for example, need to fill a local-content requirement in a particular country, and thus might need a new manufacturing business in that country.

When the ideas are identified, they go into the "fuzzy front end" of the idea funnel where they are subjected to evaluation through a stage-gate type of process. The evaluation process will consider the concept and market analysis; strategy alignment and feasibility; a rough order of magnitude business case; assumptions and risks analysis; a preliminary analysis of the required resources, operations, and development activity plan, all accomplished through the company's product development process.

Those ideas that successfully pass through the "idea funnel" evaluation process are ready for the "commercialization balancing act." The author uses this last term to signify the balancing act that Steven Johnson[17] calls "the adjacent possible" to capture "both the limits and the creative potential of change and innovation."

In the author's conversations with executives of Baker Hughes, the idea of a commercialization balancing act was discussed as a tension between creativity and entrepreneurialism versus order and process. The secret with entrepreneurial supply chains, they observed, was to make the right balance at the appropriate point in time. The challenge is to manage appropriate controls over an entrepreneurial process—seemingly self-contradictory terms. That's why, at the bottom of Figure 2.7, commercialization balancing act between creativity and entrepreneurialism on the one hand, and order and processes on the other hand, shows tension in that relationship.

A CASE NOTE FOR FURTHER STUDY: Tennant Company

The cases are available at www.harvardbusinessonline.com. Readers are encouraged to obtain copies of this case and use it to go beyond the discussion in the book. The cases were prepared as the basis for discussion rather than to illustrate either effective or ineffective handling of a particular situation.

For this chapter, the "Tennant Company"[18] case is used to illustrate some of the topics identified in this chapter. Readers may be familiar with Tennant (see www.tennant.com for more information). It is a large company that primarily produces equipment and supplies for the floor-cleaning business. The case is set from mid-2009 to early 2010, and is centered on Orbio Technologies, a new venture by Tennant to take advantage of an innovative cleaning technology developed by the company. The case includes some key elements, namely, corporate entrepreneurship, supply chains, technology innovation, and issues resulting from Tennant's move beyond the company's traditional business.

In 2000, Tennant created an Advanced Products Development Group to actively search for new ideas outside the company's core businesses. Beginning in 2002, Tennant shifted its research and development spending toward "breakthrough" products instead of incremental improvements to existing products. In October 2005, one of the scientists in the Advanced Products Development Group, actively searching for ideas in Japan, discovered that the Japanese were electrolyzing water and using it for niche cleaning applications. Tennant soon thereafter began experimenting with the ideas, from which it developed inspirations for its own use.

The CEO of Tennant decided to create a dedicated team to develop the possibilities in the technologies. He named a well-respected person to head the new venture, called Orbio Technologies, as a start-up, entrepreneurial type of company along with a senior executive to serve as an executive champion.

The CEO gave the new venture team the go-ahead to get a place of its own, nothing fancy, but at least a "glorified garage." (Remember Hewlett and Packard's garage start-up!)

As cases such as this tend to do, the case presents several questions and issues to consider, some of which are as follows. These questions are similar to ones that readers are likely to face in their own companies:

- How should Orbio fit into Tennant's supply chains, from suppliers to customers, in terms of suppliers, manufacturing, distribution, markets, and customers?
- How should Orbio leverage Tennant's applicable existing technologies?
- How should Orbio move forward with Tennant's existing customers, along with new applications outside Tennant's traditional products and markets?
- What governance structure should Tennant design for Orbio, including reporting relationships along with metrics for performance measurement and management?
- How should Tennant and Orbio establish financial transactions between the two entities, including transfer prices, royalties, and capital requirements?
- What about new technologies that Orbio might develop—who should own them and where should they be housed?
- What about managing growth? At the time, Orbio was getting all kinds of ideas that seemed to present many opportunities for growth—more than the little start-up company could handle.
- How should the company go about the hard work of building a sustainable business from a successful start-up?

Notice that this case deals with many of the same issues presented in this chapter and which continue throughout the book. Think about these questions in the context of a real company and conduct some research on what happened to Tennant and Orbio since the case began.

A FINAL WORD ON ENTREPRENEURIAL SUPPLY CHAINS

This chapter has been about why supply chains represent one of the best avenues for implementing entrepreneurial activities. Supply chains reach out from the company in both directions—upstream to suppliers and suppliers' suppliers, and downstream to customers and customers' customers. Supply chains thus serve natural boundary-spanning roles, which are ideal for gaining insight into the capabilities and needs of multiple entities in the entire chain.

Supply chains all too often are characterized merely as cost centers without much credit being given to their potential as generators of innovation and revenue growth. There is a competitive advantage of a company having a context for corporate entrepreneurship—creating new businesses from within existing businesses. Teams within an established company conceive, develop, launch, lead, and improve a new business. These new ventures are distinct from the parent company and yet they leverage the parent company's resources, capabilities, capital, and perhaps its management, customers, suppliers, technologies, and more.

Contrary to popular belief, entrepreneurial ventures may or may not require ownership. The primary purpose of entrepreneurial ventures is to create value—usually, but not always, value for the shareholders (or, for the *stakeholders*, a little more inclusive term). But how is shareholder (or stakeholder) value created. It is not necessarily by ownership, per se, as is seen in the practical and legal forms of relationships outlined in this chapter.

ASSURANCE OF LEARNING QUESTIONS

The following questions will help you to check yourself on the chapter content:

1. Why do we care about having entrepreneurial supply chains?
2. Explain, in your own words, the differences among start-ups, acquisitions, alliances, coalitions, collaboration, consortia, franchises, joint ventures, licensing, mergers, outsourcing, partnerships, or reverse supply chains as forms of different entrepreneurial supply chain ventures.
3. Describe different divesting, exiting, and harvesting strategies.

REFERENCES

1. O'Sullivan, Kate. May 2010. "Ready, Set, Grow?" CFO. 40–45.
2. Adapted from Ashton, James E., Frank X. Cook, Jr., and Paul Schmitz. June 2003. "Uncovering Hidden Value in a Midsize Manufacturing Company." *Harvard Business Review*, 81(6).
3. Chesbrough, Henry W., and Andrew R. Garman. December 2009. "How Open Innovation Can Help You Cope in Lean Times." *Harvard Business Review*, 87(12). 68–76.
4. Drucker, Peter F. 1985. *Innovation and Entrepreneurship*. New York: Collins Business. 21–29.
5. Wolcott, Robert C., and Michael J. Lippitz. Fall 2007. "The Four Models of Corporate Entrepreneurship." *MIT Sloan Management Review*. 75–82.
6. Dushnitsky, Gary. 2006. "Corporate Venture Capital: Past Evidence and Future Directions." In *The Oxford Handbook of Entrepreneurship*. Casson, Mark, Yeung, Bernard, Basu, Anuradha, and Nigel Wadeson (Eds.). Oxford and New York: Oxford University Press. 387–431.
7. Pozen, Robert C. November 2007. "If Private Equity Sized Up Your Business." *Harvard Business Review*, 85(11). 78–87.
8. Friedman, Thomas L. April 18, 2010. "Just Doing It." *The New York Times*.
9. Grove, Andy. July 5–11, 2010. "How to Make an American Job." *Bloomberg BusinessWeek*. 49–53.
10. Worthen, Ben, Tuna, Cari, and Justin Scheck. November 30, 2009. "Companies More Prone to Go Vertical." *The Wall Street Journal*.
11. Hughes, Jonathan, and Jeff Weiss. November 2007. "Simple Rules for Making Alliances Work." *Harvard Business Review*, 85(11). 122–131.
12. Dyer, Jeffrey H., Kale, Prashant, and Harbir Singh. July–August 2004. "When to Ally and When to Acquire." *Harvard Business Review*, 82(7/8). 108–115.
13. Porter, Michael E., and Mark B. Fuller. "Coalitions and Global Strategy." In Porter, Michael E. (Ed). *Competition in Global Industries*. Boston: Harvard Business School Press, 1986. 315–343.
14. Ireland, Ronald K., with Colleen Crum. *Supply Chain Collaboration: How to Implement CFPR® and Other Best Collaborative Practices*. Fort Lauderdale, FL: J. Ross Publishing, 2005.
15. Handley, Sean M., and W. C. Benton, Jr. October 2009. "Unlocking the Business Outsourcing Process Model," *Journal of Operations Management*, 27(5). 344–361.
16. Ihlwan, Moon. January 18, 2010. "Sony and Samsung's Strategic Split." *Bloomberg BusinessWeek*. 52.
17. Johnson, Steven. *Where Good Ideas Come From: The Natural History of Innovation*. New York: Riverhead Books, 2010. 31.
18. Stuart, Toby, Applegate, Lynda, and James Weber. February 8, 2010. "Tennant Company." Harvard Business School. Case #9-810-040.

CHAPTER 3

UTILIZING CUSTOMERS AND SUPPLIERS AS SOURCES OF IDEAS AND OPPORTUNITIES

LEARNING OBJECTIVES

1. Learn how to do basic industry analyses from readily available government data.
2. Be able to trace the history of CEMEX, and show how it has been a good example of entrepreneurial supply chains.
3. Learn about a company's multiple supply chains through a focus on Figures 3.4 and 3.5.
4. The food industry has some of the world's most complex supply chains. Be prepared to discuss the meaning of complex supply chains in the context of utilizing customers and suppliers as sources of ideas and opportunities, like Taylor Foods has done.

When you come to a fork in the road, take it.

—Yogi Berra

Yogi Berra is famous for his "fork in the road" quote. Robust customer and supply bases are two forks in the road for entrepreneurial supply chains. Should one pursue entrepreneurial ventures that focus on customers, or suppliers, or perhaps both, or neither? Will one way or the other lead to more innovation and growth in the enterprise, and thus to more successful entrepreneurial ventures?

Having robust customer and supply bases provides the foundation for entrepreneurial supply chains. "Robust" customer and supply bases mean having strong sets of both customers and suppliers. As stated before (and here again!), the supply chain is the part of the organization that is empowered to:

1. Service the demand, and
2. Utilize the capability of the supply side of the company.

Both of these play well into the concept of entrepreneurial supply chains.

This chapter provides an approach to understanding and structuring the entrepreneurial opportunities that may be part of the supply chains of the company—from customers' customers to suppliers' suppliers. To accomplish that, look first at industry structure and analyze companies' positions in that industry. Then, consider how to take advantage of the opportunities in multi-level supply chains in terms of recognizing their value and diving deeply into those chains as opportunities for entrepreneurial ventures.

INDUSTRY ANALYSES AND POSITIONING

Industry analyses are done to position the company vis-à-vis others. This is intended to give a starting point for determining in what direction to focus entrepreneurial ventures. Most analysts want to start with the structure of the industries in which they participate. The industry structure has the effect of setting the "rules of the road" by which competitors compete.

Industry structure is the degree to which the industry may be dominated, controlled, or strongly under the influence of one or a few firms versus an industry that is fragmented or not dominated by one or a few firms.

Industry Sectors

For the purpose of discussion, consider the manufacturing sector of the economy. *Manufacturing*, according to the North American Industrial Classification System (NAICS), includes companies engaged in the mechanical, chemical, or physical transformation of materials, substances, or components into new products. This section utilizes data and information from NAICS.

KEY IDEA
NAICS, for the most part, has replaced the Standard Industrial Classification (SIC) code system.

Sub-sectors dive successively deeper. For example, the product of an alumina refinery is an input into the primary production of aluminum; primary aluminum is the main input to an aluminum wire drawing plant; and the aluminum wire is a principal input to a fabricated wire products plant.

The following example partially illustrates one sector with its first-level sub-sectors, each of which can be disaggregated into successive levels:

Sector 311, Food Manufacturing
- Sector 3111—Animal Food Manufacturing
- Sector 3112—Grain and Oilseed Milling
- Sector 3113—Sugar and Confectionery Product Manufacturing
- Sector 3114—Fruit and Vegetable Preserving and Specialty Food Manufacturing
- Sector 3115—Dairy Product Manufacturing
- Sector 3116—Animal Slaughter and Processing
- Sector 3117—Seafood Product Preparation and Packaging
- Sector 3118—Bakeries and Tortilla Manufacturing
- Sector 3119—Other Food Manufacturing

Individual establishments may operate in multiple sectors or subsectors, each of which likely will have its own industry structure.

Structure of Industry Sectors

A *sector chart* is shown in Figure 3.1 for four different industry structures: fragmented market, unconsolidated stable market, unconsolidated unstable market, and consolidated market. In a sector chart, each participant typically is

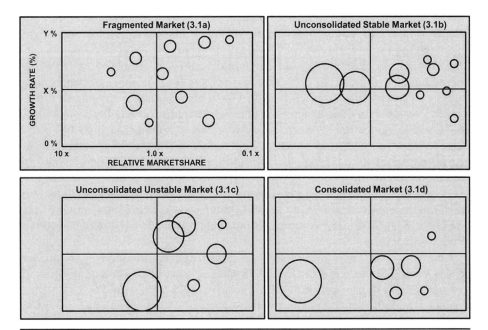

Figure 3.1 Example Sector Charts. Adapted from: Bogue, Marcus C., III, and Elwood S. Buffa, *Corporate Strategic Analysis*, 1986, The Free Press, p. 52.

represented by a circle that is proportional to its sales in that sector. The circle centers are plotted at the company's relative market share and growth rate. Thus, each sector chart contains four pieces of information to describe the sector and the competitors within the sector, including:

1. Relative market share (horizontal axis, where 1.0 is the average size enterprise);
2. Growth rate (vertical axis, represented in annual percentage growth);
3. Size of the company relative to others in the sector (relative size of the circle); and
4. Industry position relative to others in the sector (position of one circle relative to others).

In a *fragmented* market, shown in Figure 3.1a, all of the competitors are relatively small, and their growth rates may vary. At the other end of the spectrum, the industry has consolidated (Figure 3.1d), frequently with a single dominant competitor. In between are two unconsolidated stages, *stable* (Figure 3.1b) and unstable (Figure 3.1c). The *unconsolidated* stages of industry structure simply mean that no dominant player has emerged. Notice that the unconsolidated stable structure has two larger competitors, which are both growing at about the same rate, so one does not appear to be gaining dominance. Thus, the sector is *stable* in the sense that the situation is likely to remain as is for some time into the future. Notice also that the unconsolidated unstable structure has the largest competitor that is not growing as fast as the next two, which likely will overtake the largest at some time in the future.

Companies such as Waste Management, described in Chapter 2, are in a fragmented industry and have been able to grow by rolling up little companies into a larger entity, which is common. Prior to Waste Management beginning its roll-up activity, no company had a significant market share in waste collection, processing, landfills, and other services. This was a classic fragmented industry with a large number of small- to medium-sized companies. Many were privately held by the families that started them. This structure presented a classic opportunity for Waste Management.

Fragmented industries tend to present many opportunities for entrepreneurial supply chains, but in no way are entrepreneurial activities restricted to fragmented industries. Entrepreneurial supply chains can be formed regardless of the industry structure.

One way to begin to understand the extent of fragmentation in an industry in the United States is to check the U.S. Census Bureau's Economic Census for concentration ratios of various industries. As of this writing, the 2002 Economic Census, issued in May 2006, was the latest available. (See www.census.gov/prod/ec02/ec0231sr1.pdf for more information.)

A few selected sub-codes within Sector 311—Food Manufacturing are shown in Figure 3.2. Available data from May 2006 include the number of establishments

NAICS Code 311 – Food Manufacturing					
Selected Industry Sub-Codes	**Number of Establishments**	**4 Largest**	**8 Largest**	**20 Largest**	**50 Largest**
311 – All Food Manufacturing Companies	23,334	16.8 %	25.4 %	39.8 %	53.1 %
3112 – Grain and Oilseed Milling	506	47.3 %	60.7 %	75.4 %	88.2 %
31123 – Breakfast Cereal Manufacturing	45	78.4 %	91.1 %	98.8 %	100.0 %
311311– Sugarcane Mills	30	51.4%	69.8%	99.2 %	100.0 %
3114 – Fruit and Vegetable Preserving and Specialty Food Manufacturing	1,360	24.3 %	36.1 %	52.0 %	69.4 %
3115 – Dairy Products Manufacturing	1,170	24.9 %	36.1 %	55.2 %	74.6 %
31171 – Seafood Product Preparation and Packaging	648	20.5 %	28.7 %	46.0 %	68.1 %
311811 – Retail Bakeries	7,079	3.7 %	6.0 %	10.1 %	15.1 %

Figure 3.2   Share of Value of Shipments (Concentration Ratio). (See www.census.gov/prod/ec02/ec0231sr1.pdf for more information, accessed May 2010.)

in the sector (not companies because a company may have facilities serving several sectors), along with the percentage attributed to the largest four, eight, twenty, and fifty establishments in the sector.

For all food manufacturing, notice that the largest four establishments account for 16.8% of sector sales, and the 50 largest have 53.1% of sector sales. This illustrates an unconsolidated industry—a few large establishments with many small establishments. With 23,334 establishments in the segment then, 23,284 (23,334 minus 50) account for 46.9% of the total sector sales.

Notice, also, that breakfast cereal manufacturing (Sector 31123) and sugarcane mills (Sector 311311) are both highly concentrated. Breakfast cereals have 78.4% of the sector concentrated in the largest four establishments. Sugarcane mills have 51.4% in the largest four establishments. Both have 100% of the sector in the largest 50 establishments.

The retail bakeries sector (Sector 311811) is highly fragmented with only 15.1% (of 7,079 establishments) of the industry in the largest 50 establishments.

If one knows much about any of these sectors, it is fairly easy to have an instinctive understanding of their structures; but these data provide a useful quantitative appreciation. For example, sugarcane mills (Sector 311311) tend to be large, capital intensive, and strategically located where the cane is grown. So it is intuitively logical that there might be only 30 such establishments and that roughly half the capacity would be in the largest four mills.

Why the interest in sector analysis in a book about entrepreneurial supply chains? The simple reason is that this analysis shows a company what it is up against in its industry in terms of quantitative data. These data are accurate enough for first-cut analyses of the industry.

Fragmented Sectors

Fragmented industry sectors perhaps are the easiest way (but not the *only* way) to create entrepreneurial supply chains. Fragmented sectors do not have market leaders that have the power to shape the segment's competitive positioning. In a prior example, retail bakeries (Sector 311811), were positioned so that even the 50 largest competitors have only a 15.1% market share. If the reader steps back and thinks about it, this makes sense.

Porter[1] discusses fragmented industries in Chapter 9 of his book, *Competitive Strategy*, and below is a discussion adapted from it. Why is the retail bakeries sector so highly fragmented? There likely are several causes:

- *The segment has low barriers to entry.* Think of your local donut shop. The equipment, store furnishings, and fixtures are relatively inexpensive, and the store is relatively small. It is relatively easy to open a new donut shop.
- *The sector serves a localized clientele.* Your local donut shop draws customers only from a highly concentrated geographic area. Even if it is located on a busy freeway, clientele may come from a wide geographic area, but they are passing by, so effectively they become local customers in the sense that they do not drive far to reach the store.
- *Economies of scale do not amount to much.* If the donut shop were two, three, or even ten times as big, it likely could not produce donuts any better, faster, or cheaper.
- *Transportation costs are high.* Donuts do not ship easily. They are fragile; they get stale quickly; and there is no need to ship them because other shops make good donuts much closer to the customers. Switch your thinking to a ready-mix concrete plant with trucks carrying the concrete to local building sites. One does not run a ready-mix concrete truck from Miami to Jacksonville—it does not make logical, intuitive sense.
- *Inventory costs are high.* One does not store donuts or ready-mix concrete for very long—donuts go stale and concrete hardens.
- *There are no advantages of size in dealing with buyers or suppliers.* People do not purchase large quantities of donuts, and the ingredients are relatively common. Further, the amount of ready-mix concrete that is purchased depends only on the amount that is needed for the particular project. If the price were half or double the existing price, no more or less concrete would be purchased for the job. The same is true on the supply side of the ready-mix plant—only the amount of cement needed is used, regardless of the price.

You could apply the rationale to most if not all fragmented sectors. But, let's consider a specific example, CEMEX, about which you may have heard.

CEMEX: Innovation, Growth, and Consolidation in a Fragmented Industry

Amid many stories of innovation, growth, and consolidation in various fragmented industries, one, CEMEX, has a story to tell. The following discussion is adapted from the CEMEX website plus other writings on CEMEX.[2] CEMEX began as a Mexican company and now is a global building materials company that provides products and services to customers in more than 50 countries. CEMEX has a history of efforts to pursue innovative industry solutions and efficiency advancements, which have positioned it for spectacular global growth. CEMEX clearly pays attention to its supply chains and is very entrepreneurial.

CEMEX growth history. CEMEX was founded in 1906 with a plant in northern Mexico. They first expanded in Mexico. They then spread into Europe with the purchase in 1992 of Spain's two largest cement companies. In 1994, CEMEX acquired Venezuela's largest cement company, which launched its operations in South America. They became the world's third largest cement company in 1996, with an acquisition in Colombia. In 1997, CEMEX launched operations in Asia with an acquisition in the Philippines. They became North America's largest cement company with the 2000 acquisition of Southdown, a Houston-based company. In 2003, CEMEX launched a global sourcing operation for consolidated international procurement. In 2005, CEMEX doubled its size with the acquisition of RMC, adding 20 mainly-European markets. By 2006, CEMEX had over 50,000 employees at its 100th anniversary. In 2007, CEMEX initiated a major integration of Rinker Materials in the United States and Australia. CEMEX's FY2009 annual sales were approximately US$14.5B, a 28% decrease from FY2008 due to the global economic difficulties, which hit the building industries particularly hard.

CEMEX innovation. CEMEX is known for having an innovative culture and practices. It is known particularly for the innovative use of information technology both in the technical and operations side of the business and in business processes. They have a Global Center for Technology and Innovation located in Switzerland with a state-of-the-art research laboratory. They bring together industry and academia to conduct both product and process research. CEMEX often creates partnerships with academic institutions, enabling initiatives from exploratory research and continuous learning, to applied and basic research, and to the development of patents, among others.

CEMEX and Rinker Materials. Rinker Materials also has an interesting history that is germane to this story. According to its corporate website, Rinker was founded in 1926. Earlier, Rinker was purchased by CSR Limited, but now is part of CEMEX. CSR saw an opportunity for entrepreneurial supply chains in the United States. They performed a classic roll-up in the fragmented industry and consolidated their acquired companies into a much larger CSR. Rinker and CEMEX were in nearly identical businesses. In its present form, Rinker was established following the demerger of the heavy building materials businesses of CSR in 2003. Rinker group companies have operations in the U.S. and Australia, supplying aggregate (gravel), cement, concrete, concrete block, asphalt, concrete pipe and other construction materials to over 34,000 customers.

CSR Limited was an Australian company that came to the United States in the 1990s with the express purpose of consolidation in the cement and related products industries, each of which generally was a fragmented segment. For example, aggregate (rock/gravel) is a basic building block for road building, concrete, and concrete products. Aggregate is a localized product, being dug from the ground in quarries, and is difficult and expensive to transport. Generally, aggregate companies did not own cement plants or provide concrete, concrete block, or concrete pipe for their customers. The other products also generally were produced by companies that focused on one or a few products exclusively. That is, a ready-mix concrete company likely only did ready-mix concrete, a cement-block company likely only did cement blocks, and so on.

> **An Aside:**
> Full Disclosure: I was a consultant to CSR during its acquisitions and consolidation of those acquisitions in the United States. As such, I saw much of the internal strategies and operations of the company. None of that information, however, is disclosed herein.

CSR purchased many companies supplying each of these individual products and consolidated them under the CSR America brand. Then, they could go to a large road-building company and commit to deliver, on an integrated schedule, their concrete pipe on Monday, their aggregate on Tuesday, their concrete block on Wednesday, and their concrete on Thursday and Friday. They had the whole suite of products required for road building. Furthermore, some of the large construction companies that would work all over a state and could procure from one company, CSR, instead of numerous small, specialized, and uncoordinated suppliers. CSR was successful in their consolidation efforts. CSR spun off these interests, then producing more than half the company's profits, to a separate listed company, Rinker, in 2003. Rinker was subsequently acquired by CEMEX. CEMEX is a superb example of growth and innovation using entrepreneurial supply chains.

Summarizing a Framework for Analyzing the Industry Structure

As shown, using CEMEX as an example, the competitive position of a firm at least partly determines its performance in its industry. There are a series of other matters that one might consider in the industry analysis.

- *Industry segments*. There likely might be a range of competitive industry segments for the firm. As mentioned above, many companies compete in multiple segments of an industry. CEMEX competes in aggregates, cement, concrete, concrete block, and concrete pipe, as well as all of these simultaneously. Each of these can be considered a competitive segment of the business. Some customers (such as road builders) might want the entire suite of products; other, more focused customers might want only concrete block.

- *Value chain activities*. There likely also might be a range of value-chain activities spanned by the firm. For example, recall Porter's value-chain discussion in Chapter 1. Notice that several activities are included in his value-chain model: human resource management, technology development, procurement, inbound logistics, and operations. Companies frequently look for niche players in the industry, such as a company that developed software with a unique capability. An entrepreneurial company such as CEMEX or Waste Management might wish to acquire the company or its software product in order to use it in their own businesses, to keep it out of the hands of competitors, or to market and sell it themselves.

- *Geographies*. There might be a range of geographies spanned by the firm or geographic "holes" in their coverage of the market. For example, a company such as Waste Management might acquire or open waste collection and processing capabilities in a particular geographic region, and then need their own landfill to accommodate the waste. Or, a company such as CEMEX might have coverage in a geographic area for their suite of products, except for concrete pipe. The logical next move might be to start up or acquire a concrete pipe company.

ANALYSIS AND POSITIONING OF CUSTOMERS AND SUPPLIERS

There is a lot of talk about integrated supply chains, but are they the answer to corporate competitiveness? Or are they just another nifty idea that ensures full employment for management consultants and lecture material for academics?

Actually, the analysis and positioning of customers and suppliers is a three-prong process made up of strategic alignment of customers and suppliers, paths forward to achieve innovation and growth, and planning and control for existing production. Many times, however, relations between customers and suppliers are characteristic of "purchasing, circa 1970." These are tied to transactions and are highly tactical, what Mike Katzorke[3] calls "three bids, a cloud of dust, and a hearty hi-yo Silver," mimicking the old television program, *The Lone Ranger.*

Again and again, and more ominous, many suppliers are being allowed to operate differently with different parts of the buying company: first, they persuade engineering personnel to effectively write their products into the technical specifications; then, they negotiate after-the-sale levels of support with aftermarket personnel; and finally, they negotiate pricing with purchasing. Purchasing, in effect, operates primarily as a tactical, transaction-processing function with some, but not very strong, price negotiations. As a result, in areas vital for successful operation (innovation, ability to grow, quality, cost, delivery, service, cycle time, inventory, reliability, maintainability, etc.), the procurement process also is "in the 1970s" as far as results are concerned. The procurement organization in other companies focuses everything on price negotiations. This, also, is not a very enlightened approach.

What about multiple suppliers? Many buyers defend the practice of having multiple suppliers for everything. They want multiple suppliers in order:

- To ensure continuity of supply in case of a strike or other unforeseen shutdown by any one supplier;
- To strengthen the buyers' hands with an economic advantage over a fragmented group of dependent suppliers;
- To enhance competition among suppliers, who can be played off against each other into price reductions; and
- To provide maneuvering room for swings in quantities, business conditions, or technology.

> **KEY IDEA**
>
> Teaming up with suppliers many times can boost the earnings of both companies.

How would you respond to these arguments? What are the counter arguments? Please see the questions asked in the "Learning Questions" section at the end of this chapter.

Caterpillar might have responded differently to the arguments about multiple suppliers several years ago than they do now. Caterpillar's new strategy is to use suppliers to help it build its machines more efficiently. An article in *Bloomberg BusinessWeek*[4] explained that Caterpillar's suppliers in the past complained about a lack of dialogue, saying that the corporation's attitude was that they wanted suppliers simply to give them what they wanted, when they wanted it. The article quotes the company as saying that it is:

> . . . *shrinking the number of suppliers it relies on to 6,000 from 9,000 and is working more closely with 200 companies it has identified as critical to*

its growth . . . competition is going to be based on the supply chain, not an individual company.

The article cites an example of a collaborative relationship with Tenneco on a catalytic converter in which the two companies' engineers worked together on the design, reduced the complexity of the product, created a mock production line, and produced the product in a Tenneco plant in Nebraska. This collaboration cut Caterpillar's costs by 20%.

Anecdotal data from Caterpillar is interesting, but rigorous empirical research is needed. Fortunately, some data are known, with one example being published in the *Journal of Operations Management*.[5] The research involved 148 manufacturers and 592 suppliers. The authors put forward the thesis that supplier innovativeness can have positive benefits for the buyer on multiple dimensions of manufacturer performance. However, they state, interestingly, that these links are moderated by the fit between the learning styles of the manufacturer and supplier.

The five dimensions of manufacturer performance that they tested were cost, quality, product development, delivery, and flexibility. The learning style that gave the best fit was exploratory in nature. That is, when the organizational learning of both supplier and buyer was exploratory, it meant that learning and innovativeness took place in an exploratory manner. Another word, "collaboration," could be added to "exploratory," and help explain this. When the culture of both sides is to learn in a collaborative and exploratory manner, then innovation is enhanced. However, if the style of one or the other is exploitative, then the benefits from collaboration are reduced if not eliminated. An "exploitation" approach tends to reduce or eliminate cooperation and innovation.

> **KEY IDEA**
>
> Remember that your suppliers are your suppliers because they have expertise that you do not have. Treat them as valued members of your supply chain, not as adversaries to be exploited.

So, how should relations between suppliers and customers be studied? Recognize that these relationships are two sides of the same coin. Ask yourself, how do customers approach their relations with suppliers, and how do suppliers approach their relations with customers? We hear all sorts of reactions to those questions, which vary according to which side the buyer/supplier link is talking, such as:

- Customers say, "We need lower costs, better quality, faster delivery, or any of a myriad of other needs."
- Suppliers say, "We need cooperative partnerships."
- Customers say, "We need value-added benefits such as a willingness to work with us when we need something different."
- Suppliers say, "We need to grow our business with you."
- Customers say, "We need you to have the ability and desire to grow with us."
- Suppliers say, "We need to get in earlier on the product development cycle."

- Customers say, "We need innovation in technology and in business processes."
- Suppliers say, "We need you to be a better customer for us."

And on and on. . . . So, how can suppliers be positioned appropriately? Figure 3.3 shows a four-step sourcing process.

1. *Rationalize suppliers.* The objective is to identify the best suppliers available. Remember, your suppliers are your suppliers because they have expertise that you do not have. Treat them accordingly. The buyer needs to establish close linkages with the supplier, including frequent visits (perhaps quarterly, more or less, as conditions warrant) to provide direct communications and joint tangible problem solving. It is impossible to have close linkages with a large, scattered, undisciplined, and unreliable supplier base. Furthermore, it is impossible to be a good customer to a large number of suppliers. It is not the reduced supply base, per se, for which we are looking. But it is the painstaking joint efforts to attack quality issues, long lead times, high costs, or lack of innovation.

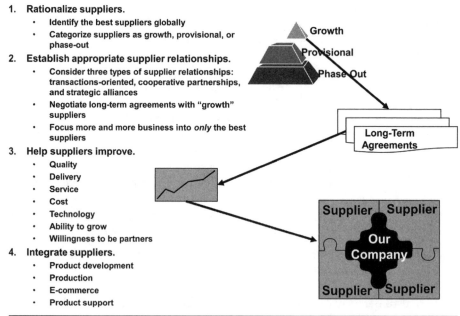

1. **Rationalize suppliers.**
   - Identify the best suppliers globally
   - Categorize suppliers as growth, provisional, or phase-out
2. **Establish appropriate supplier relationships.**
   - Consider three types of supplier relationships: transactions-oriented, cooperative partnerships, and strategic alliances
   - Negotiate long-term agreements with "growth" suppliers
   - Focus more and more business into *only* the best suppliers
3. **Help suppliers improve.**
   - Quality
   - Delivery
   - Service
   - Cost
   - Technology
   - Ability to grow
   - Willingness to be partners
4. **Integrate suppliers.**
   - Product development
   - Production
   - E-commerce
   - Product support

Figure 3.3 Four-Step Sourcing Process. Adapted from discussions with Michael R. Katzorke, coauthor of Lee, William B. and Michael R. Katzorke, *Leading Effective Supply Chain Transformations: A Guide to Sustainable World-Class Capability and Results*, 2010, J. Ross Publishing.

The supplier rationalization process identifies the best suppliers globally. These are classified as "growth" suppliers, into which more business is made available. The second-level suppliers are "provisional" and given the opportunity to become growth suppliers if they can improve to meet the growth standards; otherwise, they drop out of contention. The third-level suppliers are "phase-out" suppliers that do not meet the standards needed to continue as suppliers.

2. *Establish appropriate supplier relationships.* Establishing appropriate supplier relationships is a way to categorize suppliers for purposes of defining how to interact with them. Three types of supplier relationships generally follow the well-known *ABC* approach to inventory analysis. This phenomenon is based on Pareto's Law or the *Pareto Principle* (named after Italian economist Villefredo Pareto) who first described the "80/20 rule" in 1906. Pareto noted that, for many activities, roughly 80% of the effects come from 20% of the causes. Pareto observed that about 80% of the wealth was controlled by 20% of the people. This has become a common rule of thumb such as 80% of sales come from 20% of the customers, and 80% of the value of inventory is accounted for by 20% of the items. This is also known as "the vital few and the trivial many." This phenomenon can be used in various ways, and for discussion purposes, it is used to establish appropriate supplier relationships:

   a. *Transactions-oriented* relationships are the most numerous and least consequential. In broad terms, this category usually contains roughly 50% of the purchased items that are worth around 10% of the costs. These are purchases of "nuts, bolts, and screws" in which product quality is more-or-less standardized and per-unit costs tend to be relatively low. Cost and delivery are the key purchasing criteria.

   b. *Cooperative partnerships* entail a medium amount of collaboration. In broad terms, these usually are about 35% of the items purchased that are worth about 15% of the costs. These items are important, but not critical to the company's operations. Purchasing criteria are consistency and dependability of the relationships, and elimination of problems.

   c. *Strategic alliances* require a high level of collaboration between buyer and seller with a strong working relationship. In broad terms, these usually are about 15% of the items that are worth about 75% of the costs. There likely are technological advantages of the alliance, particularly as it applies to new products and processes. These are the "most critical" items that a company acquires.

3. *Help suppliers improve.* Helping suppliers improve usually involves joint problem solving between customer and supplier. It is highly likely that a customer's problem with a supplier is the direct result of something the customer does. The author once did a supplier survey for a consulting

client and was told by several suppliers that their delivery problems almost always traced back to short lead-time changes to the orders; the customer changed the item ordered, the quantity, or the due date, causing havoc in the suppliers' scheduling. One thing you don't want to do is to show up saying, in effect, "Hi, I'm from your customer, and I'm here to help you improve because you clearly cannot do it yourself." That's kind of like hearing, "Hi, I'm from the IRS, and I'm here to help you with your taxes!"

4. *Integrate suppliers.* The process of integrating suppliers depends upon the type of buyer/supplier relationships that exist. Recall the three types of connections cited above: transactions oriented, cooperative partnerships, and strategic alliances. Also, recognize the business activities for which integration might be useful, such as product development, production, and product support. For example, companies likely will want their strategic alliances to be involved in early product development so as to incorporate preferred technology into the products. E-commerce capabilities likely will be used primarily with transactions-oriented suppliers.

This four-step process is all about the appropriate level of supply chain integration. Flynn et al.[6] discuss and define *supply chain integration (SCI)* as follows:

> . . . *including the manufacturer (internal integration) and extending from it both directions (customer and supplier integration) . . . we define SCI as the degree to which a manufacturer strategically collaborates with its supply chain partners and collaboratively manages intra- and inter-organization processes.*

While this is a good definition, it does not differentiate the correct levels of integration, depending upon the appropriate type of relationships between buyer and seller. For example, *transactions-oriented* relationships should not fall into the definition of supply chain integration. Certainly strategic alliances, and perhaps cooperative partnerships, should be included.

Clearly, supply chain integration includes internal, customer, and supplier integration. Without strong internal integration, the others will not be successful.

RECOGNIZING THE VALUE WITHIN MULTILEVEL SUPPLY CHAINS

The focus, of course, is on entrepreneurial supply chains as the basis for innovation and growth. Clearly, multilevel supply chains stem from customers and perhaps customers' customers back upstream to suppliers and perhaps suppliers' suppliers. Unfortunately, this has not been the subject of much research, particularly in the same way that the issues are structured in this book.

There has been at least one piece of published research by Song and DiBenedetto[7] on aspects of the issue. Their research indicates that supplier involvement may be essential to a new venture seeking to develop a radical innovation. This is not particularly surprising, in and of itself; however, also important is the extent of supplier involvement as well as some of the antecedents of supplier involvement.

Song and DiBenedetto discuss the value of specific investments by suppliers in the new venture. By specific investments, they mean those with notably less value outside the relationship. They provide the following examples:

- Tailoring the production system to the requirements of the customer;
- Ensuring that the customer's requirements are met;
- Investing in specialized tools and equipment;
- Adapting technological standards to the customer's needs; and/or
- Investing in specialized worker training.

They point out that specific investments can increase the level of a supplier's involvement and thus the possible return if the venture is successful. But these investments also can increase the supplier's risk if the venture is unsuccessful. In addition, they increase the customer's risk because of the increased dependence on the supplier. Both supplier and customer need to take steps to safeguard their investments from opportunistic behavior by the other.

It is also important to consider the antecedents to successful supplier involvement. The research by Song and DiBenedetto found that the following were the most significant antecedents to success:

- The nature and extent of supplier's specific investment;
- The nature and extent of the supplier's capabilities;
- Relative power in the relationship between the supplier and customer; and
- Commitment of the customer to the supplier.

While there have been a few other studies of this type, Song and DiBenedetto are among the first to explore these effects specifically in the case of new ventures that are, perhaps more than others due to their financial constraints, particularly dependent on attracting the right suppliers and depending on them for financial support.

While Song and DiBenedetto did not suggest this, it makes sense to turn the research around and consider it as an entrepreneurial supply chain endeavor by the supplier. The supplier may be looking entrepreneurially to potential customers for investment opportunities. Their entrepreneurial supply chain integration search easily might lead to this type of opportunity.

> **KEY IDEA**
>
> Shift the focus from cutting costs to exploiting innovation and growth potential.

Recognizing the entrepreneurial value in multi-level supply chains may involve a specific plan to enable customers to serve *their* customers better. Consider a shift from cutting costs to exploiting innovation and growth potential. McKinsey & Company published an article[8] that focuses on this same idea, based on experiences of mature European basic materials industries.

Basic materials usually are thought of as commodities that are sold by the ton, based on price and availability as order winners and quality as an order qualifier. So how does one exploit innovation and growth potential in these industries? One way is to think beyond the customer to their customers and how to enable one to serve the other better. Think about, for example, viewing the supplier and customer as a single entity working together to minimize transactions costs and maximize value to the next customer in the chain. If this is accomplished successfully, this customer integration can lead to sustainable competitive advantages in industries where such advantages are difficult to come by.

To help customers serve their customers better requires a different approach— one of satisfying individual customers instead of general customer satisfaction. This means a one-on-one team-based methodology. Usually, one-on-one teams are dedicated to individual customers and focus on the requirements of their customers. For example, in the discussion of CEMEX above, one of the basic premises of consolidation in the cement-based industries was to be able to commit to deliver customers' concrete pipe on Monday, aggregate on Tuesday, concrete block on Wednesday, and concrete on Thursday and Friday. This approach helped the road-building contractor better serve its customer (whoever wanted the road built) in terms of both time and cost.

DIVING DEEPLY INTO MULTIPLE LEVELS OF SUPPLY CHAINS

Diving deeply into multiple levels of the company's supply chains for entrepreneurial opportunities implies a systematic, analytic search process. What about multiple supply chains—both incoming from suppliers and outgoing to customers?

Multiple Supply Chains

There are many versions of multiple supply chains with multiple levels on both the demand and supply sides. No one size fits all. As explained by the research of Joseph Cavinato[9], supply chains within different companies have varied widely. Sometimes, even within a given company the structure of multiple supply chains have varied widely. There are many models of supply chains; some are more amenable to innovation, growth, and entrepreneurship than others. Those who have aspirations to entrepreneurial supply chains should pay close attention to the structures and meanings of theirs. Readers who are interested in this particular advanced supply chain thinking should study the Cavinato article—it is well worth your time.

Cavinato suggests 16 different types of supply chains, shown in Figures 3.4 and 3.5. Notice the *Business Impact* on the horizontal axis in Figure 3.4, ranging from Traditional to Competitive Advantage, as well as the *Complexity*, ranging from Low to High on the vertical axis. Characteristics of the 16 types are outlined in Figure 3.5.

The first three types, arrayed on the left side of Figure 3.4, are not recommended for today's supply chains. The middle group, types 4 through 9, likely is familiar to most supply chain professionals. Type 10, Extended Supply Chains, is most common in fast-moving consumer goods industries in which collaboration from suppliers (and perhaps suppliers' suppliers) all the way through to the ultimate consumer has value. Type 11, Market Dominance and Blocking Chains, is likely to be deemed illegal in the United States, although it is legal and widely practiced in some countries.

The most useful models for our purposes are Types 12 through 16. Type 14, Innovation Chains, is of particular interest. Cavinato asserts that these are most useful in fast-paced industries with high turnover of product life cycles, such as seasonal toy companies and high-tech electronics companies. Many of these companies concentrate on the percentage of total revenue that comes from new

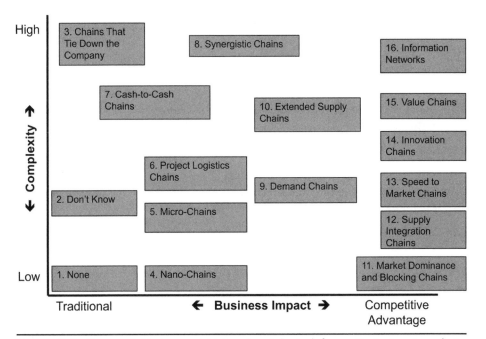

Figure 3.4 Types of Chains and Networks. Adapted from: Cavinato, Joseph L., "What's Your Supply Chain Type?" *Supply Chain Management Review*, May–June

TYPE OF CHAIN	CHARACTERISTICS	TYPE OF CHAIN	CHARACTERISTICS
1. None	Current functions are fine as is. Provides no competitive advantage.	2. Don't Know	Third-party logistics handle it. Supply chain outsourced with commodity-like logistics.
3. Chains That Tie Down the Firm	Places inordinate emphasis upon an internal aspect of the company to the detriment of the total chain.	4. Nano-Chains	Maximizes manufacturing efficiencies. Can divert corporate strategic emphasis, energies toward mostly internal activities.
5. Micro-Chains	Balance purchasing, production, and distribution. Classic logistics model.	6. Project Logistics Chains	Creates supply, flow, and logistics for specific projects.
7. Cash-to-Cash Chains	Maximizes cash flow. Can negatively affect suppliers and customers.	8. Synergistic Chains	Eliminate duplicate costs. Gain buying power. Provides no competitive advantage.
9. Demand Chains	Feed customers in ways that are efficient for them. Close collaboration with customers.	10. Extended Supply Chains	Supplier-to-customer efficiencies. Good for overall cost and flow analysis of all resources.
11. Market Dominance and Blocking Chains	Keep others out of the market. Not legal in most developed countries.	12. Supply Integration Chains	Model supplier-firm linkages. Useful for many competitive initiatives. Good for cost reduction.
13. Speed-to-Market Chains	Emphasizes product development and launch. Flexible supply chain required.	14. Innovation Chains	Push growth opportunities. Focus on creation, launch, and growth phases of product life cycle.
15. Value Chains	Focus on competing with chain partners against other chains. Emphasizes competing with the total chain.	16. Information Networks	Competitiveness in information flow. Emphasizes core set of efficient and agile processes.

Figure 3.5   Characteristics of the Types of Chains and Networks. Adapted from: Cavinato, Joseph L., "What's Your Supply Chain Type?" *Supply Chain Management Review*, May–June 2002, p. 62.

products. Managing the new product development process thus is one key to the continuous flow of innovative ideas and resulting new products. Cavinato suggests close linkages with both suppliers and customers in order to tap their capabilities and needs. He gets close to the idea of entrepreneurial supply chains when he states:

> *"This requires purchasing and supply personnel to find and create . . . relationships for the purpose of innovation rather than simple price minimization."*

For Type 15, Value Chains, Cavinato also gets close to our discussion:

> *". . . more formalized concept of developing partner-like relationships . . . [to] create an ongoing flow of technology development and product innovation between the participating companies."*

Disaggregating the Supply Chain into Relevant Activities

Which activities in the multilevel supply chains should be subject to entrepreneurial initiatives? Perhaps more rigorously, the question could be asked differently: Which activities in the value chain should be performed internally to the organization, and which should be sourced externally? This question historically has been asked as the make-or-buy decision, or as the "how much vertical integration" decision. It also has been asked as the "outsourcing" question: how much outsourcing is right, and which activities should be outsourced? All of these questions essentially involve *re-shaping the boundaries* of the enterprise. However, few if any instances exist in which these questions have been asked in an entrepreneurial or innovation context, which is what is being done here.

So, let's answer those questions head-on. Consider three process areas: *customer-focused*, *supplier-focused*, and *internal* processes. Successful entrepreneurial supply chains require strong capabilities in each of the three processes. The capabilities also need to be of two types: integration *within* each general area and integration *across* these three general areas.

KEY IDEA
Those who control the supply chains' process connections typically dominate the chains.

Consider the Key Idea for a moment: "process connections" are the primary linkages between customer-focused, supplier-focused, and internal processes.

Think about a company that is considering acquiring a certain capability from outside, whether by acquisition, outsourcing, partnering, or whatever means is appropriate. While the outsourcing decision is somewhat limiting, consider it for a moment. This has been a popular and well accepted approach to acquiring capabilities for many years. Companies have outsourced human resource administration such as payroll, pensions, and benefits management; many have outsourced elements of their finance and accounting activities; and there are numerous instances of outsourcing manufacturing and distribution functions. It is fair to say that cost reduction has been the primary objective and not innovation, growth, or entrepreneurship. That is unfortunate because companies are missing major opportunities by focusing only on cost reduction. But, significant cost reduction has not always been achieved, which should give companies reason to pause and think about such moves.

An Aside: Please note that Quinn's article focused on outsourcing innovation. His ideas are expanded here to entrepreneurial ventures, using the previously presented definition of entrepreneurial ventures to include outsourcing. An entrepreneurial venture is a more inclusive term and could include mergers, acquisitions, joint ventures, and other forms of relationships including outsourcing.

There have been several publications,[10] however, that recognize the possibilities of obtaining innovations from outside the enterprise. The pharmaceuticals industry is one of the most prolific users of outsourcing and other entrepreneurial ventures. For example, pharmaceuticals industry core competencies and entrepreneurial opportunities, shown in Figure 3.6, is adapted from Quinn,[11] and illustrates how

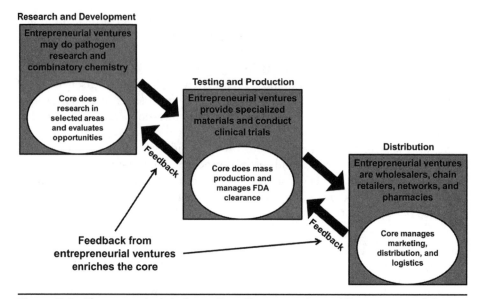

Figure 3.6   Pharmaceuticals Industry Core Competencies and Entrepreneurial Opportunities. Adapted from: Quinn, James Brian, "Outsourcing Innovation: The New Engine of Growth," *Sloan Management Review*, Volume 41, Number 4, Summer 2000, p. 15.

that industry frequently integrates its core competencies with entrepreneurial ventures.

This type of framework thinking is fairly common in electronics, food, and many other industries in addition to pharmaceuticals. In general, no single company, regardless of its industry can hope to match the totality of all the external enterprises innovating in its supply chains. This is one reason why entrepreneurial supply chains can be effective sources for innovation and growth.

So, which activities should be subject to entrepreneurial initiatives? As shown in Figure 3.6, these can range across the gamut from basic research to early-stage research to product development to various other internal processes, and to supplier- and customer-focused processes. The key questions are: where does innovation occur, and where is growth likely to happen in the industry?

Innovation can occur anywhere along the supply chain, as shown in Figure 3.6. For example, a common practice is for drug companies and other large companies to wait for the entrepreneur with his or her small company to develop the product and then purchase the company.

A non-pharmaceutical example took place a number of years ago when Emerson Electric purchased the company that made the original Weed Eater. The product was developed and brought to market by an entrepreneur. Then, when it became successful, Emerson bought the company.

Entrepreneurial supply chains should be driven by customer needs. Wayne Gretzky, the retired Canadian hockey player (who is known as the "greatest hockey player of all time") is reputed to have said that the secret to being a great hockey player is to "skate to where the puck *will* be, not to where it *is*!" This is what is wanted with entrepreneurial supply chains—go where innovation *will* be needed and where the growth *will* be. Obviously, this is easier said than done; nevertheless, that is the objective.

A rhetorical question is often asked, "Why don't we treat our suppliers in the same way we wish our customers to treat us?" We want our customers to treat us as strategic partners and as valued members of their supply chains. But we seem to want to treat our suppliers differently. The truth is that suppliers are highly valued members of supply chains. Our suppliers are our suppliers because they have capabilities that we don't have, so we should treat them well, accordingly.

HOW BAKER HUGHES UTILIZES CUSTOMERS AND SUPPLIERS AS SOURCES OF IDEAS AND OPPORTUNITIES

So, how does Baker Hughes relate to its customers and suppliers? Take the suppliers first and consider the conceptual matrix model in Figure 3.7. The company uses a supplier segmentation matrix and puts all products and major components into the matrix. For Baker Hughes, its intellectual property (IP) is extremely important, given the highly competitive and global nature of its businesses. Protecting the IP is a significant consideration when sourcing products and components. They keep a close eye on the IP world in which they live.

Notice that the horizontal axis is labeled IP Sensitivity and/or Product Complexity, and that the vertical axis is labeled Supply Chain Capability/Capacity. This 2 × 2 matrix is intended to illustrate two important considerations when dealing with both suppliers and customers. Let's take the segments in Figure 3.7 one at a time:

Low IP sensitivity and low supply chain capability/capacity: Since local-content considerations are becoming more important, this quadrant represents those products and/or components that could be manufactured in lower-cost, customer-centric regions around the world. This would satisfy the local content requirements while reducing landed cost of products. Considering that the complexity is low and there are no significant IP concerns, the risk of product transition failure is reduced. This can be a "make or buy" quadrant, and joint ventures and other arrangements also can be used to keep initial investments and the product cost as low as feasible, given delivery, quality, and other considerations.

Low IP sensitivity and high supply chain capability/capacity: Since the supply chain has already demonstrated the capability/capacity, and since IP is not a significant consideration, this usually is a traditional "buy" decision. These products

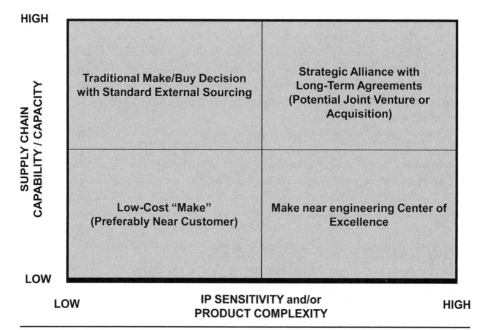

HIGH

SUPPLY CHAIN CAPABILITY / CAPACITY

| Traditional Make/Buy Decision with Standard External Sourcing | Strategic Alliance with Long-Term Agreements (Potential Joint Venture or Acquisition) |
| Low-Cost "Make" (Preferably Near Customer) | Make near engineering Center of Excellence |

LOW

LOW   IP SENSITIVITY and/or   **HIGH**
                  PRODUCT COMPLEXITY

Figure 3.7 Baker Hughes Supplier Segmentation Matrix. Conceptual model adapted from discussions with executives of Baker Hughes. Used with permission.

represent an excellent opportunity for low-cost suppliers and suppliers that can provide the best overall value in customer-centric regions.

High IP sensitivity and low supply chain capability/capacity: Baker Hughes has a clear understanding of its IP and, in their terms, they "protect it like a mother bear protects her cubs." If a product is IP sensitive and Baker Hughes owns the IP, it is usually manufactured in-house, moreover, in a country with a recognized track record of respecting IP. However, this process also recognizes *complexity* as a key sourcing criterion. Many companies have tried outsourcing high-technology/ high complexity products to low-cost sources and failed. Baker Hughes's process does a sound job of managing that risk. Products of high complexity are usually manufactured in-house and in close proximity to their engineering centers of excellence.

High IP sensitivity and high supply chain capability/capacity: There are examples in this quadrant where Baker Hughes owns the IP of a given product, but has formed strategic relationships with a handful of suppliers to produce that product. Moreover, this quadrant also houses examples where suppliers own the IP of a given product and sell to Baker Hughes. In both cases, these products are managed through strategic alliances with long-term agreements and/or joint venture arrangements, and Baker Hughes' Vice President, Supply Chain, Art Soucy, takes personal ownership of the senior level relationships.

Baker Hughes has a formal process for dealing with its top customers that attempts to establish and maintain a high degree of customer intimacy and to link the customers with its supply chain of suppliers and manufacturing. In this way, they have a linkage between the company's demand and supply, and therefore have a more cost-effective and responsive supplier-to-customer relationship. The supplier segmentation matrix as shown in Figure 3.7 is an essential component of these linkages.

The company has an active sales and operations planning (S&OP) process to enhance the demand and supply linkages. However, they freely admit that S&OP is not yet a fully capable process within the company, but it has a high priority for continued improvement.

As mentioned, local content, standards, and/or various forms of relationships (e.g., partnerships, joint ventures, and alliances) with local companies is becoming more important for doing business in many countries around the world. Therefore, it is incumbent upon Baker Hughes, like many other companies, both to satisfy local requirements and at the same time maintain the company's technologies and capabilities.

State-owned oil companies are controlling more of the world's oil and gas reserves. This means that Baker Hughes has to develop new customer relationships. Some of these relationships, as state-owned oil companies are behind the push toward more local content, are almost certainly at the direction of the governments that own them. This will continue to be an issue for many companies, not unique to Baker Hughes or to others in their industry.

An Aside: I have consulted and conducted executive education with many of these companies and countries around the world, beginning in the mid-1970s with Aramco (now, Saudi Aramco) in Saudi Arabia. I have been to Saudi Arabia numerous times and have seen the economic development of the Kingdom over the years.

Early in this experience, Aramco embarked on a program of "Saudization" with the express purpose of developing the capabilities of their nationals so that they could move up in the organization and thus displace non-Saudi employees. This was a program that lasted many years and, to an outsider, it looked to be very effective.

My focus was on "materials supply," taking hundreds of people through various educational programs, including three-month stints in the United States and providing hands-on consulting assistance. Now, Baker Hughes is responding to local-content regulations in Saudi Arabia, which is a further attempt to develop the economy of Saudi Arabia. Many other companies are dealing with the same issues, almost regardless of the industry or the country.

A CASE NOTE FOR FURTHER STUDY: Taylor Fresh Foods

The cases are available at www.harvardbusinessonline.com. Readers should obtain copies of this case and use it to go beyond discussion in the book. These cases were prepared as the basis for discussion, rather than to illustrate either effective or ineffective handling of any particular situation.

Global food chains represent the world's most complex industry, moving from seeds going into the ground to raising of crops and animals for food to our meals at homes and in restaurants. It has a few, very large players such as Monsanto, DuPont, and Syngenta in seeds. Dole is a large producer and marketer of fresh fruits and vegetables. Sysco is a global leader in selling, marketing, and distributing food products, and the ubiquitous McDonald's is all over the world. Most of the industry is built, however, on small farms, processors, distributors, retail food markets, and restaurants. Overall, it is a very fragmented industry, shown conceptually in Figure 3.8.

For this chapter, the Taylor Fresh Foods[12] case is used. Other facts are based on information from its corporate website, May 2010. This case is relevant because:

1. It shows how an extremely entrepreneurial company in a fragmented industry was able to grow substantially from a very small beginning into a large firm that is a recognized leader in its industry.
2. It deals with the complex food industry, perhaps the most complex supply chains in the world. This includes companies with multiple types of supply chains, as shown in Figures 3.4 and 3.5.
3. As discussed, fragmented industries offer particular opportunities for entrepreneurial supply chains, and Taylor illustrates how one company was able to make this happen.
4. It illustrates how Taylor expanded along several elements of the food supply chains, and how Bruce Taylor and his team were always looking for other opportunities.
5. It illustrates backward integration with suppliers, forward integration with customers, and horizontal integration with competitors.

Bruce Taylor has a MBA from Harvard and is Chairman and CEO of Taylor. He is the main character, and a key quote from Bruce sums up the case:

Our system encourages independence and entrepreneurship. . . . The challenge is: how can we be aggressively entrepreneurial in a structured way? . . . Employees are constantly on the lookout for new product ideas. . . . to understand [our customers'] needs and then help them grow using our products. We grow along with them.

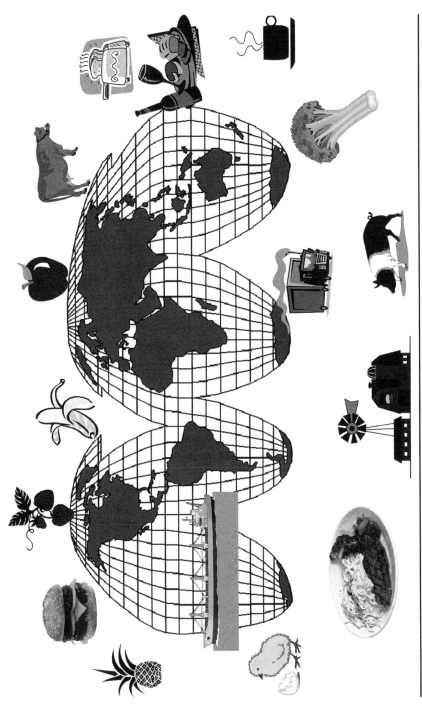

Figure 3.8 The World's Most Complex Supply Chain.

One significant point is, if Taylor helps its customers be more successful, then it, too, will become more successful. Of course, that's obvious, but then, why don't more companies practice that same simple and basic idea?

The case concentrates on Bruce Taylor's entrepreneurial focus in building his very small company, starting out on his own in 1995. At the time of the case writing, the authors of the case described his company as the leading U.S. supplier of fresh-cut vegetables and salads to institutional and foodservice buyers such as McDonald's, Darden Restaurants, and Sysco, along with retail chains such as Raley's and Safeway. For the fiscal year ending June 30, 2008, the firm reported revenues of $1.1B and operating income of $26M. At this time, Taylor's management was evaluating several product line expansions in the retail markets.

Taylor grew significantly through both organic growth and acquisitions, starting with a 1995 acquisition of South Bay Salads from U.S. Sugar in Florida. They then received a commitment from Sysco to support a California operation and acquired Valley Precut in Salinas. Major customers, Sam's Club and Darden Restaurants, were added in 1996. In 1998, Taylor acquired North American Produce and also became a major vegetable supplier to McDonald's.

In 1999, Taylor acquired several processors in Kentucky, Texas, and Florida, along with new distribution facilities for Subway, a new customer. In 2002, Taylor Farms Mexico was formed to source lettuce and other raw products from central Mexico in order to diversify supply sources. These are just a few of the diversification moves made by the company on both the customer and supply sides.

On the supply side, growing areas for many vegetables are highly concentrated, especially seasonally. This puts extra pressure on Taylor to diversify its supply sources because Taylor used many of the same base ingredients to create different products throughout the year. In 2008, Taylor had a wide variety of pre-cut and ready-to-eat salads, pre-cut vegetables and vegetable trays, and snacks. On the demand side, Taylor focused primarily on foodservice and retail customers.

The food supply industry is fragmented and capital-intensive with low margins. Competitors can imitate each other's products with relative ease. There are a few large competitors including Dole, Fresh Express, and Ready Pac. There are many regional and niche companies.

How one thinks about industry segmentation is important when considering the entrepreneurial supply chain opportunities for a company such as Taylor. For example, segments could include fresh-cut vegetables seen in retail supermarket produce sections—many of which are shipped into the United States from around the world. It is not unusual, for example, to see produce from Chile, Argentina, Israel, and Egypt, particularly during seasonal times.

Fresh-cut vegetables can be packaged into bags of baby carrots or cut broccoli for consumers to build their own salads. Salads also may be pre-mixed and pre-packaged for sale; the vegetables may be laid out into trays for party snacks; fresh vegetables may be presented in the deli section of the supermarket; or any number of other ideas may be generated to use the same raw materials. Readers should take a walk through their favorite large supermarket to see the vast array of presentations of fresh-cut vegetables. This will provide an indication of the complexity in Taylor's operation.

An Aside: To illustrate how far Taylor has come, when I visited the headquarters of Sysco for the first time in early 2011, I noticed a large poster in the lobby that advertised Sysco's "Top 100 Suppliers." Taylor was close to the top of that list. The case at the end of Chapter 8 discusses Sysco in detail.

Foodservice also has been a large market for Taylor, however, the 2008 case points out that Bruce believed this market was "maxed out." He believed that foodservice customers were reticent to place a significant portion of their business with any one supplier because of concerns about supply interruptions or serious food safety incidents. This may or may not be true, but he also apparently believed that more and more people were looking for their meals as prepared foods in supermarkets instead of in restaurants.

Notice that this case deals with many of the same issues presented in this chapter and throughout the book. A brief pause at this point is warranted to think about these in the context of a real company. Readers should do some independent research on Taylor, its industry, and its customers, suppliers, and competitors. That will be a useful learning exercise.

A FINAL WORD ON UTILIZING CUSTOMERS AND SUPPLIERS AS SOURCES OF IDEAS AND OPPORTUNITIES

This chapter has been about developing robust customer and supply bases. It began with the famous Yogi Berra quote, "When you come to a fork in the road, take it." Yogi's fork in the road analogy was used to show the choices of where in a company's supply chains they should look for entrepreneurial opportunities for innovation and growth.

One key to successful entrepreneurial supply chains is the three-way congruence among the business strategies, supply chain strategies, and entrepreneurial strategies. The goal of entrepreneurial supply chains is to maintain, gain, or enhance the firm's competitive advantage. There are several ways for this to happen, all of which present opportunities for entrepreneurial ventures:

- Decrease costs of the supply chains in the source, make, deliver, and recycle processes.
- Increase quality through product performance and conformance quality.
- Increase flexibility all along the supply chains.
- Increase innovativeness through technology applications in the supply chains.

Entrepreneurial ventures that are congruent with the business's overall corporate strategy must be ensured. One approach is to guarantee robust bases of customers and suppliers. The numerous benefits of entrepreneurial activity generally are well established and are most successful when such congruence occurs.

ASSURANCE OF LEARNING QUESTIONS

The following questions will help you to check yourself on the chapter content:

1. Is the Yogi Berra quote at the beginning of this chapter appropriate to innovation, and does it convey the ideas concerning a focus on customers and/or suppliers in the search for entrepreneurial supply chain opportunities?
2. How would you respond to the arguments in favor of customers having multiple suppliers for given commodities? What are the counter arguments?
3. How should suppliers handle competing customers to whom they sell? Suppose one customer asks a supplier for an innovation—should they keep the innovation from that customer's competitor?
4. Why do you think companies want different (and better) treatment from their customers than they are willing to extend to their suppliers?
5. What benefits do you think CEMEX gained from its global expansion? More specifically, cement and its derivative products are commodities that usually are supplied within a relatively small area, so how might CEMEX's operation in San Antonio, Texas, benefit from their globalization?
6. The idea of rationalizing the supplier base that results in a preferred supplier list of "growth" suppliers is discussed. Why might or might not this make sense for a number of companies?
7. Describe the key aspects of the Taylor Fresh Foods case and their implications for more general entrepreneurial supply chains.

REFERENCES

1. Porter, Michael E. 1980. *Competitive Strategy: Techniques for Analyzing Industries and Competitors*, New York, The Free Press. 191–214.
2. For more information on CEMEX: Ghemawat, Pankaj, and Jamie L. Matthews. November 29, 2004. "The Globalization of CEMEX." Harvard Business School Case #9-701-017; Kanter, Rosabeth Moss, Pamela Yatsko, and Ryan Raffaelli. September 16, 2009. "CEMEX (A): Building the Global Framework (1985–2004). Harvard Business School Case #9-308-022; Kanter, Rosabeth Moss, Pamela Yatsko, and Ryan Raffaelli. September 16, 2009. "CEMEX (B): Cementing Relationships (2004–2007)." Harvard Business School Case #9-308-023; Lee, Hau, and David Hoyt. December 7,

2005. "CEMEX: Transforming a Basic Industry Company." Stanford Graduate School of Business Case #GS-3 3. The cases are available at www
.harvardbusinessonline.com.

3. Lee, William B. and Michael R. Katzorke. 2010. *Leading Effective Supply Chain Transformations: A Guide to Sustainable World-Class Capability and Results*. Fort Lauderdale, FL: J. Ross Publishing.

4. Singh, Shruti Date. 2010. "Caterpillar Looks for a Few Close Friends." *Bloomberg BusinessWeek*, October 25–31. 22–24.

5. Azadegan, Arash, and Kevin J. Dooley. November 2010. "Supplier Innovativeness, Organizational Learning Styles and Manufacturer Performance: An Empirical Assessment." *Journal of Operations Management*, 28(6). 488–505.

6. Flynn, Barbara B., Baofeng Huo, and Xiande Zhao. January 2010. "The Impact of Supply Chain Integration on Performance: A Contingency and Configuration Approach." *Journal of Operations Management*, 28(1). 58–71.

7. Song, Michael, and C. Anthony DiBenedetto. January 2008. "Suppliers' Involvement and Success of Radical New Product Development in New Ventures." *Journal of Operations Management*, 26(1). 1–22.

8. Fischer, Marc, Heiner Frankemolle, Lutz-Peter Pape, and Karsten Schween. May 1997. "Serving Your Customers' Customer: A Strategy for Mature Industries." *McKinsey Quarterly*.

9. Cavinato, Joseph L. May/June 2002. "What's Your Supply Chain Type?" *Supply Chain Management Review*. 60–66.

10. For example, see Engardio, Pete, and Bruce Einhorn. March 21, 2005. "Outsourcing Innovation," *Business Week*. 84–94. Quinn, James Brian. Summer 2000. "Outsourcing Innovation: The New Engine of Growth." *MIT Sloan Management Review*, 41 (4), 13–28. Stanko, Michael A., Jonathan D. Bohlmann, and Roger J. Calantone. November 30, 2009. "Outsourcing Innovation." *The Wall Street Journal*.

11. Quinn, James Brian. Summer 2000. "Outsourcing Innovation: The New Engine of Growth." *Sloan Management Review*, 41(4). 15.

12. Bell, David E., Natalie Kindred, and Mary Shelman. December 15, 2008. "Taylor Fresh Foods." Harvard Business School, Case #9-509-008.

CHAPTER 4

HOW WE KNOW WE HAVE OPPORTUNITIES

LEARNING OBJECTIVES

1. Be able to articulate the concept of "white space" and apply it to your company.
2. Consider the company "morality" of refusing to sell their leading-edge (perhaps life-saving) medical technology to countries that will not protect their intellectual property, meaning that people may die because they lack this technology that could save their lives.
3. Understand the eight-step "framework for analysis" in defining entrepreneurial opportunities.

"A missed opportunity is worse than a defeat."

—Unknown

"Make hay while the sun shines!"

—Unknown

"Get it while you can."

—Janis Joplin

These quotes speak volumes about entrepreneurial supply chain opportunities— don't miss the opportunity! The song by Janis Joplin is emblematic of what to do about entrepreneurial opportunities: "Get it while you can." There are many quotes such as these that have applicability to this chapter; namely, how do opportunities become apparent, and what can or should be done about them?

This chapter focuses on how we know we have entrepreneurial supply chain opportunities. It is an opportunity-identification and opportunity-structuring process. How should entrepreneurial supply chain opportunities be identified and structured so that they can be managed? Many companies simply take what sometimes is considered the easy way out. Perhaps a fair way to say it is that they serve existing customers in traditional ways, but with a slight variation on existing products. For example, they might do brand extensions such as Oreo cookies has done. (**Full disclosure:** the author happens to *really* like Oreo cookies!) Nabisco put out Double Stuff Oreos, Chocolate Oreos, Mint Oreos, and others. With all due respect to Nabisco, these brand extensions are not exactly breakthrough ideas. They have built on already good ideas in ways that appeal to more customers or that entice existing customers (like the author!) to purchase more.

There is a tendency to think that every entrepreneurial supply chain opportunity needs to be a "white space" breakthrough. Simply put, *white space opportunities* normally serve new customers or markets in fundamentally innovative ways that generally are outside the company's current business model. These are opportunities that typically fit poorly within the existing organizational structure. White space opportunities almost always require new organizations or new companies.

Thus, companies are presented with a dilemma. To go into the white space means that companies will face enormous uncertainties in products and/or processes and in customers and/or markets. But, the opportunities also may be enormous—perhaps to introduce a new innovative technology, to transform an industry, create a new industry, define new markets, or to attract new customers. To decide not to enter the white space means that the company is relegating itself to its existing products and markets or to closely adjacent products and markets.

> **KEY IDEA**
>
> At the end of WWII, the U.S. spent half the world's total research and development money; today, the amount has perhaps dropped to one-third or less.

The adjacent Key Idea illustrates a significant phenomenon today. Many people admonish the United States for letting its spending on research and development (R&D) lapse, citing this statistic. However, it is more complicated than that. True, many U.S. companies have not pursued advanced R&D like they once did. Nevertheless, countries such as India and China are spending enormous sums on advanced products. Take, for example, high-speed rail. This was not developed in the U.S. by Amtrak or by locomotive manufacturers such as General Electric. In the 2011 State of the Union speech, President Barack Obama called for increased "investment" (read, federal government "spending") into high-speed rail. Whether this is possible or prudent, or if it will pay off, time will tell.

To see where some companies are spending their R&D money on breakthrough ideas such as rail, you can go to GE's website. In February 2011, it said the following:

> GE has put more than 15,000 GE locomotive engines on the world's rails— including our breakthrough Evolution™ Series, which reduces emissions by 40 percent. We also offer maintenance, repair and upgrade services, signaling and communications systems, and web-enabled tools to track security and progress.

KEY IDEA
Notice that whenever one reads about new corporate developments, there is an emphasis on providing services. One key to success is to enfold products with sets of related and innovative services.

In 2011, according to its website, GE Transportation signed a $1.4B letter of intent with China's Ministry of Railways for locomotives, locomotive sub-assembly kits, service support, and railway signaling systems. They also announced signing of a letter of intent to enter into a joint venture to advance high-speed and other rail technologies in the United States. This joint venture sounds a lot like the definition of entrepreneurial supply chain undertakings.

Pursuing too many minor opportunities may mean passing on possibilities of significant breakthroughs. Companies need to manage their limited resources of people, capital, and time. They cannot put all their resources and efforts into white space or "game-changing" breakthroughs. Recognize that companies have multiple strategic needs. There are needs for relatively minor changes, needs for major growth opportunities, and needs for significant innovative breakthroughs. Choosing the right opportunities is critical to managing the multiple balancing acts.

Having multiple growth paths presents a dilemma for corporate entrepreneurship, as shown in Figure 4.1. Consider this simple little 2 × 2 matrix, showing products and technologies along the horizontal axis, and markets and customers along the vertical axis. A company's core businesses are in the lower left-hand box with existing products and technologies and existing customers and markets. The lower right-hand box and the upper left-hand box are "Adjacencies," meaning that adjacent products and technologies are close to the existing ones, and that adjacent customers and markets also are close to the existing ones. These adjacencies thus are *accessible*, meaning that they frequently represent relatively small extensions to the existing business.

Of course, the world cannot be categorized into a generic 2 x 2 matrix or only four types of future states. Further, in Figure 4.1, only three growth paths do not make sense. The simple explanation is that each of the two axes of the matrix actually is a continuum. Companies typically have multiple products and technologies, each of which may have different associated dynamics. Also, companies typically have multiple customers and markets, perhaps with different dynamics

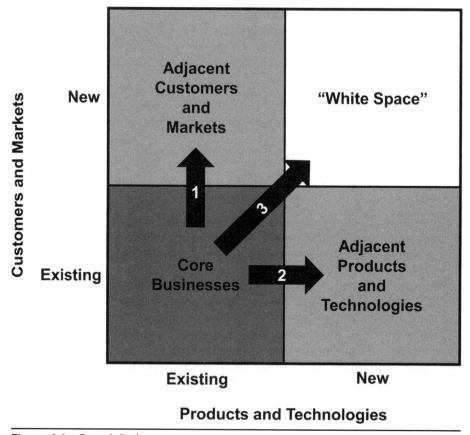

Figure 4.1   Growth Paths

associated with each. The smart approach is to segment each axis into appropriate categories. This takes the thinking from a generic 2 × 2 matrix into a much more complex and subtle set of options.

In the three generic growth paths shown in Figure 4.1, growth path 1 moves existing products and technologies into new customers and markets. For example, a company can locate in new geographies as an entrepreneurial supply chain move. McDonald's has been pursuing this strategy for years, as has Starbucks and many other establishments. McDonald's and other fast food businesses also have moved into hospitals, airports, and other types of locations—not necessarily to capture new customers but to serve them in new settings.

Growth path 2 develops new products and technologies to offer to existing customers and markets. Amazon.com began as a bookseller and then added other products to its core competencies. For example, in 2009, Amazon purchased Zappos, the online shoe retailer, reportedly for $1.2B. Amazon also enhanced its technologies of order handling and fulfillment, and almost certainly added customers. But it essentially has moved into "adjacencies" (one of which is Zappos), as they have been defined.

Growth path 3 is the most complex, and involves moving into the white space of new products and technologies combined with new customers and markets. This also is the most risky growth path. Significant risks are present: financial, operational, and reputational risks.

Companies thus should treat their possible opportunistic movements (growth path 1, 2, or 3) as projects, which will be outlined later in this chapter. But first, consider how to quantify growth paths, as shown in Figure 4.2. Recall that Figure 4.1 shows the company's core businesses in the lower left-hand corner. The existing core businesses will decline over time, and Figure 4.2 shows this happening by about two-thirds over the six-year period, with about a one-third incremental growth in the existing businesses. (The net effect is about a one-third overall decline in those business lines over the six years.) But work must occur to keep the core businesses viable. This takes a plan and the resources of people, time, and

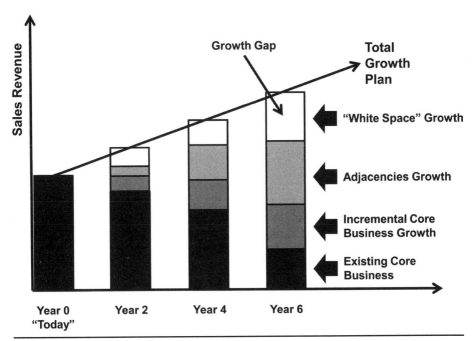

Figure 4.2   Quantifying Growth Paths

capital. Nevertheless, the example shows a net decline of sales revenues in the core businesses over the six years. This is typical.

In this example, growth in the adjacency businesses is required to grow the total business over the six years. The growth in adjacency businesses is shown to add about 50% to the existing core businesses. Again, a plan and resources of people, time, and capital are needed to achieve this growth.

Even with growth in the adjacency businesses over the six years, it is not enough to achieve the "Total Growth Plan," indicated by an arrow in Figure 4.2. The "Growth Gap" by the end of the six years requires about 50% of today's total revenues to be added to the businesses.

How can the company achieve this amount of white space growth? Could it come from technological innovations? Consider a technology life cycle, along with the company's need to choose a path, if any:

1. *Bleeding-edge technology*—may show high potential, but hasn't demonstrated its value or come into common usage. Early adopters may win big or may be trapped with a useless technology. Consider the memorable case study of VHS, introduced by JVC, versus Sony's Betamax. Some people still argue the technical superiority of Betamax, but VHS clearly won the marketing war. Early adopters who decided on Betamax lost out to those who selected VHS, regardless of the rationale for making that choice.

2. *Leading-edge technology*—has proven itself in the marketplace, but is new enough that customers may not accept it or the technology may be difficult to implement or support. Nevertheless, technology-oriented companies usually are well-advised to maintain a strong presence in leading-edge technologies. If they don't, they likely will be relegated to also-ran groups of companies, and no longer will be considered as strong technology companies.

3. *State-of-the-art technology*—is accepted and commonly used. Even advanced technology-oriented companies likely will maintain or perhaps even develop some new state-of-the-art products.

4. *Out-of-date technology*—is useful and sometimes still implemented, but only if replacement state-of-the-art or leading-edge technologies are not readily available.

5. *Obsolete technology*—has been superseded by other technology; it may be maintained but no longer manufactured. At some point, the products likely will no longer be maintained.

An example of this technology movement by Einhorn and Culpan (2010) appeared in *Bloomberg BusinessWeek*.[1] It concerns Asustek, the Taiwanese company that in 2007 introduced the first netbook, a low-priced mini-laptop that was the fastest growing segment of the PC industry for two years or so after its introduction. Netbook sales had gone flat at 12% of PC sales, due to consumers flocking to tablets such as Apple's iPad, which offered many of the same advantages of netbooks. For Asustek, that meant making a big push into tablets while trying to convince corporations and consumers that there were still advantages to netbooks.

> **KEY IDEA**
>
> The opportunities are there. You just need to know where to look.

The five categories of technology are continuously changing. Today's state-of-the-art technology will be tomorrow's out-of-date technology. But a company should examine its technology development pipeline, and where its current technologies stand, in respect to the five categories. Perhaps there are sufficient numbers of development projects in the pipeline to be able to provide the growth required to meet the growth plan, or perhaps not.

What are the appropriate levels of technology? This question becomes one of a company's most important considerations about where their opportunities might lie for entrepreneurial supply chain ventures. The simple example of Asustek's netbooks illustrates some of the profound questions that companies should ask—and answer—in order to adequately plan for their growth.

An Aside: Some years ago, I consulted with a high-technology medical equipment company on its global supply chains. The company had a strategy of research on the bleeding-edge of its technology and was introducing products on the "bleeding and leading edge." Some of their customers (prominent hospitals and medical centers) would acquire the bleeding- and leading-edge products. But other hospitals and institutions for cost purposes would stick with state-of-the-art products that perhaps were slower, lacked capacity, or lacked some of the latest features. Additionally, some users, including those in other countries, made do with out-of-date or obsolete technologies. One of the most unfortunate issues the company faced was that they could not protect their intellectual property in some countries, and thus had to refuse to sell leading-edge or state-of-the-art products there. These countries' citizens thus were denied life-saving technologies due to their governments' policies. This truly is a moral issue for those countries. Some might argue that it also was a moral issue for the company. I happen to think that the moral burden lies with the country and not with the company, but some could argue with that stand. Unfortunately, some countries still do not protect companies' intellectual property, and case after case shows that some companies simply refuse to do business in those countries.

So, basic questions have been posed for readers to consider as they struggle with learning about their opportunities. The remainder of this chapter presents a framework for analysis of entrepreneurial supply chain opportunities. The topic of opportunities has been presented as a project-oriented question. Companies could consider using the following outline to analyze opportunities. The Corning cases at the end of the chapter also can provide some ideas.

A FRAMEWORK FOR ANALYSIS

An eight-step structured approach, like the following, makes sense for analyzing opportunities, as shown in Figure 4.3. The eight steps of analysis are:

1. Understand the macro issues that are driving the company's business.
2. Begin to evaluate entrepreneurial supply chain opportunities.
3. Conduct education and training on entrepreneurship, and what it means for the supply chains.
4. Convince the organization that an opportunity exists and needs to be captured.
5. Design the supply chains for entrepreneurship.
6. Analyze the risks.
7. Assess multiple opportunities.
8. Choose which opportunities should be pursued.

Each step is developed further in the remainder of this chapter.

1. UNDERSTAND THE MACRO ISSUES

Understand the macro issues that are driving the firm and its technologies and products as well as its customers and markets. It is a cliché that dramatic change occurred in most industries over the past few years, and the macro issues likely will impact the going-forward entrepreneurial supply chain decisions for the firm.

Suppose you visit a physician who writes a prescription, and then sends you on your way without any examination or discussion. Not likely! Similarly, do not embark on an effort to create entrepreneurial supply chains before understanding the driving forces on the industry and the business. This will provide the perspective needed to move forward.

Innovation is a major transformative issue[2] that is appropriate in this context. An exploration of innovation (Mandel 2009) concluded[3] that innovation, which used to be a strength of the U.S., has been eroding and this has contributed to the economic difficulties in this country.

Many people have heard something to that effect, or a variant of it, over and over. Innovation is multifaceted, occurring in product technology, manufacturing process technology, and business processes. For example, try to think of all the different advances in technology that went into today's communications capabilities. Consider technology and innovation that moved that capability for the past 50 years or so, and included electronics, computers, phones, space technology, satellites, and many others. Furthermore, new and innovative organizations

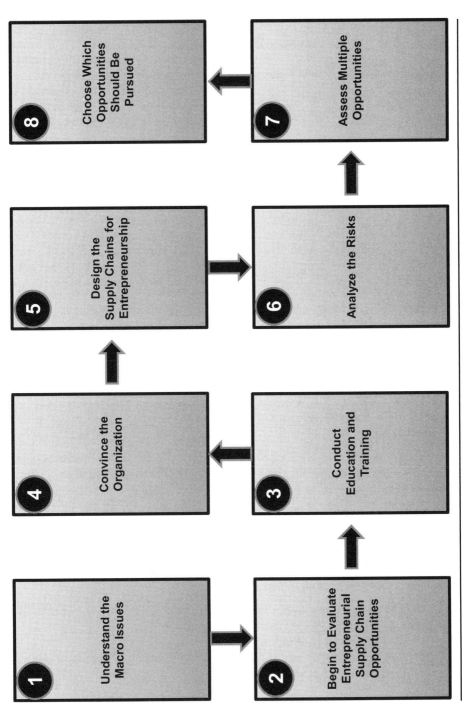

Figure 4.3   Structured Approach to Defining Entrepreneurial Opportunities.

and business processes grew up with these technologies. All of these, together, contributed to communications technology today.

<table>
<tr><td>

KEY IDEA

Leadership is the best predictor of successful innovation.

</td></tr>
</table>

And what does this say about entrepreneurial supply chain opportunities? Well, it depends! It depends on how innovative the industry is in which the firm operates. Clearly, industries with a great deal of innovation (e.g., IT, pharmaceuticals) will require that a company push innovation as a key component of its entrepreneurial supply chain strategy. If the firm is in some other industry, perhaps not as much innovation is required.

Let's not jump too quickly to the conclusion that a particular industry does not require innovation. Not that many years ago, people would have said that cement and its derivative products (ready-mix concrete, concrete blocks, concrete pipe) would have been an industry in which not much innovation occurs. How wrong they would have been! Today, primarily because of CEMEX and other like-minded innovative companies, people know better. As is said in Texas, "Who wudda thunk it?" Every industry has its innovation success stories in every part of the globe.

One way to start the identification of macro issues facing the firm and industry is with surveys that appear frequently in the business press. One survey example can be taken from the *McKinsey Quarterly*.[4]

> *An ongoing shift in global economic activity from developed to developing economies, accompanied by growth in the number of consumers in emerging markets, are the global developments that executives around the world view as the most important for business and the most positive for their own companies' profits . . .*

This excerpt from McKinsey's sixth annual survey came from respondents being asked about the forces shaping the world economy (Dye and Stephenson, 2010). This type of survey helps to provide guidance to executives trying to understand the macro issues facing their industries and companies. Of course, surveys are sensitive to time, industry, and geography, and companies need to be wary of drawing conclusions from only one survey.

Nevertheless, surveys such as McKinsey's serve a useful purpose. The five most important forces shaping the world economy, according to the findings of McKinsey's survey, are given here:

1. *Growth and risk management in emerging markets.* The three most effective ways of capturing emerging-market growth are:
   - Building a presence in the market
   - Developing partnerships or joint ventures with local companies, and
   - Recruiting and developing local talent

The importance of developing partnerships or joint ventures was discussed in Chapter 2. McKinsey's survey also illustrated some of the most important risks seen by executives in emerging markets:

- Lack of intellectual property protections (40% of respondents)
- Volatility of currency exchange (38%) and
- Geopolitical instability (26%)

The level of concern varied with different industries and with different geographies.

2. *Labor productivity and talent management.* Companies need to be more innovative in selecting, hiring, and developing talented employees. Significant variations on this issue occurred across industries and geographical regions, but the greatest concerns generally were for management talent along with technical research and development capability. For example, executives in China were most concerned about a lack of management talent, whereas executives in India were most concerned about research and development capabilities.

3. *Global flows of goods, information, and capital.*
   - Sixty-two percent of respondents foresaw a moderate increase in global flows of goods in the next five years.
   - Forty percent of respondents expected increased innovation to be the most powerful effect from increased flow of information.
   - Fifty-nine percent anticipated increased integration of capital flows in developed countries, while other countries continue to restrict capital flows.

4. *Natural-resource management.* As in McKinsey surveys from previous years, executives saw increasing constraints on the supply or usage of natural resources. Twenty-five percent said that this will have a negative effect on company profits. However, 45% of manufacturing executives expected negative effects on profits. The most common response to these trends was that companies were reducing their use of natural resources, especially energy.

5. *The increasing role of governments.* Executives in Europe and North America were worried by crippling public-debt levels: 54 percent and 61 percent, respectively, thought that public-debt levels will have a "significant" or "severely negative" impact on GDP growth. Executives in the developed markets generally were concerned that the increasing roles of governments will have a negative effect on business (Dye and Stephenson, 2010).

Clearly, individual companies must consider what this means for them. An increasing role of government could have a deleterious effect on entrepreneurship, including rules and regulations that make it difficult to start new businesses, and could mean more taxes for successful entrepreneurial ventures. Central governments that are increasingly hungry for power and money may inhibit entrepreneurs with onerous rules, regulations, and taxes. This equally applies to large companies, which are significant sources of corporate entrepreneurship.

Many people, especially in government, fail to realize that entrepreneurship is a pillar of the free enterprise system, not its enemy. Lack of government support for entrepreneurial ventures means that companies may have difficulties in countries in which government is not friendly to business.

Global trends are increasingly important in companies' entrepreneurial supply chain efforts. Many major publications and organizations conduct surveys like McKinsey's; executives should be cognizant of them and pay attention. Clearly, surveys may have different meanings for different companies, and only by paying careful attention to them can value be derived. Companies also should consider building planning scenarios around the trends that are identified as being significant to their businesses, which are discussed in the next section of this chapter.

2. BEGIN TO EVALUATE ENTREPRENEURIAL SUPPLY CHAIN OPPORTUNITIES

Begin to evaluate entrepreneurial opportunities in the supply chains. Skilled scenario-building capabilities present a useful approach to evaluating opportunities.

One of the best explanations of scenario building is in a case note by Leslie E. Grayson and James G. Clawson (1996)[5] from the Darden School at the University of Virginia. The case was based on cooperation from Royal Dutch/Shell Group, Chevron, Conoco, Compagnie Francaise des Petroles, and Sohio—all known leaders in the use of scenarios in their planning processes. The authors explained scenarios as follows:

> *Scenarios present several futures, none is 'right' or more likely than the next, and each is plausible. The theory behind scenario planning is that, if executives are aware of and modestly prepared for several possible outcomes, they will be better prepared to adjust if the world takes an unusual turn.*

Scenarios have been in use for many years. They essentially put forward two kinds of questions for corporate planners.

1. How might a hypothetical situation come about, step by step? Since much of the capability for building scenarios was developed in the energy industry, a hypothetical situation in that industry might be that the price of oil goes to five times its present price; so, how might that price develop and what caused it to occur? There could be multiple causes that develop over several years. These causes could be tracked over time, so the company could see a situation building. For example, partial cause may be explained by demographics: more people on the globe now own more automobiles. This, of course, is easy to track. However, suppose the rise in oil prices is caused by a sudden outbreak of war in the Middle East?

That's not as easy to track; nevertheless, there likely would be multiple signals that could foretell such an event.

2. What should be done if a particular situation occurs? This is the "what if . . ." question. In the example scenario, a question could be: What entrepreneurial supply chain opportunities might come about if the price of oil quintupled? Say your company was in the oil field equipment business like Baker Hughes, the subject of a continuing case study in this book. What opportunities might come about for Baker Hughes with the price of oil quintupling? Part of the scenario might involve the time frame during which this occurred—say, three months as opposed to five years. Clearly, if the price quintupled quickly, serious exogenous events likely would be driving it—war or conflict might be one possibility, as could be a shutdown of the Suez Canal.

Exploring a scenario allows exploration of how might a company, with its oil field equipment business, be affected. Likely, you could predict a significant increase in business because an increase in the price could be expected to create a substantial increase in exploration in "safe" areas of the world. Entrepreneurial supply chain opportunities could be geographic, for new products, or in mergers and acquisitions.

If an oil-price rise occurred, companies such as Baker Hughes or National Oilwell Varco (NOV) likely would be major competitors to expand their businesses, given their histories as entrepreneurial companies with strong supply chains. Many other companies in the industry also could be expected to be active.

Royal Dutch/Shell is experienced in scenario building and in integrating scenario building as an integral part of its corporate planning. Grayson and Clawson (1996) remarked that Shell originally produced six scenarios, but that they later reduced it to three. Six was too many to properly develop, monitor, and update. They give Shell's scenario planning capability the credit for helping Shell to significantly increase its market share from sixth among the so-called "seven sisters" of the global oil industry (before the 1973 oil shock) to second from the top by the late 1980s.

Another source about scenario planning is an article by Paul J. H. Schoemaker[6] in the *Sloan Management Review*. Schoemaker includes some excellent references, which should be valuable for the serious student of scenario building. He also makes an interesting point about the value of scenarios, given three classes of knowledge.

1. Things we know that we know.
2. Things we know that we don't know.
3. Things we don't know that we don't know.

All three classes should be built into scenarios, but the greatest havoc is caused by the third. Since scenario building is a strong forum for shared organizational learning, it provides a unique approach for beginning to evaluate entrepreneurial supply chain opportunities. When building scenarios for such opportunities, readers are cautioned to be aware of their biases. Definitions of several biases have been included in Appendix D, Glossary of Entrepreneurial Supply Chain Terms. Readers should consider how a few of the more common biases can influence their own thinking:

- *Anchoring and insufficient adjustment*: rooting oneself to an initial value, leading to insufficient adjustments of subsequent estimates.
- *Confirmation bias*: overweighting of evidence consistent with a favored belief; underweighting of evidence against a favored belief; or failure to search impartially for evidence.
- *Excessive optimism*: the tendency for people to be overoptimistic about the outcome of planned actions, to overestimate the likelihood of positive events, and to underestimate the likelihood of negative ones.
- *Groupthink bias*: striving for consensus at the cost of a realistic appraisal of alternative courses of action.
- *Overconfidence*: overestimating one's skill level relative to others, leading one to overestimate one's ability to affect future outcomes, take credit for past outcomes, and neglect the role of chance.

Experience with scenario building and research on it indicate that allowing biases unconsciously to invade the process is one of the greatest dangers to being able to successfully use scenarios. References cited in this section have examples of scenarios for various situations. It is beyond the scope of this book to provide additional guidance here, but readers who are serious about evaluating opportunities should look further into this powerful tool.

3. CONDUCT EDUCATION AND TRAINING

Conduct education and training for supply chain, business development, and other appropriate personnel. Please see Appendix C for an example plan.

An Aside: There is a classic story of which the source is unknown, but it's still a good story. The story is about Thomas J. Watson, Sr., when he was the head of IBM. A young engineer made a mistake that cost the company several million dollars. The engineer was called into Mr. Watson's office, fully expecting to be terminated. He tried to get ahead of the process by offering his resignation. But Mr. Watson stopped the young man by saying, "Why should you resign when we've just spent so much money educating you!" This story is *apropos* to many situations in other companies. Management does not seem to tolerate mistakes, but mistakes can be excellent vehicles for teaching and learning opportunities.

An Aside: *Education* differs from *training*, but many people confuse those terms. Education builds awareness, knowledge, and understanding. Training builds skills. Companies need both in order to build their capability to create entrepreneurial supply chains.

People get educated and trained in many different ways, as illustrated by the story about Mr. Watson: employees make mistakes and (hopefully) learn from them. That probably is the most common way of learning, unfortunately! Sometimes, the bigger the mistake, the more learning that takes place. But mistakes are both expensive and random, and better approaches are available.

Education and training programs are designed with specific objectives for specific audiences. There is a strong need for education and training about creating entrepreneurial supply chains.

Education and training at three levels in the organization build the capability to create entrepreneurial supply chains:

1. Senior management
2. Core supply chain team members
3. Entrepreneurial supply chain process participants

What kinds of education and training are needed? Some kinds are entrepreneurial supply chain education; visioning and creativity workshops; and, change management education and training. Some alternatives are facilitated discussion, classroom training, on-the-job training, job rotation, and self study.

Where can a company acquire the education and training knowledge? Companies need general as well as subject-specific sources of both. Here are a few recommendations:

- Perhaps the most well-known organization for general training is the American Society for Training and Development (ASTD). ASTD claims to be the world's largest professional association dedicated to workplace learning and development. ASTD provides resources, conferences, best practices, and other information for professional training and development.
- The International University Consortium for Executive Education (UNICON), as its name implies, focuses on university executive education. This is an organization of leading business schools and is committed to advance the field of university-sponsored executive education. UNICON is a comprehensive source of information on universities' executive education programs, which may be applicable to a company's education and training efforts. Member schools generally offer both open-enrollment and company-specific, custom-designed training programs. All are willing to work with companies to determine the appropriate subject matter and format. All members subscribe to a set of ethics guidelines for executive education.

- APICS: The Association for Operations Management and the Institute for Supply Management (ISM) are two of the most prominent professional societies that focus on supply chain management, education, and training opportunities of various sorts.

  > *Full disclosure: The author was on the Board of Directors of APICS as well as on APICS' Leadership Team (as of 2010), and on the Board of the APICS Education and Research Foundation. He has been a member of APICS since 1975, among the first group of Certified Fellow in Production and Inventory Management (CFPIM), and previously served on both boards. He also is a member of ISM and was on the Board of Directors of UNICON when he was Associate Dean for Executive Education at Rice University.*

- There are a number of books on education and training that can be helpful. For example, although a bit dated, Robert L. Craig's (Editor in Chief) *Training and Development Handbook: A Guide to Human Resource Development*, 3rd ed. (ASTD, 1987) has a wealth of information for professional education and training. Much of the information is timeless and does not go out of date.
- There are a number of general academic journals that publish articles on entrepreneurship and supply chains. Please look at the references after each chapter in this book to identify the ones preferred.
- Various education and training sources are cited in Appendix C, Sample Education and Training Programs for Entrepreneurial Supply Chains.

4. CONVINCE THE ORGANIZATION THAT AN OPPORTUNITY EXISTS AND NEEDS TO BE CAPTURED

Convince the organization of the need to move forward with entrepreneurial supply chain opportunities. "The organization" means whoever is in decision-making or influencing roles. There is an old, humorous saying (with a grain of truth!): *Change would be easy if it were not for people!* Building a formal change management program into the entrepreneurial supply chain project is necessary if the project is to be successful.

> **KEY IDEA**
>
> Change would be easy if it were not for people!

Creating entrepreneurial supply chains requires a three-level approach with people-oriented strategies, tools, and techniques applied in a coordinated manner. The three levels are (1) the entire organization; (2) groups that make up the functions and business processes; and (3) the individuals who are the process participants. Let's consider these briefly.

The organization and groups within the organization

Organizations and their functional groups need to do a few things to become entrepreneurial, among them:

- *Have a strong imperative for entrepreneurial supply chains.* The case for creating entrepreneurial supply chains must be made strongly, including at least some dissatisfaction with the *as is* situation of the organization. This is the "push" for new ways of thinking and acting, and answers the question, "*Why* are we interested in entrepreneurial supply chains?"
- *Have a vision for entrepreneurial supply chains.* The organization needs to have a vision of what the *to-be* entrepreneurial supply chain situation can be. This vision must be stronger than the satisfaction with the *as-is* situation. This is the "pull" for newness. This answers the question, "*What* do we hope to achieve with entrepreneurial supply chains?"
- *Have a process to achieve entrepreneurial supply chains.* The organization needs to have a clearly defined process for creating entrepreneurial supply chains. This is the *path forward* that people can understand and work toward. This answers the question, "*How* do we get from where we are to where we hope to get?"
- *Have a commitment to achieve entrepreneurial supply chains.* The organization needs to have a strong commitment to making the requisite changes happen. This is the gut-level dedication and belief that the company should become more entrepreneurial in its supply chains. This answers the question, "Do we really *believe* this is correct for our company?"

Individuals as the process participants

Research indicates that individuals need to do a few things to become entrepreneurial, such as:

- *Individuals must participate in the decision making.* Individuals who have not been part of the decision making are not likely to fully support the opportunities for entrepreneurial supply chains. The decisions concern both *whether* to embark with entrepreneurial supply chains as well as *which* ones should constitute the best opportunities.
- *Individuals must think that the changes are in their own best interests.* This refers to the old joke about a favorite FM radio station, WIIFM, "what's in it for me?" Frequently, this issue goes hand-in-hand with the one above—*because* they have not participated in the decision-making, *then* they believe it is not in their own best interests.
- *Individuals must believe that the changes are possible.* For whatever reason, individuals may believe that entrepreneurial supply chains are outside the capabilities of the organization to implement. They also may believe

that the industry is not receptive to entrepreneurial supply chains, or that their competitors, customers, or suppliers will stymie their efforts. These ideas must be broken down in order for entrepreneurial supply chains to succeed.

- *Individuals must break the enormous power of habit.* Individuals are creatures of habit. They may say, "We've always done it this way," or "It's always worked in the past," or something similar. Creating entrepreneurial supply chains requires a different way of thinking and doing things.

How can we convince the organization?

Next, how do we convince the organization to move forward with entrepreneurial supply chains, given the barriers above? That's an interesting and difficult question.

For one thing, recognize that change needs to occur through a series of one-time and continuous improvement actions. An organization's performance may have been flat, erratic, or even declining over time. As a result, there needs to be an assessment of the *as-is* situation.

Recognize that people hold different attitudes toward change. Some people may use one of these old sayings:

- "If we build it, they will come."
- "Let's just issue a directive that our supply chain organizations will become entrepreneurial."
- "All this is logical, so there should be no question about whether it is the right thing for us."
- "Just do it. It will be good for you."

Improvements almost never are that simple. We all know that. But what should we do? Recognize that individuals essentially have two sides to their nature.

1. *Some people are rational.* They analyze, understand, decide, and act—in a logical, rational manner.
2. *Other people are emotional.* They feel, commit, decide, and act—in an emotional manner.

The trouble is, some people are primarily rational and analytical, while others are primarily emotional and feeling. And, we all have both sides to our nature—sometimes we react rationally and other times we react emotionally. This is a classic "change management" situation for leaders who wish to bring change to the organization.

If management does not handle a change situation well, companies easily can get in a losing spiral:

1. Suppose there is inadequate attention to the implementation issues of change management early in the entrepreneurial supply chain projects, which can lead to . . .
2. . . . confusion and lack of clarity about the objectives and the path(s) forward for the projects.
3. Resistance to the change could occur as a result of uncertainty.
4. Compromises, alterations, and reductions in scope could arise as a result of the resistance, . . .
5. . . . which could result in conflict, re-negotiation, and retreat from the project's goals.
6. The final straw is failure of the entrepreneurial supply chain opportunities.

Implementation of sustainable, visible change is the essence of project leadership. A formal program of change management thus is essential for successful implementation of opportunities for entrepreneurial supply chains.

5. DESIGN THE SUPPLY CHAINS FOR ENTREPRENEURSHIP

Entrepreneurial supply chains are collaborative both inside and outside the firm. It is a good idea to map the entire supply chains in detail as far as possible on both sides of the firm. This map provides a high-quality picture of the collaborations that are needed. Alongside the supply chains' mapping, the bills of material should also be mapped in detail—again, both internal and external. Combine both maps to look for entrepreneurship opportunities.

Suppose your company can no longer deliver the growth rates that investors and others have come to expect. As pointed out in Figures 4.1 and 4.2, there are alternatives of adjacencies and white space for growth, both of which offer opportunities to design the entrepreneurial supply chain. And, there are other ways of looking at it, some of which are discussed in the next section.

New Growth Platforms

One way of thinking about designing supply chains for entrepreneurship come from Laurie, Doz, and Sheer (2006) and is known as *new growth platforms*.[7] What is a new growth platform (NGP)? Laurie, Doz, and Sheer define the concept as: "Opportunities for building new growth platforms lie at the intersection of a company's actual or potential capability set, unmet customer needs, and forces of change in the broader environment."

NGPs are platforms on which companies can build families of products, services, and businesses, and thereby extend their capabilities into new areas. A *platform* is strategic and significant to the organization. It's a big deal! Some of the needed resources may come from redeploying the capabilities that the company already has. This typically involves moving into adjacencies as shown in Figures 4.1 and 4.2.

For example, a company develops capabilities from working with a certain set of customers or within a certain market. Suppose they can redeploy those capabilities to another set of customers or another market. Laurie, Doz, and Sheer (2006) cite a company that developed micro-fluidics capabilities from working on ink-jet cartridges, and redeployed that to working on blood-testing equipment. This capability can be considered as a platform that can assist the company in moving into other products and markets—call these adjacencies or white space.

NGPs also can be developed from a company's external relationships through joint ventures, strategic partnerships, and other structures. Use of external relationships is a common practice which can result in NGPs in the pharmaceutical industry. Many of today's blockbuster pharmaceuticals products originated from small companies or research laboratories, and then were acquired through an arrangement with a so-called "big-pharma" company, as shown in Figure 4.4.

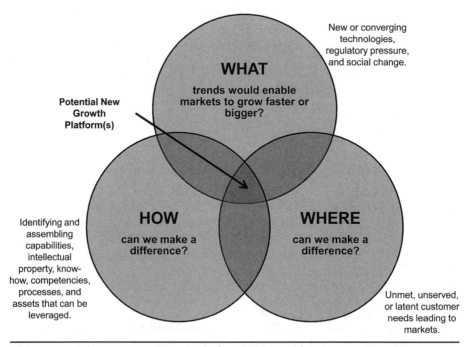

Figure 4.4   What Is a New Growth Platform? Adapted from: Laurie, Donald L., Yves L. Doz, and Claude P. Sheer, "Creating New Growth Platforms," *Harvard Business Review*, Vol. 84, No. 5, May 2006, p. 84.

Three questions typically are asked when seeking to identify new growth platforms. According to Laurie, Doz, and Sheer, NGPs lie at the intersection of answers to these three questions.

1. *What macro trends would enable markets to grow faster or bigger?* This question involves understanding issues such as new or converging technologies, regulatory changes, and social changes such as demographics. Understanding macro-issue trends that affect a company's industry is an important first step. Without understanding these trends, one would be hard-pressed to design entrepreneurial supply chain opportunities.
2. *How can we make a difference?* This question essentially asks how to begin to evaluate entrepreneurial supply chain opportunities by identifying and assembling capabilities, intellectual property, know-how, competencies, processes, and assets that can be leveraged. What does the company have, or what can it get to allow it to move forward with these new growth platforms?
3. *Where can we make a difference?* This question provides direction to the evaluation of entrepreneurial supply chain opportunities by focusing on unmet, unserved, or latent customer needs leading to markets. This also can be asked as, what can we do about it?

There is another way of looking at the question: *How do we know we have opportunities?* It's what we call the "supply chain bill of material."

Supply Chain Bill of Material

The *supply chain bill of material* is a way to combine the bill of material and the supply chain, as shown in Figure 4.5. The bill of material is one means of designing supply chains for entrepreneurship. A *bill of material* can be defined as:

> *A bill of material, formula, recipe, or ingredients list (commonly called a BoM) is an arrangement (which can be a listing or a structured hierarchy) of all the items, components, assemblies, subassemblies, intermediates, items, parts, ingredients, or raw materials, along with the quantity of each that go into a product.*

From a computer-processing standpoint, bills of material typically have two files: a product structure file and an item master file. The product structure file is shown as Table 4.1. The file has records that define the relationship between components and parent items, such as the following simplistic example from Figure 4.5. This shows that Product A has three components: Assembly B (one each), Assembly C (one each), and Item D (two each). Assembly B has three components: Subassembly B10 (one each), Item B20 (four each), and Item B30 (one each). There is at least one product structure record for every item number.

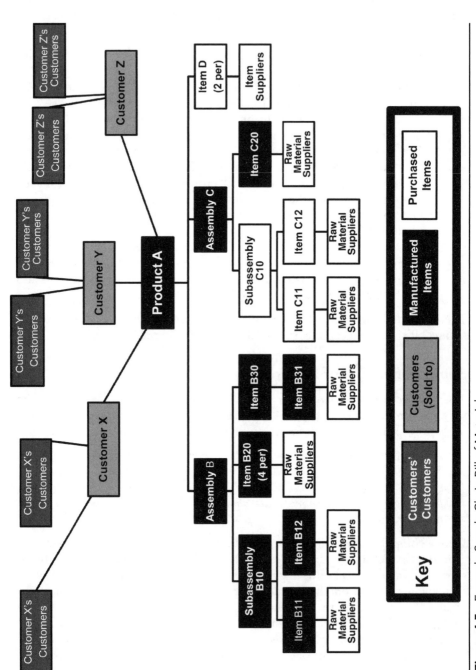

Figure 4.5   Example Supply Chain Bill of Material.

Parent Code	Component Code	Quantity per
Product A	Assembly B	1
Product A	Assembly C	1
Product A	Item D	2
Assembly B	Subassembly B10	1
Assembly B	Item B20	4
Assembly B	Item B30	1
Other items…		

Table 4.1 (Highly) Simplified Product Structure File

The item master file contains information that is unique to every item, such as the item number, its description, unit of measure (quart, gallon, meter, pound), cost information, and so forth.

One practical approach to designing supply chains for entrepreneurship is to map the structure of bills of material and their associated supply chains as shown in Figure 4.5. Notice that Product A, more-or-less in the center of the figure, is shown with its bill of material and incoming supply chains arrayed below it. Also, above Product A are the outgoing supply chains.

How does mapping bills of material help to design entrepreneurial supply chains? The simple answer is to use the map of both the bills of material and their associated supply chains to analyze the supply chain bill of material for entrepreneurial opportunities. For example, the analysis could follow several possible rationales while searching for an entrepreneurial opportunity. Suppose the company took one or more of several possible actions, such as:

- Outsource Item B31 (if producing it takes up scarce manufacturing capacity);

- Insource Subassembly C10 (if the supplier is unreliable in terms of delivery or quality or some other reason);
- Joint venture with another company on Assembly B (if this presents an opportunity to acquire more control of a critical technology);
- Acquire Customer Y or the company that produces raw materials for Item D (acquisitions, of course, may be appropriate when the returns on investments are suitable).

Of course, the more opportunities for such moves, the better. For example, Assembly B might be used in multiple products, and the investment for its joint venture can be spread over those products. Or, Customer Y may have a strong position in the industry, and may be available for acquisition at a reasonable price. The point is that looking at *supply chain bills of material* provides a unique view of entrepreneurial opportunities.

6. ANALYZE THE RISKS AND ASSUMPTIONS

What is vulnerable in entrepreneurial supply chains, and how do we know? The approach to checking for vulnerability is, first, to analyze the risks and assumptions of various alternatives. Opportunities, as well as risks, could be an acquisition, alliance, or joint venture. Each includes certain assumptions that may enhance or mitigate risks. This section introduces the idea of analyses of risks and assumptions, with more detail provided in Chapter 5.

The objectives of risks and assumptions analyses are to assess the probabilities and impacts of both positive and negative events on the venture. Risks and assumptions analyses begin with answers to questions about where the vulnerabilities in the supply chains are, what their impacts are, and what can be done about them.

Notice the linking of analyses of risks with assumptions, which is not typical. Most often, these are separate aspects of analyses. This linkage is recommended because it is important to understand how risks are inherently influenced by one's assumptions about the situation.

Risks and assumptions management can be considered as part of the overall project management plan for entrepreneurial supply chains, although it is not limited to that. One of the best sources of information on this subject is published by the Project Management Institute,[8] although they focus more on risks than assumptions.

Analyses of risks and assumptions begin with a plan, with a breakdown structure as one of the most useful inputs, as shown in Figure 4.6. Analyses of risks and assumptions begin with planning the risks and assumptions management approach, and then planning and executing the risks and assumptions management activities for the project.

The *risks and assumptions breakdown structure* (adapted from PMBOK, p. 244) shows four primary risk categories and 18 subcategories. Obviously, these would

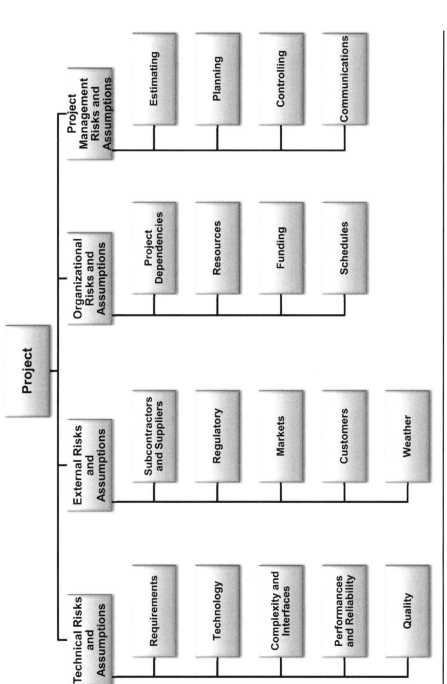

Figure 4.6 Risks and Assumptions Breakdown Structure. Adapted from: Project Management Institute, *A Guide to the Project Management Body of Knowledge (PMBOK), Third Edition,* 2004, p. 244.

be different for each entrepreneurial supply chain endeavor. The one shown here is fairly comprehensive and is a good place to start. The four primary categories of risks and assumptions shown are technical, external, organizational, and project management. There could be more, fewer, or different ones if necessary. Each category has either four or five subcategories, but they are not limited to these. The subcategories identify the risks and assumptions to a required level of detail. Each subcategory will need to have a risks and assumptions management plan, which generally includes:

- A definition of the nature of the risks and assumptions
- A methodology for assessing the risks and assumptions, including tasks to be accomplished, and
- A risks and assumptions mitigation plan that identifies individuals and/or organizations tasked with managing the risks and assumptions, along with budgets and timing for accomplishing the tasks.

Some risks and assumptions are opportunities that have potentially *positive* consequences. There are three approaches typically used to deal with these:

1. *Take advantage of* the opportunity to ensure that it is realized;
2. *Divide* the opportunity by working with a possible third party (e.g., in a joint venture or partnership) that is better able to take advantage of the opportunity; and/or
3. *Augment* the opportunity by attempting to increase the probability of its occurrence and/or maximizing its positive impacts.

Some risks and assumptions are threats with potentially *negative* consequences. There are three approaches typically used to deal with them:

1. *Avoid* the threat by changing the project plan
2. *Transfer* the threat to a third party such as an insurance company; and/or
3. *Lessen* the threat by potentially reducing the probability of the risk occurring and/or the impact of the risk.

In addition, there are two approaches to deal with *both* threats and opportunities:

1. *Acknowledge* the risk by recognizing that it is seldom possible to eliminate all risk from a project; and/or
2. Develop a *contingent* response that comes into play only if certain events occur.

Finally, a *risks and assumptions register* is often necessary to keep track of the identified risks and assumptions. This register is normally based on the risks and assumptions breakdown structure, and is a dynamic document with continuous updating to reflect current status. Registers as a rule consist of these components:

- Identified risks including their descriptions, areas of the risks and assumptions breakdown structure, their causes, and how they may affect project objectives and outcomes;
- Assigned roles and responsibilities to handle the specific risks and assumptions;
- Priorities of the risks and assumptions;
- Symptoms and warning signs of the risks and assumptions occurring;
- Probabilities of the risks and assumptions occurring;
- Agreed-upon approaches to risks and assumptions responses;
- Budgets and schedules for the responses;
- Contingency plans if the event(s) occurs;
- Secondary events that may arise as an outcome of the risks or assumptions occurring; and/or
- The relationships with the organization's thresholds for negative events.

There have been a number of surveys concerning supply chain risks. One survey was conducted among senior finance executives to examine their views on physical risks to the supply chain. The survey gathered 169 completed survey responses from CFOs and other senior finance executives across the United States.[9] Some of the identified risks were the risk of business disruption due to natural or man-made disasters, infrastructure breakdown, facilities and equipment failures, and other physical hazards along the supply chain. One of the most interesting risks identified was that the benefits of global sourcing and supplier consolidation can carry a hidden cost: increased exposure to the risk of supply chain disruption. Occurring early in the time span of global sourcing, these costs were often not considered by supply chain executives. However, as global sourcing became more prevalent, and as more disruptions occurred, these types of risks have taken on more importance. We are beginning to see more entrepreneurial supply chains that are directed toward minimizing global sourcing disruptions.

In 2011, a disastrous earthquake, tsunami, and nuclear power plant meltdown in Japan was in the news as a major global supply chain disruption, in addition to the enormous human and economic toll. Numerous stories in the press highlighted how significant corporations in that country were making all sorts of products and parts. If and when momentous supply chain challenges occur, as in the case of natural disasters, many of the solutions will be entrepreneurial in nature.

Chapter 5 provides more detail on risk management, with this section having served as a brief introduction.

7. ASSESS MULTIPLE OPPORTUNITIES FOR ENTREPRENEURIAL SUPPLY CHAINS

The next step is to *assess multiple opportunities* for entrepreneurial supply chains. When the above six steps have been accomplished, there should be a set of high-quality opportunities that might make sense going forward. Of course, it is not clear at this point just *how* high-quality the opportunities are—that's what is to be assessed at this point.

Usually *a* supply chain (singular) is not talked about; rather, it is supply *chains* (plural) that are almost always discussed. Business leaders often, however, talk as if they have a single supply chain with a single supply chain strategy, a single group of supply chain processes, and a single supply chain organization. This applies both to incoming supply chains from suppliers as well as outgoing supply chains to customers.

Consider multiple incoming supply chains from suppliers. As discussed in Chapter 3, multiple categories of suppliers contain:

(1) Transactions-oriented relationships,
(2) Cooperative partnerships, and
(3) Strategic alliances.

It is easy to think of these different types of supply chains as needing entrepreneurial coverage.

Think about a heavy equipment manufacturer with three *strategic alliances* for engines, electronics, and hydraulics. These three alliances could be considered as one type of supply chain in which the company needs a variety of relationships with the suppliers: from early supplier involvement in product development through after-the-sale product support. The objective is to achieve value-added benefits for both sides (buyer and seller) of these relationships.

What about supply chains for *cooperative partnerships*, or what sometimes is called "handshake management." The objectives here are to eliminate problems, and achieve consistency and dependability in the relationship. To achieve these objectives, companies usually employ these types of actions:

•   Implement problem-solving teams to jointly address issues and solve problems on both sides of the relationship;
•   Work with suppliers to help build capabilities between buyers and sellers;
•   Improve customer- and supplier-facing processes;
•   Provide planning information between the buyer to seller to assist the other in managing their own processes; and
•   Provide consulting advice to assist in improving processes.

Finally, transactions-oriented relationships are the "nuts, bolts, and screws" that are purchased in large numbers but at relatively little cost. This sometimes is called "competitive pressure," where the pressure is on to reduce costs—both the costs of the product and the costs of the transactions. Buyers do several types of things to achieve a cost-reduction objective; they maintain multiple suppliers so they can "play them off" one another, setting one supplier against another; they use bidding and auctions; they employ supplier-certification programs and purchase only from certified suppliers; they improve the supplier-facing processes to reduce transactions costs; or they implement direct-to-unit or direct-to-project shipments.

Multiple opportunities for entrepreneurial supply chains almost always exist. The challenges are to identify these multiple opportunities, to assess them appropriately, and to choose those which are complementary with the business and should be pursued.

8. CHOOSE WHICH OPPORTUNITIES SHOULD BE PURSUED

Choose which opportunities should be pursued and incorporate them into a comprehensive strategic plan for the entire business. The essence of these choices is represented by two questions:

1. How can the supply chain contribute to the company's growth and profitability?
2. What opportunities make sense to create supply chains that are more entrepreneurial?

Companies that succeed with entrepreneurial supply chains view the supply chains as strategic assets. Companies such as Wal-Mart, Amazon, and Dell are known for their supply chain strategies.

> **An Aside:** During a consulting engagement, I was part of a conversation with two key client executives. One asked, "We've always focused our supply chain on cost, but can there be more to it?" The other replied with another question that captured the essence of this book on entrepreneurial supply chains. He asked, simply, "How can the supply chain contribute to profit and growth?"

Choosing which entrepreneurial supply chain opportunities to pursue might involve the following questions, which need to be answered prior to going forward:

1. Have target customers been identified?
2. Have market surveys been completed?

3. Have target price points been identified?
4. Have competitive products been identified?
5. Have niche markets been identified?
6. Has entry timing been identified?
7. Has market demand been identified by segment?
8. Have potential unit sales been developed?

Having explored the question "How can we know we have opportunities?" in this chapter, two real case studies, Baker Hughes and Corning, are used next to explain how the companies approached this question.

HOW BAKER HUGHES KNOWS IT HAS OPPORTUNITIES

At Baker Hughes, Art Soucy, Vice President, Global Supply Chain, was asked about his approach to entrepreneurial supply chains when he joined the company. While he was a recognized expert on supply chain management, he did not know the industry nor, obviously, did he know the company. So the industry was his first learning curve, along with his learning curve on the company.

To learn about the industry and the company, Art took a trip around the world, meeting with customers and suppliers, visiting Baker Hughes' facilities to get to know the employees and their capabilities. He kept asking people whom he met, "What are our most pressing opportunities—both positive that we can enhance, and negative that we need to fix?" As you can imagine, he got many, many suggestions—far more than he could handle!

When Art returned home, he began to try to make sense of these responses, beginning with the most pressing issues on which they could take action quickly, and then the ones that presented the most strategic opportunities. There were five that he called the "supply chain strategic initiatives." Since all of these were not entrepreneurial supply chain opportunities, per se, only three are included here. While he was looking for improvement opportunities and not necessarily for entrepreneurial opportunities, such opportunities were noticeable:

1. *Transportation and logistics.* The company ships product all over the world and they were able globally to reduce from 251 freight forwarders to six primary ones. Art said the following about this change. "It's just impossible to keep tabs on 251 freight forwarders all over the world."

   While not an entrepreneurial supply chain opportunity for Baker Hughes, each of these six freight forwarders had its own chances at becoming an entrepreneurial venture. Each obtained long-term agreements that were leveraged by the volume of business that Baker Hughes was able to give them.

2. *Sales and operations planning (S&OP).* Prior to Art's initiative, the company had different processes among their operating companies. S&OP, of course, is a formal monthly integrated planning and management process

that typically begins with demand planning, and then progresses through supply and production planning, new product development planning, and then financial planning, and perhaps other elements of the management process. The intent is to balance demand and supply, incorporate product development activities, include major initiatives, and determine the effect of all this effort on financial plans.

An outside consulting firm evaluated Baker Hughes S&OP processes and, frankly, did not give them good grades. Art then initiated an improvement effort led by a respected internal person. This began to pay dividends with improvements in critical components of S&OP.

Often important, but usually unstated when discussing S&OP, is the impact of entrepreneurial possibilities on the business. When an acquisition, merger, or other entrepreneurial supply chain opportunity is on the horizon, S&OP usually provides a perfect vehicle for incorporating entrepreneurial possibilities into the business' plans. The company's strategy, for the most part, is to fold acquisitions into existing businesses, or to start up new product lines or other forms of new businesses within existing ones. A well-functioning S&OP process is quite useful to this strategy.

An Aside: My experience with S&OP goes back to my doctoral dissertation. Unfortunately, I was not smart enough to coin the term *sales and operations planning*, but instead used the academic term, aggregate planning. The trouble was, no one knew what aggregate planning meant. The term was too vague, had not been adopted by industry at the time, and there were no processes around it. My dissertation objective was to propose an implementation structure and processes using an actual company as a test site. The plan was marginally successful in implementation, but very successful in its primary objective—earning a doctoral degree!

Someone later came along and called it "sales and operations planning"—balancing demand and supply. The term "S&OP" stuck. However, S&OP now is too narrow for its current use. It is more than balancing demand and supply. As stated, it includes a number of other considerations, particularly, product development and financial. But, it is what it is—S&OP—and it'll probably always be S&OP.

3. *Strategic sourcing.* In 2010, over 25% of Baker Hughes' manufacturing capacity was in Western Europe (United Kingdom and Germany), and most of the rest was in the United States (Texas and Oklahoma). These locations, while serving much of the company's historical demand, had three drawbacks: high-cost locations; physically a long way from the emerging

markets in South America, Africa, Middle East, and Asia/Pacific; and more of the company's demand coming from countries with local-content laws, regulations, and requirements. Art recognized that he had to reconfigure his supply chains to address these three issues. This reconfiguration created entrepreneurial opportunities for the company.

These issues are in line with what other companies are experiencing, in Baker Hughes' industry as well as in others. Strategic sourcing has become recognized as a key supply chain activity that links corporate strategy to the supply chain strategy and to the sourcing strategy. For example, if the company has a strategy to penetrate areas of the world where product cost is important or where local content is important, the sourcing strategy for both make items and buy items must reflect those considerations. Baker Hughes has taken steps toward entrepreneurial supply chain ventures in Mexico, Russia, China, Malaysia, Thailand, Saudi Arabia, and elsewhere. These can be "greenfield" plants, acquisitions, or joint ventures. They also sold or closed several facilities.

As the conversation with Art concluded, the author asked, "What did you miss?" Art replied, "I completely missed 'the communication thing.' I simply underestimated how hard managing the change process would be." This discussion is covered in Chapter 7.

A CASE NOTE FOR FURTHER STUDY:
Corning Incorporated

Cases are available at www.harvardbusinessonline.com. Readers should obtain copies of these cases and use them to go beyond discussion in the book. These cases were prepared as the basis for discussion, rather than to illustrate either effective or ineffective handling of any particular situation.

In this chapter, three cases about entrepreneurial and innovative supply chain activities of Corning Incorporated[10] from the Stanford and Harvard business schools are used:

- "Corning Incorporated (A): Reinventing New Business Development"
- "Corning Incorporated (B): Bringing Rigor to Early-Stage Opportunity Identification"
- "Corning: 156 Years of Innovation"

Corning creates and makes keystone components that enable high-technology systems for consumer electronics, mobile emissions control, telecommunications and life sciences. It has long been known for its dedication to technology, innovation, and entrepreneurial activity. Corning's Form 10-K, which includes the *Annual Report* for the fiscal year ending December 31, 2009, provides background information. Corning was established in 1851, and its name was changed from

Corning Glass Works in 1989. Corning considers its business to be in five segments: display technologies, telecommunications, environmental technologies, specialty materials, and life sciences. Corning operates approximately 60 manufacturing facilities in 13 countries. Net sales for fiscal 2009 were approximately US$5.395B.

Corning was one of the first companies to form a corporate research group in 1908. Through the years, they experimented with numerous approaches to assessing opportunities, both technology and market. After 2000, Corning started a unit called Strategic Growth to collaborate with their corporate research organization and to proactively develop new, large (at least $500m), and profitable opportunities. Strategic Growth was intended to be an innovative approach to fostering organic growth. The goal of Strategic Growth was to build two to four $500m businesses per decade.

The Strategic Growth organization tried to capture the essence of what Corning did best—the innovation recipe, shown in Figure 4.7. One conclusion was that they were really good at glass and optical physics technologies (both R&D and manufacturing), things that other people could not do, i.e., really difficult projects that result in technology that becomes the *keystone component of systems*.

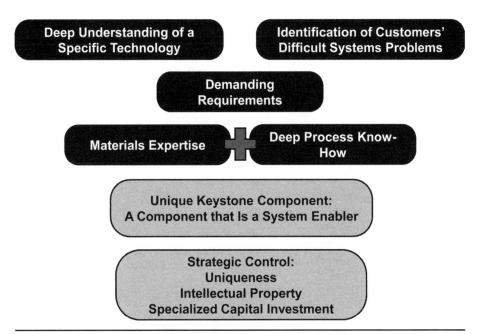

Figure 4.7 Corning's Innovation Recipe. Adapted from: "Corning Incorporated (A): Reinventing New Business Development," page 30.

Furthermore, Corning concluded that they were really good at the combination of materials expertise and deep process know-how.

Strategic Growth was charged with investigating the white space markets and technologies in which Corning was not already participating directly. These were adjacent markets and technologies.

Corning's stage-gate process is shown in Figure 4.8, and is adapted from the Corning (A) case. Notice the five stages of the process separated by four gates.

1. Build Knowledge → "Generate Ideas"
   Gate 1 → Decision Point
2. Determine Feasibility → "Perform Experiments"
   Gate 2 → Decision Point
3. Test Practicality → "Carry Out Projects"
   Gate 3 → Decision Point
4. Prove Profitability → "Engage in Production"
   Gate 4 → Decision Point
5. Manage Life Cycle → "Achieve Profits"

An Aside: This stage-gate approach is not unusual for product and process development today, and other companies' models are similar. Of course, different companies will use different terminology to define their stages and gates. I worked as a consultant and educator with several companies to help them develop stages and gates along these lines for their own purposes. Research that was done in conjunction with those engagements showed a wide diversity of approaches and vocabulary to describe a similar type of process.

Stages and *gates* perform different functions. *Stages* describe activities in which work is accomplished as defined above. *Gates* are decision points. Gates typically have associated questions that must be adequately addressed before work can progress to the next stage. Gates are intended to ensure that too much time and resources are not expended without adequate review and decisions.

Prior to Stage 1, there is usually an early opportunity identification (Pre-Stage 1). Some companies call this the "fuzzy front end" to denote that ideas are unclear, vague, and uncertain at this point. This usually is a form of advanced research that has not been developed into product or process concepts.

If a project successfully passes Gate 3, then Corning begins a new start-up business unit to commercialize the new product(s) and the associated processes.

The second, Corning (B) case focuses on the "fuzzy front end," what Corning called the Pre-Stage 1—Early Opportunity Identification. The nature of this stage is somewhat undisciplined and lacking in rigor, typically with a "technology-push" mentality. Someone would investigate a promising technology, and then a business team would try to find markets and customers for it. Corning wanted to switch

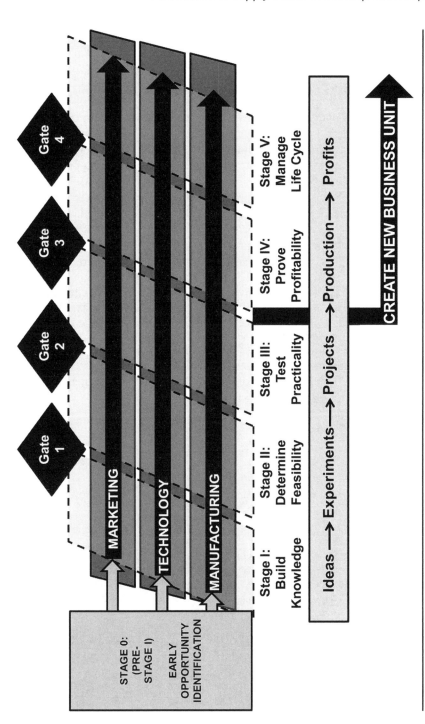

Figure 4.8 Corning's Innovation Stage-Gate Process. Adapted from: "Corning Incorporated (A): Reinventing New Business Development."

to a "market-pull" mentality so as to work "outside-in." They wanted to look for clear problems and issues, and then assemble the resources to work on them.

One of the difficulties, however, was where to look for the opportunities. Corning needed a way to "get smart fast," as they put it. They decided on an approach to hold a workshop to which they invited outside experts in a number of fields to speak: demographics, the environment, communications, computing, manufacturing, health, and others. They then followed this workshop with an internal structured brainstorming and visioning session for what these ideas meant to Corning. (See Appendix A for an example of how such a visioning process like this might be accomplished.)

These ideas were then screened against Corning criteria and narrowed to a smaller set on which white papers were developed. This was followed by a "bakeoff" of the white papers in order to decide on a relatively few ideas to take forward into further development. This process "narrowed the funnel," with only the most promising ideas surviving. The most promising ideas were resourced and moved into the Stage 1 process.

In summary, then, rigor was added to the early-stage opportunity process through the following six steps:

1. *Workshops* to identify major trends using external experts;
2. *Ideation* and visioning for facilitated internal brainstorming to help focus on areas of potential opportunity;
3. *White papers* to identify potential opportunities for Corning and to justify in-depth opportunity analyses;
4. *In-depth opportunity analyses* for market and technology assessments and to test the opportunities;
5. *Presentation of idea(s) to Corning Technology Council (CTC)* to review the findings and recommendations, and to decide whether to advance the idea to Stage 1 or abandon the opportunity; and
6. *Stage 1 projects* to execute critical experiments and decide whether to expand the effort.

An Aside: Based on experience and discussions with other innovative and entrepreneurial companies, the Corning approach has value. Readers should consider it for their companies. However, there are some questions to ask about criteria for apparently considering only opportunities with the potential of $500M in sales, and with the objective of only two to four per decade. Other companies in technology-rich industries might aim for many "singles and doubles" (to use baseball terms), realizing that they also will hit a few "home runs." Also, Corning's time frame of several years seems too long for taking an opportunity from ideation to commercialization; too much can change over several years.

A FINAL WORD ON HOW WE KNOW WE HAVE OPPORTUNITIES

This chapter has focused on approaches to determine what opportunities might reasonably exist to create entrepreneurial supply chains. An eight-step approach was presented, as follows. Understand the macro issues affecting the industry. Begin to evaluate entrepreneurial supply chain opportunities using various techniques including scenario building. Conduct education and training for supply chain, business development, and other appropriate personnel. Convince the organization of the need to move forward with entrepreneurial supply chain opportunities. Design the supply chains for entrepreneurship considering the possibilities of new growth platforms and supply chain bills of material. Analyze the risks and assumptions to understand the vulnerabilities of the various alternatives. Assess multiple opportunities to determine just how high quality the opportunities are. And, finally, choose which opportunities will be pursued.

So, how do we know we have opportunities? This chapter discussed an entrepreneurial supply chain opportunity-identification and opportunity-structuring process so that these opportunities can be managed. Two case studies, Baker Hughes and Corning, were used to illustrate how two real companies accomplish this important task.

ASSURANCE OF LEARNING QUESTIONS

1. Describe the key aspects of the chapter and their implications for your organization.
2. Examine your own organization and compare its supplier management processes with the descriptions in the chapter.
3. For your company, brainstorm some possible adjacent and white space opportunities along the three growth paths, as shown in Figure 4.1.
4. Explain the advantages and disadvantages of the stage-gate process, as outlined in the Corning cases.
5. What problems is a company likely to encounter when it moves entrepreneurially into the white space between its existing businesses? What opportunities is it likely to encounter?

REFERENCES

1. Einhorn, Bruce, and Tim Culpan. June 14, 2010, "Technology: A Netbook Pioneer Enters the iPad Age." *Bloomberg BusinessWeek*. 31–32.
2. Lee, William B., and Michael R. Katzorke. *Leading Effective Supply Chain Transformations: A Guide to Sustainable World-Class Capability and Results*. Fort Lauderdale; J. Ross Publishing, 2010.
3. Mandel, Michael. June 15, 2009. "Innovation Interrupted." *BusinessWeek*.

4. Dye, Renee, and Elizabeth Stephenson. May 2010. "Five Forces Reshaping the Global Economy: McKinsey Global Survey Results." *McKinsey Quarterly Premium Edition*.
5. Grayson, Leslie E., and James G. Clawson. 1996. "Scenario Building," Darden Business Publishing Note #UV0539, University of Virginia.
6. Schoemaker, Paul J. H. 1995. "Scenario Planning: A Tool for Strategic Planning." *Sloan Management Review*, 36(2), 25–40.
7. Laurie, Donald L., Doz, Yves L., and Claude P. Sheer. May 2006. "Creating New Growth Platforms." *Harvard Business Review*, 845, 80–90.
8. Project Management Institute. 2004. *A Guide to the Project Management Body of Knowledge (PMBOK)*, 3rd ed. See "Project Risk Management" in Chapter 11, 237–268.
9. CFO Research Services, "Physical Risks to the Supply Chain: The View from Finance," CFO *Magazine*, March 2009.
10. Denend, Lyn, and Robert A. Burgelman. June 10, 2008. "Corning Incorporated (A): Reinventing New Business Development," Stanford Graduate School of Business, Case #SM-167A; "Corning Incorporated (B): Bringing Rigor to Early-Stage Opportunity Identification," Stanford Graduate School of Business, Case #SM-167B. Bowen, H. Kent, and Courtney Purrington. April 23, 2008. "Corning: 156 Years of Innovation." Harvard Business School, Case #9-608-108. The cases are available at www.harvardbusinessonline.com.

CHAPTER 5

MANAGING THE RISKS OF ENTREPRENEURIAL SUPPLY CHAINS

"You've got to be careful if you don't know where you're going, because you might not get there."

—Yogi Berra

This quote from Yogi Berra is an example of risk management—be careful if you don't know where you're going! Risk management of the opportunity is one of the most important considerations for managing an entrepreneurial supply chain project.

Take a look at any company's 10-K Form, which all public U.S. companies must submit annually to the Securities and Exchange Commission; it then becomes part of the public record. There is a required section on Risk Factors for the business, which typically point to risks in the company's supply chains as well as to other risks in development of new products or services: risks in the competitive landscape, in the industry, and other risks. Readers should review these risk factors for their competitors or possible future competitors. Most companies freely admit that risks abound in their industry and for their company, and that those risks may affect their business performance and stock price.

Sometimes opportunities are brilliantly disguised as risks. One can look at the risk factors in a 10-K and see opportunities imbedded in them. Most companies begin the risk factors section with something like the following statement, which is not real, but representative:

> *An investment in our common stock involves various risks. When considering an investment in our company, one should consider carefully all of the risk factors described, as well as other information included in this report. There may be additional risks, uncertainties, and matters not listed, that we are unaware of, or that we currently consider immaterial. Any of these could adversely affect our business, financial condition, results of operations, and cash flow and, thus, the value of investment in our company.*

The statement typically will go on with more language, represented here, most of which likely will affect the supply chains:

- Demand for our products may be outside of our control. Changes in the global economy may adversely affect our customers' spending for our products.
- Volatility of prices for our products and our competitors' products may adversely affect demand for our products and services.
- Our customers may not be able to pay amounts owed to our company.
- Our suppliers may not be able to deliver in a timely manner.
- Changes in industry capacity utilization may adversely affect our business.

The statement is trying to cover all the bases, and make sure that the organization warns potential investors of all the pitfalls of investing in their company. The organization does not want to get sued if someone's investment goes sour! They may get sued anyway, but this statement could be a partial defense.

Risk is a combination of consequences and the likelihood of an event occurring. Most people think of risks being events that have a relatively *high* probability of occurring, such as difficulties with suppliers, demand not being what they expect, or competitors bringing forth new products. However, it is not always the case that high-probability risks are all that could go wrong for entrepreneurial supply chains.

An article by Daniel Fisher and Christopher Helman (2010) in *Forbes*[1] addressed the issue of low-probability/high-impact risks, including:

> *A meltdown of a nuclear power plant could affect surrounding regions, including supply chains that run through the vicinity of the plant. It could cost lives, as well as cost the plant owners hundreds of billions of dollars. It also could affect power availability to wide areas.*

Remember the Three Mile Island partial nuclear core meltdown that occurred in 1979? That incident did more to damage America's nuclear energy programs than any other single incident in history. The public scare was out of proportion to the actual damages or health impact.[2] Nevertheless, the nuclear power program in the United States was brought to a standstill at the time by politicians and activists. In addition, the long-term impact of the earthquake, tsunami, and nuclear power plant radiation leaks in Japan in 2011 is unknown. However, the impact on the nuclear power industry will be significant, regardless. The Japanese disaster almost exactly parallels the article by Fisher and Helman, which also discussed more low-probability/high-impact risks:

> *A liquefied natural gas (LNG) explosion could occur in a port with a tanker carrying products that burn more intensely than oil or gas, and will not stop until all the fuel is burned. Such an explosion could occur at sea with perhaps less, but still significant, loss of life than if it occurred in a port.*

Although the article did not mention them, many ship disasters have occurred over the years. One such disaster occurred at Texas City, TX, in 1947, when a ship fire detonated approximately 2,300 tons of ammonium nitrate used primarily for fertilizer. The resulting fires and explosions reportedly killed at least 581 people. Interestingly enough, the Port of Houston did not allow loading of ammonium nitrate because of the danger, and that is why the ship was in Texas City, a few miles away from Houston. Speaking of Houston, the area around Houston, TX, contains the nation's largest concentration of petrochemical plants. The low-probability/high-impact risks reported by Fisher and Helman, indicated:

- A chemical plant explosion and fire in Houston could kill 600 people and cost $20 billion. It not only could affect supplies of the plant's products, but also surrounding plants and their product outputs—to say nothing of the deaths and injuries.
- If a Category 5 hurricane hits New York City, it could create a 25-foot storm surge up the Hudson River. It could disrupt communications and supply chains headquartered in or run throughout the region, costing more than $320 billion.
- A super volcano such as Italy's Mount Vesuvius could threaten 2 million people because of dense urban development around the mountain. Mount Rainier could erupt, as it did 5,700 years ago when it sent a mud flow into what are today the suburbs of Seattle. Or, as in the volcano eruption in Iceland in 2010, air travel could be disrupted over a wide area of the globe.

In addition, Fisher and Helman cite BP's 2010 oil spill disaster in the Gulf of Mexico, which killed 11 people. The disaster cost BP $70 billion in lost market capitalization—one estimate of the ultimate total cost to the company. Companies operating in the oil and gas value chain, as a result, will likely face greater regulatory scrutiny, operational and administrative procedures, liability, and consequently higher risk even if they had nothing to do with that catastrophe. Each internal corporate discipline, including the supply chain, will face change in order to adjust to new government regulations and liability protections. BP may need to reassess strategies and opportunities, as well as oversight of the risk management function of the company.

Of course, the global oil and gas industry has a long history of dealing with risks and disasters, continuously learning and trying to improve their safety record. The 1988 disaster aboard the Piper Alpha,[3] a production platform in the North Sea, is the worst offshore oil disaster in terms of lives lost and industry impact; 167 people were killed, with 59 survivors. The rig was owned by Occidental Petroleum, and the explosion was attributed to poor design, inadequate maintenance and safety practices, and inappropriate decision-making procedures. The British government established an official inquiry, which resulted in a significant rewriting of the rules for offshore safety. However, that did not prevent BP's 2010 disaster, which shows the need for continuous learning about risk management—not just in the oil and gas industry, but in all others also.

There are hundreds of supply chain risk examples, but here is only one more: On September 29, 1982, a "Tylenol scare"[4] began when the first of seven individuals died in metropolitan Chicago after ingesting Extra Strength Tylenol® that had been deliberately contaminated with cyanide by someone with no connection to Johnson & Johnson (J&J), manufacturers of Tylenol. Within a week, the company pulled 31 million bottles of Tylenol tablets back from retailers, making it one of the first major recalls in U.S. history. Tylenol sales initially collapsed, but eventually recovered. The incident necessitated that makers of both prescription and over-the-counter medications introduce tamper-evident packaging as a standard procedure. This has become a famous case study of well-executed crisis management, and J&J has reaped substantial positive publicity for its handling of the incident—the time it occurred and in its response with new packaging.

However, in 2010, Johnson & Johnson was cited for problems in its quality control procedures in an article in *The Wall Street Journal*,[5] which stated:

> *J&J's handling of problem Tylenol has become a focus of a congressional investigation into manufacturing problems. J&J has issued more than a half dozen recalls of popular over-the-counter medicines over the past year, and temporarily shuttered the Fort Washington, PA, plant where it makes many Tylenol products.*

In an accompanying video, *The Wall Street Journal* made the point that *Barron's* publishes its annual list of the "World's Most Respected Companies," and Johnson & Johnson was at the top of the survey for the second year in a row.

Supply chain risks are not to be taken lightly. The above examples show that low-probability risks occur frequently enough so that planning for such events is prudent.

UNDERSTAND MACRO RISKS FACING THE COMPANY

Macro issues facing the organization should be the beginning point for managing the risks facing the entrepreneurial supply chains.

> **KEY IDEA**
>
> It is a cliché to say that dramatic change has occurred, and that this change is accelerating.

There are a number of macro risk issues that directly influence entrepreneurial supply chains. Five macro risk issues are:

1. *Globalization.* It is virtually the same Coca-Cola, Nestle, Volkswagen, or Sony product anywhere one goes in the world. One can walk into an Outback Steakhouse in Texas and get an Australian-themed experience in spite of the fact that Texas is justly famous for its own steak houses. Consumer fads travel, seemingly in days, around the world. But what does this mean for entrepreneurial supply chains? Simply, opportunities for new enterprises (either start-ups or corporate entrepreneurship ventures) know no national boundaries. Globalization is not a far-off, abstract concept that economists and politicians use. It is real. It is here. We all know it, whether we like it or not.

> **KEY IDEA**
>
> Zara created what was an extremely fast global supply chain for their industry to make it easier to manage rapidly moving consumer demand.

Not only can globalization present entrepreneurs with opportunities, it also contains risks. Competition can come out of the blue, from anywhere in the world. (Witness Texas steak houses with competition from Australia.) Readers who are considering entrepreneurial supply chain ventures might be advised to recognize and articulate both global risks and global opportunities in their enterprises.

2. *The global idea market.* The globalization of the idea market perhaps can do as much as anything to increase supply chain effectiveness and efficiency throughout the world. The globalization of supply chains has significantly increased the rate of technology and information transfer.

   For the entrepreneurial supply chain, the global idea market can be a two-edged sword. It presents opportunities for an entrepreneur to move his or her ideas quickly around the world. On the other hand, it means that competition from anywhere can appear very quickly. Presumably, the entrepreneur has a new and better idea, and thus could become the "predator" rather than the "prey."

3. *Giant wealth transfer.* International balance of payments status also can have a positive or negative impact on entrepreneurial supply chain ventures. If the enterprise is a U.S. company, and if the U.S. dollar is relatively weak, then buyers in countries with a currency that is strong relative to the dollar can purchase U.S. goods and services comparatively

cheaply. This stimulates U.S. exports. It also makes non-U.S.-made goods comparatively more expensive to purchase in the United States.

As of 2010, there was substantial controversy about the relative values of U.S. versus Chinese currency. The argument was made that China undervalued its currency to make its products more attractively priced in the West, and to stimulate its exports and dampen demand for non-Chinese products in China. Even if, at other times, it is not the Chinese currency versus the U.S. dollar, but another country's currency, there will always be currencies that will appear to be out of balance with each other.

Relative values of currencies are risks for entrepreneurial supply chain ventures. They also can be opportunities if entrepreneurs are looking for low-cost manufacturing sites around the world.

The Economist periodically publishes a tongue-in-cheek, but useful, "Big Mac index"[6] which tracks the price of McDonald's Big Mac around the world:

> *The index is a lighthearted attempt to gauge how far currencies are from their fair value. It is based on the theory of purchasing power parity, which argues that . . . exchange rates should move to equalize the price of an identical basket of goods between two countries.*

The Economist's "identical basket of goods" consists of a single item, the Big Mac hamburger produced in nearly 120 countries. Their conclusion indicates that, versus the U.S. dollar, the Chinese Yuan is undervalued by 48%, the euro is overvalued by 16%, the Brazilian real is overvalued by 31%, and the Swiss franc is overvalued by 68% based on this index as of the time of the writing. However, *The Economist* admits that their index is not precise since the burger's cost also depends on such local inputs as rent and wages which tend to be lower in poor countries.

4. *Wall Street's short-term demands.* Short-term demands by investors (should we call them *speculators?*) have distorted decision-making within entrepreneurial ventures. This impacts entrepreneurial ventures in two ways. First, it makes financing of entrepreneurial ventures more difficult because readily-available sources of "patient money" are difficult to come by. Entrepreneurial supply chain ventures may take time to pay a return on the investment, which makes it difficult to obtain financing when everyone is looking for a short-term return. Second, ventures that start with corporate entrepreneurship funds also face this short-term focus.

5. *Innovation.* Innovation is the heart and soul of entrepreneurial supply chains. The whole purpose of these ventures is to bring innovative thinking, and innovative products and services, to the marketplace. A 2009 article in *BusinessWeek* explored innovation, primarily in the United States, and concluded:[7]

An Aside: I consulted with a large, well-known company and visited a number of their business units around the world. I was told, almost unanimously by division heads, that they would not take what all agreed were needed supply chain actions because the profits would come "too late to make the numbers." The business-unit heads would be off to their next jobs by the time the payoffs occurred. This company had a policy of leaving business-unit heads in their jobs usually for about two or three years. If they "made their numbers," they would get a bigger job. If they did not, they "would be given a good recommendation to go work for the competition," as the saying went. Clearly, this company's short-term Wall Street focus affected their approach to entrepreneurial supply chains—they had none—and entrepreneurial actions were in short supply in that company.

> *During the last decade, U.S. innovation has failed to realize its promise—and that may explain America's economic woes. . . . We live in an era of rapid innovation. Countries that fail to keep up with innovations are destined to lag others that are more innovative. Current press reports indicate that China, for example, is substantially more innovative than the U.S. in clean energy. This clearly is a risk to the United States and to entrepreneurial companies that are focused on clean energy.*

Entrepreneurial supply chain innovations typically are multifaceted. Innovations occur in product technology, manufacturing process technology, business process technology, and many others. Successful entrepreneurs tend to be innovative in at least one of these.

UNDERSTAND RISKS IN THE COMPANY'S BUSINESS STRATEGY

What determines success in an industry? Effective risk management cannot be accomplished without a solid understanding of the company's business and industry, and what drives success.

One example of a company's strategic risks is illustrated by *Bloomberg Business-Week*.[8] Evergreen Solar makes silicon wafers that go into solar plants. In 2008, they decided to build a plant in Massachusetts, given the optimism that they saw about the U.S. federal government's drive for alternative energy. The bankruptcy of Lehman Brothers cost Evergreen about $300 million in equity. They got financing from the federal and state governments, but not nearly enough to make a go of manufacturing in the U.S.

The Chinese government then approached the company with a generous offer for them to move their manufacturing to China. The CEO said, "That left us no choice but to stop making panels in the U.S. and shift our focus to China. The access to capital for start-ups there is staggering." The result was that 800 people in Massachusetts lost their jobs; the article does not say how many people in China were hired. "My hope is that someday more jobs will come back here," the CEO said.

Evergreen Solar makes for a very interesting and relevant case study for this book. An August 17, 2011 article[9] in *The Wall Street Journal* brings the story up to date with Evergreen's bankruptcy filing for its U.S. business. It illustrates the risks of a technology-based start-up that relied on "green-energy" government subsidies that were favored by the Obama administration. In its Chapter 11 filing, Evergreen cited the difficulties in competing against Chinese solar companies that "receive considerable government and financial support." This also cites the fact that "it's a lot better to pay workers $1 an hour in China rather than $15 an hour in Massachusetts." The company blamed the U.S. government's failure "to adopt supportive policies." Further, Evergreen also bet on the wrong technology so that when prices changed for a key input it "stripped away Evergreen's competitive edge and left it with a higher-cost manufacturing process." This story illustrates how U.S. federal and Massachusetts state governments lost hundreds of millions of dollars of taxpayers' money trying to support politically favored companies and technologies.

In another example, the author was on the Board of Directors and chairman of the Compensation Committee of a large, well-run company for a number of years. During his tenure, he and other directors advocated that the company strengthen its risk management focus. Fortunately, the company did not have any serious incidents; nevertheless, it was well prepared in case something happened.

Roles of companies' Boards of Directors (including audit committees and compensation committees) are being updated concerning their oversight of the companies' risk management system and activities. Certainly, not all Boards will take the same approach, but generally they are being urged to provide a comprehensive risk oversight system tailored to the specific needs of their companies. The National Association of Corporate Directors (NACD) published a comprehensive report on board-level risk oversight.[10] They pointed out that while the nature of the information required by the board will vary from company to company and from risk to risk, the following are examples of the risk information the board might address:.

- *Governance risks* require the board to weigh the risks and rewards of different courses of action, especially with the corporate strategy.
- *Critical enterprise risks* include definitions of the risks along with the impact of the risks and the probability of them occurring.

- *Board-approval risks* can result from management's requests for approval, such as for mergers, acquisitions, and major capital expenditures.
- *Business-management risks* can occur in normal, everyday activities such as risks in reporting, operations, financial, human resources, compliance, or reputation.
- *Emerging and non-traditional risks* could be risks of natural events, demographic shifts, or cyber-risks.

Companies should examine their organization's and the industry's macro issues, as well as their business strategy for inherent risks that need to be incorporated into a comprehensive risk management plan for entrepreneurial supply chains. Such a comprehensive plan needs to be a joint examination by the Board of Directors and the management team. This reflects the belief that most companies' risk management has not kept pace with current challenges.

Since this is a book on entrepreneurial supply chains, risks inherent in the supply chain strategic plan are emphasized, as shown in Figure 5.1. The Supply Chain Risk Mitigation Strategic Plan elements are disguised from a real company and provided by Michael R. Katzorke, CEO of Bryce Consulting Group. Notice that the figure contains several selected elements from the company's supply chain strategic plan (some are left out). For each element of the plan, the company's management identified the important risk issues and a risk mitigation plan. For example, one of the elements in the supply chain strategic plan was to implement the commodity team concept—see the first strategic plan element in Figure 5.1. In their definition, commodity teams were co-located teams including appropriate people from various engineering disciplines, quality management personnel as well as personnel from finance and accounting, manufacturing, service parts support, and purchasing—whatever areas of the company from which capability was needed. The commodity teams were to focus on specific types of items in the product, such as machined parts, castings and forgings, electronics, hydraulics, and the like.

The company was experiencing limited acceptance for the commodity team concept even though it had been approved by senior management. This presented a risk, and the selected risk mitigation plan was to create three cross-discipline, cross-site teams during the targeted year, and to show that they could function well. Other teams would be created in subsequent years.

Careful attention to risk management for entrepreneurial supply chain ventures is necessary because they can be very risky. The processes shown in Figure 5.1 can be useful in this effort.

THE RISKS AND ASSUMPTIONS MANAGEMENT PLAN

The relationship between risks and assumptions was explained in Chapter 4. Risks are important to understand, but so are assumptions about risk. Readers

OBJECTIVE: SUCCESSFUL SUPPLY CHAIN 20XX STRATEGIC PLAN ACHIEVEMENT		
STRATEGIC PLAN ELEMENTS	**RISK ISSUES**	**RISK MITIGATION PLAN**
Implement commodity team concept	Limited acceptance for commodity teams	Create three cross-discipline and cross-site commodity teams to see how they work
Link supply chain objectives to business objectives	No unified vision between groups	Create line-of-sight linkage from supply chain to business objectives
Create sense of urgency for the speed of change	Need for cultural shift from firefighting to strategic focus for supply chains	Conduct education and training programs on need for strategic view
Ensure that supply chain metrics drive enterprise-wide behavior	Lack of linked and consistent metrics, definitions, and measurements	Standardize enterprise metrics, reporting, and link to supply chain metrics
Implement optimal organization structure	Current structure supports silo mentality	Create total enterprise supply chain organization
Implement early supplier involvement (ESI)	Current ESI is limited	Create incentives for Engineering to actively implement
Upgrade demand management capability	Too much forecasting and lack of connectivity with customers	Enhance forecast accuracy metrics and use to drive connectivity efforts
Improve material availability and reduce overall inventory levels	Too much excess and obsolete inventory combined with too many shortages	Strengthen sales and operations planning process with master scheduling
Reduce transactional work by supply chain personnel	Lack of appropriate automation	Implement Ariba software
Improve make-or-buy decision process	Process is inconsistent and lacks reliability	Implement Bryce strategic sourcing process

Figure 5.1 Supply Chain Risk Mitigation Strategic Plan Elements.

were referred to "Chapter 11—Project Risk Management" in the *Project Management Body of Knowledge (PMBOK® Guide)*[11] for a summary of risk management. The guide is written from a project management viewpoint, and is one of the most comprehensive documents for readers who are contemplating entrepreneurial supply chain ventures.

The *PMBOK® Guide*, however, does not adequately address project assumptions. Every entrepreneurial supply chain venture is predicated on a set of assumptions. Assumptions, for planning purposes, are considered to be hypotheses, suppositions, beliefs, conjectures, or premises, which are used to build a business plan, accordingly. Assumptions affect all aspects of entrepreneurial supply chains, and occur from their conception to their termination. Project teams for new ventures frequently identify, document, and validate assumptions as part of their planning processes. Assumptions and risks are closely related—assumptions generate risks because risks occur when assumptions turn out not to be true, especially if the firm has acted (or not acted) on them. Assumptions analysis explores the accuracy of assumptions and identifies risks inherent in the assumptions if they happen to be inaccurate, inconsistent, or incomplete.

In Chapter 4, Figure 4.6, the risks and assumptions breakdown structure (RABS) showed examples of categories and subcategories of risks and assumptions. A RABS results from risk management planning. It describes how risk and assumptions management will be structured and performed in an entrepreneurial supply chain venture. It is contained in or as a subsidiary of the overall business plan. The risk and assumptions management plan can be informal and broadly framed, or it can be formal and highly detailed, based on the needs of the venture. Information in the plan varies by application area and the venture's size.

The risk and assumptions register contains the list of venture's risks and assumptions, the results of their analyses, and the responses. The RABS, shown in Figure 4.6, and the risk and assumptions register (RAR), shown in Figure 5.2, should be worked together.

Notice that the example RAR in Figure 5.2 contains a description of the risks and assumptions, as well as a potential response to each. Also, the root causes of the risks and assumptions are listed along with probabilities of occurring. These link the register with the breakdown structure (schedule, technical, demand, regulatory, resources, and project dependencies). The register also highlights the responsible individuals and the dates for resolution. When the RAR and the breakdown structure are kept up to date, they provide a current "to-do" list along with the collected record of the risks and assumptions. Records should be kept of the dispositions of risks and assumptions when they have been taken care of.

Of course, the registers that are developed and used in real life tend to be more complete and contain more information. Microsoft Excel or Access software, or other commercial software, can be used for this database.

The RABS and RAR are not the complete management plan—it goes beyond those two tools. The risk and assumptions management plan contains the

Risk and Assumptions Register (RAR)

Date Last Updated	Risks and Assumptions	Potential Response	Root Causes and Their Probabilities	Responsible Individual(s)	Schedule for Resolution
xx/xx/xxxx	First risk – negative (describe)	Avoid – change the business plan's schedule	Schedule too tight (30-40% chance)	Nick	yy/yy/yyyy
xx/xx/xxxx	First assumption – negative (describe)	Transfer – add to subcontractor A's contract	Technical assumption (60-80% chance)	Becky	yy/yy/yyyy
xx/xx/xxxx	Second assumption – positive (describe)	Exploit – make sure this happens	Assumptions about customers' demand (50-75% chance)	Susan	yy/yy/yyyy
xx/xx/xxxx	Third assumption – positive (describe)	Enhance – lobby for no regulatory changes	Assumptions that regulations will not change (60-80% chance)	Ryan	yy/yy/yyyy
xx/xx/xxxx	Second risk – negative (describe)	Mitigate – increase early funding	Risk that resources will be insufficient (50-50% chance)	Beverly	yy/yy/yyyy
xx/xx/xxxx	Third risk – negative (describe)	Contingent based on missing early milestones	Risk that project dependencies could affect milestones (10-20% chance)	Katie	yy/yy/yyyy

Figure 5.2   Risk and Assumptions Register.

following six components adapted from the *PMBOK* framework, which should be incorporated into the business plan:

1. The *risks and assumptions management planning* process involves planning and controlling the activities related to managing risks and assumptions in the entrepreneurial supply chain venture.
2. *Risks and assumptions identification* consists of identifying and describing the risks and assumptions that may affect the venture.
3. *Qualitative risks and assumptions analysis* is a discipline that is used frequently in various settings. This analysis seeks to gather an in-depth understanding of the risks and assumptions, and the reasons for their occurrence. Qualitative analysis investigates what, why, how, where, and when the risks and assumptions may occur. Qualitative analysis is different from quantitative analysis in the sense that qualitative analysis deals with non-numerical descriptions. Qualitative analysis tends to be exploratory in nature, and sometimes is used to explain the quantitative analysis. Further, qualitative analysis involves combining the probabilities of occurrence with the impact.
4. *Quantitative risks and assumptions analysis* involves numerically analyzing the root causes and determining their probabilities of occurrence. Measurement is central to quantitative analysis because it provides the fundamental connection between qualitative analysis and mathematical expressions of quantitative relationships. Qualitative and quantitative analyses frequently are accomplished in combination with each other.
5. *Risks and assumptions response planning* involves developing response options and associated actions to enhance opportunities and reduce threats to the entrepreneurial supply chain venture.
6. *Risks and assumptions monitoring and control* involves following up on the risks and assumptions, potential responses, root causes, individuals responsible for resolution, and agreed resolution schedules. It includes keeping the RAR up to date. It also involves identifying new risks and assumptions and archiving those that have been resolved.

Risks and assumptions are two of the most important components of the entrepreneurial supply chain venture. They are important to the strengths, weaknesses, opportunities, and threats (SWOT) analysis of the undertaking. Paying close attention to risks and assumptions is highly recommended.

DEFINE RISKS AND ASSUMPTIONS FOR THE SUPPLY CHAINS

The RAR and the RABS, are important to document and monitor those issues that might affect the entrepreneurial supply chain venture—positively and negatively. From where do these issues arise? Two sources were identified: risks and assumptions that are inherent in the *macro* issues affecting the enterprise along with those that are included in the company's business *strategy*. Also, risks and assumptions generated from both *external* and *internal* sources might be considered. But let's discuss some specifics.

Risks and Assumptions Inherent in Macro Issues

Economic risks and assumptions. Many industries are subject to different economic conditions. Access to borrowed funds affects ability to finance acquisitions or to start new businesses. Economic conditions also affect spending plans as well as companies' abilities to repay amounts owed.

Cyber-risk[12] *and cyber-assumptions.* Companies and governments have become increasingly concerned about surveillance of computer systems that control the electric grid and other critical infrastructure, including companies' own critical business data. The concern is that companies and governments have highly developed hacking capabilities that enable them to infiltrate even the most sophisticated computer systems.

Liability risks and assumptions. Managing a company's liability has become increasingly important in the last few decades, particularly in the United States, as it has become increasingly litigious. An attorney friend of the author put it this way in a private conversation: "Beware of indeterminate liability, for indeterminate reasons, to indeterminate parties, for an indeterminate time. You can't win!"

Rather than legally define *liability* here, suffice it to say that there are many kinds of liability. Product liability, for one, concerns manufacturers, distributors, suppliers, retailers, and others who make or sell products and are held responsible for any injuries those products might cause. Product liability laws generally are established at the state level, and vary widely from state to state. Each type of product liability claim requires different elements to be proven to present a successful claim.

Risks and Assumptions Inherent in the Company's Strategy

Strategic risks and assumptions. Businesses' strategies define the ways that a firm allocates its resources to maximize their value. How well companies execute their strategy can involve both assumptions and risks. Any strategic change, say, increasing international expansion through an entrepreneurial supply chain venture, may be adversely affected by local laws and customs, legal and regulatory requirements, or political and economic conditions. Yet, the assumptions can be that it will be a roaring success. As discussed above, risks and assumptions sometimes work in mysterious ways!

For example, a company's ability to manage an entrepreneurial supply chain venture effectively represents both risks and assumptions. Presumably, the firm assumed that its capabilities were sufficient to complete a successful venture; otherwise, the firm would not have embarked on it. The risks are that such capabilities are not sufficient.

Competitive risks and assumptions. Competition is tough, but what should a company's strategy say about the competition? The essence of a strategy is specification of how the entrepreneurial supply chain enterprise will compete in the marketplace. But compete against whom, in what ways, and to what effect? Michael Porter presented a good framework for competitor analysis in *Competitive Strategy*,[13] which has been adapted in Figure 5.3.

In an analysis of a competitor, according to Porter, there are two primary considerations: what drives the competitor, and what the competitor is doing and can do. In the category of what drives the competitor, two main questions arise: what are the competitor's future goals, and what assumptions does the competitor hold about itself and its industry? In the category of what the competitor is doing and can do, two major questions appear to be relevant: what are the competitor's current strategy and current capabilities, including both strengths and weaknesses?

But the most important consideration, according to Porter, is the question of the competitor's response profile to competitive threats. He poses four questions about whether the competitor is satisfied with its current position, the likely moves or strategy shifts it may make, where it may be vulnerable, and what will

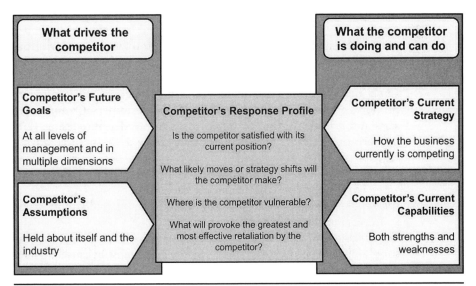

Figure 5.3 Components of a Competitor Analysis. Adapted from: Porter, Michael E., *Competitive Strategy: Techniques for Analyzing Industries and Competitors*, The Free Press, 1980, p., 49.

provoke the competitor's greatest and most effective retaliatory moves to a competitive threat.

Early-stage entrepreneurial supply chain ventures should take the time to analyze in detail the major competitors that may surface for the undertaking. Porter's framework is useful in this regard.

Using the OMBOK for Risk and Assumptions Analysis

The *Operations Management Body of Knowledge (OMBOK)*[14] from APICS: The Association for Operations Management has a fairly complete summary of risk analysis. Assumptions and risks about the venture's strategy typically will include many in the taxonomy that follows, which is adapted from the *OMBOK*. This represents a reasonable set of competitive risks and assumptions for consideration in entrepreneurial supply chain ventures. Assumptions are that these are all congruent, and the risks are that they are not.

The following taxonomy is a good example of what should be used for an in-depth analysis of the risks and assumptions for the entrepreneurial supply chain venture, and is adapted from the *OMBOK*:

1. *Operations strategy* for the venture corresponds to the overall business' strategy as well as being coordinated with the other functional strategies of marketing, finance, and product development.
    a. *Transformation processes* use the firm's resources to convert inputs into the desired outputs which meet the needs of the customers.
    b. *Competitive priorities* are designed to create advantages for the entrepreneurial supply chain venture in the marketplace. These priorities typically are driven by business plan objectives and customer preferences for products and services of the venture.
    c. *Order qualifiers and order winners* are the aspects of the company's products and services that are valued by the customers. *Qualifiers* are screening criteria for the customers to even consider purchasing. *Winners* are the unique characteristics that create a competitive advantage for the seller.
    d. *Activity-system maps* define how the venture's strategic components are delivered and how they reinforce each other.
    e. *Operations strategic fit* defines how the operations and supply chain strategies are aligned with the corporate strategy.
    f. *Economies of scale and/or scope* usually are difficult for entrepreneurial supply chain ventures to achieve in the beginning because of their typically small size. Nevertheless, the ability to increase the scale and/or scope of the venture is important to long-term sustainability.

g. *Considerations in adding capacity (timing and sizing)* are maintaining resource balance, frequency of capacity additions, and the use of external capacity.

h. *Understanding constraints* centers on understanding the weakest link in the process flow, which is typically the link with the least capacity or a bottleneck operation.

i. *Sustainability, ethics, and social responsibility* require trust and integrity among partners in the supply chain.

j. *Operations metrics* are quantitative indicators that show improving, maintaining, or declining process performance.

2. *Supply chain strategy* considers all the elements (above) of the operations strategy with some additional considerations including the following:

a. *Building strategic partnerships* is based on overall business strategy and typically is limited to suppliers of strategically important goods or services as stated earlier in this book.

b. *Insource/outsource (make or buy)* decisions generally are made to improve service or cost for the supply chain.

c. *Drivers of supply chain performance* are no different than the performance drivers for the end member of the supply chain, the customer or consumer.

d. *Synchronization* is the simultaneity and speed of movement of information, funds, and goods or services through the supply network.

e. *Integration of suppliers, internal supply chains, and customer systems* is the essence of supply chain effectiveness.

f. *Breadth of activities (designing, planning, and controlling)* correspond with the activities of a single business but on a scale that incorporates the needs and capabilities of several businesses within a supply chain and has the goal of enabling the entire network to function as a single virtual entity.

g. *Reverse logistics* is the need in some companies and industries to take products back to their source, frequently for warranty repairs, recycling, or remanufacturing. It's what the SCOR model calls "return."

h. *Product sustainability* involves sustainable use of resources and not harming the environment.

i. *Regulatory compliance* is a necessary condition for doing business wherever in the world the company operates.

j. *Global considerations* means that further risks arise because of globalization of the supply chains. Global considerations also present opportunities to grow the entrepreneurial venture.

3. *Operations management links to other functional areas* within the firm create risks that things will "fall between the cracks" at every boundary.
    a. *Corporate strategic and business plans* usually consist of the corporate strategy, the annual operating plan, and the functional or business unit operating plans.
    b. *Operations and enterprise economics* usually impact the operations of the supply chains including how value is created, where breakeven points occur, best operating levels, and many aspects of managerial accounting.
    c. *Marketing,* operations, and supply chains all interact to create value for the customers.
    d. *Human resources,* of course, is considered to be a functional area, but the company's human resources include all its people as well as those aspects of the business that make them productive.
    e. *Organizational development and managing change* are intended to build high levels of organizational effectiveness.
4. *Product/service development* involves development of new products and service offerings.
    a. *Life-cycle planning* is particularly important for entrepreneurial supply chain ventures.
    b. *Design for manufacturing and assembly* is the practice of designing products, including setting the tolerances and specification of the materials and components, so that the required processes and equipment are efficient.
    c. *Concurrent engineering* involves cross-functional teams during the product development phases so as to minimize time to market.
    d. *Computer-Assisted Design and Computer-Assisted Manufacturing (CAD/CAM)* are electronic tools to aid in product and process design and manufacture.
    e. *Basic process types* (such as job shops, assembly lines, cells, and so forth) used for producing goods or services must match the volume and flexibility needed.
    f. *Group technology* is a process to simplify product and process design.
    g. *Quality function deployment (QFD)* shows relationships and dependencies of product capabilities and quality as understood from the customers' points of view.
5. *Strategic capacity decisions* involve the nature and extent of productive capacity for products and services.
    a. Learning curves effect strategic capacity decisions as productivity improves with increased experience in manufacturing. These are sometimes called *experience curves.*
    b. *Strategic use of project management* is the methodology by which goals are assigned and resources and plans are developed and monitored to

achieve these goals. Entrepreneurial supply chain ventures frequently are managed as projects.

Risks and Assumptions Inherent in External Issues

Natural events risks and assumptions. Weather-related risks (such as hurricanes, tornadoes, earthquakes, floods, ice storms, or volcanoes) can cause significant supply chain disruptions. Consider, for example, Hurricane Katrina that hit New Orleans and the Gulf Coast in 2005, and Hurricane Ike that hit Galveston, TX in 2008. Natural events also are important considerations around the world. Floods can be significant in Brazil, India, and other places. El Niño is a prolonged period of above-average water temperature off the west coast of South America, and La Niña is a period of colder-than-average water—both can have an effect on rainfall in Latin America and hurricanes in the Gulf of Mexico. In China, heavy floods and droughts can have a direct impact on hydroelectric power, which plays an important part in China's economy.

Public relations risks and assumptions. Adverse publicity can cause a loss of confidence in a company's products and thus impact its reputation. As mentioned, Johnson & Johnson handled the Tylenol crisis in 1982 well at the time it occurred, and subsequently by leading the industry with tamper-proof packaging. Public relations represent an important component of a company's risk and assumptions management. For example, the Public Relations Society of America (PRSA)[15] is the nation's largest group of public relations and communications professionals. They provide training, set standards of excellence, and uphold principles of ethics for the global public relations profession. As a leading voice in the industry, they also advocate for greater understanding and adoption of public relations services. PRSA has about 21,000 members, and maintains a database of case studies, including crisis management. Many entrepreneurial supply chain ventures effectively utilize public relations professionals to "get the word out" about their products and services.

Industry risks and assumptions. Price and product competition can change rapidly due to technological innovation including the introduction and market acceptance of new technologies and products. Overall movement toward industry consolidation or fragmentation among competitors or customers occurs every day. The ability of customers, channel partners, contract manufacturers, and suppliers to obtain financing or fund capital expenditures is changing. Many companies are suppliers to the same customers, so problems or defaults on the part of individual suppliers can ripple through the industry.

An Aside: Please do not make any implications about this, because it is entirely made up. Consider an imaginary scenario of a concentration of aircraft manufacturers in Wichita, KS, commonly known as the "Air Capital of America." Many companies that are well-known in the industry, such as Hawker Beechcraft, Boeing, Cessna, Lear, and Airbus have workforces there. Many suppliers to this industry also are located there. Suppose, as an illustration, a serious problem that was undetected occurred in one of these major suppliers. Then, all companies in the industry could be affected simultaneously. This is a type of supplier risk that could affect an entire industry.

Legal risks and assumptions. The assumptions historically seem to have been that governments have been favorably disposed to business. But that no longer seems to be the case. Governments seem to be increasingly anti-business. Especially as they get more desperate for revenues, governments increasingly target businesses.

For example, after the BP oil spill in the Gulf of Mexico in 2010, the Obama administration put in a moratorium on deep-water drilling in the Gulf for six months, even after being warned that rigs would move out of the United States, people would be put out of work, and the government itself would lose royalties. That happened. The first rig reportedly[16] moved to Egypt on July 10, 2010:

> *Diamond Offshore announced Friday that its Ocean Endeavor drilling rig will leave the Gulf of Mexico and move to Egyptian waters immediately— making it the first to abandon the United States in the wake of the BP oil spill and a ban on deep-water drilling.*

Diamond Offshore had nothing to do with the BP accident. Neither did Devon Energy, which had leased the Ocean Endeavor to drill in the Gulf of Mexico. Supply companies and service companies, which also had nothing to do with the accident, were put out of work by this move. Further, shrimp fishermen, restaurants, and many other people and businesses were damaged—first by the oil and then by the rash actions of government. Companies need to beware of the possibility of industry-wide repercussions that might result from the actions of competitors.

Risks and Assumptions Inherent in Internal Issues

Merger and acquisition risks and assumptions. Beginning, but failing to complete, a merger or acquisition can negatively affect a company's performance. The company may have to pay significant costs relating to the curtailed merger or acquisition without receiving the benefits of the transaction. Management attention likely will be distracted from the business for a period of time during which the deal is being worked. In addition, the company's reputation almost certainly will be damaged if a transaction is announced but not consummated.

If the merger or acquisition does go through, significant management attention and costs will be incurred to complete the transaction and to integrate both companies. These business combinations almost always are predicated on certain synergies occurring, many of them in the supply chains. Their success will depend, at least in part, on the company's ability to realize the anticipated benefits—or so it is assumed. This represents risks based on these assumptions.

Demand risks and assumptions. Fluctuations in demand for products and services from a company's entrepreneurial supply chain venture can occur for any number of reasons: changes in global economic conditions, customers' spending plans, customers' required lead times, demand originating with specific customers, plus many others. These can result in variations among sales channels, product costs, mix of products sold, and the timing, size, and mix of orders from customers.

Volatility of prices in an industry can affect demand for products and services of all companies in the industry—not just entrepreneurial ventures. In most industries, companies that are faced with lower prices for their products tend to decrease their capital expenditures, and higher prices generally lead to increased capital outlays in the industry. However, sustained high prices for certain commodities (say, for oil and gas) can lead to decreased overall economic activity, and thus to decreased spending in most sectors.

Demand for the enterprise's products and services frequently is subject to factors beyond the control of the company. This likely will affect the company's operating results—positively or negatively. Changes in the global economy could impact a company's customers' spending levels and thus, the company's revenues and operating results.

Supply risks and assumptions. Supplies of raw materials and components for products may not always be available at reasonable prices, even though the assumptions generally are that they will be. This can be especially difficult for entrepreneurial supply chains, which typically are relatively small enterprises, perhaps without much bargaining power with suppliers. It also can occur because of global supply and demand for certain commodities that may strain upstream capacities. For example, spikes in economic activity can increase demand for commodities such as copper, nickel, and paper. Increased demand on capacity-limited firms can lead to allocations of products among its customers. Customers that treat suppliers with respect and dignity are more likely to be given fair treatment; whereas customers that have taken advantage of them are more likely to be given something less.

> **KEY IDEA**
>
> Your suppliers are your suppliers because they have capabilities that you do not have. Thus, treat them as valued members of the supply chain and not as adversaries to be exploited.

Imbalance of supply and demand can cause shortages or cost problems even for large, powerful companies in specific industries. For example, *The New York Times*[17] illustrated this point about Apple's iPhone manufacturing after researchers did a "teardown" of the product, which is assembled in China:

> ". . . *the smallest part of Apple's [iPhone] costs are in Shenzhen, where assembly-line workers snap together microchips from Germany and Korea, . . . a touch-screen module from Taiwan, and more than 100 other components. [But] manufacturing in China is about to get far more expensive" [due to soaring labor costs, strengthening currency, and inflation].*

The supply chain represents a significant risk to entrepreneurial ventures, as the iPhone example shows. Given a complex supply chain like this one, the lack of a relatively minor part can shut down a plant and stop shipments to its customers. If this had happened, it could have been devastating to Apple, since demand for the iPhone was so strong.

Product risks and assumptions. Risks are inherent in new product introductions along with a myriad of assumptions that are made about the introductions. Success of an entrepreneurial supply chain venture in new and evolving markets, including emerging and advanced technologies, depends on certain assumptions as well as risks in the enterprise. But new products can give rise to liability claims if the technologies do not work as assumed when they are designed and manufactured. There is always a certain dependence on technology assumptions as well as a vulnerability to certain risks in any product.

Operations risks and assumptions. Operations risks have been the object of extensive study by Michael A. Lewis (2003).[18] Lewis outlines an operations-related event typology with examples:

- *Capacity/facilities strategy.* In 1984, the Union Carbide plant in Bhopal, India, released quantities of poisonous methyl isocyanate gas into the atmosphere. Estimates of the number of fatalities were in the range of 3,000–10,000. From an operations perspective, it is significant that the plant had operated at a maximum of 50% capacity because of declining global demand. This caused management to assume (apparently incorrectly) that they could cut back expenditures on facilities maintenance without harm.
- *Process technology.* In 1990, Perrier ordered a product recall as a result of benzene contamination. Contamination had been caused by a failure to replace charcoal filters, and management apparently had assumed that no impairment or harm would occur. Not long after, Nestle acquired the firm.
- *Supply chain management.* In 1990, IBM posted US$6 billion in profits; and in 1992, they reported the largest loss in U.S. corporate history, US$5 billion. What happened in two years? Actually, it was the result of a series of poor supply chain assumptions and decisions over the previous decade. For example, they had made two fundamental supply chain mistakes about

excluding the Windows operating system and not sourcing Intel's 80386 chips.

- *New product development.* In the mid-1970s, Dow Corning rapidly developed an entrepreneurial new product, a silicone-based breast implant. They assumed that they would be able to take advantage of a booming cosmetic surgery market. Although the firm manufactured almost 5,000 other products, in 1995 it was forced to file for Chapter 11 bankruptcy.
- *Workforce and organization.* In 1998, Northwest Airlines pilots voted to strike, resulting in extensive media coverage and huge customer dissatisfaction. Similarly, the General Motors strike in 1998 also led to a high-profile debate about the nature of operations management. Both Northwest and GM took years to rid themselves of the stigma of the strikes. Certain assumptions had been made that subsequently turned out to be wrong about the impact of changes to workforce, work rules, and organizations.
- *Control systems.* In Johnson & Johnson's Tylenol crisis in September 1982, cyanide-contaminated capsules were not the company's fault. However, another incident in February 1986 with cyanide-laced Tylenol *was* traced back to specific production facilities and control systems that were incapable of preventing such occurrences despite assumptions to the contrary. Tylenol abandoned the capsule form of the product and by July 1986, the company had regained most of the market share that it had lost.

Examples such as these are plentiful, but the point is that operations management presents companies with many opportunities for risks. Entrepreneurial supply chain ventures should be careful about their assumptions regarding management of operations and the potentials for these risks to occur.

Labor and labor relations risks and assumptions. Entrepreneurial supply chain ventures can face a shortage of qualified labor such as occurs in different industries and geographies at different times. Many companies have multiple unions representing their labor force, any one of which can cause significant disruptions in the business. Multi-employer pension plans are common across industries—companies do not directly manage these plans, but are subject to the performance of their administrators.

Labor and labor relations risks frequently are discussed as turnover, or the rate at which an employer loses employees and has to replace them. Simple ways to describe it are "how long employees tend to stay" or "traffic through the revolving door." Turnover is measured for individual companies and for their industry as a whole. If an employer is said to have a high turnover relative to its competitors, it generally means that employees of that company have a shorter average tenure than in other companies in the same industry. High turnover can be harmful to a company's productivity if skilled workers are often leaving, and the worker population contains a high percentage of novice workers. However, unskilled workers typically have a higher turnover and are easier to replace than skilled ones.

High turnover often means that there are underlying causes which may indicate negative risk factors for the business. These causes may be numerous, such as unhealthy or unsafe working conditions. Companies should periodically do studies of why people leave their company and attempt to correct issues that give difficulties. Do not just assume that reasons for leaving are intuitively obvious.

Inventory risks and assumptions. The ability of an entrepreneurial venture to maintain appropriate inventory levels and purchase commitments is important to its success. In early stages, this may cause strains on working capital and cash flow, so financial risks and assumptions go hand in hand with inventory.

Financial risks and assumptions. For the entrepreneurial supply chain venture, there are a number of financial risks and assumptions. Examples are variations in costs of product raw materials and components, fluctuations in gross margins and the factors that contribute to such fluctuations, the ability to achieve targeted cost reductions, increasing fuel costs, or prolonged periods of product inflation or deflation. Actual events, circumstances, outcomes, and amounts can differ from prior judgments, assumptions, and estimates used in determining the values of certain assets, liabilities, and other financial items. Changes in tax laws or accounting rules also can affect reported earnings.

DETAILED CONTROL OF ON-GOING RISKS

Many companies, in an effort to maintain detailed control of on-going risks, keep spreadsheet-based registers of assessments and mitigation plans. One example, modified from a real company, was supplied by Mike Katzorke, CEO of Bryce Consulting Group. Assembly WXYZ, along with its supplier, Zelta, shown in Figure 5.4, is giving the company particular difficulty. The question for the company is a possible re-sourcing decision with this as the risk assessment for such decision. Notice that six risks are identified. For each risk, the initial probability of the risk occurring is estimated along with the impact if the risk occurs. An initial score is calculated as the probability times the impact, which is then color-coded for emphasis. Next, a risk mitigation action is defined along with the effects of such mitigation actions. Finally, the "owner" of the mitigation action is specified along with the due date for accomplishing the action.

HOW BAKER HUGHES MANAGES THE RISKS OF ENTREPRENEURIAL SUPPLY CHAINS

Baker Hughes performs periodic surveys of key executives to identify risks along with statements of mitigation strategies based on quantification of the risks facing the company. A major effort goes into the Risk Factors section of Baker Hughes's 10-K, which is used here for fiscal year 2010, ending December 31, 2010. Its risk factors are a useful reference of the major risks facing entrepreneurial supply

Assembly WXYZ
Supplier = Zelta

Re-Sourcing Risk Assessment		High = 5 Medium = 3 Low = 1		0-4 = G (Green) 5-14 = Y (Yellow) 15-24 = O (Orange) 25 = R (Red)			Init Prob = Initial probability of the risk occurring. Init Imp = Initial Impact if the risk occurs. Initial Score = Initial Probability x Impact. Red Prob = Reduced probability of the risk occurring. Red Imp = Reduced impact if the risk occurs. Rev Score = Revised Probability x Impact						
Last Revised on February 1, 20XX												
Risk #	Risk Category / Issue	Init Prob	Init Imp	Initial Score	R/O/Y/G	Mitigation Action	Red Prob	Red Imp	Rev Score	Rev R/O/Y/G	Owner	Due Date
1	Schedule. Introduction misses plan for 2nd quarter due to grinding machine bottleneck.	5	5	25	R	Short run: obtain outside capacity. Long run: procure new machine.	3	3	9	Y	Jim	May1 and Oct 1
2	Durability. Redesign may delay first part introduction.	5	3	15	O	Introduce at XY after transition. Concurrently engineer redesign.	1	3	3	G	Mary	June 1
3	Sourcing. New coating source not found in country	3	3	9	Y	Investigate global sourcing	1	3	3	G	Bob	April 15
4	Suppliers. Communication with supplier logistically difficult	3	3	9	Y	Establish on-site engineering presence. Hold monthly pre-production review meetings.	1	3	3	G	Bill	May 1
5	Operations Plan. Inventory exceeds business plan goal	3	3	9	Y	Negotiate buffer stock agreement with supplier.	1	1	1	G	Susan	July 1
6	Policies. Supplier pursues breakout orders for spare parts	3	3	9	Y	Implement Supplier Agreement # 99-026 that prohibits this.	1	3	3	G	Mark	March 1

Figure 5.4 Risk Assessment and Mitigation Tracking Form. Adapted with permission from copyrighted material supplied to the author by Michael R. Katzorke, CEO of Bryce Consulting Group, September 2010.

chain ventures. If readers take out references to the oil and gas industry and substitute another industry, the risk factors would be applicable, except for those that refer to the company's settlement with the U.S. Department of Justice and the Securities and Exchange Commission. The full text of the Form 10-K contains significant explanatory notes beyond what is reproduced below.

The following are direct quotes from the Baker Hughes FY2010 Form 10-K, which is a public document. While all factors cited below are relevant, the BJ Services merger is important because that section speaks directly to the risks in a relatively recent entrepreneurial supply chain undertaking:

- Risk factors related to the worldwide oil and natural gas industry
  - Demand for oil and natural gas is subject to factors beyond our control, which may adversely affect our operating results. Changes in the global economy or credit market could impact our customers' spending levels and our revenues and operating results.
  - Volatility of oil and natural gas prices can adversely affect demand for our products and services.
  - Our customers' activity levels and spending for our products and services and ability to pay amounts owed us could be impacted by economic conditions.
  - Supply of oil and natural gas is subject to factors beyond our control, which may adversely affect our operating results.
  - Changes in spare productive capacity or inventory levels can be indicative of future customer spending to explore for and develop oil and natural gas which in turn influences the demand for our products and services.
  - Seasonal and adverse weather conditions adversely affect demand for our services and operations.
- Risk factors related to our business
  - We operate in a highly competitive environment, which may adversely affect our ability to succeed.
  - The high cost or unavailability of infrastructure, materials, equipment, supplies and personnel, particularly in periods of rapid growth, could adversely affect our ability to execute our operations on a timely basis.
  - Our business is subject to geopolitical, terrorism risks, and other threats.
  - Our failure to comply with the Foreign Corrupt Practices Act (FCPA) would have a negative impact on our ongoing operations.
  - Compliance with and changes in laws or adverse positions taken by taxing authorities could be costly and could affect operating results.
  - The May 2010 moratorium on drilling offshore in the U.S., as well as changes in and compliance with restrictions or regulations on offshore drilling in the U.S. Gulf of Mexico and in other areas around the world,

has and may continue to adversely affect our business and operating results and reduce the need for our services in those areas.

- Uninsured claims and litigation could adversely impact our operating results.
- Compliance with and rulings and litigation in connection with environmental regulations may adversely affect our business and operating results.
- Demand for pressure pumping services could be reduced or eliminated by governmental regulation or a change in the law.
- Control of oil and gas reserves by state-owned oil companies may impact the demand for our services and create additional risks in our operations.
- Changes in economic conditions and currency fluctuations may impact our operating results.
- Changes in market conditions may impact any stock repurchases.
- The merger with BJ Services may create additional risks for the company.

From the supply chain standpoint, just like the rest of the company, risk management is focused on the above points. Also, risk management is especially focused on suppliers and supplier risk. Baker Hughes, like many companies, is taking steps to substantially reduce its supply base. One approach is by looking at supplier quality processes as illustrated in the conceptual model in Figure 5.5. The forward-facing dimension is a "looking back" dimension in the sense that it focuses on the past. The horizontal axis is plotted as Quality Escapes, with Quality Notifications plotted along the vertical axis.

Suppliers with a large number of quality escapes but a low number of quality notifications are plotted in the lower-right-hand quadrant and labeled as High Risk Suppliers. They are higher risk because they have a history of more-than-normal defects that get into Baker Hughes. Risky Suppliers are plotted in the upper-right-hand quadrant. These suppliers have a large number of quality escapes but a large number of quality notifications also. The other dimension, "looking forward," completes the risk-assessment framework. High confidence in supplier management brings forth low-to-moderate risk. Low confidence in supplier management results in medium-to-high risk.

Baker Hughes' supplier audits are aligned with this framework. That is, suppliers that fall into the right-hand quadrants of this framework will receive a more stringent audit, for obvious reasons.

Finally, since Baker Hughes operates all over the world, the business risks and the intellectual property (IP) risks are different. It behooves the company's management to be cognizant of and to manage these risks differently.

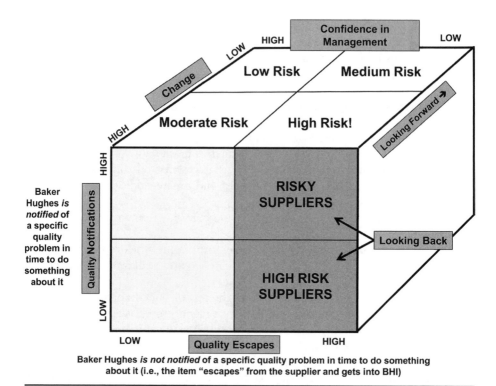

Figure 5.5 Baker Hughes Supplier Quality Risk Assessment Framework. Conceptual model adapted from discussions with executives of Baker Hughes. Used with permission.

A CASE NOTE FOR FURTHER STUDY: Cisco Systems, Inc.

The cases are available at www.harvardbusinessonline.com. Readers should obtain copies of this case and use it to go beyond discussion in the book. These cases were prepared as the basis for discussion, rather than to illustrate either effective or ineffective handling of any particular situation.

This section is adapted from several sources, the primary one being "Cisco Systems, Inc.: Collaborating on New Product Introduction."[19] Although this is not a chapter on new product introductions, this case is appropriate for risk management of entrepreneurial supply chains for three reasons. First, many entrepreneurial supply chain ventures involve risky new product introductions. Second, Cisco is a large, entrepreneurial company that is greatly admired. Third, this case presents a number of risk situations faced by Cisco in introducing a significant new product.

Cisco describes itself as "the worldwide leader in networking that transforms how people connect, communicate and collaborate." According to the corporate website, Cisco's FY2009 revenue was US$36.1B with net income of US$6.1B—a good result in a bad economic year. Their Q3FY10 employee count was 68,574.

Cisco's website makes the following points about their innovation focus: 30 major labs, 20,000+ engineers, $5.2B annual R&D investment (14% of FY2009 revenue as compared with 6% for IBM, 15% for Microsoft, 16% for Intel, and 3% for HP), 700 patents filed annually, and 5,000 patents issued. Cisco has an active acquisition strategy for market acceleration, market expansion, and new market entry. They also have an active partnering strategy to go to market with mutually beneficial, best-in-class, long-term partners.

The case opens with a Cisco management meeting of over 100 employees on November 13, 2007. The purpose of the meeting was to get the go-ahead to manufacture a new high-end router that was supposed to add to Cisco's competitive position. The project's code name was "Viking." This product, like most of Cisco's new product introductions, was managed as a project.

The case evaluates entrepreneurial supply chain issues in a company that both outsources and offshores its global manufacturing. It draws attention to the multifaceted and complicated difficulties of developing and producing complex, advanced-technology products for a global market. Readers can consider what it takes to achieve success in new product introduction for entrepreneurial supply chains as well as how to manage the inevitable risks. The project team faced numerous risks with going forward:

- Before they shipped the first product, the project had only one year to line up manufacturing, supply chain, and marketing—an extraordinarily hurried time frame for a company in this industry.
- The project wanted to begin manufacturing in a low-cost country, China, in contrast to its usual practice of beginning to manufacture a complex product in the United States and then transitioning to a country like China. This was a risky move on their part, because of the lack of a track record with this type of product.
- They wanted to give the manufacturing to Foxconn, a contract manufacturer; but, Foxconn had never before produced such a complex product for Cisco.
- They wanted to give Foxconn a wider-ranging role than normal in the supply chain.

An Aside: Foxconn claims to be the world's largest contract manufacturing company, headquartered in Taiwan, with employees in Asia (primarily China), Europe, and the Americas. Foxconn's website claims a compound average growth rate in excess of 50% as of 2010. Foxconn had gotten some negative press after the Cisco case was written; an article in *Bloomberg BusinessWeek* was directed toward a number of suicides among its work force.[20] (A similar article was published on May 27, 2010, in *The Wall Street Journal*.) The reporters apparently spent some time in Foxconn's vast manufacturing facility in Shenzhen that employs more than 250,000 people making products for Apple, Dell, Microsoft, HP, and others. (Cisco was not mentioned.) The reporters cited working conditions being especially tough. "Conversation on the production line is forbidden, bathroom breaks are kept to 10 minutes every two hours, and workers get yelled at frequently," according to the *Bloomberg BusinessWeek* article. Whatever the true facts of the case are, (and I admit that I do not know them) apparently, Foxconn's customers had gotten the message and promised action, but this type of incident illustrates some of the risks in offshore contract manufacturing.

Cisco had a history of successful new product introductions and integration of acquisitions. They brought over 250 new products to market in FY2008. A new product introduction stage-gate process is shown in Figures 5.6, 5.7, and 5.8. This approach is not significantly different from many other new product introduction stage-gate processes, but its effectiveness lies in the company's ability to implement it. Also, although Cisco is a large company, its processes for new product development and implementation do not differ significantly from other entrepreneurial supply chain ventures, regardless of their size. Cisco's

Figure 5.6   Cisco's New Product Introduction Process (Phase 1—Strategy and Planning). Adapted from: Shao, Maria and Hau Lee, "Cisco Systems, Inc.: Collaborating on New Product Introduction," Stanford Graduate School of Business Case #GS-66, June 5, 2009, p. 21.

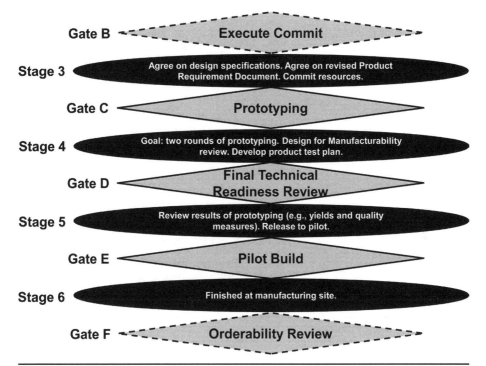

Figure 5.7   Cisco's New Product Introduction Process (Phase 2—Execution). Adapted from: Shao, Maria and Hau Lee, "Cisco Systems, Inc.: Collaborating on New Product Introduction," Stanford Graduate School of Business Case #GS-66, June 5, 2009, p. 21.

entrepreneurial ventures usually would be called "corporate entrepreneurship," as discussed previously.

Phase I of the stage/gate process is shown as Figure 5.6. This phase starts with what some companies call the "fuzzy front end" of the process and consists of *brainstorming* (Cisco's word) product design ideas. Brainstorming usually implies something more simplistic than Cisco's approach, but this process actually is more akin to strategic product planning, out of which many product concepts may emerge, including some that may be recycled or discarded.

Gate A, in Cisco's terminology, is *Concept Commit*. This gate is intended to ensure that a satisfactory product requirement document and business plan have been approved. Some companies call this a *concept and market analysis* of a particular model or family of products, which is intended to determine whether there is a potential market for the concept, the size of the market, the fit within

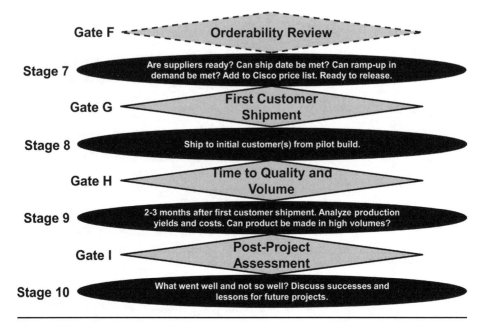

Figure 5.8 Cisco's New Product Introduction Process (Phase 3—Deployment). Adapted from: Shao, Maria and Hau Lee, "Cisco Systems, Inc.: Collaborating on New Product Introduction," Stanford Graduate School of Business Case #GS-66, June 5, 2009. p. 21.

the company's strategic plan, and the initial business case for the concept. Some of the questions that generally must be answered at this point are:

1. Have market segments been identified?
2. Have customer input and expectations been obtained through diverse channels?
3. Has the required technical performance been specified?
4. Has a product or product family concept been developed to meet customer expectations and required technical performance?
5. Has conformity with the strategic plan been confirmed?
6. Have required technologies been identified?
7. Have rough-order-of-magnitude facilities requirements been identified?
8. Has a rough-order-of-magnitude business case with risk and assumptions analyses been developed?

Phase 2—Execution, shown in Figure 5.7, begins with the *Execute Commit* gate. This gate leads to agreement on design specifications, agreement on the product requirement document, and commitment of resources. This phase goes through several stages of prototyping, a final technical readiness review, and a pilot build. After the pilot build, responsibility shifts to manufacturing from engineering. Near the end of the execution phase comes an "orderability" review, which is intended to ensure that Cisco can hit the target ship date in the volume and quality level required.

After the orderability review, the project enters Phase 3, shown in Figure 5.8, meaning that the product is ready for release and first customer shipments. Two or three months after production begins is another checkpoint, *Time to Quality and Volume*, which ensures that Cisco's contract manufacturing sites are producing to Six Sigma quality and can make the product cost-effectively in high volumes. Finally, there is a post-project assessment that captures learning that can be incorporated into future projects.

Cisco claimed to have a "globally networked and adaptive supply chain." The company had moved aggressively to outsource manufacturing, and by the time of the case, virtually all its manufacturing was done on contract with a relatively few companies. Cisco's contract manufacturing partners were taking on increasing responsibility for overall supply chain management.

Cisco's approach brings some inherent risks that can be especially difficult in high-tech industries, but are not limited to those types of companies. Cisco has an extensive listing of what they consider to be their risk factors in their SEC Form 10-K. A few of them are mentioned here that pertain particularly to its supply chains:

- *Product life cycles risk*. High-technology products typically go through their product life cycles very quickly. The result is that companies must maintain a pipeline of new product development with flexible and responsive supply chains. This frequently is stated as "faster, better, cheaper," and the supply chains must be capable of changing direction quickly.
- *Industry competitive risk*. Segments in which Cisco competes are subject to intense competitive risk. Competitors in their segments include such companies as Alcatel-Lucent, Ericsson, Hewlett-Packard (HP), IBM, Microsoft, Motorola, and Juniper.
- *Cost pressure risk*. Cisco was sensitive to unremitting cost pressure on its products. The "aside" on Foxconn on page 172, and Cisco's ability to respond to this cost pressure, shows the possible result of this cost pressure.
- *Contract manufacturing risk*. Cisco used contract manufacturing extensively, if not exclusively. When so doing, it makes the company vulnerable to the actions or inactions of the contract manufacturer.
- *Outsourcing and off-shoring to China*. Many companies that have moved contract manufacturing to China have regretted that move due to quality and other problems. Mattel,[21] for one, had a significant problem with toys containing lead paint. They recalled millions of toys from customers as a result. Having said that, however, many companies continue to outsource

and off-shore contract manufacturing to China due to cost pressure. Nevertheless, companies should carefully evaluate their risks in doing so.

- *Supply chain risk.* Competitors tend to rely on many of the same suppliers in an extremely complex supply chain. Any company's supply chain risk is increased when it does not do its own manufacturing.

It is important when companies face significant supply chain risks that they plan for risk mitigation. The case cites some of the actions that Cisco has taken in this regard.

A FINAL WORD ON MANAGING THE RISKS OF ENTREPRENEURIAL SUPPLY CHAINS

The "BP Oil Spill" in the Gulf of Mexico prompted an article in *The Wall Street Journal*[22] about BP's CEO, Tony Hayward, which has implications for entrepreneurial supply chains:

> . . . *his story serves as a cautionary tale of how a single mishandled crisis can eclipse an entire career and of the multiplying demands on the top corporate job. [His] various gaffes—saying he "wants his life back"—and sour appearances before legislators showed a degree of tone deafness* . . .

It's not just the risks that companies face; perhaps more importantly it is how a crisis is handled that ultimately determines the total impact. This is an important lesson for anyone in an executive position.

Of course, most companies do not cause major oil spills, so your organization probably will not make the same mistakes that BP did. However, you have other worries. A recent poll by *CFO* magazine[23] cited the top risks as identified by senior finance executives, as:

1.	Financial exposure	51%
2.	Supply-chain/logistics disruption	37%
3.	Legal liability/reputational harm	35%
4.	Technology failure	33%
5.	Security breach	23%
6.	Natural or man-made disasters	21%
7.	Physical-assets failure	8%

Respondents were asked to select up to three risks of concern to their companies. Notice that all seven of these risks have been addressed in one form or another in this chapter. Companies can address them by determining how much to spend to have a sense of balance with their risk tolerance. This survey, along with sources of risks mentioned in this chapter, can help executives of entrepreneurial supply chains to prepare themselves for the next crisis—not the last one.

Readers should define as many assumptions as possible about the risks to their own entrepreneurial supply chains. This exercise forces one to ask about the important issues that might make a difference in the company's future, and helps to reduce the possibility of being caught unaware.

ASSURANCE OF LEARNING QUESTIONS

1. Consider the five macro transformative issues listed at the beginning of the chapter, apply them to your entrepreneurial supply chain venture, and figure out what they likely mean to you.
2. Put Cisco's new product development process into your own words as it might apply to your venture.
3. Our adaptation of *OMBOK* uses the following definition of risks and assumptions: "Operations metrics are quantitative indicators that show improving, maintaining, or declining process performance." Provide five examples of operations metrics that are applicable to entrepreneurial supply chain ventures and explain why they are important.

REFERENCES

1. Fisher, Daniel, and Christopher Helman. June 28, 2010. "If You Think That Oil Spill Is Bad . . . " *Forbes*. 30–31.
2. Kemeny, John G., October 1979. *Report of the President's Commission on the Accident at Three Mile Island; The Need for Change: The Legacy of TMI.* Washington, D.C.
3. "Piper Alpha." *Wikipedia*. http://www.wikipedia.org/wiki/piper_alpha. Also, the BBC produced a DVD documentary, "Spiral to Disaster," about the Piper Alpha.
4. See "Tylenol." *Wikipedia*. http://www.wikipedia.org/tylenol.
5. Rockoff, Jonathan D., "J&J's Quality Control Draws Scrutiny," *The Wall Street Journal*, September 28, 2010.
6. For data on the Big Mac index, see http://www.Economist.com/markets/bigmac.
7. Mandel, Michael. June 15, 2009. "Innovation Interrupted." *BusinessWeek*. 34.
8. Brady, Diane. January 31–February 6, 2011. "Hard Choices: Michael El-Hillow." *Bloomberg BusinessWeek*, 80.
9. Gold, Russell, "Overrun by Chinese Rivals, U.S. Solar Company Falters." August 17, 2011. *The Wall Street Journal*, B1.
10. National Association of Corporate Directors. 2009. "Report of the NACD Blue Ribbon Commission on Risk Governance: Balancing Risk and Reward." See http://www.NACDonline.org for more information.

11. Project Management Institute. 2004. "Chapter 11: Project Risk Management." *A Guide to the Project Management Body of Knowledge (PMBOK®)*, 3rd ed., 237–268.

12. Gorman, Siobhan. "U.S. Plans Cyber Shield for Utilities, Companies." July 8, 2010. *The Wall Street Journal*. A similar article is "Cyberwar." July 3, 2010. *The Economist*, 11.

13. Porter, Michael E. 1980. *Competitive Strategy: Techniques for Analyzing Industries and Competitors*. The Free Press. New York.

14. *Operations Management Body of Knowledge Framework (OMBOK)*. 2009. APICS: The Association for Operations Management.

15. For more information, see Public Relations Society of America at http://www.prsa.org.

16. Dlouhy, Jennifer A. July 10, 2010. "Disaster in the Gulf: First Rig Sails Away Over Ban." *Houston Chronicle*, 1.

17. Barboza, David. July 5, 2010. "Supply Chain for iPhone Highlights Costs in China." *The New York Times*.

18. Lewis, Michael A. March 2003. "Cause, Consequence, and Control: Towards a Theoretical and Practical Model of Operational Risk." *Journal of Operations Management*, 21(2), 205–224.

19. Shao, Maria, and Hau Lee. "Cisco Systems, Inc.: Collaborating on New Product Introduction." Stanford Graduate School of Business Case #GS-66, June 5, 2009. Also see Tempest, Nicole. "Cisco Systems, Inc.: Acquisition Integration for Manufacturing." Stanford Graduate School of Business Case #OIT-26, Rev. February 3, 2004.

20. Wong, Stephanie, Liu, John, and Tim Culpan. June 3, 2010. "Why Apple and Others Are Nervous About Foxconn." *Bloomberg BusinessWeek*.

21. Hoyt, David, and Hau Lee. October 15, 2008. "Unsafe for Children: Mattel's Toy Recalls and Supply Chain Management." Stanford Graduate School of Business Case #GS63.

22. Sonne, Paul. July 26, 2010. "In Crisis, Hayward Struggled to Find Right Tone." *The Wall Street Journal*, A7.

23. Rogers, Celina. July/August 2010. "Risk Management: Learning Too Much from History?" *CFO*, 13.

CHAPTER 6

DUE DILIGENCE AND THE BUSINESS PLAN

LEARNING OBJECTIVES

1. Understand the reasoning behind due diligence and why it should be applied in certain situations.
2. Be able to articulate the similarities and differences in due diligence for mergers, acquisitions, and start-up enterprises.
3. Learn the rationale for business planning in addition to due diligence. How are they similar or different?
4. The Valhalla Partners case presents a reasonably complex approach to due diligence. Be able to state why it would be advantageous for a company to spend the time and money for this approach.

"Plans must be simple and flexible.
They should be made by the people who are going to execute them."
—General George S. Patton

"What makes a plan capable of producing results is the commitment of key people to work on specific tasks."
—Peter F. Drucker

Both quotes by General George S. Patton and Professor Peter F. Drucker say essentially the same thing, but from two different perspectives. Both men were well-known in their respective fields, and came to the same conclusion regarding plans and planning. Plans need to be simple and flexible, and made by those who are committed and will be responsible for carrying them out. So it is with notions of due diligence and the business planning process.

To exemplify due diligence and the planning process, suppose you decided to drive to Boston from Chicago. One alternative is to start driving east because Boston is generally east from Chicago. You probably can find your way to Boston by making highway selections along the way. Unfortunately, this approach will take longer than if you planned a route ahead of time. Had you connected on the Internet to a website designed to provide maps, you could receive a map with directions for the most direct route to Boston from Chicago. This illustrates an emphasis on due diligence (which is pre-planning) and business planning.

Notice that Chapter 5, Managing the Risks, is before this due diligence chapter. Some readers may question why, because real risk management comes *after* the due diligence is done and a deal is consummated. However, thinking about risk identification and risk mitigation should come *before* due diligence. That way, due diligence can be structured to include the risk factors.

As an individual, group, or organization proceeds along the entrepreneurial supply chain path, they may decide to purchase a company, a division, assets of another company, or an alternative. In situations where the type of targeted organization is not for sale or cannot be purchased, they may decide to start a separate business entity or create a new division to accomplish their objectives. Other entrepreneurial supply chain options are coalitions, joint ventures, mergers, and partnerships, as described in Chapter 2. In any case, due diligence needs to be performed and a business plan needs to be prepared for whatever the particular situation is under consideration. These obviously will differ from one situation to another; nevertheless, the essential processes will be the same.

This chapter provides an overview of due diligence and business planning processes that are recommended, regardless of the particular situation. We first will examine the due diligence processes, and then turn to business planning. These are the basic processes through which the available entrepreneurial options are considered. Appendix B will take these ideas forward and provide an example business plan for an entrepreneurial supply chain venture.

DUE DILIGENCE

> **KEY IDEA**
>
> Due diligence, as important as it is, does not really have a well-accepted definition of what's in and what's out of the process.

There are a number of variations on the term, due diligence, not all of which involve an investigation of a business situation prior to taking some action, as discussed here. Due diligence normally occurs after the parties to a venture have decided that the deal is feasible, after a preliminary understanding is reached, but before a final agreement is made.

Objectives of Due Diligence

Due diligence has two, somewhat conflicting, objectives. First, an objective should be directed toward gaining a complete understanding of the proposed venture in all of its complexities and interrelated pursuits, processes, activities, functions, and geographies. Second, the objective should be to do this as quickly and cost-effectively as possible.

Unfortunately, much due diligence is cursory, superficial, and almost entirely devoted to financial issues. It frequently ignores critical areas such as products and markets, technology and product development, operations, or human resources. The due diligence team often does not include industry experts who can speak to the forces driving the industry and its competitors. The financial numbers, in and of themselves, are necessary, but neither sufficient nor informative enough.

Before embarking on due diligence, especially of start-ups or small ventures that do not have the backing of a larger company (as would be the case in corporate entrepreneurism previously discussed), a brief study of why small firms fail is appropriate. This provides some handles on the true focus of due diligence.

A set of sobering statistics on small firms is provided by Cressy.[1] For example, he cited some European studies, which indicated that the survival of start-ups was remarkably low, as known from random information obtained by the author over the years. In one study of German start-ups by Cressy, 24% went out of business within two years, and 37% failed within five years. Another study of UK start-ups showed that 45% went out of business in the first two-and-one-half years, and 80% were gone in the first six years. He cited other studies with similar results. He did not indicate what kinds of companies these were, although the experience of service industries and manufacturing tended to be similar. He also said that if firms survive for the first two years, their long-run survival chances were high.

Cressy also cited evidence that "the true constraint on business survival was not financial, but rather human, capital" (p. 181). On the financial side, the evidence showed that the correlation between financial assets and survival did not hold. Larger amounts of human capital can be characterized by the level of the entrepreneur's realism regarding the pursuit of his or her goals, industry-specific work experience, managerial capability, and whether the start-up was a purchase (perhaps indicating that it had been a going business before being acquired or, as Cressy observed, indicating the existence of networks of businesses). Cressy concluded that enhanced education and training of would-be entrepreneurs would be important contributors to the small-business success rate, perhaps more so than economic subsidizing of start-ups.

Due diligence investigations should involve various aspects of the situation and include management capabilities and management processes,

> **KEY IDEA**
>
> Due diligence is checking out the risk versus reward trade-off.

products and services offered and the technology status thereof, geographies covered by the company including international transactions and relationships, legal issues (not to forget the United States' Foreign Corrupt Practices Act), both current and potential competitors and the competitive environment, customers, suppliers, financial, marketing, operations (manufacturing sites, facilities, distribution centers, and manufacturing technologies), product development, human resources and employee benefits (including immigration status of employees), accounting, tax, debt instruments, information technology, environmental, intellectual property, real and personal property, insurance and liability coverage, and so on. In other words, due diligence should include all relevant areas and concerns of the venture.

Who Should Do Due Diligence

Sometimes due diligence is performed by those who are directly involved in the proposed entrepreneurial supply chain venture, such as management of an acquiring company who performs due diligence on the target of an acquisition venture. Other times, outside entities are employed to conduct due diligence, such as banks, private equity firms, public accounting firms, and consultancies.

However, an organization *should not perform its own due diligence* because of the strong potential for injecting bias into the process. In many instances, management so wanted to consummate a transaction that they (deliberately or not) biased the due diligence process or results to show the preferred outcome. Conversely, a case can be made for using management and employees of the acquiring company rather than outsiders to perform the due diligence. Supporters of this argument usually are in favor of it because of the greater knowledge insiders have, as opposed to outsiders. Further, many will say (sometimes rightfully) that outsiders just submit their reports and then walk away without any responsibility to make the deal work. Clearly, there are arguments on both sides.

An Aside: I can be cited for my own biases, having performed several large due diligence projects as an outsider during my consulting career. However, there was a conscious effort to have integrated teams consisting of outsiders and insiders, as well as industry and functional experts. In one particularly large, complex, multinational, and hostile takeover, the due diligence team was over 100 people who needed to get the essential due diligence finished in a short time period and provide a go/no-go recommendation to the acquiring company. But the due diligence process actually continued for about three months after the deal was signed because of "claw-back" provisions in the contract. Further, there was a need to assist the acquiring company to "get its arms around" the acquired company. The due diligence team was used successfully throughout the entire process.

A selling company may also complete some due diligence of its own on the acquiring company. Management of the seller probably will want to determine whether the buyer has adequate financial capability to purchase the company. If all or a portion of the purchase price is stock, the due diligence of the seller is even more necessary and detailed.

The seller also wants to know whether the operational capability of the purchaser is adequate to absorb the selling organization. Another concern is what will happen to the employees of the selling company. For example, employees will want to know whether there will be significant layoffs, or whether employees will have the opportunity to join the purchasing company.

Possibilities for Due Diligence

Three possibilities for due diligence in an entrepreneurial supply chain venture are shown in Figure 6.1, which simplifies a myriad of opportunities for illustrative purposes. Two general classes of due diligence are (1) ventures that involve two or more companies, and (2) ventures that involve a start-up enterprise.

Ventures that involve two or more companies can include any of the possibilities presented earlier in this chapter: acquisitions, alliances, coalitions, and so

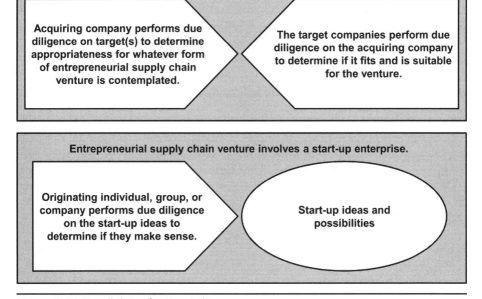

Figure 6.1   Possibilities for Due Diligence.

forth. As indicated on both sides of the transaction, all parties want to determine the appropriateness for whatever form of entrepreneurial supply chain venture is contemplated. The acquiring company and the target company both have essentially the same objectives—to determine if this is the right thing to do.

Start-ups also require due diligence that is not significantly different from that between two or more companies. The originating individual, group, or company performs due diligence on the start-up ideas to determine if they make sense and can fulfill the objectives.

As stated in the "Key Idea" sidebar, due diligence involves checking out the risk versus reward trade-off. Put another way, it involves seeking to determine how big the win, or how big the loss, could be. At the same time, it involves seeking to determine the chances of success, and how much time and capital it will take to get there. Further, it involves seeking to determine the fault lines between success and failure.

THE DUE DILIGENCE PROCESS

The following is not legal, tax, or accounting advice—only an attorney, a tax expert, or an accountant can do that. But the author understands the due diligence process and was involved several times in due diligence projects, knowing when to engage attorneys, tax experts, and accountants. Different specialties in those fields are needed for individual due diligence projects, and some recommendations are made in this section for them.

The due diligence process involves four steps: planning the due diligence, conducting the due diligence, drawing conclusions from the due diligence, and making recommendations based on the due diligence, as shown in Figure 6.2.

A number of articles and books have been written on the topic of due diligence, such as those by Bing[2] and Pickard.[3] Both books include questions that might be part of the due diligence process. Bing's book provides, in addition, a good discussion on various aspects of the process, including planning and conducting due diligence as well as constructing the checklist for due diligence. He also discusses a number of specific areas of inquiry such as legal, capital structure and ownership, management, products and services, R&D and technology, markets, competition, customers, and manufacturing. Pickard's book contains lists of questions on almost every conceivable subject related to due diligence. Using Bing and Pickard together can provide a good starting point for planning the due diligence process.

Whenever a company goes into an entrepreneurial supply chain venture, there is a need to understand the motivations of the other party, assuming that this is a transaction that involves two parties and not a start-up. This should be part of the due diligence process but frequently is not. The following types of questions illustrate what is needed to understand these motivations. Notice that these questions could be asked on either side of the transaction:

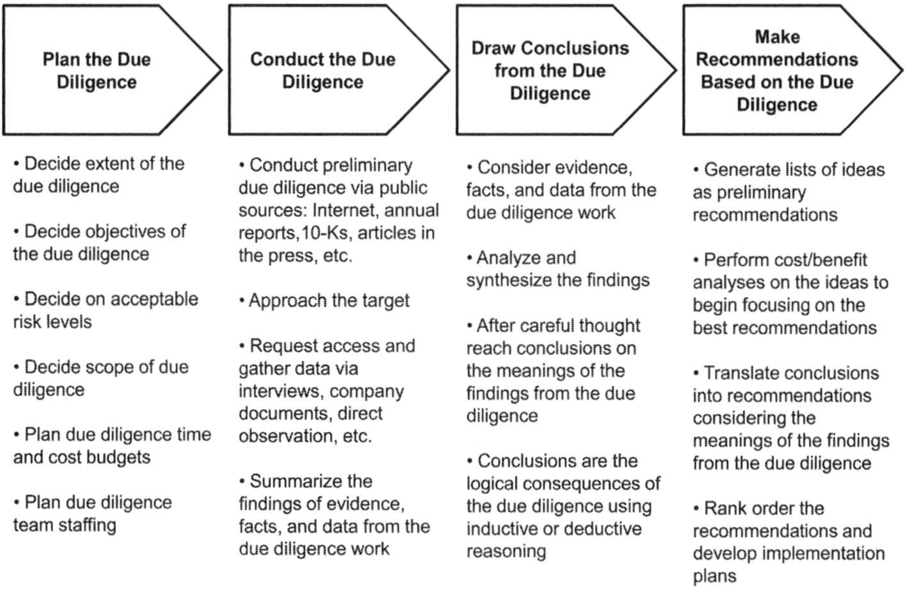

Figure 6.2 The Due Diligence Process. Adapted from material in: Bing, Gordon, *Due Diligence Techniques and Analysis: Critical Questions for Business Decisions*, Quorum Books, 1996.

- What are the needs of the other party relating to the venture? What do they want to get out of the undertaking? What are their motivations for going forward? How do these needs match up with yours?
- What have been the most significant factors in the past success of the other party? How have they achieved that success? Are these factors compatible with this venture?
- What are their plans for the venture after it is consummated? For example, do they want to be involved in active management of the venture, or might they want to take away some intellectual property for their own use? How do these plans match up with yours?
- What would be the greatest obstacles that would be faced in achieving those plans?
- What time frame is being considered for closing the transaction?
- What kind of ownership-transition period does the other party foresee?
- In the case of an acquisition, if the new owner wanted to invest additional capital into the business, what should it be used for?
- In the case of a joint venture, partnership, alliance, and so forth, if one party wanted to invest additional capital, how would that happen and what would it likely be used for?

- If an agreement on price and terms can be reached, is there any reason why this transaction cannot go forward?
- What are the governance options and plans for the venture? What are the advantages and disadvantages of the different options?
- What are the plans for the business if the deal does not go through? What are the options for both sides?

The following general areas of inquiry are adapted from several sources, including Bing and Pickard. This represents a few suggested areas and, depending on the particulars of the acquisition, although there likely will be others:

- *Capital structure and ownership*. A basic part of any due diligence process is to determine how the business is legally and financially structured, and who owns what part of the business. This clearly is to ensure that the buyer knows what is being purchased. Going forward also provides a series of questions that must be answered. What are the options for capital structure and ownership, and what are the advantages and disadvantages of each option? What are the current plans? If this is a two-sided (or more) transaction, is there agreement on capital structure and ownership? If not, what happens going forward—can the transaction really proceed without such agreement?
- *Competition*. Who are the competitors, and how are they currently positioned *vis-à-vis* the target? In what direction(s) are they moving, toward adjacent customers and markets, adjacent products and technologies, or white space opportunities? What impact does this have on the venture's likely success?
  - How is the target's technology relative to its competitors? What is preventing a competitor from introducing a better, faster, or cheaper product, or perhaps one with less or more features and options?
- *Corporate culture*. How does the target's corporate culture match yours? Are they compatible? How about the desired culture in the new venture?
- *Corporate governance*. Who has control of the new venture, and how was this determined? Is the other party comfortable with this? Many ventures have floundered on this very question.

An Aside: The Russian venture involving BP (TNK-BP) a few years ago had difficulty with governance, i.e. who was in charge? In 2008, a dispute occurred between the major shareholders as BP and its Russian partners seemed to have differing visions for the company's corporate governance and future strategy. During the dispute, some BP executives reportedly experienced visa problems, and the American CEO, Robert Dudley, was accused by the Russians of having violated Russian law. He subsequently was jailed briefly and ousted as CEO of the company.

- *Customers and markets.* There are a number of relevant questions regarding customers and markets for the venture:
  - Who are the current customers, and what are their decision-making processes?
  - Why do current customers choose to buy from the target company? What are the costs for customers to switch their buying habits from the target company to other providers?
  - What value proposition does the target offer to its customers? Is it compelling relative to their alternatives?
  - How large is the potential market, and are projected growth rates realistic?
  - Are existing customers representative of the larger market?
- *Engineering, research and development, product development, and technology.* Where does the venture stand currently with regard to these? What is the status of the product development pipeline? What are the future plans? What are the capabilities of the technical people in the venture, and how do they stack up *vis-à-vis* the competition?
- *Facilities and equipment.* What facilities and equipment does the target have, will they be available in the future, where are they, and what is their condition?
- *Finance and accounting.* Does the target company need cash now? If so, how much and why? What assumptions and risks does the company have regarding revenue and expenses? Has a competent accountant been engaged who can audit the target firm's books?
- *Human resources, recruiting, compensation, and benefits.* How do the target company's policies and practices match yours? Will you have to modify yours, or will you have to modify those of the target? What do you know about the capabilities and competencies of the work force?
- *Information systems and technology.* Integration of the target's operations with the acquiring company's cannot be accomplished without integration of the information systems. Some companies have a standing policy that whenever an acquisition takes place, the first team of people that go into the newly acquired company consists of the accountants and the information systems people. The information systems then are immediately transferred over to the acquiring company's systems where possible.
- *International business.* Here is another area that has significant risks, especially in terms of the U.S. Foreign Corrupt Practices Act. A number of companies have been snared in that trap, so competent attorneys should be used to investigate any hint of difficulties.
- *Legal.* Has a competent attorney been engaged who has experience in mergers and acquisitions? If so, he/she likely will want to see copies of all agreements relative to settled litigation as well as to look at all on-going legal proceedings.

- *Management.* It's important to know who currently manages the business, their capabilities, and their desires going forward. Do they wish to stay and under what circumstances? Does the purchaser wish for current management to stay and under what circumstances? How capable are the current employees, particularly the key employees? Going forward, is current management good enough to see the company through to success? In the future, how can the company attract and retain enough of the right kind of talent that it needs to be successful?
- *Manufacturing, distribution, and purchasing.* The due diligence team should visit and examine closely the manufacturing and distribution operations with an operations expert. Purchasing also should be a significant focus for due diligence because of both risks and opportunities. The risks are that purchasing presents the need for strict controls. The opportunities are that improvements in purchase price go straight to the bottom line—a $1 saving on the purchase price of a component translates directly to a $1 increase in operating income.
- *Marketing, advertising, promotion, pricing.* The entire marketing mix should be examined in due diligence by a qualified marketing expert. This includes the amount of funding of the overall marketing effort and how it is distributed to the mix of initiatives. Pricing should be an area for scrutiny because of the opportunities for improprieties.
- *Products and services.* What products and services does the target offer currently? How are they segmented? Due diligence requires an assessment of the target's current products and services and the stages of their life cycles. For example, are products and services at the beginning or near the ends of their life cycles?
- *Real estate.* What real estate holdings does the target currently have, and what is their condition? Perhaps an important issue for due diligence with respect to real estate is the environmental conditions. Environmental remediation can be a costly and time-consuming task.
- *Risk management.* Please revisit Chapter 5 for an overview of risk management.
- *Sales and customer service.* How are products and services sold, and do they differ by product/service line? If the company has a sales department, the due diligence team should obtain copies of its sales handbook, as well as other sales-related documents that describe the sales process. Qualified sales professionals should be part of the due diligence team.
- *Taxes.* The focus on taxes during due diligence should be on determining what taxes are owed and paid to what jurisdictions and whether payments are up to date. Competent professional tax people should be used in the due diligence process to ensure that the acquiring company does not get caught in a non-payment situation.

Finally, a risk/return reality check can be completed for the following areas.

- *Employee/supplier/customer response and relationships.* Are they good, bad, or indifferent?
- *Financial.* Are sufficient reserves in place to get through a down period? What will be the internal rate of return (IRR) on this investment?
- *Industry.* Is this the industry both sides *really* want to be in?
- *Liability.* Where are the possible liabilities?
- *Seller's desire to do the deal.* Is the business *really* for sale? What are the seller's motivations?
- *Technology.* How fast will it change, and in what ways? What impact will it have on the business and its future?
- *Terms and conditions.* Has the seller been reasonable with the terms and conditions?
- *Valuation.* Is the valuation appropriate?
- *Value added.* What do both sides *really* bring to the party? What value added does the acquiring company provide?

To complete an acquisition, the acquired company must be valued. Some methods for determining the valuation for a firm are outlined by Lerner and Willinge.[4] They present several valuation methods with discussions and an example calculation of each. For the novice in valuation, this note provides a good overview. For those who want a more in-depth discussion, the note provides a good set of references. Of course, it is critical to engage an experienced accountant and/or merger and acquisition specialist who can perform the valuation. Companies also frequently seek a "fairness opinion" from a qualified person or firm to ascertain:

- *Net Present Value (NPV).* NPV is a theoretically sound approach that is relatively easy to understand. However, data may be difficult to obtain and may be somewhat suspect. Further, the "answer" is sensitive to cash-flow, the discount rate, terminal value, and other assumptions and estimates. Users frequently use three sets of estimates (worst, most likely, and best case), and calculate a range of values for the business.
- *Adjusted Present Value (APV).* This approach is theoretically sound and relatively easy to understand as a variant on NPV. However, it is more complicated than NPV, and it has the same disadvantages as NPV. APV simply allows adjustments in various inputs such as the capital structure, the effective tax rate, and net operating losses of the target company.
- *Asset options.* This approach also is theoretically sound, and it overcomes some of the drawbacks of APV and NPV. However, this approach is not commonly used in practice and is not easy to understand. Further, real-world situations may not be easy to solve.
- *Comparables.* This is a "quick-and-dirty" way to get an approximate valuation by looking at other firms that display similar characteristics of size,

risk, and growth rate. This approach is commonly used in practice because it is easy to understand and provides a good intuitive basis for a valuation. However, access to data sometimes is difficult, and the data often are not comparable. For example, the price/earnings ratio is a commonly applied metric, but "earnings" can be seriously affected by accounting policies.

- *Monte Carlo simulation.* This is not a theoretical model; it is an analytical tool. Monte Carlo simulation makes assumptions about all combinations of input variables using probability distributions. A large number of calculations then are run, and a probability distribution of a large number of "answers" is obtained. The availability and ease of use of simulation packages makes this a popular tool for testing out large number of variables.
- *Venture capital.* This approach is simple to use, easy to understand, and commonly used in practice, particularly in the private equity industry. However, it suffers from being oversimplified in certain situations. The process starts with an estimate of the terminal value at a future point in time. This is then discounted back to the present using a target rate of return, which is high enough to justify the investment of the venture capitalist. This approach has been criticized for the excessively high target rates of return that are typically employed—frequently 40%–75%. The VCs justify this for the risk they claim to incur and for other reasons, but we believe this should not be a criticism of the method, per se, but of the input values that are used.

Typically, not just one, but rather a combination of valuation methods is utilized. Assistance from consulting firms, accounting firms, and investment banks may be required to determine appropriate valuations.

Once the valuation is completed, the purchaser must prepare an offer. There are a number of legal considerations that the purchaser will need to take into account during the acquisition process. Here, it is important to engage a competent corporate attorney who has experience in mergers and acquisitions of the same type and size as the one contemplated.

Letter of Intent

Among the first documents lawyers will draft is a *letter of intent (LOI)*. The reason for an LOI is to decide whether an agreement between the buyer and seller about price and terms is possible. Moreover, the letter of intent can be useful in determining whether a deal is worth pursuing before spending time and money in the process. If a company finds that the best arrangement it can negotiate with a seller is not good enough to justify pursuing the acquisition, it should look for another target.

A letter of intent usually is not binding in its entirety. However, it may contain, say, specific non-disclosure agreements which are binding. Furthermore, the LOI may include an agreement on the part of the seller not to continue to search for another buyer as long as the LOI is in effect. The reverse may also be true; the buyer may agree not to search for another acquisition as long as the LOI is in effect.

A letter of intent also sends a signal to a business owner about the seriousness of buying the business. Sellers are more willing to negotiate with a purchaser they believe to be credible and serious. Some people who say they are interested buyers are only "testing the waters" in hopes of finding a "steal." Sellers do not want to waste their time and money on buyers of this kind. An LOI also gives the owner an incentive to provide more information to a prospective purchaser. Some sellers will not provide prospective buyers with complete information until they ascertain the buyer's level of commitment, and a letter of intent signifies commitment.

A formal offer usually comes after the LOI. Once the valuation is completed, the purchaser must prepare an offer. There are a number of legal considerations that the purchaser will need to take into account during the acquisition process with the aid of competent legal representation.

Management and Non-compete Agreements

Other common contracts associated with the purchase of a business are agreements on management and agreements not to compete. This agreement may consist of one or two documents, depending on what they cover.

For one, a *non-compete agreement* is basically a contract whereby the seller agrees not to compete directly or indirectly with the business that he or she has just sold. The agreements serve to protect the buyer from having the owner sell the existing business and then start an identical business shortly thereafter while taking substantially all of the customers or employees of the existing business.

A *management agreement* may be a contract for the existing management to stay in place for an agreed time, with an agreed set of duties, at an agreed compensation.

Items Included in Legal Agreements

Some of the items that should be included in legal agreements related to a business purchase appear below. These legal agreements should be drafted by competent attorneys to fit the individual circumstances of an acquisition. The contracts will contain paragraphs dealing with these issues:

1. A statement on the sale/purchase of the business
2. The purchase price
3. Method of payment
4. Adjustments to the purchase price

5. Buyer's assumption of contracts and liabilities
6. Seller's representations and warranties
7. Seller's obligations pending closing
8. Risk of loss clause
9. Covenant not to compete and management contract (if any)
10. Conditions precedent to closing
11. Closing date, time, and location
12. Indemnification by seller
13. Seller's security deposit
14. Arbitration of disputes
15. Escrow arrangements

Often, the amount offered by the purchaser to the seller is a premium above the valuation of the company. The parties then work together until they agree, and thus a deal is made between the purchasing and selling company. In reality, sometimes a deal cannot be consummated. The potential buyer and seller then move on to other opportunities.

Of course, the financing must be completed. One option is to pay cash. Another option is to use the purchaser's stock to acquire the seller's company. Of course, a combination of cash and stock also can be employed.

With respect to the effects on management of the merger/acquisition for the purchased company, experience indicates that continuity of management in the purchased company is sometimes desirable but typically difficult to maintain. The turnover rate for managers in the purchased company is usually at least double the turnover rate for managers in non-merged firms.

Next, the process of preparing business plans for starting a new division or company to accomplish entrepreneurial supply chain options is discussed.

THE BUSINESS PLAN FOR THE ENTREPRENEURIAL SUPPLY CHAIN VENTURE

How can the due diligence be tested on its risks and assumptions? By developing a business plan. Business plans for start-up entrepreneurial supply chain ventures and for corporate entrepreneurial supply chain ventures are similar, but have a few differences.

A business plan is needed before moving forward, regardless of the type of venture. This is true whether the venture is an acquisition, start-up, collaborative venture, joint venture, or other form of entrepreneurial supply chain endeavor.

Below is a sample business plan outline adapted from Williams and Napier, *Essentials of Entrepreneurship*.[5] Appendix B provides a complete example of a business plan. Readers can also check out the websites of companies in which they are interested, paying particular attention to their Form 10-K. While the websites and Forms 10-K certainly are not business plans and do not contain business plans, nevertheless they are useful guides as to how to present certain information in creative ways. After all, a company's website is a selling document in addition to being an information-dispensing document.

Most business plans should be approximately 40 pages maximum with background details in a separate volume of appendices. A business plan is a narrative and quantitative statement, depicting *what* is to be done; *why, where, and how* it is to be done; *when* it is to be done; and *who* is to do it. An example business plan is given here:

1. The *Enterprise Mission Statement* typically starts the business plan. This is a short, one- or two-sentence statement that outlines the reasons for the entrepreneurial supply chain enterprise. The *enterprise mission* reflects the motivations of both the entrepreneur who creates the entity and the market which will be served by it (and hence will pay money for its products or services).

2. The *Executive Summary* is a one- to three-page discussion of what the business will be all about, who will be involved, where it will be located, and why there is a need for the business. It should include a succinct statement about the nature of the business, what financing is required, and what will be done with the funds. For an entrepreneurial supply chain venture, there should be some detail as to the connectivity with supply chains.

3. The *Business Description* includes a detailed portrayal of the business. The activities of the company can be defined and explained in this section. An enterprise definition may be included as a statement about what the firm either presently does or will do in the future. It should be sufficiently encompassing to stimulate thinking; it should not constrain creativity, but it should be narrow enough to provide direction. At this point, the specific opportunity is defined.

4. The *Industry Analysis* section contains the economic, social, demographic, and political characteristics of the industry in which the proposed venture will operate. What are the markets and the main types of customers for the industry, and does the industry definition contain domestic competitors or international competitors? In addition, there should be an analysis of the dynamics of the industry in terms of entries, exits, and mergers and acquisitions. The industry structure, found in Chapter 3, in terms of fragmented versus consolidated, and stable versus unstable, also should be analyzed.

5. The *Competition* should be outlined in detail, including current and potential competitors as well as other kinds of competition. There should be a statement about the products and services offered by the competitors and to what extent they are directly or indirectly competitive. Further, it should contain an estimate of the market share of these competitors.

An Aside: An example of "other kinds of competition" is from the history of Southwest Airlines, which was formed originally to fly between Houston, Dallas, and San Antonio, TX. There is a commonly accepted yet unverified story that their business plan contained the usual statements about their competition being other airlines. However, a statement allegedly was contained to the effect that their biggest competitor was likely to be the automobile, not other airlines. This turned out to be true in its early days.

6. The company's *Strategic Plans* in the business plan document describe what products and services the company is going to offer to which class of customer in which specific geographic areas. Strategic planning takes into account the broad goals of the organization, and deals in horizons of several years. According to Thompson, Strickland, and Gamble,[6] the venture's strategy should face three central questions in evaluating its business prospects:
   - What is our present situation?
   - Where do we need to go from here?
   - How should we get there?

   Thompson, Strickland, and Gamble go on to say the following about strategy: "A company achieves sustainable competitive advantage when an attractive number of buyers prefer its products or services over the offerings of competitors and when the basis for this preference is durable."

7. The *Marketing and Sales Plan* is an important component of the business plan. Comprehensive marketing and sales plans frequently are written for both the total business and for each market segment and/or each product or service line. These plans should include, at a minimum, the market position, the pricing strategy, and a market awareness plan.
   a. Many people suggest that there should be an underlying marketing philosophy, such as Wal-Mart's "Save Money, Live Better."
   b. The slogan of Ernst & Young, "Quality in Everything We Do," is another example; it truly emphasizes a quality theme. As a brief aside, one of E&Y's publications is titled, "Exceptional: Entrepreneurship + Innovation = Growth."

8. The *Product and Service Development Plan* should include a stage-gate process for development of new products and/or services. There also should be a product/service philosophy in terms of new product development. For example, companies can move in any or all of the following directions: (1) into adjacent customers and markets using existing products and technologies, (2) into adjacent products and technologies

for existing customers and markets, and/or (3) into the white space of new customers and markets combined with new products and technologies. This could be the basis for a product/service philosophy along with statements concerning how much "bleeding/leading-edge" new product development will take place versus how much "line extensions" will be appropriate for the business.

9. The *Organizational Structure and Management* section contains a brief biographical sketch of each key management person, usually with a brief description of each person's job title and duties.

10. The *Risks and Assumptions* section identifies, assesses, and prioritizes the uncertainties facing the enterprise as it goes forward. Many risks and assumptions were discussed in Chapter 5 along with possible mitigation approaches.

11. The *Pro Forma Financial Statements* include projected income statements, balance sheets, and cash flow statements. When these statements are prepared, all risks and assumptions should be well documented and defined. The forecast time period utilized is often five years. However, the number of years can vary depending on the company's needs and the industry norms. An illustration of how the company's cash flow might happen through time is shown in Figure 6.3. When a venture begins, and usually

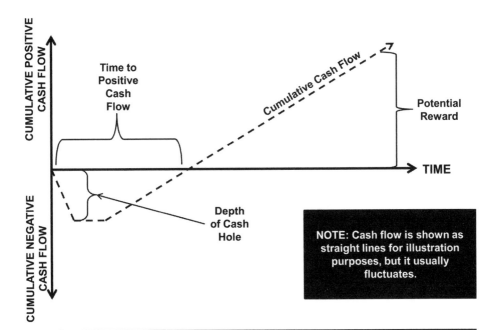

Figure 6.3 Cash Flow through Time. Adapted from: Sahlman, William A., "How to Write a Great Business Plan," *Harvard Business Review*, July–August 1997, pp. 98–108.

for the first few months (and maybe years), the cash flow is negative. Then it begins to turn around, and ultimately it heads up, erasing the previous negative cash deficit. Three critical pieces of information are shown in this figure: the time to positive cash flow, the depth of the cash hole that is dug with the negative cash flow, and the potential reward of cash at a particular time in the future. Note that for the sake of simplicity, the cash flows are shown as straight lines, although that by no means will always be the case.

12. The *Operating Plans* are the plans to operate the business in the months immediately ahead while progress is made toward the objectives of the strategic plan. Operating plans should cover a rolling 18 months. This means that the operating plans always cover the current fiscal year plus at least six months into the next fiscal year.

   a. Operating plans usually include operations, marketing, and product development. A technique, commonly known as *sales and operations planning (S&OP)* should be the basis for the company's operating plans. The domain of S&OP usually is 3–18 months into the future, in which the basic objective is to balance demand and supply. It is not strategic in nature because strategic plans usually go out for five years or more. Further, it is not execution because those plans usually go out for three to six months. The S&OP objectives are fourfold:

      i. Balance demand and supply;
      ii. Manage uncertainty;
      iii. Establish accountability; and
      iv. Integrate plans and decisions.

   b. The basic structure of a monthly process for a manufacturing company is shown in Figure 6.4. S&OP focuses on three elements of general management responsibilities: grow the business (new products review and demand review); run the business well (demand review, supply review, financial review, and the executive S&OP review); and add to the business' capabilities (special projects review and new products review).

   c. The six-step S&OP as shown in Figure 6.4 is a formal, monthly process. Around the first of the month, the Special Projects Review and the New Products Review take place. These are led by the appropriate senior leaders and attended by the middle management personnel who are directly involved. Special projects might include major new (or major upgrades of) facilities and equipment. The Special Projects Review ensures that these projects are part of the overall intermediate-term planning of the company and that they are completed on schedule and on budget. The New Products Review focuses on the pipeline of new products, likely using a new-product development stage-gate process. It ensures that no surprises in budget or schedule

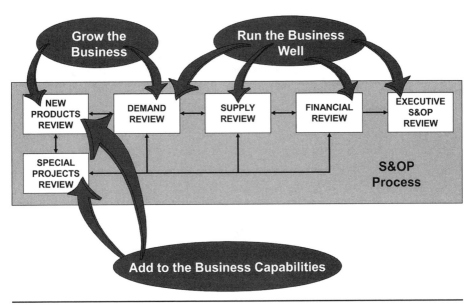

Figure 6.4   Sales and Operations Planning Process.

occur as new products move through the development process. These are the two pieces of the puzzle that add to the business' capabilities.

d. The next two elements of the process are intended to *grow the business*: the New Products Review and the Demand Review. This is not a second New Products Review; rather, that element simply fulfills two objectives of general management responsibilities. The Demand Review usually is chaired by the Vice President of Sales and Marketing (or a person with a similar position), and is attended by people who have responsibility for the company's demand. Usually, this is a review based on product families as defined by the Sales and Marketing organization. It is typically a family-by-family review of the demand plan looking out for 18 months. The idea is that the 18-month demand plan is reviewed and analyzed monthly. Each month contains an analysis of actual demand versus planned demand to ascertain the causes of the discrepancies, and this information is used to review and possibly change the demand plan going forward. Also attending the Demand Review are people from the supply side (likely manufacturing, procurement, and distribution) of the organization. This way, they get a view of what is happening on the demand side.

e. The next four elements of the process are intended to *run the business well:* Demand Review, Supply Review, Financial Review, and

Executive S&OP Review. This is not a second Demand Review. The Supply Review and Financial Review are similar to the Demand Review in that they typically are chaired by their respective senior leaders, the Vice President of Operations, and the Chief Financial Officer. They are attended by the appropriate middle management and professional personnel. The Executive S&OP Review is the final and most important session in the process. It is where everything comes together and unresolved issues get aired and decided. This session usually is chaired by the business leader and attended by the Leadership Team, plus selected others as needed.

    f. At this point, you probably are wondering why S&OP is included as part of the business plan. The answer is simply that S&OP provides *management's handles on the business*. S&OP should be part of the venture's operations planning process from the beginning.

13. The *Milestone Schedule* segment of the business plan includes a timetable and/or Gantt chart indicating key milestones to be accomplished for the new venture to succeed. Once the milestones and required deadlines are determined, they need to be monitored on a continuing basis.

14. The *Strengths, Weaknesses, Opportunities, and Threats (SWOT)* analysis is a mainstay of business planning. *Strengths* may include location, facilities, manufacturing capability, differentiated products or services, prices, and human resources. *Weaknesses* may relate to the firm's size, if it is a start-up, or to its organization as a joint venture if there is some instability in the JV. *Opportunities* may lie in its technology that is new and unique. Major threats, or risks, can include the type of business, marketing strategy, competition, and market size.

15. The *Legal Form* section contains the rationale for the specific legal form selected. Most companies are regular corporations, but some can be Subchapter S corporations, partnerships, and other legal forms. The lawyers and CPAs providing services for the company can supply assistance on the appropriate legal form, and any significant taxation implications. This section should include a justification for the selection of the particular legal form.

16. The next section is concerned about developing a *Harvest Strategy*, assuming that this is a venture that has an exit strategy. Assuming the venture is successful, the question of how the owners want to handle the orderly transfer of the business is considered. The timing of when the initial venture management team transitions to new positions and other people transition to the management team is defined. The preparations necessary for continuity are identified. The objectives and timetable for the exit also are specified.

17. The *Appendices*, if needed, are at the end of the document or contained in a separate volume. Items often included in this section are intellectual

property information, products and services information, research documents on the markets and industry, and other data deemed relevant.

HOW BAKER HUGHES DOES DUE DILIGENCE AND BUSINESS PLANNING

Baker Hughes carries on an active program of acquisitions in its industry and has developed a well-thought-out process for accomplishing that. A senior executive made the simple and correct statement to the author that "it's all about managing risk and reward."

The company embarked on a series of initiatives aimed at rationalizing its existing technology portfolio and closing strategic gaps. This includes targeted acquisitions as well as specific internal product development activities.

In 2010, Baker Hughes closed on a significant acquisition of BJ Services Company, a provider of pressure pumping and other oilfield services. The acquisition closed a significant gap in Baker Hughes' technology portfolio. The company knew a great deal about BJ Services prior to the acquisition process commencing, since (1) it is in the same industry, and (2) Baker Hughes previously owned BJ Services but spun it off a number of years ago to reduce its product portfolio.

What kinds of due diligence does the company perform prior to its acquisitions? First, they have a stage-gate process from which they decide what elements and questions of the stages and gates make sense for the venture under consideration. Second, they put together a due diligence team of (mostly) full-time people, depending on the size and nature of the acquisition. Third, they execute the stage-gate process.

A rigorous compliance audit is an essential part of their process. This includes an in-depth and exacting analysis of the target company's relationships with its agents and other entities.

Baker Hughes then does some preliminary business planning prior to consummating the acquisition. This begins with a summary and then in-depth planning for the target's strategy, assets, people, and technology. A key part of its business planning is how the target will fit into the company's global infrastructure in order to achieve its synergies.

A CASE NOTE FOR FURTHER STUDY: Valhalla Partners

The cases are available at www.harvardbusinessonline.com. Readers should obtain copies of this case and use it to go beyond discussion in the book. These cases were prepared as the basis for discussion, rather than to illustrate either effective or ineffective handling of any particular situation.

This section is adapted from several sources, the primary one being "Valhalla Partners Due Diligence."[7] See the endnote for other resources that may be of interest. This case considers due diligence from the perspective of a venture capital firm, Valhalla Partners, which is considering an investment in Telco Exchange, an enterprise that helps large firms manage their complex telecommunications expenses. Telco is 14 years old, has about $2 million in annual sales, and is run by a 70-year old CEO with his son as Chief Technology Officer. Telco originated from an existing business that developed software for internal use, and then decided that sufficient markets existed to spin it off as a stand-alone business.

The real purpose for including this case is to study the due diligence process of Valhalla, a $177 million venture capital firm that believed it had developed a better way of doing due diligence. They believed due diligence would give it a competitive advantage against other venture capital firms, and provide the basis for more profitable investments. Telco, the target, was the first deal on which a new due diligence process was applied. The Valhalla due diligence process is illustrated in Figure 6.5

The new Valhalla due diligence process had 12 steps, and was more complex and time-consuming than the process typically used by venture capital firms. Despite numerous cases, articles, and books, there are widely varying approaches for conducting due diligence according to "best practices."

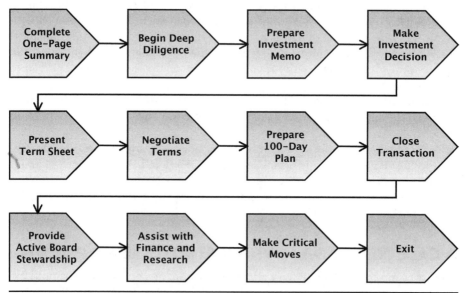

Figure 6.5   The Valhalla Due Diligence Process. Adapted from: Sahlman, William A., *Valhalla Partners Due Diligence*, Harvard Business School Case #9-805-033, September 21, 2001.

Much can be learned about the due diligence process by studying how others go about it. Specifically, there is value in learning how companies reduce the risks and enhance the positive aspects of the transaction.

Valhalla took the approach of spending more time in due diligence than generally is the practice of venture capital firms, despite worrying about wasting time. Further, they were determined to work more closely with management than usual so as to develop a closer relationship that would pay dividends after the transaction was closed. Throughout their planning, Valhalla was concerned with how entrepreneurs would react to intense scrutiny. However, Valhalla was determined not to lament later that, "We wish we'd discovered that earlier."

These are the 12 steps of the Valhalla approach to due diligence:

1. *Complete a one-page summary.* The one-page summary provides a brief description of what the target does, how long it's been in business, and other relevant general information about the target.

2. *Begin deep diligence.* Valhalla's due diligence approach is deeper than is typical. The general guiding principle is that "mistakes are costly." They want to avoid mistakes that would have caused another decision to have been made.

3. *Prepare investment memo.* Valhalla's investment memo on Telco was 22 pages, plus summaries from reference checks on Telco's management team. The objective was to prepare a clear description of the company and its strengths, weaknesses, opportunities, and threats, although not a SWOT analysis, per se. The investment memo took a great deal of time to prepare, and there were questions as to whether it was worth it. (As with any due diligence, questions always arise as to how much is sufficient, appropriate, and cost-effective.)

4. *Make an investment decision.* The investment decision rested on three questions for Valhalla, which were:
   - *Is it real?* Is there a strong market demand, and is it growing?
   - *Can they win?* Does Telco have an advantage against its competitors, and can they continue that advantage as things change over time?
   - *Is it worth it?* Does this present a persuasive investment story, assuming respectable performance by Telco over time?

5. *Present term sheet.* Sometimes, a term sheet is called a letter of intent or a memorandum of understanding, although sometimes a memorandum of understanding is signed by both parties whereas the other two may be signed by only one party. Whatever the form, it usually is simply a non-binding agreement to negotiate in good faith.

6. *Negotiate terms.* Almost inevitably there is some disagreement between the investor(s) and the company as to some components of the proposed terms of the deal. Usually this concerns the monetary valuation, but that is not always the case.

7. *Prepare 100-day plan.* The 100-day plan is a detailed plan for after the closing. The 100-day plan was developed after negotiation of the term sheet, but before closing of the transaction. It had several key components for Telco, but obviously would vary from company to company. In any case, it should provide a sense of what's important to the company in the short term. Telco's plan addressed the following issues, which specifically were unique to Telco, but generally were of the type that would be applicable to most companies.
   - Review, identify, select, recruit, and hire key individuals, such as:
     i. "C-suite" executives;
     ii. Certain professional and managerial personnel; and
     iii. Member(s) of the Board of Directors.
   - Work with company management on a variety of needs, such as:
     i. Appropriate revenue recognition policies;
     ii. Appropriate stock-option plan;
     iii. A (possible) new name and branding strategy;
     iv. Proper analyst relationships;
     v. A "strategic message" to characterize the company, its industry, and its position in the industry;
     vi. A pricing strategy for multiple products, channels, and customers; and
     vii. Appropriate accounting firms and banks.
8. *Close the transaction.* The transaction closing is the formal signing of contract(s) for the deal.
9. *Provide active board stewardship.* Valhalla intended to provide active support and oversight to the Board of Directors.
10. *Assist with finance and research.* Valhalla felt that they could provide assistance to Telco with finance and research.
11. *Make critical moves.* Critical moves were defined in the 100-day plan.
12. *Exit.* Most venture capitalists have a defined exit strategy when they go into a possible transaction. Valhalla's exit strategy included an assumed date (four years into the future), an assumed revenue and after-tax income performance, assumed valuation multiples at the exit, and estimated possible exit valuations.

KEY IDEA
How much risk is known versus unknown beforehand, regardless of how much due diligence is performed? How much due diligence is enough?

The case makes the final point that an important underlying question is about how much risk is really knowable beforehand versus how much would be unknowable regardless of how much due diligence is performed. The decision of Valhalla was to go ahead with the investment. They recruited a new CEO, but the company's performance fell short of plan due to the sales process being more complicated than imagined even though users raved about the software. As of the writing of the case, the company's performance remained below plan and Valhalla had not yet achieved its planned exit.

This, of course, raises the question about how much due diligence is enough.

Articles on Business Planning

This chapter considers both due diligence and writing a business plan. In the case of Valhalla Partners, there are two aspects of their due diligence process that could be turned into business plans (the investment memo and the 100-day plan) although neither could be called a business plan, per se. In any case, they would need a business plan for going forward.

From hundreds of articles and books about writing business plans, consider three sources[8] in this chapter. The article, "How to Write a Great Business Plan" by William A. Sahlman, develops a framework for writing a business plan, emphasizing that numbers are important to include, but should be toward the back of the business plan. Sahlman creates a framework based on four interdependent factors critical to every venture, including questions regarding each factor: people, opportunity, context, and risk and reward.

Another source is "How to Write a Winning Business Plan" by Stanley R. Rich and David E. Gumpert. They discuss three key constituencies whose viewpoints need to be considered: the market, potential investors, and the entrepreneur or inventor. Rich and Gumpert indicated that too often the business plan is written from the entrepreneur or inventor's viewpoint, and does not emphasize enough about the market and investor viewpoints. When considering the market, they suggest the business plan establish market interest, document market interest, and document all market claims. To emphasize the investor viewpoint, they want to know when and how the investors can cash in their chips. It is best not to be too optimistic or include too many exhibits to cover all possible contingencies. Investors base their prices on valuations using five-year forecasts. To get the best price, have some potential customers use the products and try to demonstrate substantial interest in the marketplace.

The third source is the chapter "Writing a Business Plan: The Basics," from the book *Entrepreneur Toolkit: Tools and Techniques to Launch and Grow Your Business* by Harvard Business School Press. Some key topics are: why a business plan is necessary, what type of format is best to convey the information needed by investors, why the executive summary is significant, how the segments of the plan should be prepared, and ways to differentiate the message from other plans.

A FINAL WORD ON DUE DILIGENCE AND THE BUSINESS PLAN

This chapter has introduced the concepts of due diligence and corporate entrepreneurial options for growing a company, including the process of developing business plans for a separate new venture and a new division within an existing company. These topics should help to determine:

- What types of due diligence are appropriate when considering various entrepreneurial supply-chain options.
- Deciding whether to organize individual entrepreneurial supply-chain options within a company's existing organizational structure, or whether the creation of a new business is the best approach to take advantage of an entrepreneurial supply-chain opportunity.
- Preparation of a business plan for an internal organization or new business venture separate from the company.

ASSURANCE OF LEARNING QUESTIONS

1. Specify some due diligence topics you may consider when thinking about the acquisition of a company or assets.
2. What are some corporate entrepreneurial options for growing your company?
3. Describe approaches for preparing a business plan for creating a new business entity outside your company, and then describe an organizational structure within your company.
4. Research Valhalla Partners. Determine how they are doing as a company and how some of their clients are performing. Valhalla's website as of February 2011 has the tag line, "helping information technology entrepreneurs change the world." How do you think they accomplish that?

REFERENCES

1. Cressy, Robert. "Determinants of Small Firm Survival and Growth." In Casson, Mark, Yeung, Bernard, Basu, Anuradha, and Nigel Wadeson (Eds.). *The Oxford Handbook of Entrepreneurship*. Oxford and New York: Oxford University Press, 2006.
2. Bing, Gordon. *Due Diligence Techniques and Analysis: Critical Questions for Business Decisions*, Westport, CT: Quorum Books, 1996.
3. Pickard, Scott S. *Due Diligence List*. San Jose, CA: Writers Club Press, 2002.
4. Lerner, Josh, and John Willinge. "A Note on Valuation in Private Equity Settings." Harvard Business School Case #9-297-050, Rev. March 18, 2011.

5. Williams, E. E., and Napier, H. A. *Essentials of Entrepreneurship*, Chicago: T&NO Book Company, 2010.
6. Thompson, Arthur A., Jr., Strickland, A. J., III, and John E. Gamble. *Crafting and Executing Strategy: The Quest for Competitive Advantage*, 17th ed., New York: McGraw-Hill Irwin, 2010.
7. Sahlman, William A. "Valhalla Partners Due Diligence." Harvard Business School Case #9-805-033, September 21, 2004. See also, Roberts, Michael J., and Lauren Barley. "How Venture Capitalists Evaluate Potential Venture Opportunities." Harvard Business School Case #9-805-019, Rev. December 1, 2004.
8. Sahlman William A. "How to Write a Great Business Plan." *Harvard Business Review*, July/August 1997; Rich, Stanley R., and David E. Gumpert. "How to Write a Winning Business Plan." *Harvard Business Review*, May/June 1985; "Writing a Business Plan: The Basics." *Entrepreneur Toolkit: Tools and Techniques to Launch and Grow Your Business*. Harvard Business School Press, 2004.

CHAPTER 7

IMPLEMENTING ENTREPRENEURIAL SUPPLY CHAINS

LEARNING OBJECTIVES

1. Understand the management of change as companies move toward more entrepreneurial supply chains.
2. Be able to explain the stage-gate approach to change management.
3. Develop an understanding of the six "behavioral change levers," how they fit together, and how they are useful in large-scale change projects.
4. 3M is an outstanding example of an entrepreneurial company. You should research 3M and learn as much as possible about what makes it successful.

"Great change dominates the world, and unless we move with change we will become its victims."

—Robert F. Kennedy

Robert F. Kennedy's quote about change defines a big issue facing companies to-day—how to move *with* change to not become a *victim* of change. Creating entre-preneurial supply chains and focusing them on innovation and growth represent significant change in most companies. This chapter takes a look at managing the change process of implementing innovative and entrepreneurial supply chains.

Clearly, the issue of managing change is more applicable to corporate entre-preneurship than to start-up enterprises. Start-up endeavors begin with change, so change tends not to be as big an issue as are corporate entrepreneurship under-takings. Ventures that originate with corporate entrepreneurship usually must change their current ways of doing business—sometimes this change can be major.

> **KEY IDEA**
>
> Stage-gate processes are divided into stages separated by gates. Stages usually are activities, analyses, and/ or deliverables, and represent work to be accomplished. Gates are decision points that consist of assessment and decision criteria. Gates usually result in decisions to go ahead, stop, hold for more information, or recycle for more work.

Implementing change that is sustainable, visible, and effective is vitally important to create innovative and entrepreneurial supply chains in existing organizations. In order to ensure successful implementation, a formal program of change management is recommended, and several ways to do this are presented in this chapter.

One change management program, the "stage-gate" process, is shown in Figure 7.1. The end objective, shown as the third circle with arrows aligned and pointing in the same direction, is strategic alignment toward the desired new state. This is a three-gate, two-stage change process, explained as:

1. *Gate 1—As-Is.* In an uncoordinated and unfocused organization, this is the beginning of the change management process. It is the first gate of the stage-gate process. Gate 1 represents the *as-is* situation and is defined by an

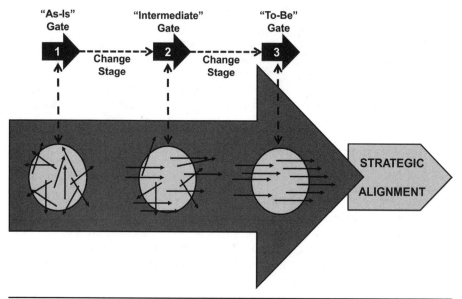

Figure 7.1   The Stage-Gate Process of Change Management. Adapted from: Kotter, John P., *Leading Change*, Harvard Business Review Press, 1996.

as-is assessment. The distance between Gate 1 and Gate 2 is shown as a change stage, corresponding to activities in the change management process.

2. *Gate 2—Intermediate.* Some processes have not yet been changed. This is an intermediate point of the change management process. Multiple intermediate stages and gates usually are part of the change process.

3. *Gate 3—To-Be.* All arrows are headed in the same direction, suggestive of a coordinated and focused organization. This is the end point of the change management process.

There are enormous barriers to change within organizations. One of the best references on change management is by John Kotter.[1] Kotter's discussion on removing barriers is illustrated in Figure 7.2. He discusses empowering a broad base of people to take action by removing barriers to implementation of the change vision; in this case, the vision involves entrepreneurial supply chains. Kotter addresses four barriers as particularly important: structures, skills, systems, and supervisors. The objective of change management is strategic alignment toward entrepreneurial and innovative supply chains, that is, everyone lined up and going in the same direction.

The general message about change should now be clear. Not all the organization can change at one time—it is a *process* that takes time and is accomplished in stages. That is the essence of a formal stage-gate change management process.

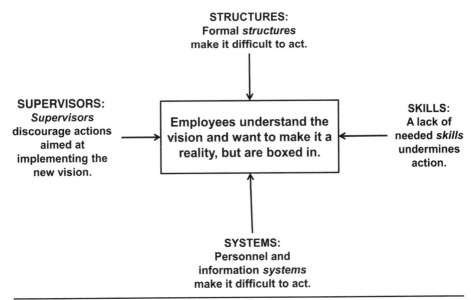

Figure 7.2 Barriers to Change. Adapted from: Kotter, John P., *Leading Change*, Harvard Business Review Press, 1996, Page 102.

For most entrepreneurial supply chain efforts, companies need to provide a rationale for a series of changes. Creating entrepreneurial supply chains frequently imposes a great deal of change on the organization. The big change is to move:

<table>
<tr><td>

KEY IDEA

Attitudes toward change can vary widely from person to person. "Change will be good for you." "If we build it, they will come." "Change would be easy if it were not for people!"

</td><td>

- *From a culture* in which supply chains are viewed as low-level, transactional, and error-prone organizations . . .
- *To a culture* in which supply chains are capable of a high level of entrepreneurial activity, innovation, and growth, and which contribute significantly to the organizational strategy.

</td></tr>
</table>

This likely will require a set of formal processes to stimulate entrepreneurial activity, innovation, and growth. In all probability this will require moving *from less formal* to *more formal* ways of doing business. Almost all major entrepreneurial, innovation, and growth initiatives will require changing organizational structures, reporting relationships, and job descriptions. Further, efforts to ensure motivation to get and stay committed usually are necessary.

An Aside: 3M, one of the world's most innovative and entrepreneurial corporations, reportedly gives its scientists up to 15% of their time along with some funding to pursue projects of their own interest. The result is a corporate goal of having 25–30% (both percentages appear in publications) of revenue based on products that did not exist five years earlier. Clearly, this is a formal organizational arrangement that sets aside informal but purposeful sources of time and money.

Most major entrepreneurial efforts will also require aggressive time schedules for implementation. Simply put, motivation for change is difficult to sustain for extended periods of time without visible indications of progress.

Of course, people hold different attitudes toward change. The "Key Idea" sidebar illustrates some of these attitudes. Some say "Change will be good for you"—kind of like your mother used to say when you were a child and she had some horrible tasting medicine for you to take. Some say "If we build it, they will come." Still others say, not always tongue in cheek, "Change would be easy if it were not for people." Clearly, there are other sayings about change and implementing change, but you get the point that attitudes toward change can vary!

Effective implementation of entrepreneurial supply chains addresses both sides of human nature, as shown in Figure 7.3. Everyone has a rational side and an emotional side, yet all people are different. One's rational side leads a person to think, analyze, understand, decide, and act based on reason and analysis. One's emotional

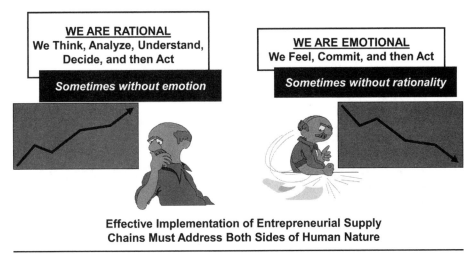

**Effective Implementation of Entrepreneurial Supply
Chains Must Address Both Sides of Human Nature**

Figure 7.3   Human Nature Has Two Sides.

side leads a person to feel, commit, and act based on feelings. Understanding and addressing both sides of people's human nature is necessary in order to build support for the changed focus of the supply chains.

DEVELOP A FORMAL CHANGE MANAGEMENT PROGRAM

One framework for a formal change program is presented in Figure 7.4. It has five components, corresponding roughly to five steps in the process. It is not unlike the overall approach described in Chapter 4. Step 1, the As-Is State, calls for an assessment of the current state of affairs for the organization in terms of its readiness for change. Step 2, the To-Be State, outlines the future state of the organization. Step 3, the "Gap Analysis," delineates the process of comparing the as-is to the to-be situation in order to determine where the gaps exist. *How* the change process takes place is through the change levers in Step 4. *Who* is responsible for the change process are the change agent teams in Step 5. Let's now take these five steps in more detail.

Step 1: Assess Readiness for Change from the "As-Is" State

The Step 1 focus is on the as-is state of the organization and whether it is ready for change. The key issues in the readiness for change assessment are, first, what are the circumstances for the assessment of readiness for movement toward en-

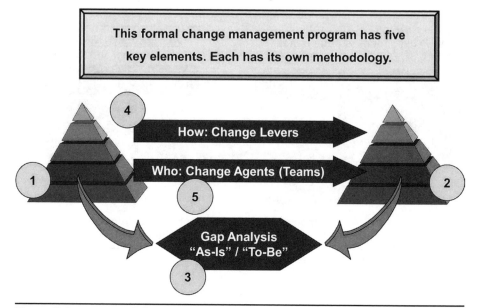

Figure 7.4   Framework for Implementing Entrepreneurial Supply Chains.

trepreneurial supply chains; second, what are we trying to accomplish in the move away from the as-is state?

In the case of a firm trying to move its supply chain to become an entrepreneurially focused organization, the as-is circumstances may be bureaucratic, transactions-oriented, and error-prone. The assessment of its readiness to change almost certainly will concentrate on issues such as its culture, the knowledge levels of its personnel concerning the definition of a "good" or a "class A" supply chain organization, and the level and source of dissatisfaction with the status quo.

Step 2: Define the "To-Be" State

A famous quote from Yogi Berra states the essence of Step 2: "You've got to be careful if you don't know where you're going, 'cause you might not get there." Defining the to-be state requires two elements: (1) explain the rationale for the end state of where we're going; and (2) specify how the organization, business processes, and systems must work together in the to-be state.

Step 3: Perform a Gap Analysis

The gap analysis compares the current as-is situation with the desired to-be situation. At its heart, the gap analysis answers these questions:

- What is the current as-is situation?
- What is the desired to-be situation?
- What is the difference between the two situations?

There can be a number of gaps related to entrepreneurial supply chains. There can be a perception gap, a behavioral gap, a results gap, an organizational gap, an information gap, a strategy gap, and so on. Gap analysis provides a basis to measure the required investments of time, money, and people required to achieve the to-be situation.

Along with the gap analysis, frequently comes a change management plan of how to get from where we are to where we want to be. The change management plan integrates with the project plan. Say, for example, we have a five-phase entrepreneurial supply chain project plan, with these steps identified:

1. Prepare for the project
2. Develop blueprint for entrepreneurial supply chains
3. Perform initial implementation tasks
4. Plan launch
5. Launch

Work the change management plan with the project.

Step 4: Determine How to Implement the Change Levers

> **KEY IDEA**
>
> Failure to achieve behavior change is a primary cause of failure in large-scale projects.

Some change levers were already mentioned in this book: leadership, communications, commitment, education and training, workforce and organizational transition, and results orientation. Think of each lever arrayed against the objectives, key actions, responsibilities, and schedules for each phase of the project. For example, consider for each phase of the project how leadership would have its objectives, key actions, responsibilities, schedules, and performance requirements characterized in an implementation format. That is, ask what would be the objectives for the leadership, what would they be expected to accomplish, what key actions would be required from the leadership, who would have the responsibilities for the actions, how would the leaders performance be measured, and what would be the schedules for the actions. Ask the same sorts of questions about each change lever. The change levers are discussed in substantially more detail later in this chapter.

Step 5: Select the Change Agent Teams

For change projects of any magnitude, a set of change agent teams is required to tackle different aspects of the project. The focus should be on strategic alignment of people, business processes, resources, and tools, as shown in Figure 7.5. Entrepreneurial supply chains require focus and strategic alignment throughout the company. The people, business processes, resources, and tools should all be aligned simultaneously.

While alignment is necessary, it is not always sufficient. Many entrepreneurial supply chain strategies have serious flaws and distract from the overall strategy. Sometimes these flaws are in individual elements. For example, the firm may lack the appropriate quantity, mix, and capability of any of the people, business processes, resources, or tools.

What does *strategic alignment* mean? Alignment of the *people* means that people agree with the strategic direction, understand it, and are capable of implementing it. For an entrepreneurial supply chain, the company needs its people to agree on the need for entrepreneurship along the supply chain, understand what *entrepreneurship* means, and be capable of implementing entrepreneurial behaviors.

> **KEY IDEA**
>
> If change is easy, why is the press so full of stories about organizations that cannot achieve it?

For strategic alignment of the *business processes*, the organization needs processes and metrics that encourage entrepreneurial behavior. For example, the nature of entrepreneurship means that every idea will not flower into a full-blown business opportunity. Thus, there must be some tolerance for failure. If the company's metrics punish failure

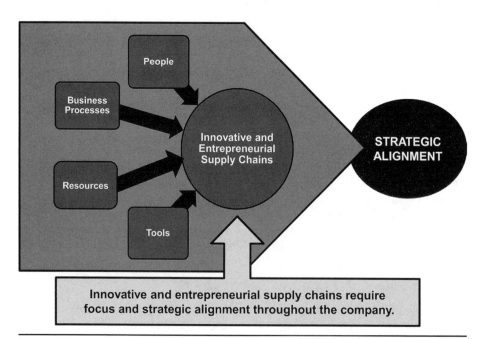

Figure 7.5   Entrepreneurial Supply Chains Require Strategic Alignment.

then do not be surprised if you do not get acts of entrepreneurship—people do not like to be punished for their actions.

The firm's *resources* may not be capable of making an important contribution to entrepreneurialism if, say, the organization cannot appropriately share resources across business units.

Finally, the firm's *tools* may not have sufficient capability. For example, business intelligence and analytics can be difficult to use for the typical business user, so new software may be needed.

In addition, there is a need to keep these four elements of change in perspective and notice how they work together:

- If the efforts are focused only on *people* and *tools*, we've automated chaos! Left out are the *business processes* and *resources* that support entrepreneurship and innovation.
- If the strategic alignment is focused only on *business processes, resources,* and *tools*, we've made the implicit statement that "people don't count around here." There has been a failure to recognize the strategic role of people and resources in entrepreneurial supply chains.
- If the strategic alignment is focused only on *people, business processes,* and *resources*, we've left out anything about *tools*. The implicit statement that "the people are Luddites!" has been made, and it is implied that technology is not needed.

The overall message is to include all parts of the puzzle.

The spirit of the formal change program should move traditional supply chains to entrepreneurial and innovative supply chains, as shown in Figure 7.6. Starting with existing (traditional) behavior, add people-oriented change levers (leadership, communications, commitment, education and training, workforce and organization transition, and a results orientation), which are then executed at the organizational, group, and individual levels, to drive new entrepreneurial and innovative behavior. The theory of planned organizational change incorporates behavior-based programs, and the approach of this book is consistent with this theory.

KEY IDEA
Change is difficult. Managing change is *really* difficult.

However, widespread misconceptions exist about change, and how to achieve and manage it. People say a variety of things about change. Unfortunately, a number of false impressions about change reinforce leaders' beliefs that a significant change management program is unnecessary. Consider examples such as the following statements, variations of which have been widely used.

- "Our people are used to change, so this will be just fine with them."
- "Pressures that caused us to change will be viewed rationally."

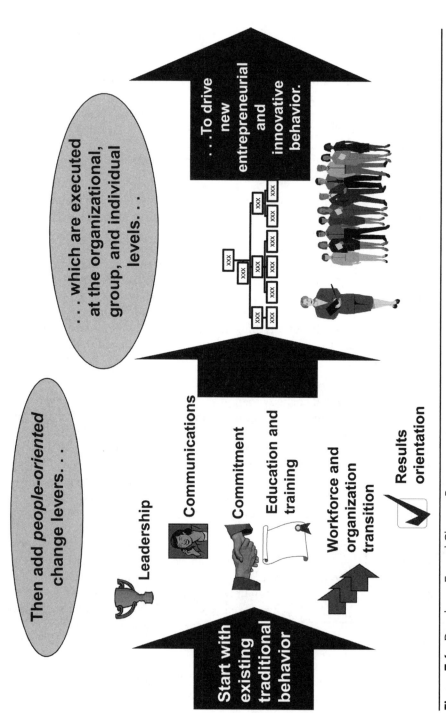

Figure 7.6 Develop a Formal Change Program.

- "During the change process, those who appear 'OK' really are."
- "Senior management behavior during the transition is invisible to the rest of the organization."
- "The weak people are the ones who are likely to leave because of the change."
- "People 'hear' what management communicates."
- "Change just takes strong leadership."

Individuals, groups, and organizations must *behave* differently if performance is to improve. Behavioral change and performance improvement don't just happen; a change management *program* is required. Frequently, the impact of the coming change is not obvious in the early phases of the project, so resources are not devoted to manage the change process. But research and practical experience demonstrate that change management must *begin early* in order to be effective; organizations often end up doing too little, too late.

Outline of a Change Management Plan

The outline of an effective change management plan could look something like this:

1. Executive Summary
2. Definition of and Rationale for Formal Change Management
3. Roles and Responsibilities of the Change Management Teams
4. Change Management Plans for the Total Project and Site Implementations
   a. Assessments: As-Is, To-Be, and Gap Analysis
   b. Leadership Plan
   c. Communications Plan
   d. Commitment Plan
   e. Education and Training Plan
   f. Workforce and Organization Transition Plan
   g. Results Orientation Plan
5. Timelines and Resources

Change levers can be integrated with a project plan, as shown in Figure 7.7. Notice the five phases of the project plan: prepare for the project, develop a blueprint for entrepreneurial supply chains, perform initial implementation tasks, plan launch, and launch. Each of these phases has a set of lower-level activities identified, such as determining costs and benefits, approving funding, project kickoff, various education and training activities, and so forth.

The six change levers at the bottom of Figure 7.7 cut across the entire project plan, integrating with each phase. For each change lever and each phase of the project, the change management plan outlines objectives, key actions,

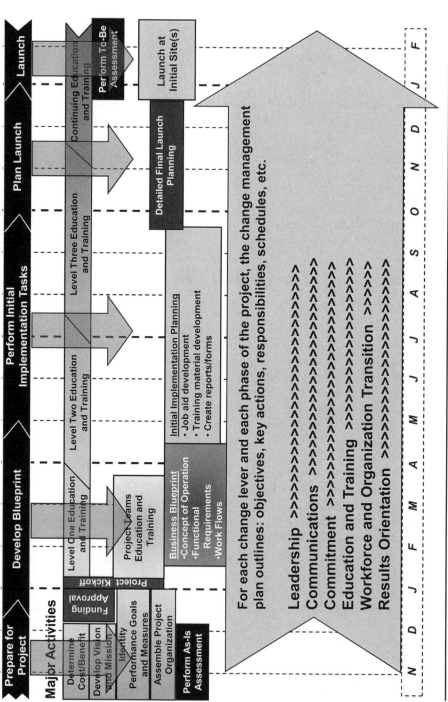

Figure 7.7 Programmed Change Levers. Source: The plan is adapted from a project management template from Oliver Wight Management Consulting.

responsibilities, schedules, and so forth. For example, leadership as the first change lever will map into project preparation, developing the blueprint for entrepreneurial supply chains, initial implementation tasks, planning for the launch, and launch.

Let's look at the levers one at a time.

Leadership *of the Transition to Entrepreneurial Supply Chains*

Leadership plays a strong, unique, and central role in the change management process. Leaders send strong signals to individuals through their messages; leaders send stronger signals through their actions about which behavior change messages are "real." Leaders sometimes need to change their own leadership styles to match the new demands for entrepreneurial and innovative supply chains, and must personally work to secure support for the change. From time to time, leaders must make tough "people decisions" required to make the new business orientation work.

Leaders need to visibly show commitment to the project throughout its life cycle. This includes allocating resources, empowering teams, communicating the change and the vision for the future, and inspiring confidence in the new business processes for the entrepreneurial and innovative supply chains.

Leaders need to align the organization by ensuring senior management commitment, find champions to lead individual initiatives, recognize and reward proponents, and identify and persuade resistors. They then must maintain this alignment throughout the project. Leaders need to serve as role models for behavior change by exhibiting attention to:

1. Goal: "Leaders recognize and fulfill their new roles."
   - Create a leadership strategy that will produce the alignment, involvement, and contribution necessary to successfully implement the innovative and entrepreneurial supply chain business blueprint.
2. Key actions:
   - Recognize that the leaders identified here are not just the formal leaders of the organization but include the informal leaders throughout the organization.
   - Develop relationships between the leadership and the core and change management teams to ensure a partnership throughout the implementation.
   - Gain the shared commitment and accountability of key leaders for the new business blueprint.
   - Educate and develop key leaders on their role as change agents.
   - Provide key leaders with real-time feedback and coaching regarding leadership issues such as alignment, involvement, and contribution.
3. Indicators of success:

- Implementation of the project is on time and within budget.
- Employee beliefs about the organization's leadership are positive:
    - *Alignment:* the workforce is focused and committed to a common vision and goals.
    - *Involvement:* participation in the project is high among affected employees.
    - *Contribution:* employees have clear and meaningful ways to make a difference in the project's success.
    - *Commitment:* employees act out of personal interest and accountability in the project.
- Targeted business results are achieved.

Communication *of the Transition to Entrepreneurial Supply Chains*

An effective communications program requires a set of sound principles, a set of clearly articulated goals and objectives, sound overall plans, effective execution, and continued monitoring and feedback. Early in the change process, there is a need to develop and implement a detailed communication plan in terms of what

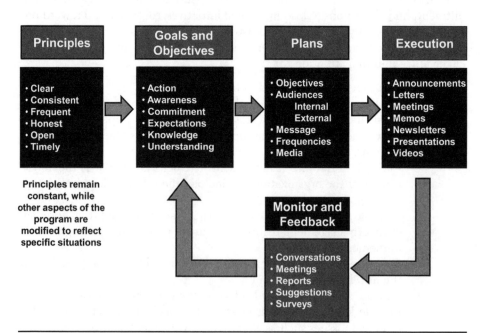

Figure 7.8   Effective Communications Programs.

messages to communicate, to whom, when, and how (what media). A structure of the process might look like the one shown in Figure 7.8.

The project team needs to communicate the project purpose, scope, and time-table via newsletters, memos, meetings, and presentations. As the project progresses, the communications program needs to continue. Throughout the project, status and progress reporting are needed, and the message needs to be personalized in terms of "what-this-means-to-me." The communications plan could look like this:

1. Goal: "Clear communication to and understanding by all stakeholders."
   - Stakeholders' clear understanding of . . .
     - The purpose and business case for innovation and entrepreneurship.
     - The picture and vision of what success means.
     - The plan and path forward for implementation.
     - The part each person, group, and organization plays in the process.
   - Active two-way communications between stakeholders and project management.
     - Open and honest communications . . . repeated.
     - Active feedback and critique throughout the project.
2. Key actions:
   - Develop, continuously update, and implement communications plans.
   - Actively solicit and act on feedback from all stakeholders.
   - Monitor and assess the effectiveness of the communications.
3. Indicators of success:
   - The various stakeholders understand how entrepreneurship and innovation impacts them.
   - Feedback from the various stakeholders is incorporated into the project.
   - The communications program is tailored to local needs.

Commitment *to the Transition to Entrepreneurial Supply Chains*

Commitment to the change program is achieved through targeted participation and involvement. Building commitment is a process. People take more responsibility for implementing ideas that they helped to create. When people participate and are committed, they feel more "in the loop" and trust the organization. Involvement helps people to feel more "in control" over their lives in times of change. More creativity results from allowing many people to participate in the change process, as well. People either participate in change, or they anticipate change and speculate on it. Anticipation and speculation usually are not effective ways to manage change and may be incorrect.

Commitment to creating innovative and entrepreneurial supply chains is increased by utilizing project teams in a variety of ways, such as:

- Change imperative team(s) early in the process can help establish early commitment;
- Visioning team(s) can help people understand the to-be state of affairs with innovative and entrepreneurial supply chains;
- Redesign and build team(s) can help people participate in the redesign and building of supply chain processes;
- Implementation team(s) can help the organization successfully implement the new and/or revised innovation and entrepreneurial supply chain processes; and
- Continuous improvement team(s) use feedback from the implementation so as to continuously improve the processes.

Key people should be involved in creating the change, in a variety of ways:

- Early in the process, identify target individuals and groups who will lead, or at least not resist, the change. There are organizational and cultural diagnostic tools that can be used to identify, analyze, and assess major issues and common themes, and these should be used.
- Informal influence leaders should be involved throughout the process; if informal leaders are not on the side of change, it will not happen or it will not happen with efficiency.
- Key resistors need to be brought into the process; they can do more damage outside of the process than inside it.
- Conduct challenge sessions with senior management and project teams.
- Involve process owners and participants in process redesign, building the new processes, and implementation.
- Utilize appropriately chosen focus groups to develop creative solutions.

Work to build a strong consensus for the change and the ultimate vision throughout the process, from the earliest point onward:

1. Goal: "Committed individuals and groups working together."
   - Impacted employees believe in the value of the project enough to change.
2. Key actions:
   - Involve stakeholders in project design and decision-making to ensure ownership in the results.
   - Build the perception and belief that the project is in the stakeholders' own best interests and that change is both possible and desirable.
   - Reinforce participation through recognition and reward.

- Communicate support and resources to be provided so stakeholders believe they can be successful in the new organization.
- Recognize and deal with typical responses to change.
3. Indicators of success:
   - Stakeholders are involved in design efforts.
   - Employees contribute to design teams, feedback sessions, and implementation teams.
   - Employees believe that their efforts are rewarded.
   - Employees' attitudes toward the project are positive.

Education and Training *for the Transition to Entrepreneurial Supply Chains*

Education and training programs should be designed with specific objectives for specific audiences. *Education* is different from training:

- Education builds "knowledge about . . ." and "understanding of . . ."
- Training builds "skills in using or doing."

The following are examples of education and training programs.

1. Senior management
   - Content:
     - Innovation and entrepreneurship education programs
     - Visioning and creativity workshops
     - Change management education
   - Instructional methods:
     - Facilitated discussion
     - Case studies
2. Core team members
   - Content:
     - Innovation and entrepreneurship education programs
     - Innovation and entrepreneurship skills training
     - Visioning and creativity workshops
     - Change management education
   - Instructional methods:
     - Facilitated discussion
     - Case studies
     - Lectures
     - Exercises
3. Process participants
   - Content:
     - New roles and responsibilities in innovative and entrepreneurial supply chains

- Innovation and entrepreneurial supply chain functionality and operation
- Instructional methods:
  - Facilitated discussion
  - Classroom training
  - On-the-job training
  - Job rotation
  - Self-study
  - Exercises

Education and training is an important behavioral change lever.

1. Goal: "Enhanced awareness, knowledge, understanding, and skills."
   - Individuals should have appropriate awareness, knowledge, and understanding about the relevant business processes for entrepreneurial and innovative supply chains.
   - Individuals should have appropriate technical skills required to maximize entrepreneurial and innovative supply chains.
   - Individuals should have appropriate interpersonal and team skills required to do their new or revised jobs.
2. Key actions:
   - Assess competencies of individuals against defined job requirements.
   - Identify education and training needs to fill competency gaps:
     - Technical
     - Non-technical
   - Determine education and training delivery mechanisms.
   - Deliver education and training.
3. Indicators of success:
   - Employees have appropriate levels of awareness, knowledge, and understanding to become entrepreneurial and innovative.
   - Employees have the skills necessary to effectively perform new and changed jobs.
   - Entrepreneurial and innovation business processes are utilized effectively and appropriately.
   - Employees are satisfied with education and training received.

Workforce and Organization Transition *to Entrepreneurial Supply Chains*

When the organization, business processes, and jobs are redesigned, people need to be re-matched with the organization. Some people will lack the required new skills, and training will be required. Some new capabilities will be needed, and hiring programs will need to be adjusted. Some people will not desire or will not be able to adjust to the new environment, and will need assistance to find alternative career paths.

1. Goal: "Redefined organization, jobs and job roles, and responsibilities."
   - Job designs and organization structure align with the new entrepreneurial and innovative business processes.
   - Impacted individuals feel that workforce transition issues are handled fairly and objectively.
2. Key actions:
   - Job design: define new jobs and competencies as required.
   - Organization: realign organization to fit new entrepreneurial and innovative business processes.
   - Transition:
     - Match the right people to the right jobs.
     - Identify actions necessary for employees to become effective.
3. Indicators of success:
   - Employees feel that they are fairly treated.
   - Employees feel energized and enthusiastic about possibilities within the new organization.
   - Employees know what is expected of them and how to do it.
   - New organization fits the new entrepreneurial and innovative business processes.

Results Orientation *Transition to Entrepreneurial Supply Chains*

1. Goal: "Measured performance improvement."
   - Agreement on the organization's improved target performance goals.
   - Target performance measures are met, including successful implementation of entrepreneurial and innovative supply chains.
2. Key actions:
   - Determine target performance measures and set performance standards.
   - Ensure that employees know what is expected of them and how their contribution fits into the overall objectives.
   - Redesign measurement and reward systems to support new jobs, organization structure, and overall expectations.
   - Manage to achieve target performance.
3. Indicators of success:
   - Improved individual and organization performance targets are met.
   - Entrepreneurial and innovative supply chains are successfully implemented.

HOW BAKER HUGHES IMPLEMENTS CHANGE

When Art Soucy was hired, Baker Hughes faced enormous challenges with its supply chains, and significant change was required. Baker Hughes' implementation of change was focused on how the company put significant innovations into practice in its supply chains. Some of these innovations involved making the supply chains more entrepreneurial. But more importantly, the innovations were concerned with overall improvements, up to and including major transformations of the supply chains.

When Art Soucy took over as Vice President, Supply Chain at Baker Hughes, he was charged with making a number of important changes. He was asked the direct question: "How would you describe the magnitude of the changes you faced with the supply chains when you began in this job?"

"Transformational!" That may have been an understatement, given the magnitude of what had happened to the company in the not-so-distant past.

Art was hired in April 2009. Prior to May 4, 2009, Baker Hughes was organized primarily through seven product-line divisions and secondarily through four "super-regions" that spanned North America, Latin America, Europe, Africa, Russia Caspian, the Middle East, and Asia Pacific (MEAP). It is fair to say that the company operated in a highly decentralized manner with semi-autonomous units around the world.

On May 4, 2009, the company implemented a new organization structure by geography and product lines. Global operations were reorganized into a number of geo-market organizations, reporting to nine regional presidents who, in turn, reported to two hemisphere presidents. Separately, product-line marketing and technology organizations reported to a president of products and technology. Reporting to the Chief Operating Officer are the presidents of Western Hemisphere, Eastern Hemisphere, Products and Technology, Chief Information Officer, and Vice President, Supply Chain (Soucy).

The geographic organizations are responsible for sales, field operations, and well-site execution. This means that the client-focused operations' reporting structures are aligned with the countries in which the company does business. The products and technology organization is global and responsible for product development, technology, marketing, and delivery of cross-product-line solutions to enable customers to enhance their reservoir performance.

Soucy's supply chain organization also was global. He became responsible for procurement, in-bound logistics, manufacturing, and out-bound logistics to support the above organizations in a cost-effective (and highly legal) manner. As of 2010, manufacturing operations were located in the United States (Texas, Oklahoma, Louisiana), United Kingdom (Scotland, Britain), Germany, South America (Venezuela, Argentina), Singapore, and the Middle East (United Arab Emirates, Saudi Arabia).

Since taking over his responsibilities, Soucy initiated new entrepreneurial manufacturing enterprises in Mexico, China, Russia, and Thailand. He also has sold several operations. There were a number of reasons for new ventures that included access to low-cost manufacturing (to offset the concentration on high-cost U.S., UK, and Germany), to comply with local-content requirements, and to be physically closer to the customers.

Soucy was hired to help implement the company's shift in its strategy from a highly decentralized to a much more centralized structure. Hence, there was a major focus on change and effective change management within that organization because a change program of this magnitude is an extraordinarily risky exercise.

The six primary elements of the formal change program are called "behavioral change levers," using the metaphor of a "lever" to accomplish change. This harkens back to Archimedes' quote, "Give me a place to stand and with a lever I can move the world." The six elements are: leadership, communications, education and training, commitment, workforce and organization transition, and results orientation.

Baker Hughes has not explicitly used the six-step framework for its change management program, as outlined in Figure 7.6. Nevertheless, based on discussions, Soucy indicated that it made sense for what he tried to accomplish. He stated that the company's performance was strong on those same six people-oriented change levers. He particularly approved of his leadership support, saying it had been "great." He also had good things to say about how the transition process worked, with people generally responding very well to what had to be accomplished, although he admitted that there (not surprisingly) was some "questioning from below." All in all, the process appeared to have been carried out fairly effectively for a large-scale change effort. Of course, the change effort was not completely finished, and is ongoing.

A CASE NOTE FOR FURTHER STUDY: 3M Corporation

The cases are available at www.harvardbusinessonline.com. Readers should obtain copies of this case and use it to go beyond discussion in the book. These cases were prepared as the basis for discussion, rather than to illustrate either effective or ineffective handling of any particular situation.

This section is adapted from multiple sources.[2] Because 3M Corporation has been written about extensively, these are only a few of the available sources.

On its corporate website, 3M says that it is: "A global technology company delivering innovative solutions to life's everyday needs. . . . Serving customers through six business segments, 3M finds ways to make life better and easier." As to its history, the company was founded in 1902 to mine mineral deposits for abrasives, but that proved to be of little value. They later moved into sandpaper and dozens of other products, all having a technological base.

Innovation at 3M

3M has long been known as an innovative company. They have defined *innovation* in different ways.

- An innovation is a *user* innovation when the developer (firm or individual) expects to benefit by using it. This creates "demand pull" for the innovation— "You make it, and I will buy it and use it."
- An innovation is a *manufacturer* innovation when the developer expects to benefit from manufacturing and selling it. This creates "supply push" for the innovation—"If 3M makes it, they will buy it and use it."

3M's preference was user innovations. That is what led them to "lead user" research. (See the von Hipple, Thomke, and Sonnack reference, and the cases by Thomke, listed at the end of the chapter). This approach was an attempt to understand leading-edge customer needs and thus help 3M return to its roots of working more closely with customers. A *lead user* is someone who experienced needs ahead of others and was motivated to innovate on his or her own. These individuals were invaluable sources of innovative ideas.

3M eliminated its market research department in favor of lead user research. The Vice President of Corporate Marketing was quoted in the Thomke (A) case (2002, page 6) as saying, "We didn't learn anything from our market research department. . . . Traditional market research couldn't deliver the goods. . . . So we ended up eliminating the market research department to learn about customer needs!" Furthermore (on the same page of the case cited just above), the head of research and development was quoted as saying, "Traditional strategic planning does not leave enough room for innovation." (These are interesting quotes. Your author does not recall ever seeing anything like them before.)

Lead user research followed a disciplined four-stage approach with some allowance for overlap between the stages. This is not much different from the stage-gate process for product development:

1. Project planning
2. Trends and needs identification
3. Preliminary concept generation
4. Final concept generation. This stage usually includes a two-and-a-half-day workshop on the concept.

Entrepreneurship at 3M

Another Harvard Business School case, "3M: Profile of an Innovating Company,"[2] discussed how 3M developed and maintained the culture and practice of innovation. Early in its history, the company developed an appreciation (and tolerance) for the power of individual entrepreneurs—no matter how idiosyncratic they may be. Furthermore, matching technology to customers' needs became a general guiding principle for the company. Its early legacy was of technological innovation, market responsiveness, institutionalized entrepreneurship, and sharing of knowledge among employees.

However, 3M did not think of itself as a "high-tech" company. Rather, it preferred to describe itself as "a creative company that needs a high level of technology." Thus, *growth through innovation* became its mantra. 3M had a formal objective that "25% of its sales should come from products introduced within the most recent five-year period." [Please note: these cases and articles speak to 3M's objective—sometimes it's 25% of its sales and sometimes it's 30% of sales. Obviously, there is not much difference, but different sources quote different numbers.]

The company recognized that niche markets could be profitable, so it encouraged this individualized entrepreneurial behavior. Further, management recognized that many products and technologies subsequently found applications far beyond the ideas of the original entrepreneur.

The company also did not punish mistakes, which they called *well-intentioned failure*: "Management that is destructively critical when mistakes are made kills initiative, and it is essential that we have many people with initiative if we are to continue to grow." Perhaps the most well-known "failure" at 3M is the story of the scientist who was trying to develop a strong adhesive, but it turned out to be a very weak one. The Post-It® notes product line was the result!

Also, part of 3M's change management process was organizational. They observed that when a division reached a certain size, it had a tendency to spend too much time and effort on existing products and markets and not enough on new ideas. They implemented a plan to break out new businesses, to appoint a new management team, and to charge them with a renewed emphasis on innovation and growth. But, as 3M grew, this approach generated too much fragmentation of effort, so they reorganized again into sectors through which they could gain more focus on innovative ideas. This helped to identify underperforming businesses, such as the copier business, which was spun off into a joint venture. This led to a more disciplined technology development process.

An interesting exhibit is contained in the "3M: Profile of an Innovating Company" case (p. 18). It is 3M's "technology tree," which shows how one technology grew out of others. Other companies could consider this type of representation to understand the importance of building on technologies.

The "3M Optical Systems" case illustrates how 3M has created a culture of institutionalized entrepreneurship. The expectation within 3M was that even front-line managers will take action, behaving as an entrepreneur and a champion of ideas developed in his or her part of the business. However, culture starts at the top. A CEO needs to set the tone as a strong supporter of entrepreneurship and innovation for the organization. He or she must make sure that the standards, principles, philosophical values, and convictions that are the underpinning of the company are maintained and strengthened.

Strategic Stories at 3M

Another part of 3M's success is in its strategic planning process (see the reference to "Strategic Stories" in the endnote). The point of 3M's process is that people remember stories. A good story (and good strategic plan) defines relationships, a sequence of events, cause and effect, and priorities. These elements are likely to be remembered as parts of a complex whole, which argues for strategic planning through storytelling. This approach is very similar to scenario planning, which was pioneered by Royal Dutch/Shell, and was discussed in chapter 4 earlier in this book.

An Aside: An update to these 3M cases appeared in *Fortune* magazine as part of a 2010 series on Fortune 500 companies. The article cites data to describe 3M[3]:

- 3M had $23.1 billion in revenue and $3.2 billion in net income in 2009, placing them number 106 on the Fortune 500 list. 2010 sales were up 21% and net income was up 43% in the first half of 2010.
- 90% of U.S. homes use transparent tape.
- 1,000 layers of optical film are required to produce a product, like a window reflector, that is no thicker than a sandwich bag.
- 3,072 shares of 3M stock today equal one of the original shares issued in 1946.
- 40,000 global patents and patent applications are held by 3M with about 25% having been filed in the United States.
- 1 trillion 3M diaper tape tabs have been sold in the United States.
- The amount of Scotch Transparent Tape, a 3M product, which is sold *annually* in the U.S. would circle the globe 165 times.

The *Fortune* article observes that "3M has long been synonymous with innovation . . . [and] has deployed a range of practices to promote out-of-the-box thinking." These include giving its researchers up to 15% of their time to pursue their own ideas. 3M awards annual grants allocated by their peers, of up to $100,000, to company scientists for research.

"Our business model is literally new-product innovation," the article quotes Larry Wendling, who oversees 3M corporate research. The goal is "to generate 30% of revenue from new products introduced in the past five years." For one thing, they have achieved this by keeping R&D spending at high levels even during the recession of the late 2000s. They have kept the focus on empowering researchers to "restore the luster" of 3M.

A FINAL WORD ON IMPLEMENTING ENTREPRENEURIAL SUPPLY CHAINS

This chapter has presented some ideas, concepts, tools, and techniques that deal with the management of large scale and significant change. It rests on the theory that implementation of innovative and entrepreneurial supply chains require change to the business processes perhaps in all companies except start-ups.

Readers should develop a formal change program for the transition to innovative and entrepreneurial supply chains. This includes assessing readiness for change, preparing a change management plan, and utilizing the six change levers to implement change.

3M has been described as one of the United States' most innovative and entrepreneurial companies, and readers can learn a great deal from 3M's practices.

ASSURANCE OF LEARNING QUESTIONS

The following questions will help you to check yourself on the chapter content:

1. What do you think of the assertion that "human nature has two sides" (shown in Figure 7.3)? How can you incorporate these ideas in your change management plans?
2. Explain the real meaning of the six change levers: leadership, communication, commitment, education and training, workforce and organization transition, and results orientation.
3. Explain what 3M does to try and be effective as an innovative and entrepreneurial company.
4. Many companies have tried to replicate the Toyota Production System (TPS) without Toyota's success. (TPS was not discussed in this book.) Do you think that 3M's innovation and entrepreneurial success can be replicated in other companies? Why or why not?

REFERENCES

1. Kotter, John P. *Leading Change: An Action Plan from the World's Foremost Expert on Business Leadership*. Boston: Harvard Business Review Press, 1996.
2. A few of the many citations of 3M and its management practices are found in: Bartlett, Christopher A., and Afroze Mohammed. "3M: Profile of an Innovating Company." Harvard Business School Case #9-395-016, January 3, 1995. Bartlett, Christopher A., and Afroze Mohammed. "3M Optical Systems: Managing Corporate Entrepreneurship." Harvard Business School Case #9-395-017, Rev. May 28, 1999; Shaw, Gordon, Brown, Robert, and Philip Bromiley. "Strategic Stories: How 3M Is Rewriting Business Planning." *Harvard Business Review*, May/June 1998; Thomke, Stefan. "Innovation at 3M

Corporation (A)" and "Innovation at 3M Corporation (B)." Harvard Business School Cases #9-699-012 and #9-699-013, Rev. July 23, 2002; von Hipple, Eric, Thomke, Stefan, and Mary Sonnack. "Creating Breakthroughs at 3M." *Harvard Business Review*, Sept./Oct.1999. These are available at www.harvardbusinessonline.com

3. Gunther, Marc. September 27, 2010. "3M's Innovation Revival: How the company that brought you 55,000 products from Scotch tape to Thinsulate, got its mojo back." *Fortune*, 73–76.

CHAPTER 8

REAPING THE PAYOFF

LEARNING OBJECTIVES

1. Gain awareness of why the ideas behind entrepreneurial supply chains are not new.
2. Be able to discuss continuous improvement and how it is (or might be) used in your company.
3. Learn about innovation in its various forms, and why Drucker said that "to be effective, an innovation has to be simple."
4. Develop an understanding of how Baker Hughes and Sysco reap the payoff of entrepreneurial activities.

"[Plans] must lead to action; desultory talk without operational content produces paralysis."

—Dr. Henry A. Kissinger

"Most innovations, especially the successful ones, result from a conscious, purposeful search for innovation opportunities, which are found only in a few situations."

—Peter F. Drucker

Interviewer: "Tell me, Mr. Sutton, why do you rob banks?"
Willie Sutton: "Because, that's where the money is."

—Anonymous

Dr. Henry Kissinger's quote is appropriate for reaping the payoff from an entrepreneurial supply chain venture. The key questions involve *what* will be done, *who* will do it, *when* will it be done, and *what* will be the results. Plans that lead to action are what the business venture is all about. This book is subtitled, *A Guide to Innovation and Growth*, but innovation does not just happen. It is the result of a "conscious and purposeful search" as Drucker says. This book outlines some of the ways that such conscious and purposeful searching can occur and what is the expected result. The third quote has been famous for years. It illustrates why we have entrepreneurial and innovative supply chains—because that's where the money is!

This chapter deals with how companies can measure and manage the payoff and continuously improve the entrepreneurial supply chain process. It is a "where we go from here" analysis.

A HISTORICAL NOTE ON REAPING THE PAYOFF THROUGH INNOVATIVE AND ENTREPRENEURIAL SUPPLY CHAINS

Commodore Cornelius Vanderbilt has been cited as the second richest person in the history of the United States. He certainly "reaped the payoff" by making his fortune through innovation and entrepreneurial supply chains in the 1800s when that terminology had not been invented.

An Aside: I graduated from Vanderbilt University in Nashville, TN, with an undergraduate degree. As such, I have always been interested in Commodore Vanderbilt (1794–1877), but did not know much about him until reading a really interesting book called *The First Tycoon* by T. J. Stiles.[1] Stiles provides an outstanding description of the essence of entrepreneurial supply chains, although he does not use that term. Mr. Vanderbilt had never heard that term, either, but nevertheless that is what he created in an innovative way—time after time—and got wealthy doing so.

Early in his book, Stiles discusses an incident (pp. 12–13) with the Duc de la Rochefoucauld-Liancourt, who was standing in the late 1790s on the Battery at the southern tip of New York's Manhattan Island. Capturing the Frenchman's imagination were the Americans' busy stores and workshops, new buildings being erected, ships passing by in the harbor, and other signs of an economy that was full of life. He boldly predicted that America would attain a degree of prosperity, which in the future would render this part of the world a successful rival of Europe. If he had only known how right he was. Also, if he only knew of entrepreneurial supply chains!

The New York Times[2] estimated that Vanderbilt was the second richest person in U.S. history, second only to John D. Rockefeller, another supply chain entrepreneur. But Rockefeller's wealth obviously was built in the oil business. (Bill Gates was estimated to be number 5 on the all-time list, and Warren Buffett was listed as number 16.)

KEY IDEA
If the government was entrepreneurial and innovative, then high-speed rail would have been developed by AMTRAK.

Stiles's book should be required reading in business schools for at least three reasons. First, it describes the rise of entrepreneurship in the United States during the early-to-mid 1800s. Vanderbilt reportedly began his entrepreneurial career at the age of 16, ferrying freight and passengers between Staten Island and Manhattan—the predecessor of the modern Staten Island Ferry. He used what was known then as a "periauger," a shallow-draft sailboat with two masts. There is some dispute about whether he actually owned the boat or whether it was owned by his father. Nevertheless, the story goes that he received at least half the profits (if his father owned the boat) or all the profits (if he owned it). The book illustrates Vanderbilt's numerous other entrepreneurial ventures throughout his life and how they made him the richest person in the United States at the time.

Second, the book portrays the development of modern integrated supply chains, particularly in the transportation of goods and people. Ferries and other boats were used for transportation around New York, New England, New Jersey, and Philadelphia, PA, and around Long Island Sound and Upper and Lower New York Bay and the Hudson River. Vanderbilt built his businesses so that he dominated water-borne transportation using sailing vessels and, later, steamships. The integration occurred because the water transportation required connecting with railroads, which led Vanderbilt into the railroad business.

Third, the book describes business practices that, were they used today, likely would have landed Vanderbilt and many others in jail. There was stock manipulation, insider trading, fraud, and all sorts of double dealing. Vanderbilt apparently fancied himself as a very honest (albeit very tough) businessman, according to the standards of the day.

Cotton was one commodity that contributed to Vanderbilt's rise. Cotton, of course, at the time typically was grown on plantations in the southern part of the United States. It was cultivated, harvested, and processed largely based on slave labor. Originally, much of it was shipped from the South through New York (later, directly from Southern ports) to New England and to Europe. Vanderbilt began to dominate cotton shipping from the South in the 1830s.

Vanderbilt believed in vertical integration, although he apparently did not use those words. *Vertical integration* is where a single owner takes control of businesses at every step of the supply chain, from mining raw materials, growing crops and animals, and drilling for oil and gas, to production of finished goods. A vertically integrated company could capture profits (or reduce costs) at every point. Perhaps more important, in an age when few industries existed, it helped to ensure supply that otherwise might be diverted to a competitor (p. 201). Vanderbilt's water and railroad enterprises were vertically integrated, and he sometimes achieved integration through means that would not be entirely legal or ethical today.

The term *consolidations* seems quaint, an old-fashioned version of the currently popular phrase "mergers and acquisitions," yet it was fraught with portentous meaning in the 1860s. Vanderbilt's consolidation of railroad companies into others, and then into an empire, would mark a profound change in the way business was conducted in the United States (p. 367).

REAPING THE PAYOFF THROUGH CONTINUOUS IMPROVEMENT

Continuous improvement is one of the cornerstones of "reaping the payoff" from entrepreneurial activities and is humorously shown in Figure 8.1. The point is that we must continuously improve on the original ideas that led to the formation of the entrepreneurial supply chains in the first place. Some of these improvements are breakthrough ideas and some are minor, but we need both.

Figure 8.2 conceptually shows the process of continuous improvement. The first circle demonstrates the beginning of the process without any improvement. The arrows are all pointing in different directions, illustrating that the entire

Figure 8.1   Improvement Ideas Are Not Always Obvious to Everyone.

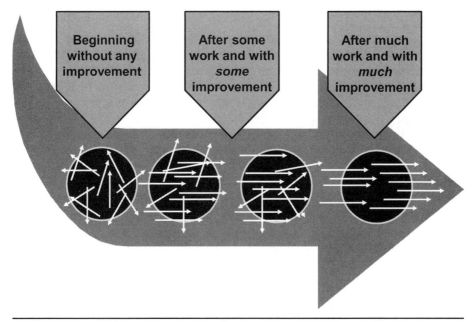

Figure 8.2 So, Why Are We Interested in an Improvement *Process?*

organization is uncoordinated and lacking a common direction. The middle circles in Figure 8.2 illustrate *some* improvement after *some* work. Then, of course, the last circle shows a coordinated, synchronized, and organized process. The figure is intended to demonstrate abstractly the approach to continuous improvement for entrepreneurial supply chains. That is, continuous improvement consists of a series of relatively minor improvements, the sum of which leads to major improvements.

Continuous improvement is just that—a continuous process of making incremental improvements, that is, many small improvements rather than a few large-scale or radical changes. The small improvements are likely to be easier and less expensive to implement than far-reaching or extreme improvements. A continuous improvement process is an ongoing effort to improve products, services, or processes. Improvement can be measured in multiple ways, such as efficiency, effectiveness, speed, cost, and flexibility. However, it is doubtful one ever reaches the end of the process; more improvements always can be made.

The essence of a continuous improvement process is shown in Figure 8.3. When we look at how different companies approach continuous improvement,

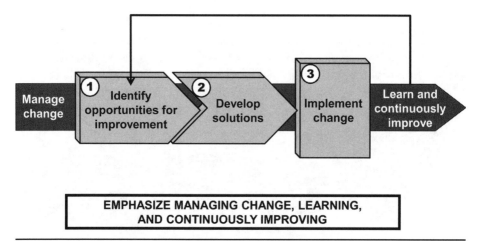

Figure 8.3   Three-Phase Continuous Improvement Approach.

many variations on this three-phase process are observed. However, the three steps capture the fundamental nature of the approach:

1. *Identify opportunities for improvement.* Discussed in Chapters 3 and 4, the process of identifying opportunities has the objective of defining the nature and perhaps the size of the entrepreneurial supply chain improvement prospect.
2. *Develop solutions.* Chapters 5 and 6 dealt with this subject. Solution development tends to result from a deep and rigorous set of analyses with the outcomes being agreement and commitment to achieve the necessary change.
3. *Implement change.* Covered in Chapter 7, implementation is about making change happen. It involves taking the agreed-upon recommendations, developing specific action steps, executing these steps, and ensuring that the benefits are achieved.

Notice that the process moves from "manage change," on the left of Figure 8.3, to "learn and continuously improve," on the right. Throughout the improvement process, there is a need to manage the change process, as discussed in Chapter 7. There also is the need to learn and continuously improve both the change process and the business processes that are the focus of the change.

During change, "learning" is the operative word. In this context, the word does not refer to learning in the academic or scholarly sense; rather it means to learn how to get better at what is being done. We try something, see what the results are, and then modify or change the process—getting better at both the change process and the business processes that are the focus of the change. We find out what works and what doesn't work, becoming more skilled in the process, and thus discover and understand more. Also, people frequently say, "We learn how to learn." During the process of continuous improvement, learning how to learn naturally takes place. In the interest of showing how learning continues, a framework adapted from the author's work as a consultant with Deloitte & Touche is provided in Figure 8.4. This framework consists of eight interlinked components, each of which provides a unique and useful perspective on the continuous improvement process. A practical way to use this framework is to start at the end—the right-hand-side of the figure—and to analyze it backwards. For example, if the objective was to improve a company's product development processes as part of an overall entrepreneurial supply chain improvement project, start with a definition of customers and customers requirements, and go (backwards) from there.

Customer requirements would be what the customers want to see out of the product development process. But who are the "customers"? Are they internal or external to the organization? Real (buying) customers obviously would be customers of the process, but also what about various organizations within the company? Manufacturing must be able to make the product, finance must be able to provide funds for development and at least initial manufacturing, and procurement must be able to source the components, perhaps throughout all the company's organizations. So, a definition of "who is/are the customer(s)" and "what do they want" might be a first step in improvement. Generally, this is a

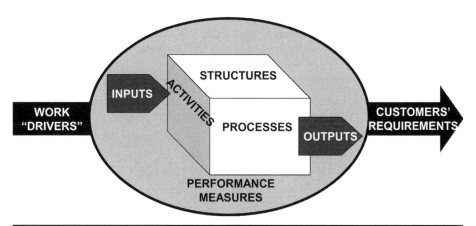

Figure 8.4 Analytical Tool Framework. Adapted from: "Renewing Organizational Infrastructures: Program Manual," a Deloitte & Touche Consulting Client Service Program. There is no date on the material in your author's possession, but it likely is from the late 1980s or early 1990s.

good first set of questions in any supply chain improvement activity, especially when creating entrepreneurial supply chains.

Performance measures, as shown in Figure 8.4, provide a means, first, to examine and evaluate current performance based upon existing measurement systems. This likely would occur at the beginning of an improvement project. Supposedly, the company already has a product development process and an existing set of performance measures. Second, performance measures provide a way to consider how well the organization meets the customer requirements and what improvements might be required to meet them more fully. It also is important to consider how the performance measures affect organizational behavior, and vice versa. Third, after the improvement project is finished, performance measures provide an ongoing test to ensure that the improvements have actually accomplished the objectives of the project. For almost any supply chain improvement project, performance measures might be composed of some variation on efficiency, effectiveness, speed, or cost. But, obviously determining performance measures is more complex than just individual metrics. The following are examples of the more complex questions to be asked for a new product development process.

Process Design
- How flexible is the new product development process?
- How well does the new product development process link with customers?
- Is the new product development process reliable?
- Will the new product development process provide the desired results?
- Is the new product development process scalable?
- Can the new product development process be used for different types of products?
- Does the new product development process match corporate values?
- How does the new product development process compare with best practices across various industries?

Process Change
- To how many and what types of initiatives should the new product development process be applied?
- How should new ideas be incorporated and improvements implemented to the new product development process?

Process Thinking
- Do people understand the new product development process in general?
- Do people understand the new product development process in detail?
- Do people understand the case for change with the new product development process?
- Do people link the new product development process with the overall objective of creating entrepreneurial supply chains?

Outputs from the improved product development process would be many. The improvement project could focus on the delivery of products and services to the customers as they have been defined above. The ultimate output of the new product development process would be achieving a stable production rate and customer acceptance in the marketplace. Some examples of specific outputs likely would be something like what are contained in the following statements:

> *The new product development team's responsibility to the customer is the idea that development has not succeeded until volume rates and deliveries are met and the customers are happy with the product. The customers are the final validation of the process. As part of the output from the process, the operational and maintenance training materials are finalized. The lessons learned from the program are drafted, accepted, and disseminated. All organizational development, training, and manpower issues are completed. The deliverable is a smoothly running new product and production process, ready for use by the entire organization. Further, the final gate review process is completed.*

Activities and processes, also shown in Figure 8.4, portray how work is accomplished. Many times, these are described as a hierarchical structure. Think about *processes* being composed of multiple *sub-processes*, which are composed of multiple *activities*, and which are composed of multiple *tasks*—like the following outline.

1. *Processes* tend to be *cross-functional, cross-businesses,* and *cross-geography.* The new product development process certainly would cross various business units, and might include marketing to identify market segments and customer requirements, engineering to design the product, manufacturing engineering to design the production processes, manufacturing to make and ship the product, accounting to price the product, sales to sell the product, and so on across most organizations within the company. Clearly, this meets the criteria of a process.
2. *Sub-processes* tend to be contained within one *discipline* or *function,* such as "design the product" within the engineering discipline. Sub-processes, by definition, are subordinate to the overall process.
3. *Activities* tend to be contained within specific *groups,* such as mechanical engineering, that designs the mechanical components of the new product. Activities are subordinate to sub-processes.
4. *Tasks* tend to be performed by specific *individuals,* such as an individual mechanical engineer who is responsible for designing a single component or group of components. Tasks are subordinate to activities.

Structures tie all the above together through processes, organizations, functions, groups, and so forth like the "glue" that joins these as one.

Inputs could be a resources, operations, and development master activity plan (ROADMAP) for the new product development process. Resources could be human resources and capabilities of various types from engineering, manufacturing, quality assurance, reliability, supply chain, facilities, marketing, sales, finance, accounting, and so forth. Operations could include facilities, equipment, and technology upon which the organization is based. Input requirements likely would be based on the outputs, activities, processes, structure, and performance requirements of the organization.

Work drivers will be the outcome of the overall master activity plan for the development of a specific new product. The detailed plan for a particular new product likely will contain at least dozens if not hundreds of activities and thousands of tasks. Each task and each activity may result in one or more work orders of some sort, which become detailed "work drivers." In another context, invoices received from suppliers could be work drivers for the accounts payable organization.

A core project team and other interested groups that are focused on continuous improvement put it all together, as shown in Figure 8.5. This integration begins at the top with senior leadership such as the "C-Suite" executives, senior leadership team, vice presidents, and business unit leaders. Many companies will have a core project team for continuous improvement that will include people such as a steering committee, project sponsors, project leadership, functional expertise, analytical resources, technical resources, or consulting resources. Finally, other interested parties could include key employees or managers. Figure 8.5 indicates that all of these individuals and groups are integrated around the continuous improvement project.

What is trying to be achieved with the continuous improvement process is shown in Figure 8.6: both improvement and innovation. While the term *continuous improvement* tends to refer to a series of relatively small, incremental changes, the term *innovation* tends to refer to larger, more substantive changes.

As readers have probably figured out, continuous improvement is akin to *operations improvement* and to striving for *operations excellence*. But don't stop there because these are terms that refer to improving on more-or-less existing modes of operation. What if we break out of those ways of thinking and look for new ways of doing things, like what Michael Hammer[3] calls *operational innovation?*

Hammer cited Wal-Mart, Toyota, and Dell as companies that achieved success through operational innovation—essentially rethinking how to do work in their industries. He suggested that innovations in areas such as procurement, new product development, and post-sales customer support as places where operational innovation could have the most effect on achieving key strategic goals. Interestingly, these are all areas of interest for entrepreneurial supply chains.

Hammer mentioned Taco Bell as an unlikely candidate for operational innovation and discussed how they began to think of their restaurants in manufacturing rather than fast-food terms. For example, they outsourced food preparation to

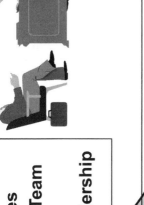

Senior Leadership

"C-Suite" Executives
Senior Leadership Team
Vice Presidents
Business Unit Leadership

Core Project Team
Steering Committee
Project Sponsors
Project Leadership
Functional Expertise
Analytical Resources
Technical Resources
Consulting Resources

Other Interested Parties
Key Employees
Other Employees

Figure 8.5   Integrated Organizational Approach.

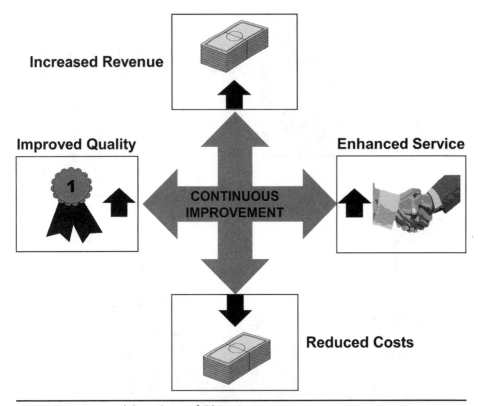

Figure 8.6   Focused On a Suite of Objectives.

outsiders, centralized the production of key components, and concentrated on assembly rather than fabrication in the restaurants. The author has seen examples of companies that essentially did the same thing as Taco Bell by thinking in terms of other industries which, on the surface, seemingly had little in common with their own operations.

REAPING THE PAYOFF THROUGH INNOVATION

Before we begin the discussion of reaping the payoff through innovation, let's ask ourselves: "What is an innovation?" A useful reference source is the Oxford American Dictionary and Thesaurus (2003), which provides the following definition and synonyms:

> **Innovation:** *The act or process of inventing or introducing something new; a new idea, invention, or way of doing something; the creation and delivery*

of new customer value in the marketplace that also provides a sustainable return to the entrepreneurial supply chain venture.

Innovation: *originality, inventiveness, creativity, imagination, novelty, modernization, alteration, change.*

Ideas of Drucker, McKinsey, Baumol, Schumpeter, and Rogers

Peter F. Drucker[4] once discussed the discipline behind innovation. He said that, "In business, innovation rarely springs from a flash of inspiration." He cited seven sources of innovation, all of the citations below resulted in entrepreneurial supply chain ventures:

> **KEY IDEA**
>
> "To be effective, an innovation has to be simple . . . Indeed, the greatest praise an innovation can receive is for people to say, 'This is obvious! Why didn't I think of it? It's so simple!'" SOURCE: *Peter F. Drucker*

1. *Unexpected occurrences* are often dismissed, disregarded, or resented. Yet history shows that many successful innovations and entrepreneurial ventures resulted from unexpected events. Take 3M's famous Post-It® notes, about which most people are familiar, that resulted from a failed adhesive experiment.

2. *Incongruities* often appear in different forms. Drucker cites an incongruity in cataract surgery of the 1960s, in which a part of the surgery was incongruous with the rest of the procedure. Alcon Laboratories added a preservative so an enzyme could be used in the surgery. Suddenly, cataract surgery was transformed, with many more people taking advantage of it.

3. *Process needs* for innovation occur as part of the process of doing something else. Companies such as Baker Hughes mentioned how needs can occur for new process technologies that enable them to produce new or improved products; or, a supplier may have ideas for making a component that will enable them to improve another product.

4. *Industry and market changes* often create massive opportunities for innovation. Pundits cite how retailing companies such as Sears and Kmart fell by allowing arrogance to blind them to changes in U.S. retailing trends. They did this without the help of innovative companies such as Amazon .com, which was just in its infancy when Kmart first began running into trouble. Amazon.com arose from developments in Internet technology that enabled them to revolutionize retailing online.

5. *Demographic changes* create fairly predictable opportunities because demographics typically change relatively slowly. Demographics refer to population characteristics such as age, location, gender, ethnicity, income, and level of education. Entrepreneurial supply chains are fairly common

in consumer goods. For example, fluctuating birth rates can change demand for baby products in the short-to-intermediate term and for products that cater to teenagers in the long term.

6. *Changes in perception* can occur because of new awareness, knowledge, and/or understanding. Witness the recent rise of discussions about "sustainable development" and "sustainable supply chains." In this context, *sustainability* means that the needs of the present are met without reducing the ability of future generations to meet their needs. But hasn't the need for sustainable development been around for centuries? Of course it has, but we have become more aware of it and have begun to understand it better only in recent years. That's a change in perception that has given rise to multiple innovations and entrepreneurial ventures as a result.

7. *New knowledge* often is required for innovations to occur. Frequently, new knowledge actually is a convergence of several strands of knowledge that someone finally puts together to create something new. Amazon.com was mentioned several times as having been enabled by Internet technology and by new ideas about entrepreneurial supply chains.

McKinsey's survey of senior managers shows that they typically give lip service to innovation, but how much further they are willing to go is sometimes unclear. A 2007 survey by McKinsey[5] cited some 70% of corporate leaders as saying that innovation is among their top three priorities for driving growth. However, the survey also indicated that companies do not manage as if they believe that. They responded to the survey by saying that they manage innovation in an *ad hoc* manner. Their responses indicate where some of their priorities lie:

- 64% said, "We determine where to focus innovation efforts."
- 52% said, "We make commercialization decisions."
- 50% said, "We decide who will work on innovation projects."

And, yet, the following low-response comments illustrate these ad hoc approaches:

- 24% said, "We set innovation budgets."
- 22% said, "We set innovation performance metrics and targets."

Further, less than 50% of the top management respondents said that innovation is a core part of the leadership agenda. The takeaway from this survey is that executives said innovation is very important, but their companies' approach to it was often minimalist and informal, and leaders lacked confidence in their innovation decisions, maybe for good reason! Altogether, the survey results were not very encouraging.

William J. Baumol[6] ties innovation to entrepreneurship. He distinguishes between "replicative" and "innovative" entrepreneurs. He believes that "the vast majority of all entrepreneurs appear to be of the replicative variety." It seems logical to assume that the innovative entrepreneur generally is the creator of the small start-up firm. However, to the extent that innovation is a function of funding, he points out that the larger firms increasingly provide the bulk of (so-called) innovation funding in the United States. But, it also is logical to assume that large firms' innovation spending incorporates little of the creative, risk-taking approaches that one usually associates with the entrepreneur. Conceivably, that's why we get the line extensions which we have discussed previously. Also, maybe that's why Baumol seems to heap less praise on successive models of washing machines and refrigerators—each new model is a bit longer-lasting, a bit less susceptible to breakdown, and a bit easier to use—all of which are the result of continuous improvement. Perhaps that is why a currently popular phrase is "corporate entrepreneurism." However if one is a cynic, one might say that corporate entrepreneurism is an oxymoron!

> **KEY IDEA**
>
> "Innovation is not a homogeneous product." SOURCE: *William J. Baumol*

Joseph A. Schumpeter[7] was a supporter of innovation and entrepreneurship—which of course puts him right in line with this book. He acknowledged that innovation takes various forms, and he believed that innovation is a critical aspect of organizational change. He said that one can innovate with new products, new methods of production, new markets, new sources of supply, or new organizations. This reinforces Baumol's "Key Idea" in the sidebar, that innovation is not a homogeneous product. Innovation varies.

Schumpeter also popularized the idea of creative destruction, which perhaps is his most famous contribution to the history of management thought. This is not unlike the discussions in this section of the ideas of others who wrote on innovation. He characterized creative destruction as a basic result of innovation and entrepreneurship. Simply put, when innovation occurs and entrepreneurial ventures are formed, they have the tendency to break up the established order.

Everett M. Rogers[8] generally is credited with popularizing the ideas behind how innovations are spread among people and organizations. Figure 8.7 explains Rogers' ideas on innovation diffusion: 2.5% of people are innovators; 13.5% are early adopters; 34% are early majority people; 34% are late majority people; and 16% are laggards. "Innovators" are usually predisposed to take risks in trying something new. "Early adopters" tend to set the tone for others to accept the innovation. They are considered to be opinion leaders who are looked to by others with respect. "Early majority" individuals generally look to others for leadership, but are open to trying an innovation once it is shown to be useful. "Late majority" people are skeptical and tend to wait until most people have adopted the innovation. Finally, "laggards" sometimes never get the word! They exhibit almost no opinion leadership, and sometimes are described as "being dragged kicking and screaming" into the mainstream.

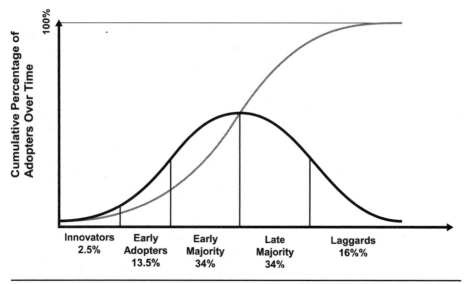

Figure 8.7   Diffusion of Innovations. Source: Rogers, Everett M., *Diffusion of Innovations*, 1962, Free Press.

Rogers proposed in his book that four elements influence the spread of a new idea: the innovation itself, the communication channels through which the message is propagated, time as determined by the rate of adoption, and a social system which could be considered to be organizations. His definition of *innovation* is similar to the one given above.

Rogers also stated that the process of innovation diffusion takes place through five stages: knowledge, persuasion, decision, implementation, and confirmation.

So, what does all this mean for the subject of this book? From Drucker, innovation is the result of discipline and there are a number of sources (he cites seven) of innovation, each of which has some relevance to entrepreneurial supply chains. From comparing the McKinsey survey with Drucker's ideas of innovation being hard work, we see why real innovation is so rare in large companies—executives are insincere about innovation and forget the hard work that it requires. Baumol reminds us that innovation and entrepreneurship are tied together; without innovation, it is hard to have entrepreneurship. Schumpeter's ideas of creative destruction illustrate what happens when innovative entrepreneurs are successful and dislodge established companies. Finally, Rogers demonstrates how innovations are diffused throughout organizations and the economy. All of these tie into the ideas of creating entrepreneurial supply chains.

REAPING THE PAYOFF THROUGH CLOSED OR OPEN INNOVATION

The ideas behind "open innovation" have gained popularity in the past few years. But, if there's an "open innovation," it stands to reason that there must be something called "closed innovation." But what's the difference?

Innovation is the introduction of something new. The new can be, according to Schumpeter, new products, methods, sources of supply, markets, or organizations.

Let's talk first about closed innovation. What we now call closed innovation historically has been the approach of organizations that have the "not invented here" (NIH) syndrome. Simply put, *closed innovation* occurs when innovations are conceived, developed, and implemented solely within a given business, business unit, or organization.

Someone once said: "If you want it done right, do it yourself." This idea seems to appeal to companies that are strongly vertically integrated and/or have strong centralized management control. Also, it can appeal to companies that have an outstanding research and development (R&D) organization that thinks it has all the expertise needed by the company. But, whatever the reasons, many companies do not want to allow information about their innovations to get out.

The seemingly deep-seated idea of closed innovation is that innovation cannot be fully successful without control and ownership of the intellectual property (IP) that results from the innovation. Many companies feel that their R&D activities are so proprietary that they must be kept internal and secret from their competitors. They also seem to feel that it is the only way for them to be first to market with new discoveries and developments.

On the other hand, the primary disadvantage of closed innovation is that those involved cannot collaborate with anyone else who might have a more diverse set of knowledge and information. One popular expression is that when R&D is done totally internally, people within the same organization "all drink the same Kool-Aid." Those involved "know what they know" and perhaps at best "know what they don't know," but they certainly "don't know what they don't know." Some people call these the "knowns," the "known unknowns," and the "unknown unknowns." Maybe others know what these people don't know (if all that makes sense)!

Open innovation occurs when innovation activities are open to people outside of the particular business unit. This can be either outside the entire business or simply in another business unit within the same company. Open innovation can occur in a variety of ways according to *Inside Supply Management*,[9] the magazine of the Institute of Supply Management:

- Business unit to business unit;
- Crowdsourcing with internal employees;
- Collaborating with suppliers;

- Partnering with external solutions providers;
- Licensing/buying an existing solution; and
- Crowdsourcing with the external public.

Procter & Gamble (P&G) is one company that has been doing open innovation successfully for a number of years and has written about it in the *Harvard Business Review*.[10] P&G calls its approach "Connect + Develop," that is, they *connect* with others and *develop* the ideas that they obtain. They seek to find good ideas and bring them into the company to enhance and capitalize on their own internal R&D, manufacturing, marketing, purchasing, and other capabilities. According to the corporate website in 2011:

> "*P&G's Connect + Develop open innovation strategy has established more than 1,000 active agreements with innovation partners. Connect + Develop allows us to share our R&D, commercialization, and brand strength with partners worldwide, bringing great ideas to market—and into the lives of consumers—faster.*"

They go on to say that over 50% of their product initiatives involve significant collaboration with outside innovators.

KEY IDEA
"#1 Most Innovative." SymphonyIRI Group recognized P&G as the most innovative manufacturer in the consumer packaged goods industry for the last decade with its "Outstanding Achievement in Innovation" award. SOURCE: *P&G 2010 Annual Report*.

P&G cites a number of examples including Olay® Derma-Pod. The fastest-growing Olay sub-brand is the Derma-Pod, a small, one-use portion of Olay with a unique applicator. This deal focused on packaging and design, and was done with Cardinal Health.

On March 24, 2011, P&G announced a master agreement with Teva Pharmaceuticals to create a partnership in consumer health care by bringing together both companies' existing over-the-counter medicines and complementary capabilities to accelerate growth. The press release mentioned "innovation" several times and projected annual sales in excess of US$1B. Teva will have responsibility for manufacturing outside of North America. While the press release did not mention "Connect + Develop," the venture's description sounds like the result of open innovation. In any case, this appears to be a strong example of "corporate entrepreneurial supply chains."

So why are open and closed innovation being discussed in a book on entrepreneurial supply chains? Simply put, the very nature of entrepreneurial supply chains is an open process. We've said many times that the supply chains connect suppliers and suppliers' suppliers with customers and customers' customers. These are open-loop systems, not closed-loop systems—meaning, that relationships with suppliers and customers are defined by their openness. When companies truly have open-loop entrepreneurial supply chains, they are open to innovations and ideas from wherever they may happen.

REAPING THE PAYOFF BY THE MOST ADMIRED COMPANIES FOR INNOVATION

Every year, *Fortune* magazine conducts a survey for its "Most Admired Companies" list. Since innovation is a key attribute of this book, the top ten of the 2011 list[11] of most admired companies were, in order: Apple, Google, Berkshire Hathaway, Southwest Airlines, Procter & Gamble, Coca-Cola, Amazon.com, FedEx, Microsoft, and McDonald's. Unlike in the past, *Fortune* did not break out its rankings for innovation except to mention Apple as number 1.

Fortune listed the attributes on which they based their ranking. They listed the top companies on each attribute both before the recession (2007) and after the recession (2011). Apple came out on top in the attribute of "innovation" both pre- and post-recession. Here are the nine attributes and the leading companies in 2007 and 2011:

- Ability to attract, develop, and keep talented people
  - 2007: General Electric   2011: Goldman Sachs
- Effectiveness in conducting its business globally
  - 2007: Nestle   2011: McDonald's
- Innovativeness
  - 2007: Apple   2011: Apple
- Quality of management
  - 2007: Procter & Gamble   2011: McDonald's
- Quality of products and services
  - 2007: Anheuser-Busch   2011: Amazon.com
- Responsibility to the community and environment
  - 2007: UPS   2011: Statoil
- Soundness of financial position
  - 2007: ExxonMobil   2011: Google
- Value as a long-term investment
  - 2007: Berkshire Hathaway   2011: Google
- Wise use of corporate assets
  - 2007: ExxonMobil   2011: McDonald's

KEY IDEA

Successful entrepreneurship requires innovation.

Fortune commented significantly on which companies came out on top of the rankings, and interestingly, of the nine attributes about which *Fortune* asked in the survey, eight had new companies leading the category.

GE had long been considered as the best in the world at developing people, but no longer. In 2011, it was Goldman Sachs. P&G no longer was considered best at the quality of management, now it was McDonald's. In fact, McDonald's was the leader in three attribute categories, and Google the leader in two. These are interesting changes in *Fortune*'s ranking; the magazine commented: "Good times may be when you make the most money—but bad times may be your greatest opportunity."

REAPING THE PAYOFF THROUGH EFFECTIVE ENTREPRENEURIAL SUPPLY CHAIN STRATEGY

So, what is an entrepreneurial supply chain strategy, and why bring it up again? Strategy is the pursuit of competitive advantage. Michael Porter[12] says the following about that:

> *Competitive strategy is the search for a favorable competitive position in an industry, the fundamental arena in which competition occurs. Competitive strategy aims to establish a profitable and sustainable position against the forces that determine industry competition.*

KEY IDEA
Strategy is the pursuit of competitive advantage.

Could it be that a company's strategy could simply be stated as: "*Our strategy is to be entrepreneurial and innovative.*" Thompson, Strickland, and Gamble,[13] in a popular textbook on strategy (in its 17th edition), say the following about what makes a strategy a winner:

1. "How well does the strategy fit the company's situation?
2. Is the strategy helping the company achieve a sustainable competitive advantage?
3. Is the strategy resulting in better company performance?"

If a company's strategy is to be entrepreneurial and innovative, and if it fits the above three points, it is possible that a company can have a successful strategy of being entrepreneurial and innovative. However, there needs to be a "how-to" vision linked to that strategy—a vision that says something about how the company intends to develop and implement the business model that will achieve the strategy. Saying you want to be entrepreneurial and innovative is necessary, but far from sufficient.

KEY IDEA
40% of the companies in the S&P 500® were not there 10 years ago.

This is true particularly if the company wants to base its entrepreneurial and innovative strategy on its supply chains, as in the context of Figure 8.8. The Balanced Scorecard has become a popular mechanism to focus attention on several components of a management system, such as:

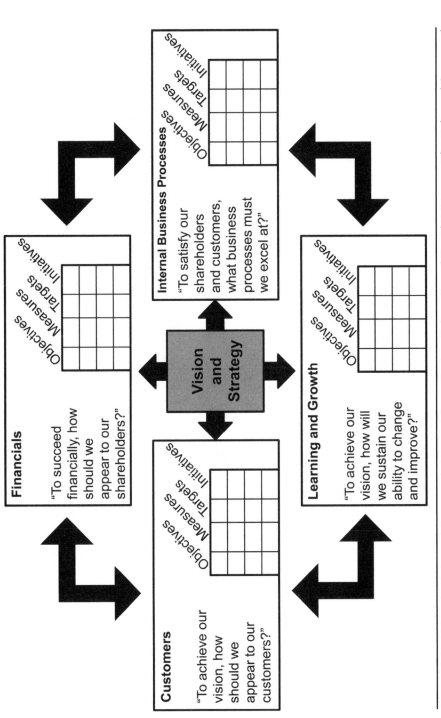

Figure 8.8 Using the Balanced Scorecard. Adapted from: Kaplan, Robert S. and David P. Norton, *The Balanced Scorecard*, Harvard Business School Press, 1996.

1. *Clarifying and translating vision and strategy.* A vision needs a strategy linked to it to become entrepreneurial and innovative. A strategic plan is then needed to do this. As in the "Key Idea" sidebar, a strategic plan identifies where we are currently, where we're going, how we plan to get there, and what performance targets will define as the point of arrival at "there."

> **KEY IDEA**
>
> A strategic plan identifies where we are currently, where we're going, how we plan to get there, and what "there" is, i.e., the performance targets that define the point of arrival.

2. *Communicating and linking strategic objectives and measures.* It is a simple fact that people will not buy into a strategy unless they understand it and have it linked to something tangible that they comprehend. When the Balanced Scorecard is implemented properly, it is linked up and down the organization so that all levels and units have visibility into how they fit into the total puzzle. This requires a significant communications program and laying out a set of linked performance measures.

3. *Planning, setting targets, and aligning strategic initiatives.* What is the exact point of arrival, and how do we know when we have arrived? The strategic plan should look about five years ahead. That is, there should be a five-year plan of what will be the strategic initiatives and what the performance targets will be. This plan should encompass the four elements of the Balanced Scorecard in Figure 8.8: the financials, customers, internal business processes, and learning and growth. It also should include how these four elements fit together and mutually reinforce each other.

4. *Enhancing strategic feedback and learning.* This takes place through quarterly reviews of performance. Notice that each of the four elements in Figure 8.8 contains objectives, measures, targets, and initiatives. These are the pieces of the quarterly reviews of performance.

In summary, Thompson, Strickland, and Gamble present the strategy-making, strategy-executing process (pp. 24ff), as shown in Figures 8.9, 8.10, and 8.11. The Entrepreneurship Maturity Model is a good synopsis of the process discussed throughout this book, and is a useful framework for succeeding in entrepreneurial supply chain endeavors.

Figure 8.9 illustrates a fairly straightforward five-phase process that builds on a strategic vision, from which objectives are set, and a strategy is crafted, implemented, and executed. From there, developments are monitored, performance is evaluated, and corrective adjustments are made. Then, these are all revised as needed in light of actual performance, changing conditions, new opportunities, and new ideas. This approach looks relatively simple in concept, yet it is excruciatingly difficult in practice.

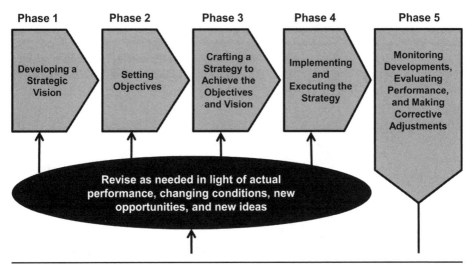

Figure 8.9   The Strategy-Making, Strategy-Executing Process. Adapted from: Thompson, Arthur A., Jr., A. J. Strickland III, and John E. Gamble, *Crafting and Executing Strategy: The Quest for Competitive Advantage, Concepts and Cases, 17th Edition*, Page 24, McGraw-Hill Irwin, 2010.

Figure 8.10 is another fairly simple illustration of a difficult process, "capturing the value with entrepreneurship capability," building directly on Figure 8.9. Most companies and many people have at least a modicum of capability on the first level, "what a business is able to achieve with current entrepreneurship capability." That assumes, of course, that they follow a logical process, such as outlined in this book. Otherwise, they will not accomplish any more than they have in the past. As the old saying goes, "The height of futility is continuing to do the same thing and expecting different results."

The next level of Figure 8.10 shows "what a business could achieve practically with enhanced entrepreneurship capability." Think of this as the level of capability that could be achieved by implementing focused ideas, concepts, tools, and techniques, some of which are presented in this book. This is the *delta* over and above the current capability, also known as "winning"! Finally, the top level of Figure 8.10 illustrates in theory what a business could achieve with advanced entrepreneurial capability. Of course, the three levels in this figure are merely conceptual, with no quantification on the measurements. Nevertheless, they are useful to help think about the different levels of capability to which a company might aspire.

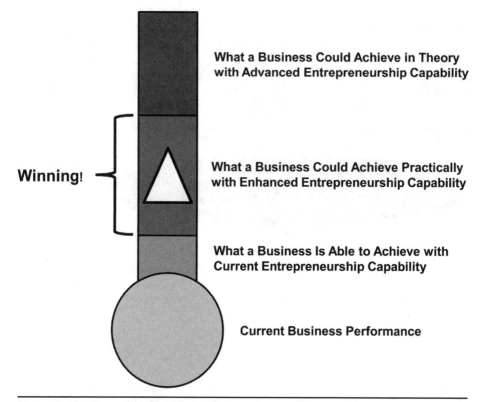

Figure 8.10   Capturing the Value with Entrepreneurship Capability.

Figure 8.11 is a more complex illustration of the process, showing an entrepreneurship maturity model. This model points out a four-phase "maturity": think long term, begin to deliver value, expand and build capability, and scale up to achieve long-term value. Notice that the four levels of capability are arrayed against "business performance," with performance increasing as maturity increases. Each level of maturity contains a description of its meaning.

HOW THEY REAP THE PAYOFF AT BAKER HUGHES

In the five years immediately prior to this writing, Baker Hughes has made 19 acquisitions and four divestitures. In the oil and gas industry, broadly defined, the company certainly has not done the most acquisitions and divestitures, but neither has it done the least. However, they have been one of the more successful companies with entrepreneurial ventures.

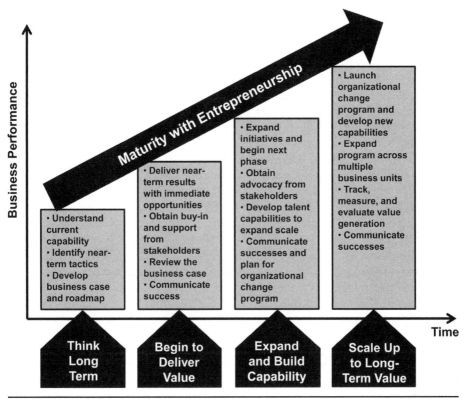

Figure 8.11   Create an Entrepreneurship Maturity Mode.

In April 2010, Baker Hughes closed on a major venture when they acquired BJ Services, a large provider of pressure pumping and oilfield services. BJ Services was the third-largest provider of pressure pumping services, whereby slurry, often sand and water, is injected into an oil or gas well to stimulate production. Pressure pumping is used in unconventional gas plays such as shale formations to break up rock. This qualified as an entrepreneurial supply chain venture in the sense that the acquisition filled a missing link in Baker Hughes' go-to-market strategy of being a full-service company vis-à-vis its largest competitors, Schlumberger and Halliburton.

An interesting note regarding this transaction is that BJ Services earlier was part of Baker Hughes, but was spun off in 1990. However, the two companies have worked closely in the meantime; whenever the company needed pressure pumping services, they called on BJ Services and vice versa whenever BJ Services needed products or services that Baker Hughes could provide.

The financial benefits from the BJ Services acquisition were to be both revenue enhancement and cost synergies. The revenue enhancement was almost all of BJ Services' revenue, since there was relatively little overlap in the two companies' businesses. Baker Hughes told the financial communities that the cost synergies would be about $75M in year 1 and year 2. Most of that was in SG&A.

Over 20 task forces were set up from the two legacy companies to manage the integration and reap the benefits. Since the two companies essentially did not have any overlapping products or services, the operations aspect of the integration was relatively straightforward. On the other hand, the SG&A aspects of the integration were more complex. Pay and benefit scales were different and had to be reconciled, and headcount needed to be rationalized.

So how did they reap the benefits from acquisitions? One thing that has made Baker Hughes' acquisitions successful is that they have a global infrastructure into which they can integrate acquisitions. Oil and gas is a global industry, and companies wishing to be major players in the industry must have a global presence. This means, for example, that the company can relatively quickly take the products or services of an acquired company into a global market, whereas the acquired company may have been too small to do that before being acquired by Baker Hughes. So, one way they can "reap the benefits" is to be able to leverage this global infrastructure.

A CASE NOTE FOR FURTHER STUDY: Sysco Corporation

The cases are available at www.harvardbusinessonline.com. Readers should obtain copies of this case and use it to go beyond discussion in the book. These cases were prepared as the basis for discussion, rather than to illustrate either effective or ineffective handling of any particular situation.

> **KEY IDEA**
>
> Sysco's Mission: To market and deliver great products to our customers with exceptional service. Sysco's Vision: To be our customers' most valued and trusted business partner. SOURCE: www.sysco.com

Sysco[14] was founded in 1969 and went public in 1970. Its entrepreneurial founder, John F. Baugh, is said to have had a vision of a national company distributing products for food service enterprises. On its website,[15] Sysco claims to be "the global leader in selling, marketing, and distributing food products to restaurants, healthcare and educational facilities, lodging establishments, and other customers who prepare meals away from home. Its family of products also includes equipment and supplies for the foodservice and hospitality industries." Sysco is headquartered in Houston, TX, and as of July 3, 2010, Sysco operated 180 distribution facilities throughout the United States, Canada, and Ireland, with approximately 46,000 employees. With 14,000 sales and marketing professionals, Sysco's sales force was larger than those of the next nine largest competitors combined.

The company annually distributes over 1 billion cases of food and related products to over 400,000 customers in the United States, Canada, and around the world. Sixty-two percent of Sysco's customers are restaurants, 11% are hospitals and nursing homes, 6% are hotels and motels, 5% are schools and colleges, and 16% are "other."

Sysco is subject to the U.S. Federal Food, Drug, and Cosmetic Act, which is administered by the U.S. Food and Drug Administration (FDA), as well as numerous regulations promulgated thereunder. Similar regulatory bodies in Canada and other countries in which Sysco operates have their own requirements to which Sysco is subject.

Sysco has been widely recognized by *Fortune* magazine and others. In *Fortune*'s "most admired companies" published in 2010,[16] Sysco was ranked as number 1 overall in the Wholesalers: Food and Grocery industry. (*Fortune* said that due to a poor response rate for that ranking, only overall industry scores were reported. Individual attribute rankings were not reported.) However, in *Fortune*'s rankings of March 16, 2009, Sysco was ranked as follows in its industry:

> *Sysco ranked first in financial soundness, innovation, long-term investment, people management, quality management, quality of products and services, social responsibility, and use of corporate assets. They ranked second in global competitiveness.*

Please note that the *Fortune* "most admired" rankings published in 2011 did not include Sysco—they dropped the Wholesalers: Food and Grocery category altogether.

In the Fortune 500 listing published in 2011,[17] Sysco ranked 67th among the 500 companies in size, and number 1 among "Wholesalers: Food Industry," with $37.2B in sales and $1.2B in profit. This was substantially ahead of the second company, CHS, in the industry. CHS was number 103 in size with $25.3B in sales and $502M in profit.

Sysco describes itself as having a foundation of an entrepreneurial culture. They make an important point for an entrepreneurial company when they say on their website, "we are only successful if we help them [our customers] be successful." The case writer asserts that the Sysco entrepreneurial culture produced three important results:

1. An entrepreneurial, iterative do-it-better mentality;
2. An openness to change; and
3. A passionate focus on the details of execution day in and day out.

At its essence, Sysco is a company that excels at execution.

William B. Day, Executive Vice President, Merchandising and Supply Chain, has an interesting title that links merchandising with supply chain, a good idea for a company with entrepreneurial supply chains. Sysco's website discusses its 50,000-plus "business reviews" with its customers. Sysco's business review process is an in-depth consultation that covers everything from menu planning to inventory management, all with the goal of helping its customers' run their businesses more efficiently and profitably. This is an entrepreneurial activity that helps Sysco's customers sell more of Sysco's products. Thus, everyone benefits—they all sell more, and learn from each other.

An Aside: Business reviews with customers are an important consideration for any company that aspires to be more entrepreneurial; plus, expanding the idea to business reviews with suppliers is an interesting and useful addition. Companies with entrepreneurial supply chains need to look carefully for opportunities to connect better with both suppliers and customers. This was discussed in more detail in Chapter 3, but it bears repeating as one important way to reap the payoff from entrepreneurial supply chains.

The case writer observes that Sysco's "growth historically had come primarily from domestic geographical expansion, product expansion, new-customer segments, and operating efficiencies. Underlying its results had been a growing market for the number of meals eaten outside the home." (Note: The growth rate for meals eaten away from home has slowed since the case was written, and this presented Sysco with challenges to its historical growth rate.)

Sysco has an interesting entrepreneurial venture that operates in an adjacent space from their traditional food service distribution business. This is Guest Supply, a lodging industry operating company that distributes personal care guest amenities (shampoo, lotions, etc.), equipment, housekeeping supplies, room accessories, and textiles to the lodging industry. This clearly is adjacent to Sysco's primary business of serving food service establishments and the food service units of hotels, hospitals, and schools. This is out of the ordinary for Sysco, as the company generally is careful about entering adjacent products and markets. However, it has been a successful undertaking. Guest Supply operates nationwide and independently from Sysco's other businesses.

The case writer, Professor Edward D. Hess of the Darden School of the University of Virginia, is well known for his research into how companies grow. He cites Sysco's evolutionary growth pattern as having happened in the following order of steps, where Sysco:

1. Expanded geographically;
2. Increased product offerings to include nonfood supplies for existing customers;
3. Segmented customers into four price-point segments for greater focus;
4. Expanded into specialty and ethnic foods;
5. Added services to help its customers be more successful;
6. Focused on cost efficiencies; and

7. Redesigned its supply and distribution chain for additional cost efficiencies.

Sysco entrepreneurially introduced its own private labels in 1975. Clearly, they had to set up the supply chains to be able to accomplish this, recognizing that many suppliers would not produce and/or package private-label products, especially if they were in competition with their own brands.

Their broad range of private-label products enhances Sysco's entrepreneurial culture. Sysco-branded product lines deliver the quality and variety their customers demand and extend the product portfolio beyond what is available from the branded-products companies. Sysco has effective relationships with most if not all of the well-known major national and regional brands. Thus, Sysco is able to offer its customers a selection of their private-label products combined with well-known national and regional brands. These provide both distinctive and cost-effective solutions to the needs of its customers. The company also has many specialty and one-of-a-kind products for the unique needs of customers. In total, Sysco offers their customers approximately 400,000 stock-keeping units (SKUs) of which roughly 40% are Sysco brands. This breadth and depth of products contributes to Sysco's own entrepreneurial capabilities and also allows it to support its customers' entrepreneurial undertakings.

From information on the Sysco website, it appears that their entrepreneurial and innovative culture began with Sysco's founder, John F. Baugh, who passed away in 2007. He is described as "a true visionary, a legendary entrepreneur." He apparently set up the company's decentralized structure that gave significant autonomy to the operating companies and empowered their leadership to act entrepreneurially in their market area. It appears that this culture has been successful for the company, and it evidently continues to this day.

Sysco has expanded globally. Worldwide, Sysco conducts business in more than 100 countries. Their International Food Group was created to distribute both food and non-food products to international customers. This appears to be a major growth area for Sysco.

Throughout the case, the word, "entrepreneur," was mentioned many times. Clearly, the case writer felt that Sysco was a superbly entrepreneurial company. Your author agrees.

A FINAL WORD ON REAPING THE PAYOFF

This chapter has focused on reaping the payoff from entrepreneurial supply chain ventures. It began with a historical discussion of Commodore Cornelius Vanderbilt and how he developed his empire using the ideas and concepts of entrepreneurial supply chains, although he did not know the term. Commodore Vanderbilt became the second richest person in the history of the United States, and clearly reaped a substantial payoff from those ventures!

Once an entrepreneurial supply chain venture is launched, continuous improvement is necessary. Continuous improvement programs work well and play out to reap the payoff.

Innovation plays an important role in reaping the payoff from entrepreneurial supply chain ventures. Of all the keys to success, innovation perhaps is the most powerful.

Finally, the Baker Hughes case illustrates how one company reaps the payoff. Also, in the case of Sysco, a large food-service distribution company, this shows another company's success at entrepreneurial supply chains.

ASSURANCE OF LEARNING QUESTIONS

The following questions will help you to check yourself on the chapter content:

1. Research the life of John D. Rockefeller and about how he made successful businesses with entrepreneurial supply chains. Put together a brief write-up that compares and contrasts him with Commodore Cornelius Vanderbilt.
2. Continuous improvement is a powerful concept that is used extensively in all sorts of companies. If your company has a continuous improvement program, look into how it is run and how successful it is.
3. Integrate the ideas of Drucker, Baumol, Schumpeter, and Rogers into your own definition of *innovation* and what it means to you.
4. This chapter focused primarily on corporate entrepreneurship. How do you think these ideas would differ, if at all, for start-up companies?
5. Research Sysco beyond what was presented in this chapter. What do you think have been the top three ideas that have made the company successful?

REFERENCES

1. Stiles, T. J. *The First Tycoon: The Epic Life of Cornelius Vanderbilt*. New York: Vintage Books/Random House, Inc. 2009.
2. Uchitelle, Louis. July 15, 2007. "Age of Riches: The Richest of the Rich, Proud of a New Gilded Age." *The New York Times*.
3. Hammer, Michael. April 2004. "Deep Change: How Operational Innovation Can Transform Your Company," *Harvard Business Review*. (84–93)
4. Drucker, Peter F. August 2002. "The Discipline of Innovation." *Harvard Business Review*.
5. Barsh, Joanna, Capozzi, Marla, and Lenny Mendonca. October 2007. "How Companies Approach Innovation: A McKinsey Global Survey." *McKinsey Quarterly*.

6. Baumol, William J. *The Microtheory of Innovative Entrepreneurship*. Princeton University Press, 2010. Princeton, 2010.

7. Schumpeter, Joseph A. *The Theory of Economic Development*. Translated from the Original German by Redvers Opie. Harvard University Press, Boston, 1936.

8. Rogers, Everett M. *Diffusion of Innovations*. Free Press, New York, 1962.

9. Yuva, John. "Closed and Open Doors of Innovation." *Inside Supply Management*, 22(2), 26–30.

10. Huston, Larry, and Nabil Sakkab. March 2006. "Connect and Develop: Inside Procter & Gamble's New Model for Innovation." *Harvard Business Review*. (58–66).

11. Colvin, Geoff. March 21, 2011. "The World's Most Admired Companies." *Fortune*.

12. Porter, Michael E. *Competitive Advantage: Creating and Sustaining Superior Performance*. The Free Press, New York, 1985.

13. Thompson, Arthur A., Jr., Strickland III, A. J., and John E. Gamble. *Crafting and Executing Strategy: The Quest for Competitive Advantage, Concepts and Cases*. 17th ed. McGraw-Hill Irwin, New York, 2010.

14. Hess, Edward D. "Sysco Corporation." Darden Business Publishing, University of Virginia, Case #UV0874, 2007.

15. See http://www.sysco.com for more information (accessed January 2011).

16. *Fortune*, March 22, 2010.

17. *Fortune*, May 23, 2011.

18. Hofheinz, Paul, "Europe's Tough New Managers," *Fortune*, September 6, 1993, p. 111.

19. Templin, Neil and Jeff Cole, "Manufacturers Use Suppliers to Help Them Develop New Products," *The Wall Street Journal*, December 9, 1994, p. 1.

APPENDIX A

VISIONING ENTREPRENEURIAL SUPPLY CHAINS

LEARNING OBJECTIVES
1. Articulate how creativity and visioning work together and, particularly, how they help to develop a vision for entrepreneurial supply chains.
2. Develop an understanding of how a visioning retreat might work for your company, including potential topics, list of attendees, and deliverables.
3. Understand why "the journey is more important than the destination."
4. Learn about VF's "growth plan" and how it might apply to your company.

"Where there is no vision, the people perish."
—Proverbs 29:18, King James Version

"At no time am I a quick thinker or writer: whatever I have done in science has solely been by long pondering, patience, and industry."

—Charles Darwin

Human beings need to have a vision of what *is* possible and even what *should be* possible. There are actually four components to a vision. The vision is a long-term view, but it starts in the here and now, and shares some components of the path forward. This will be the essence of this chapter.

```
┌─────────────────────────────────────┐
│               KEY IDEA              │
├─────────────────────────────────────┤
│ What's in a vision?                 │
│ 1. Where are we now?                │
│ 2. Where are we going and why?      │
│ 3. How do we get there?             │
│ 4. What barriers are in the way?    │
└─────────────────────────────────────┘
```

The quote from Darwin underscores the tough slogging process of getting to a vision: long pondering, patience, and industry. Clearly, Darwin was one of history's great scientists, but his visions of a natural order did not come easily. He had to work at it. That is true of many visions.

An Aside: In a speech by President John F. Kennedy, at Rice University's football stadium in 1961, he promised that the United States would put a man on the moon, and bring him back safely, by the end of the decade. That was a powerful vision! It also was backed by hard science: the scientists and engineers knew the point from which they were starting (called the "as-is" situation); they mostly knew the path forward in terms of what scientific and engineering breakthroughs would be required, in what order, on what schedule; and they generally knew the barriers that stood in their way. They felt confident enough to give President Kennedy the go-ahead to make his statement.

But there's another lesser-known part of Kennedy's speech: an obvious digression from the main point of his speech but it made an important point in a humorous way. "Why does Rice play Texas in football? Not because it's easy, but because it's hard!" Now that's certainly true, but the President of Rice University later was quoted as saying, "Once in awhile we even beat them—not often, but often enough to keep hope alive!"

Readers should realize that "visioning entrepreneurial supply chains" is not easy—it is difficult. Furthermore, trying to visualize a future state of affairs includes an attempt to understand the starting point, path forward, and barriers that may lie in the way.

CREATIVITY AND VISION

A dictionary and thesaurus[1] gives the following synonyms of *creativity* as: "imaginative, inventive, originative, artistic, original, ingenious, [and] resourceful." Another important word is *creative,* defined as: "inventive and imaginative [and] creating or able to create." There is also the word *create,* synonyms of which are:

"make, cause, produce, form, bring into being, originate, conceive, generate, invent, imagine, think up, frame, forge, fashion, fabricate, manufacture, develop, design, contrive, devise, produce, dream up, initiate, engender, give rise to, spawn, [and] beget."

That's enough—you get the point! There are many ways to describe *creativity,* but we are interested in linking it to visioning and, especially, to visioning entrepreneurial supply chains.

So, what is the process of creativity all about? Please pardon your author for a personal experience if he describes briefly his own creative process in writing this book. Everyone's creative process is unique of course, but maybe there are a few things in common. First, you might want to start with a (probably simple) set of ideas. In this case, that started with three simple concepts that have been among his core beliefs for a long time:

1. *Companies, in general, do not have enough entrepreneurial focus.* Although it may sound harsh, many companies, particularly large ones, lapse into bureaucratic ways of operating because it is easy and entrepreneurship is hard.

2. *Supply chains can offer an important source of ideas and opportunities for entrepreneurial activities.* This is because supply chains, broadly defined, touch both the demand and supply sides of the company. People working on the supply side, or on certain portions of the supply side, are in a unique position to see what suppliers are doing and to gather ideas for opportunities and needs relating to suppliers that can spur entrepreneurial ventures. The same is true on the demand side. On either side, perhaps there is an acquisition or start-up opportunity, or some other entrepreneurial opportunity. Supply chain people should be alert to those opportunities. The same idea should be true if the company has needs that can be fulfilled by entrepreneurial acquisitions, start-ups, partnerships, or joint ventures.

3. *Supply chain personnel do not naturally think entrepreneurially.* They need to develop a vision of the entrepreneurial possibilities, compared with the current reality, as well as to develop the necessary ideas, concepts, tools, and techniques to do something about it. Senge[2] calls this "creative tension". He says:

   ". . . the gap between the vision and current reality is a source of energy. If there was no gap, there would be no need for any action to move toward the vision. Indeed, the gap is the source of creative energy. We call this gap creative tension."

But, what is the *need*; where is the *demand*; and who is the *audience* for the creative vision? These, too, are part of the creative process.

Starting with these three basic concepts and these three questions, the author proceeded to sketch out a description of the potential audience and those needs which would drive demand for a book on entrepreneurial supply chains.

This process created a question of "What content is needed?" An overall outline for the book was then built on the three concepts, and a detailed summary, along with features that would make the book attractive to readers. All this was accomplished in stages, with each stage of the work building on the previous stages.

Next, extensive research was required. The author had been through the process of creating and enhancing entrepreneurial supply chains several times with consulting clients. Plus, he had taught MBA courses and executive education programs on this and related subjects. But he did not want simply to replicate past consulting or teaching, recognizing that other people are experts. The author wanted to ensure that the book contained a diversity of opinion and experiences, so research was extremely important. No doubt you may notice a number of references in every chapter, and a major case study in every chapter along with the Baker Hughes continuing case.

Ultimately, the most important question was, "What do I want to create with this book?" It was not to say, "I published a book!" No, it would be something that would have a lasting impact, that people would truly want to read and have meaning for the future; have something to say that others can use.

Ultimately, the vision had to be broken down into smaller, practical, creative problems. Writing an entire book is a lot of work! The quote from Darwin is appropriate to a book-writing context: "At no time am I a quick thinker or writer: whatever I have done in science has solely been by long pondering, patience, and industry." The author understands perfectly what Darwin was trying to say. Like playing the University of Texas in football—it is difficult!

THE HARD WORK OF GETTING TO A VISION

One of the best books on vision and visioning is by Joseph Quigley.[3] Quigley included little nuggets of wisdom regarding vision throughout his book, and this is one of his best: "Make your vision as clear as your profit goals. Profit alone is not enough to motivate your people. Expand the scope of your vision to address more of the whole person." Quigley does an excellent job of discussing the role of visions and the visioning process in today's organizations; his book is highly recommended.

KEY IDEA
"Vision is the art of seeing things invisible."

Getting to a vision of entrepreneurial supply chains embodies transformative change for most organizations (see Lee and Katzorke Appendices 1 and 2).[4] One way of thinking about managing transformative change is shown in Figure A.1, which includes five steps:

1. *Prepare* for transformation to entrepreneurial supply chains. Since this will be a major change for most organizations, careful preparation is necessary if it is to be successful.

2. *Vision* the entrepreneurial supply chains. The visioning process begins with understanding the baseline or "as-is" situation. It proceeds step-by-step through successively detailed definitions of how the entrepreneurial supply chains should work. Recognize, however, that this step-by-step really is an iterative back-and-forth process. Start with the baseline as-is, go a few steps, then jump to the *benchmarking* process (step 3, next), then back to the beginning. Don't worry about even jumping to the *design* stage (step 4, below) and do some definition of the "to-be" design. This iterative back-and-forth typically is the most effective approach and yields the best result.

3. *Benchmark* entrepreneurial supply chains. A number of companies considered to have at least some elements of entrepreneurial supply chains are highlighted in this book. The benchmarking process could begin with research on some of these companies. References at the end of each chapter tell where to begin the research.

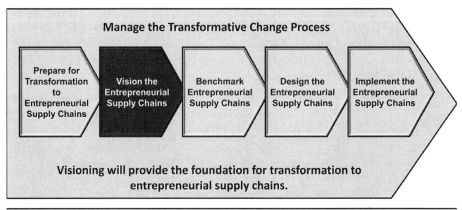

Figure A.1 A Five-Step Approach to Managing Transformative Change. Adapted from: Lee, William B. and Michael R. Katzorke, *Leading Effective Supply Chain Transformations: A Guide to Sustainable World-Class Capability and Results*, Page 179, J. Ross Publishing, 2010.

4. *Design* the entrepreneurial supply chains. Design is a detailed definition of the conceptual vision of the supply chains. This includes detailed process definitions, showing the gaps between "as-is" and "to-be" situations.
5. *Implement* the entrepreneurial supply chains as the final stage of the process.

CULTURAL VISION FOR ENTREPRENEURIAL SUPPLY CHAINS

> **KEY IDEA**
>
> Changing a company's culture is an enormous undertaking.

Without an understanding of the organization's culture, potential barriers to creating entrepreneurial supply chains can be overlooked. Resistance to change almost certainly will happen. In this section, some ideas on how to understand the organization's culture, how to recognize whether there is a need to change it, and how to devise a plan for doing so are presented. The attitudes and behaviors of people (called *organizational culture*) can be either the most positive force for, or the greatest barrier to, change.

So, what is organizational culture? There are hundreds of ways to think about it. In simple terms, organizational culture includes the shared set of routine, customary, ordinary, and expected norms and rules which characterize and strongly influence the attitudes and behaviors of people in an organization or group. These norms and rules affect actions, management style, approaches to problem solving, measures of success and lack of success, and what is appreciated within the organization. Organizational culture perhaps can be described best and simplest as "the way we do things around here."

Failure to change the culture (or the wrong culture change) can be one of the biggest difficulties for an organization.

An Aside: I recently read a fascinating book by Loren Steffy[5] on the "BP oil spill" in the Gulf of Mexico that took place in late April 2010. (When one lives in Houston, it's difficult to stay away from the oil and gas industry, and Steffy is a respected columnist for the *Houston Chronicle*.) While there are multiple opinions on this subject, Steffy did a superb job in describing the successes and failures of offshore oil exploration and production for this critical natural resource. A major point that Steffy weaves throughout the book concerns the culture of BP. In essence, he says, BP gave lip service to having a culture of "safety first," but actually had a culture of "profits first." Steffy cites multiple examples of "do more with less" and similar messages that indicate a culture of "put safety first, but don't spend money to upgrade deteriorating equipment and facilities" (paraphrasing Steffy). While people will agree and disagree with this character-ization, it's an insightful thought that applies in different ways to different orga-nizations. Steffy's conclusion was that BP's culture ultimately was what caused a series of mishaps, including leaking pipelines in Alaska; a deadly explosion at a refinery in Texas City, TX; trading misdeeds; and the massive spill and result-ing environmental catastrophe in the Gulf of Mexico. A similar message came through in a 2010 PBS Frontline program, "The Spill". The report communicates essentially the same material about BP's difficulties and BP's corporate culture. **Full disclosure:** I have done consulting and education work for BP but nothing related to the oil spill.

An organization's culture can be either its greatest asset or its greatest liability when working on entrepreneurial supply chains and other large-scale organiza-tional change efforts. The point is not specifically about BP—it's about a culture of entrepreneurship in supply chains, which is a good thing and not a bad thing! A company can give lip service to entrepreneurial supply chains, but by its ac-tions can communicate that it is not really serious about it. Suppose the company professes to support a culture of entrepreneurship, but at the same time punishes people who move to implement new ideas, particularly if they conflict with other objectives such as, say, short-term profits. That is why it is important to take an honest look at the organization's culture—both professed and actual—and take steps to change that culture if necessary.

Elements of the transformative change process are shown in Figure A.2. Within the organization are the components of the organizational structure, people, and organizational culture. The observable characteristics are the organi-zational structure and the individual people and groups. Largely implicit, but for the most part invisible except by their actions, are individual perceptions, group norms, and culture.

A process should be undertaken to measure the company's culture, seeking a "hard" way to understand the "soft" data on culture. The attempt should be made to identify the organization's readiness to change with entrepreneurial supply chains, identify barriers to change, and measure the degree of change required. To do that, a questionnaire designed for the specific company being assessed is a good idea. There are numerous consulting firms that have questionnaires that would be happy to work with your company to get a handle on your culture.

KEY IDEA
What does it mean to "vision the culture"?

However, measuring an organization's culture is fraught with difficulties. Edgar H. Schein is a well-known and insightful researcher on organiza-tional culture. One of his best-known books[6] has been around for awhile and is now in its fourth

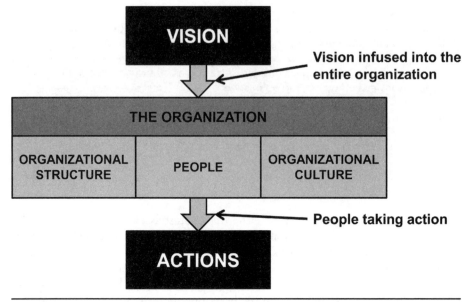

Figure A.2   Turning Vision into Actions.

edition. It contains many astute and thoughtful gems on the subject. Throughout the book, Schein discusses various problems that are inherent in measuring culture, saying that, at best, measurements are incomplete pictures of the culture and must be interpreted as such.

In any case, culture is a system of learned behavior and incorporates a set of shared ideas by people within an organization. Thus, when we talk about a *culture of entrepreneurship* within a company, particularly when it is applied to supply chains, it usually means that employees have learned certain ideas, concepts, tools, and techniques pertaining to entrepreneurial supply chains, much like what is discussed in this book.

KEY IDEA
Deep, lasting culture change requires an integrated approach that re-models a company's social systems. SOURCE: Ram Charan.

Since entrepreneurial supply chains are not normally found in organizations, some proactive efforts need to be taken to instill this culture. Home Depot reportedly is one company that took a series of practical steps to change its culture, as discussed in the *Harvard Business Review*[7] article by Ram Charan. Home Depot used a variety of tools to help employees internalize a system of learned behavior and a set of shared ideas around the new culture. This is important because the tools were used to change Home Depot's organizational culture, which could be adapted for an entrepreneurial supply chain culture change:

- *Data templates* were used to organize and standardize performance data for regular business reviews. These could be used regardless of the "from and to" culture change.
- Senior management used what they called a process of *Strategic Operating and Resource (SOAR) Planning*, which revolved around an annual eight-day planning session to balance priorities and select the investments that were most likely to lead to achieving their targets. Again, this could be used regardless of the "from and to" culture change.
- *Disciplined talent reviews* were employed frequently and consistently to emphasize the need for candor and fairness in judging employee performance.
- *Middle management learning forums* (specifically, store managers) helped to drive the culture change down into the organization, to make certain that they understood the requirements for the change, and to ensure implementation of the strategies intended to lead to the desired culture changes.
- *Monday morning conference calls* among the company's top executives were used to share business results and to emphasize accountability for the culture change.
- *Employee task forces* were used to get direct feedback and to gain support for the culture changes. These task forces were staffed by employees from all levels of the company.
- An array of *leadership development programs* raised the bar for future leaders. These included programs such as Future Leadership, Store Leadership, and Merchandising Leadership. Some leadership suggestions appear in Appendix C—Sample Education and Training Programs for Entrepreneurial Supply Chains. One program was a five-day "learning forum" that about 2,000 middle-management employees attended. They were encouraged to see the company as the CEO did, and to generate ideas for new growth opportunities. Apparently, when they realized that their ideas matched those of the leadership team, they welcomed the changes.
- *Mapping of the HR processes* was useful in identifying ways in which they could be improved as well as highlighting ways to sustain cultural change.

Home Depot also used a variety of metrics, such as the following, to achieve their objectives:

- Show employees that things are not going as well as they thought, using metrics such as customers' perceptions.
- Reinforce desired behaviors such as understanding the relationships among revenue, margins, and inventory turns.
- Provide a platform for collaboration such as between merchandising and supply chains.

As indicated above, each of these metrics could be adapted for an entrepreneurial supply chain culture change project.

Another good source for ideas to help develop a cultural vision is a model by Mark W. Johnson.[8] His model fits well with an entrepreneurial supply chain focus. He suggests a three-stage approach: incubation, acceleration, and transition, shown in Figure A.3. *Incubation* is the process of identifying and testing the basic ideas of the new cultural business model. In this case, it means testing the new entrepreneurial supply chain business model culture. Johnson says that the immediate goal here is "not business success but new learning." The incubation stage focuses on testing the business concept, preferably in a small test laboratory. He says there is a need to "test early, test cheaply, and test often." It's the idea of investing a little to learn a lot. At this stage, we test not only the business model but also the culture that is needed to support it.

Acceleration is the stage when you "hit the accelerator" to really get the new business concept going with its new business culture. Over time, the new culture becomes internalized as "the new normal" in terms of metrics and "rules of the road." As internalization occurs, the organization becomes ready to expand the

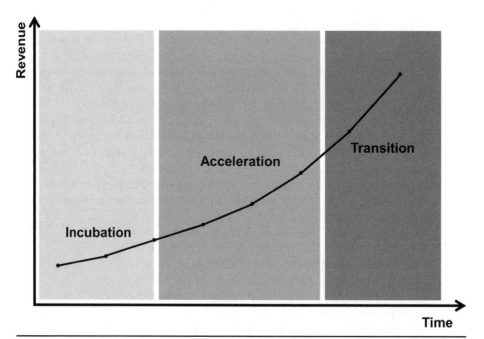

Figure A.3   Stages of Business Model Implementation. Adapted from: Johnson, Mark W., "Implementing the Model: Taking a New Business Model into Action," Chapter 7 in *Seizing the White Space: Business Model Innovation for Growth and Renewal*, Harvard Business Press, 2010.

concepts of entrepreneurial supply chains and begins to accelerate the model's development. This means the model is gaining traction. Johnson suggests this stage as the time to try different forms of expansion. For example, companies moving forward with entrepreneurial supply chains can try acquisitions, mergers, joint ventures, partnerships, or coalitions to see what works best. During experimentation, there is a need to closely monitor the business results and how the various pieces of the enterprise are working together. We could simply take the relevant chapters of this book and use them as important elements of the enterprise to test how:

- It works to use customers and suppliers as sources of entrepreneurial ideas and opportunities.
- The business knows it has good opportunities.
- The business is able to manage the risks of entrepreneurial supply chains.
- Due diligence and business planning work out best.
- The implementation process for the entrepreneurial supply chains.
- The visioning process.
- Ideas and processes for education and training of personnel.

Johnson's third stage is *transition* to an on-going enterprise. Basically, the question at this point is whether the new venture can be folded into an existing business or whether it needs to stand alone as its own business unit. Both of these are significant possible moves.

A case by Hess, regarding Best Buy,[9] is cited as an example of a company that transformed itself three times from a company with commissioned sales people in its stores to salaried sellers of products to salaried customer-solutions people. In the process, it moved from an entrepreneurial company to a highly top-down, centralized company, and then back to an entrepreneurial model at the store level. Hess comments that "organic growth is more than just a strategy—it is a system." Accordingly, an entrepreneurial supply chain approach is more than just a strategy—it is a system. It is a system that requires culture, structure, HR policies, and execution processes that are aligned and linked to the company's growth strategy. Best Buy had to embark on a massive education and training effort to teach store employees entrepreneurial skills.

> **KEY IDEA**
>
> An entrepreneurial supply chain approach is more than just a strategy—it's a system.

Best Buy has grown both organically and via acquisitions. Its organic growth first was through geographical expansion. Then, it expanded its product offerings, added services, focused on operating efficiencies, and finally, created or acquired new concepts. Its acquisition strategy included using acquisitions to enter new countries (China and Canada), to penetrate new customer segments (Magnolia Hi-Fi, Pacific Sales Kitchen and Bath Centers), and to offer services (Geek Squad). In 2003, Best

Buy expanded into China by establishing a Shanghai office for sourcing products, thus enhancing its operating efficiencies.

AN ENTREPRENEURIAL SUPPLY CHAIN VISIONING RETREAT

A retreat can be an effective way to develop or confirm a vision for entrepreneurial supply chains. Usually, however, in and of itself, it does not provide enough time to develop a complete vision from beginning to end. So a retreat needs to be supplemented with other vision development processes.

Nevertheless, there are several reasons why a company may want to do a substantial part of its visioning in the form of a retreat:

1. Use a retreat to consider whether it makes sense to create entrepreneurial supply chains in the first place. A retreat can be an ideal venue to investigate this question and to explore its implications.
2. Use a retreat to encourage creativity within the company and to develop new ideas about entrepreneurial supply chains for the company. Retreats tend to have fewer distractions to creative thinking, particularly if composed of appropriate people and structured to stimulate creativity.
3. Use a retreat to analyze the organization's culture and determine how supportive it is of entrepreneurial supply chains. A retreat can provide an opportunity to discuss the culture with some degree of confidence.
4. Use a retreat to create some portions of a vision for what the company's entrepreneurial supply chains are likely to look like when implemented. As mentioned above, the retreat likely will not provide enough time to create an entire vision; nevertheless, some of the critical work can be accomplished in this format.

With a retreat, companies receive the benefits not only of appropriate participation in generating ideas but also it is likely to result in better decisions. The group collectively will have a wider perspective and a greater number of ideas than a few people working in isolation.

An Example Outline of a Visioning Retreat

The author has facilitated many retreats on a variety of subjects with many companies in different industries. The following example is an outline of an entrepreneurial supply chain visioning retreat scenario. It is a composite of several retreats conducted over the past few years.

Some general guiding principles were used to keep the visioning retreats on track:

- The facilitator met with participants individually and in small focus groups prior to the retreat, and solicited their input on its goals and processes. This information was fed back to the leadership team without attribution, and the retreat goals and processes were adjusted accordingly.
- Management generally wanted the visioning retreats to reinforce the idea that what they were trying to accomplish was innovative. The retreats usually were the creation of the CEO and the leadership team, who had never done anything like this before. They set the objectives, hired an experienced facilitator, selected about 30 key leaders to participate, and ensured that the logistics were handled appropriately. The retreats usually were set for two days offsite at a resort hotel within a short drive from the corporate headquarters. Participants were to arrive in the afternoon of the day before the retreat, have dinner as a group, and stay for two nights. If desired, they were invited to arrive early and play golf in the afternoon. The retreat was seen as a big deal for the company and the participants.
- The visioning retreats had primary objectives to achieve a set of actionable deliverables, leading to the creation of entrepreneurial supply chains. However, to get decisions implemented, there had to be a strong commitment from those who would have to take action based on those decisions.

The following outline is typical of what was put into place for a visioning retreat. Some commentary on the retreats also is presented. Drafted answers to the following questions were provided as part of the retreat materials, which were supplied to participants in advance:

1. What are the processes for the retreat?
   a. *Focus*, *align*, and *engage* around a few key behaviors.
      - Keep an open mind.
      - Actively listen to others.
      - Participate effectively.
   b. A "contract" was drawn up among the participants that specified their commitments to each other and to appropriate behavior during the retreat. Furthermore, the leadership team members almost always attended and were active as participants. Everyone agreed formally to a series of statements about their behavior, some of which were as follows:
      - "We agree to be present for the entire retreat, be on time, silence all communications devices, and be focused on the work of the retreat at all times."
      - "We are aware that our (leadership team's) presence could have a deleterious effect on the participants' willingness to contribute and to say what they really think. We promise that we are all equal during the retreat and that nothing said by participants will

be held against them. We want honesty and openness in all our discussions."
- "We promise to let the facilitator run the retreat and that no one will dominate the discussions."
- "We promise that everyone will participate as and when they feel appropriate, and that no one will simply sit by and not contribute."

2. Why are we here, and what should we accomplish in the visioning retreat?
   a. A draft answer to these questions usually was provided as part of the advance retreat materials, for example: "To decide whether entrepreneurial supply chains make sense for our organization, and if so, to design a plan and achieve consensus on a process and structure along with how to deploy it to create entrepreneurial supply chains for the company."
   b. The group would debate and agree on a statement of purpose with slight modifications, along with a definition of *entrepreneurial supply chains for the company*. This usually took well over an hour.
      - In retrospect for a couple of the retreats, a draft definition of entrepreneurial supply chains should have been given out ahead of time. Some confusion could result if participants did not have a common frame of reference with a definition in advance. A glossary also should be prepared with terms that were going to be used during the retreat, along with a better definition of the desired deliverables. The advance thinking at the time (somewhat of a mistake) was that forcing participants to wrestle with definitions would result in more effective learning and better results, but instead, it resulted in taking too much time with less-than-optimal results.

3. What are the desired results for the visioning retreat?
   a. A draft answer to this question was provided as part of the advance retreat materials. The desired results of the retreat are to:
      - Align our understanding of these questions:
         - What are the current supply chain processes that are appropriate for entrepreneurship?
         - How should we think about entrepreneurship in the company?
      - Identify actions required to achieve entrepreneurial supply chains in our company.
         - Define specific actions that we need to do now.
         - Agree on clear accountabilities for each of these actions.
         - Agree on specific milestones and schedules for the actions.

- Define overall structure, staffing, and reporting processes to enable success in meeting our company objectives concerning entrepreneurial supply chains.

b. The groups debated and agreed on these as the desired results. Usually there was some minor modification.

4. Why are we doing this?
   a. In one retreat, the CEO's statement about why the retreat was happening, as follows, was presented for debate and agreement or modification: "We're frequently on lists of 'most admired' companies. But that's because of our engineering and our products. We want to be admired, also, for our operations, for how we run the business, and for being an entrepreneurial company."
   b. The group debated and agreed with this statement, but asked these rhetorical questions: What is the change imperative, and why are *we* doing this? This discussion took about an hour. In the end, the group agreed with the statement.

5. What is the scope of the problem? The advance materials for the visioning retreat provided an outline of the scope, stating:
   a. We do not have a superior model to guide our product development efforts. The advance material contained a version of a large (about 3' × 3') wall chart that was used to collect ideas using Post-It® notes. Participants were encouraged to add ideas to the chart as the ideas were developed. The wall chart contained four quadrants labeled as core businesses, adjacent products and technologies, adjacent customers and markets, and white space opportunities.
   b. We have difficulty getting out of our core business model with existing products and existing customers.
      - We attempt to move our existing products and technologies into adjacent customers and markets. But we really do not staff, say, with appropriate and sufficient numbers of knowledgeable sales and technical people to be able effectively to penetrate these new customers and markets.
      - We do not put sufficient product development resources toward adjacent products and technologies even for our existing customers and markets. This means, for example, that we make it difficult for our customers to work with us to make sometimes relatively small modifications to our products and services to better meet their needs.
      - We do not give much consideration to opportunities to move into the white space of new products and technologies and new customers and markets. We have a tendency to just say, "We're not in that business, and move on."

   c. We are not leveraging our sources for innovative and entrepreneurial ideas. The advance material also contained a version of a large (about $3' \times 3'$) wall chart that was used to collect ideas using Post-It® notes during the sessions. Participants were encouraged to add ideas to the chart as the ideas were developed. There were five areas of the chart: current customers, current suppliers, competitors, potential customers, and potential suppliers. Prior to the retreat, participants were asked to do some research into what was happening and the potential with each of these. They were then in a position to discuss their ideas during the session, and to build on each others' ideas.

- We need to spend more time discussing how to leverage our customers and suppliers for entrepreneurial opportunities. We have few if any discussions about how to tap into our current customers and suppliers, or other possible customers and suppliers, for innovative ideas.
- Our competitors possibly could provide opportunities for entrepreneurial advantage if we would spend some time focusing on them for entrepreneurial purposes. This is also true of other possible sources of innovative ideas such as different kinds of companies along with universities and trade associations.
- Sometimes, "idea factories" such as IDEO, a design and innovation consulting firm, are sources of ideas for innovation and growth, although they were not used in retreats attended by the author.

   d. Our product development efforts are not yielding sufficient new products. Perhaps one reason is that we are not organized correctly for new product development (NPD) nor do we fund it correctly. We used the Four Models presented in Chapter 2, as a platform for discussions of NPD and how the company should organize and fund NPD (see Figure 2.4). We also used a $3' \times 3'$ wall chart with Post-It® notes to collect ideas. The discussion centered on how the company might move away from its current approach. (The *Opportunist* in the conceptual model in Chapter 2 is the closest to our current approach.) These actions were considered to possibly move to:

- *The Advocate* approach. To do this, the company needs an advocate to be an evangelist for entrepreneurial supply chain opportunities, even though the funding would come from individual business units.
- *The Enabler* approach. To do this, the company needs to set up dedicated funding sources at the corporate level, and to develop a process for business units to apply for funding for their ideas. Ownership for the opportunity would remain with the business unit.
- *The Producer* approach. This likely would be the most complex and difficult approach to implement. The company needs a centralized group that has a mandate for corporate supply chain

entrepreneurship. The approach relies on business units to develop ideas for entrepreneurial supply chain ventures, which would be turned over to the central corporate group to implement.

6. How should we operate differently? The advance materials for the visioning retreat provided a draft of a path forward:

   a. We need shifts in our mindsets.

- We need to shift from "muscle is a core competence" to a mindset of "post-heroic ways of doing business."
  - "Muscle is a core competence" is a mindset that leads organizations to give kudos to people who "solve" problems by making a short-term fix as opposed to a long-term resolution of a real, underlying problem. They may be fond of saying something like, "We'll just muscle it through."
  - "Post-heroic" ways of doing business means that an organization has formal linkages for its planning and execution processes, such as:
    - The organization's strategic plan is linked formally to its annual operating plan.
    - The annual operating plan is linked formally to the monthly sales and operations planning and execution processes.
    - The monthly sales and operations planning processes are linked formally to the weekly master production scheduling process, which is, in turn, linked to the daily execution of supply chain activities.
- So, how should we operate differently? Suggestions that were offered by the participants included:
  - Move from today's functional silos to tomorrow's fully integrated organizations.
  - Move from today's decoupled processes to tomorrow's linked planning and control processes.
  - Move from today's batch/push supply chains to tomorrow's demand flow supply chains.

7. What should be our path forward? What is the journey?

   a. Recognize there is not a "silver bullet" to implement entrepreneurial supply chains. Instead, put into place a series of fundamental "building blocks" before we can really say that they have been implemented.

   b. A key building block is recognition that "The journey is more important than the destination" because the destination for entrepreneurial supply chains keeps getting pushed out. When can we say that we truly have entrepreneurial supply chains? Will we always find that we have more to do or that we can always get better?

> **KEY IDEA**
>
> The JOURNEY is more important than the DESTINATION.

    c. People frequently ask the author, "When do we know that we have entrepreneurial supply chains?" The tongue-in-cheek answer is, "You don't, because it's a journey, not a destination." You can always say, "We've done this, that, or something else entrepreneurially, but we also have X, Y, and Z to do now." Improvement is the norm.

    d. A second building block is to get senior management on board. The roles of senior management are fairly simple but powerful, such as:

- Accept responsibility for an entrepreneurial company and for entrepreneurial supply chains;
- Ensure linkage and alignment of the entrepreneurial plans; and
- Manage the process to guarantee implementation by visibly supporting the ideas behind entrepreneurship.

    e. A third building block is to find a starting place, as shown in Figure A.4. This is a simple 2 × 2 matrix of easy to difficult (vertical) versus low impact to high impact (horizontal). Like the other example above, use

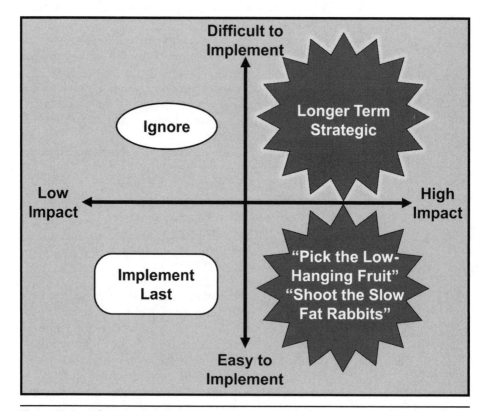

Figure A.4 Where to Start?

as a 3' × 3' wall chart and supply sticky notes to the participants for their ideas. As participants go through the course of the retreat, they can keep their ideas for later by using these wall charts.

- Clearly, the important part of Figure A.4 is in the high-impact ideas.
- The easy-to-implement, high-impact ideas are where we make easy choices (pick the low-hanging fruit). We usually say to implement at least some of these first, so as to provide some "quick wins" along the journey.
- The upper-right corner of Figure A.4—the difficult-to-implement, high-impact ideas—have a longer term or strategic impact. These may be the second batch of ideas to implement.
- The left side of Figure A.4 contains the low-impact ideas. If the ideas are low-impact/difficult-to-implement (upper-left corner), it is best to just ignore them. If the ideas are low-impact/easy-to-implement (lower-left corner), then we usually say to implement them last because by the time we get to them we may have other ideas that completely rearrange the priorities.

8. How should the visioning retreat be closed?

   a. No visioning retreat should be closed without a formal action plan to which the participants have committed. Before leaving the retreat, they should commit to:

- Certain actions and to deliverables from those actions.
- Assign responsibilities for the actions and deliverables.
- Agree to deadlines and target dates for the actions and deliverables.
- Determine how progress will be measured.

   b. The "messy room" is a well-known closing game that has been used effectively for many years by retreat facilitators (see Figure A.5). (Further discussion can be found in a book[10] about managing retreats.) It makes the point that implementation of the outcomes from a visioning retreat often is a messy process that goes through several possible results. Many times, during the retreat, the participants can be seen going through these four possibilities in sequence. They may be exploring all other possibilities before arriving at the final stage of embracing the change. Some might say they "do the right thing but only after exploring all avenues to get out of it."

- The first possible result is to "Be Satisfied with the Status Quo," in which people see little need to change what they are doing. They are not necessarily ecstatically happy, but they are not unhappy either. This means that retreat participants see little need to implement entrepreneurial supply chains in lieu of their existing behaviors within the organization. This result may not be the one desired by the retreat organizers, but at least it indicates that the participants are not ready to make substantive change.

Figure A.5   The Messy Room. Adapted from: Campbell, Sheila and Merianne Liteman with Steve Sugar, *Retreats That Work: Designing and Conducting Effective Offsites for Groups and Organizations*, 2003, Jossey-Bass / Pfeiffer, A Wiley Imprint, pp. 290–292.

Recognize that they may merely move through this stage on their way to more substantive results.

- The second possible result is to "Deny the Need to Do Anything," which may range from a simple refusal to face the facts that can be overcome with some discussion to a refusal to act because of a hard-core disbelief in the suggested changes. Some people may not believe that their company should be engaged in entrepreneurial supply chains. A somewhat middle ground in this denial debate may be lack of desire to do the work that is required to implement entrepreneurial supply chains. Denial is a well-known response to a push to make change. This could be an end point with the group simply refusing to go further, or it may be an intermediate stage in their journey to the final resolution.

- The "Live in the Messy Room for Awhile" possible result reflects the messiness of change. Experts in change management talk about how "messy" it is to decide what, how, when, or who will do what—all on the way to getting it done. The visioning retreat can result in some order and going-forward structure being put on the "messy room." If this is the end result, this is progress, although perhaps not as much as some people might desire. Alternatively, it again may be an intermediate stage in their journey to the final destination.
- The final possible result is to "Embrace the Change" and to arrive at a consensus to do so. This is the most desirable result from the visioning retreat. Some companies may jump very quickly to this stage because it is intuitively obvious even to the casual observer that it's the right thing to do. Other companies get there slowly and only over a long period of study. Still other companies never get to embracing entrepreneurial supply chains as the right thing to do for them.

Using these steps as the closing game gives the participants an opportunity to discuss the changes they want to make, and what stage the organization is in relative to each. Blind voting is a good way to start a discussion because it will highlight differences of opinion in the room. Further, it gives participants an opportunity to discuss why differences occur, and what can be done about them. Campbell and Liteman suggest that the whole group of retreat participants be divided into four sub-groups. Each sub-group is assigned one of the four stages to discuss, and to answer the following three questions on a flip chart:

1. How do we know when we are in this stage?
2. What are the advantages and disadvantages of this stage relative to our overall effort to change the organization?
3. What might we do to be successful in this stage and to move on to the next stage only when it is appropriate?

Each sub-group then presents its conclusions and recommendations to the total group and leads a discussion based on their ideas. This closes the retreat. A good closing discussion involves the following questions:

- We all have ideas, now are we committed to following through on the results of the retreat?
- Go around the room and ask each person individually to answer the question, "What is in it for me?"

HOW BAKER HUGHES DOES VISIONING

Baker Hughes has a relatively new but well-structured visioning process called Strategic Marketing Planning (SMP). Their process is quite well thought out and appears to work for them.

In the middle of a discussion, a matrix was put on the board as shown in Figure A.6. Participants were asked if it represented their thought process. The answer was, "Yes." The two axes Technology Products and Services and Customers and Markets each have Existing and New. The lower-left corner, represented as Now, are the company's existing products and technologies along with existing customers and markets. The figure shows three possible growth paths.

The horizontal growth path, into potential New Technology Products and Services, shows the company possibly moving into products and services for Shale Gas. These would be adjacent products and technologies offered to existing

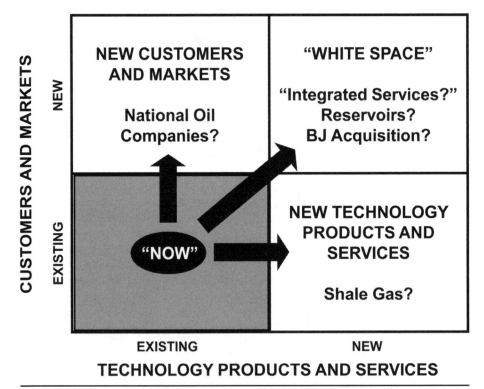

Figure A.6   Conceptual View of Strategic Marketing Planning. SOURCE: A conceptual model of Baker Hughes' Strategic Marketing Planning—adapted from discussions with BHI executives.

customers and markets. The vertical growth path, into potential New Customers and Markets, shows the company possibly moving into working more closely with National Oil Companies. The third growth path is diagonal, upward and to the right, into the potential White Space of both New Technology Products and Services and New Customers and Markets. This shows the company possibly moving into Integrated Services, more reservoir work, and acquisition of BJ Services. Notice that the examples in each of these three new quadrants have question marks associated with them to indicate that there may be questions. The point of this graphic is not to illustrate the exact examples, so much as to demonstrate the potential directions that the company might take in its visioning efforts for entrepreneurial supply chain ventures. As one can imagine, this is a very sensitive area of discussion for Baker Hughes, so examples are theoretical and not necessarily representative of actual plans.

A CASE NOTE FOR FURTHER STUDY: VF Brands

The cases are available at www.harvardbusinessonline.com. Readers should obtain copies of this case and use it to go beyond discussion in the book. These cases were prepared as the basis for discussion, rather than to illustrate either effective or ineffective handling of any particular situation.

A case[11] about VF Corporation, commonly called VF Brands, involves its line of apparel brands. VF's brands include Lee, Rustler, and Wrangler jeans, as well as The North Face and Jansport outdoor products, Nautica sportswear, and others. When VF acquires a new brand, the company keeps its brand identity and most, if not all, of its operating philosophies and practices. That's why most people have heard of their brands; but few likely have heard of the parent company, or, at least, they don't know that the brands are owned by VF. While there is no data to support this assertion, the author suspects that many people associate VF with its corporate predecessor, Vanity Fair.

VF is an entrepreneurial company whose supply chains are important ingredients for its success. Its entrepreneurial approach more-or-less followed Hess's outline, albeit not in Hess's sequence:

- Product expansion with exploding numbers of styles, colors, sizes, and other variations;
- Geographic expansion to become a global company;
- Service expansion downstream to retail outlets;
- Operating efficiencies with supply chain redesigns and improvements, resulting in what they describe as "fast and flexible" supply chains; and
- Continuing acquisition of brands and integration of new brands into its supply chains.

The case discusses the company's data-driven methodology and execution in terms of both its new products and existing operations. As of the end of 2010, VF described itself as a $7 billion-plus apparel company, with a diverse, international portfolio of over 30 brands and associated products that reach consumers around the world.

VF and the Apparel Industry

VF Brands claimed to be the largest company in the apparel industry in 2010. On its corporate website, it also claimed to have the industry's most efficient and complex supply chain. Not unlike others, however, VF's supply chains span multiple geographies, product categories, and distribution channels. It is unclear exactly what leads VF to claim to be the *most* efficient and complex, but it is a large and complex supply chain, and it likely is efficient, but whether it's *the most efficient and complex* could be arguable.

The case (dated 2009) discusses VF's "Growth Plan," publicized on its website as the following:

> *Launched in 2004, our Growth Plan began the process of transforming VF into a global lifestyle apparel company. The Plan identified six Growth Drivers crucial to our success. These Drivers ensure a balanced approach to growth across multiple fronts, from acquisitions to international expansion to increased direct-to-consumer businesses.*

They go on to say that the Growth Plan was updated and confirmed in 2008, and discuss the company's innovation focus. They claim that, for VF, innovation is a holistic *process*, one that touches every aspect of the business including supply chain management and global growth. VF apparently considers that their innovation relates both to something new as well as to renewal of something that currently exists. It is also apparent in reading between the lines that VF considers itself to be an innovative apparel company.

So how does VF differ from the rest of the apparel industry? It might be easy to characterize the apparel industry as entrepreneurial in the sense that companies are constantly coming and going, reconfiguring themselves, buying and selling brands, and developing new fashions, styles, and colors—and almost everything new. But it is more complicated than that.

A good example of that differentiation is ZARA[12] (not part of VF), the entrepreneurial and innovative Spanish retailer that has expanded globally with an extremely quick-response fulfillment system for its retail stores. ZARA observes what is selling and what is not in their stores, and continually adjusts what it produces and merchandises on that basis. It reportedly is able to restock a retail store within days, as opposed to weeks for other retailers. Inditex owns over 100 companies around the world, with ZARA perhaps being the best known. Inditex's net sales are approximately €11.0B.

An Aside: Not long ago, my wife and I were in Buenos Aires, Argentina, having just disembarked from a cruise. We were walking down Florida Street, a major retailing area, and came across a ZARA store. I wanted to go in and see the store because I had used a case about ZARA recently to teach an MBA course. (Wanting to visit a women's apparel store is a highly unusual event for a person who thoroughly dislikes shopping!) The store was beautiful, well laid out, and fully stocked with fashionable merchandize. The manager spoke English and was willing to talk when asked if it was true that her store could get restocked with any item within two weeks, even though it is a long way from Spain. She confirmed, indeed, that was the case. We talked for awhile about how the company operates, and she confirmed what had been written in the case. This was a very informative and enjoyable encounter that fortunately did not cost too much when my wife decided to do some shopping while waiting!

The VF case illustrates the difficulties of visioning and implementing a new supply chain concept. The ZARA case, however, is also extremely interesting for supply chain professionals, and readers should do further research into that case and the company.

The VF Supply Chain

Chris Fraser, VF's President, Supply Chain International, had advocated for a new supply chain strategy that he called the "Third Way." Traditionally, the apparel industry has used one of two supply chain strategies, along with some variations. The case makes the point that 49% of retail apparel sold in the U.S. in 1992 was made domestically, but by 1999, only 12% was made in the United States. The main reasons were intuitively obvious—cost is important in a labor-intensive production process, and barriers to entry are low. Hundreds of thousands of small contract manufacturers existed around the world, and they were intensely competitive with each other. Further, and perhaps not so obvious, was the fact that tariffs and quotas negotiated among governments were constantly changing, and thus the economics of producing in one country versus another also constantly changed. This caused a constant shifting of the countries of origin for apparel.

The first approach is used by ZARA and others with their own manufacturing and distribution, so that they can control the quality and responsiveness of the supply chain. ZARA used a combination of vertically-integrated manufacturing, small-lot production, and information technology to achieve this and provide ZARA with its quick-response capability. The second approach is complete outsourcing of manufacturing to low-cost countries with the apparel companies controlling the design and marketing of the products. The first approach maximizes quality and responsiveness, and the second approach minimizes costs. Also, some apparel companies control their own retail, such as ZARA and others. Other apparel companies go to market through large retail chains such as Nordstrom's and Macy's. Which approach is best depends on the company's strategy to achieve competitive advantage in the marketplace. (The reader can choose which one is best.)

> **An Aside:** An interesting article was published in *Bloomberg BusinessWeek*[13] about U.S. apparel manufacturers that are getting new business as Asian factories get more selective about taking new orders. United States customers are disgruntled about overseas production. Plus, off-shoring trends have run into difficulties as rising costs for labor and transportation make Asia more expensive. The article especially focused on apparel manufacturing, one of the hardest hit U.S. industries with domestic production falling from 41% of the industry in the 1990s to just 3% in 2008. Apparently, this is now in the process of reversing.

Fraser's Third Way was intermediate to these two approaches to competitive advantage, and was intended to capitalize on VF's manufacturing and sourcing expertise in certain products. His idea was to get the "best of both worlds." He first presented the concept five years previous to the case, but had encountered skepticism from within the company. As of 2010, the company had experimented with the Third Way concept with a few suppliers, but he had not been able to gain full acceptance within VF of his ideas. This is a typical example of a company's attempt to develop a vision of a new supply chain approach and to implement that vision.

VF had organized itself into five major coalitions, each of which was responsible for design, marketing, and sales of its product lines. Each coalition had its own go-to-market strategy, depending on its competitive strength in the marketplace. Fraser would have to convince all five coalitions of the soundness of his Third Way approach in order to gain full implementation within VF. Fraser's idea was that VF's manufacturing capabilities provided it with a significant competitive advantage, since they had been benchmarked as among the best in the world. VF also had developed a supplier network that he felt was among the world's best. In total, Fraser felt that its supply chain provided a substantial basis for the company's growth. Using entrepreneurial supply chain ideas, VF could play off the different strengths in its supply chain.

VF's complexity presented Fraser with both threats and opportunities. VF had over 600,000 stock keeping units (SKUs), and they did not even count size variations in that number—only style and color. Further, each coalition had its own priorities and needs from the supply chain. For example, product lines that compete with ZARA had to have quick-response lead times. Other product lines were in highly cost-sensitive segments. Others were in high-end fashion merchandise segments, which had their own requirements.

Fraser's Third Way supply chain strategy had several characteristics. He had developed these concepts and had been trying to convince the organization about them for over five years:

- Supplier agreements would last for several years instead of the usual one-year agreements that were common in the industry. Like longer agreements in other industries, VF's, in essence, would be in the form of "capacity purchasing" (although that term was not used) in which VF would agree to purchase a certain amount of capacity from the supplier. VF then could vary the volume and mix of its products within the limitations of the capacity purchase. This provides both VF and the supplier with a win-win situation—the supplier gets a long-term volume guarantee from VF, and VF gets to change its product mix with very short lead times.
- The suppliers would invest in and dedicate production capacity to VF, in contrast to the usual practice of taking on all customers to fill up their capacity.
- Joint development of production schedules would take place, based on sharing of forecasts.
- Both VF and the supplier would work on process improvements with the savings being shared between the two.
- The supplier would own the plant and equipment, but VF would invest in certain specialized equipment when necessary.
- VF would share its purchasing strength and agreements with the suppliers, and would agree to buy back any unused fabric or raw material.
- The supplier would be paid on a cost-plus basis with agreed margins.

While the case did not say explicitly, your author (in reading between the lines) believes that the supply chain thus would become the basis for a much more entrepreneurial culture as a result of these innovations.

The Third Way was originally proposed in 2005, but by 2009 only five partnerships had been formed: backpacks in Thailand, outerwear in China, and jeans in Bangladesh, Morocco, and China. All were successful except for the Moroccan supplier, and VF had to acquire them. Fraser commented that they had found it much easier to convince new suppliers rather than existing suppliers to sign up for the partnerships. Existing suppliers were reluctant to change their processes and ways of doing business or to share their cost data with VF.

The case ends with Fraser feeling that his Third Way approach had reached a decisive point because of VF's ambitious international expansion plans. He saw three options at that time: develop further the Third Way strategy, enlarge VF's internal manufacturing capacity, or expand traditional sourcing. He knew that whatever choice the company made would have a profound impact on the company's competitive position for many years to come.

Of concern is the amount of time it took (five years) to arrive at a decisive point, and a definitive decision still had not been made. Could Fraser have taken a different approach and been more successful in his quest for a new entrepreneurial supply chain strategy? Or, maybe it is the wrong strategy for VF, and Fraser should have been let go a long time ago? What do you think?

What Would Kotter Say?

The VF case did not say much about how Fraser's Third Way vision was developed, communicated, or how its implementation began. But it's obvious that the vision should have been substantially put into operation in less than the five years between the time it was developed and the case was written. Now we'd like to explore some of Kotter's ideas about implementing change as a way to understand more about what might have been done to make VF's vision more easily successful.

Bear in mind that this next section is somewhat speculative because what Fraser did, did not do, or what he might have done or not done to affect change is not really known. Also, while the Third Way sounds like the correct strategy for VF, the case simply is silent on that point.

John P. Kotter[14] is an authority on leading change in organizations. He has written extensively about his research as a professor at the Harvard Business School (now an emeritus professor). His book, *Leading Change*, is generally considered to be one of the most useful books on organizational change.

According to Kotter, the organizational vision should be a fundamental statement of an organization's aspirations. It should appeal to individuals' hearts and minds, that is, it should appeal both emotionally and rationally as discussed in Chapter 7 around Figure 7.3. It needs to offer a clear understanding of where the organization is today (the "as-is"), where it is going in the future (the "to-be"), how it intends to get there, and what barriers might be in the way. Recall the speech regarding President Kennedy's promise to put a man on the moon (and the promise to bring the astronaut back home, safely!) That was a very stirring and emotional speech, but it clearly had rational, logical science and engineering behind it—the essence of vision.

Visioning for the entrepreneurial supply chain is depicted in Figure A.7. The Vision Hierarchy is adapted from Kotter's book, and conveys that the vision fits in a hierarchy. Kotter said that underestimating the power of vision is one of the biggest failures of senior management when they seek to transform an organization. Additionally, linking that vision to strategies, plans, and actions also needs the power of vision and makes it operational. Kotter goes on to suggest some keys to successful implementation of organizational change, none of which does the VF case give any evidence that Fraser followed:

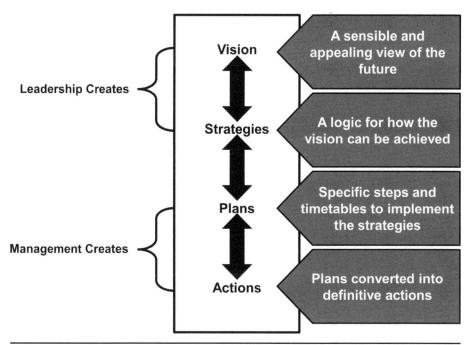

Figure A.7 The Vision Hierarchy. Adapted from, Kotter, John P., *Leading Change,* Harvard Business Review Press, 1996.

1. *Communicate the new vision to all employees.* This means that all available means of communication should be used, beginning with highly personalized messages. Even the most compelling vision requires effective communications to generate agreement, consensus, and dedication to the change.

2. *Remove structural barriers.* Internal barriers erected by organizations can inhibit change. One barrier for VF might have been its "coalitions" of brands with divided responsibility for managing the brands, and especially the disconnections between brand management and supply chain management. This structure fragments both resources and authority. Although the case does not mention this situation, management of the supply chains evidently has less power and clout in the organization than does brand management. That's probably as it should be, nevertheless too much difference between the two is not good.

3. *Provide needed training and education.* Fraser wanted to change the fundamental nature of the supply chain organization, but people likely did not have the capabilities to function under a new paradigm. Kotter

recommends that a lack of needed capabilities weakens the actions that should be taken.

4. *Align systems to the vision.* In many cases, various systems (using the term "systems" in a broad sense to mean how the organization is managed) make it difficult to act in the new organizational model. Kotter uses the firm's human resource systems as examples:

   a. The performance evaluation forms may contain virtually nothing concerning the core of the new organizational standards.

   b. Compensation decisions may be based more on not making mistakes than on creating positive change.

   c. Promotion decisions may be subjective and not linked to the desired change efforts.

   d. Recruiting and hiring decisions may not support the new mode of operation by not focusing on acquiring the needed capabilities.

5. *Dealing with difficult middle management.* Some people have characterized middle management with the term *frozen middle* to indicate that frequently this is where a primary barrier to change exists. Many times, middle management has the most to lose from a change and thus puts up the most resistance. This occurs often in cases where empowerment of lower-level employees is a key idea in the change, and middle management sees this as a diminution of its power. They thus discourage any actions that they see as being aimed at implementing the new vision.

So, the question of "What would Kotter say?" is relatively easy to answer if one reads Kotter's book. It can be summarized in a few words: *Don't graft a new paradigm onto the old culture.* This emphasizes the importance of the firm's culture and of how supportive it is of new ways of operating. There usually is no question about the need for a cultural change to implement an entrepreneurial supply chain organization.

A FINAL WORD ON VISIONING FOR THE ENTREPRENEURIAL SUPPLY CHAINS

This appendix has addressed visioning. A detailed step-by-step roadmap through the visioning process is provided as follows:

1. *Prepare for Visioning* with education and training for core team members, assembling "as-is" and "to-be" documents, and determine common ground for the vision.

2. *Conduct Visioning Session 1* with the first day spent in understanding the baseline and the second day spent in "stepping out of the box" with new ideas.

3. *Investigate and Analyze Alternative Visions* that came out of the Visioning Session 1 and conduct further assessments of discussions and ideas that were part of the session.
4. *Conduct Visioning Session 2* with the first day spent in creating a shared vision and the second day spent establishing the evaluation criteria and pulling it all together.
5. *Wrap up the Visioning Process* by finalizing the entrepreneurial supply chain vision statement along with the going-forward plan to effect the changes.

These points are useful to keep in mind for readers who are making an effort to develop a vision for entrepreneurial supply chains in their companies.

ASSURANCE OF LEARNING QUESTIONS

The following questions will help you to check yourself on the chapter content:

1. Visit the website of VF Corporation and read about the company. From information on the website, what would you surmise makes VF successful within a fragmented apparel industry? Look also at some competitors, such as Liz Claiborne with FY 2009 net sales of less than half of VF's at $3.0B; Phillips-Van Heusen with 2009 net sales of $2.4B, and ask the same question. Which companies do you think will be more successful in the long run, and why?
2. Check out the ZARA website and the referenced case, and put "ZARA" into a search engine. What can you say about their home base in Spain? Is it fair to compare ZARA with VF? What about comparisons of ZARA with other apparel companies? If ZARA fails, why might this happen, and what might be the impact on its competitors?
3. Outline an approach for your company to develop its own entrepreneurial supply chain vision. What might that vision contain, and how might it be implemented?
4. "What do you think?" was asked earlier in the section on VF when discussing the amount of time it took (five years) to arrive at the point that a definitive decision had to be made. Could Fraser have taken a different approach and been more successful in his quest for a new entrepreneurial supply chain strategy? Or, was it the wrong strategy?

REFERENCES

1. McKean, Erin (Ed.). *The Oxford American Dictionary and Thesaurus with Language Guide*, 2003, New York and Oxford: The Oxford University Press.
2. Senge, Peter M. *The Fifth Discipline: The Art and Science of the Learning Organization*. Doubleday Currency, 1990. New York. p. 150.

3. Quigley, Joseph V. *Vision: How Leaders Develop It, Share It, and Sustain It.* McGraw-Hill, New York, 1993.
4. Lee, William B., and Michael R. Katzorke. *Leading Effective Supply Chain Transformations: A Guide to Sustainable World-Class Capability and Results.* J. Ross Publishing, Ft. Lauderdale, 2010.
5. Steffy, Loren C. *Drowning in Oil: BP and the Reckless Pursuit of Profit.* New York: McGraw-Hill, 2011.
6. Schein, Edgar H. *Organizational Culture and Leadership*, Fourth Edition, New York; Jossey-Bass, 2010.
7. Charan, Ram. April 2006. "Home Depot's Blueprint for Culture Change." *Harvard Business Review.* 60–70.
8. Johnson, Mark W. "Implementing the Model: Taking a New Business Model into Action." In *Seizing the White Space: Business Model Innovation for Growth and Renewal*, Boston: Harvard Business Press, 2010.
9. Hess, Edward D. "Best Buy Co., Inc." University of Virginia Darden School Case #UV0761, 2007.
10. Campbell, Sheila, and Merianne Liteman with Steve Sugar. *Retreats That Work: Designing and Conducting Effective Offsites for Groups and Organizations.* Jossey-Bass/Pfeiffer, A Wiley Imprint, New York, 2003.
11. Pisano, Gary, and Pamela Adams. November 5, 2009. "VF Brands: Global Supply Chain Strategy." Harvard Business School Case #9-610-022.
12. Ghemawat, Pankaj, and Jose Luis Nueno. "ZARA: Fast Fashion." Harvard Business School Case #9-703-497, Rev. December 21, 2006.
13. Leiber, Nick. March 28–April 3, 2011. "Suddenly, Made in USA Looks Like a Strategy." *Bloomberg BusinessWeek*, 57–58.
14. Kotter, John P. *Leading Change.* Boston: Harvard Business Review Press, 1996.

APPENDIX B

SAMPLE BUSINESS PLAN FOR AN ENTREPRENEURIAL SUPPLY CHAIN OPPORTUNITY

LEARNING OBJECTIVES

1. Know how to write a business plan for an entrepreneurial supply chain opportunity.
2. Grasp how the various pieces of a business plan communicate the essential message for the opportunity.
3. Understand the essential elements of the business plan—what is important and what is not important.

"A man's accomplishments in life are the cumulative effect of his attention to detail."
—John Foster Dulles

"The world can never be learned by learning all its details."

—Ralph Waldo Emerson

"The devil is in the details."

—Saying

These three quotes illustrate the main point of this appendix. The business plan contains the details of entrepreneurial supply chain endeavors, where we lay out what we are planning to do, and why, how, and who.

For readers interested in entrepreneurial business plans, a good resource is a book by Edward E. Williams and H. Albert Napier, *Preparing an Entrepreneurial Business Plan.*[1]

Most people probably do not think of funeral homes as part of supply chains, much less as entrepreneurial supply chain opportunities. Nevertheless, they are. It's obvious to say that "everyone dies" and that something must be done with the remains. However, funerals are much more than disposal of human remains—they are ceremonies that recognize, honor, and recall the life of the person. Funerals may range from the simple to the complex, and from inexpensive to costly. Funerals involve both products and services, most of which in the U.S. usually are sold and provided by a funeral home. Funeral customs vary by religion, geography, and socioeconomic status.

In the language of supply chain management, funeral homes and funerals are high fixed-cost businesses with uncertain demand and make-to-order production from stocked components. It is a serious and complex industry. The profitability of a high fixed-cost businesses is dependent largely on break-even points and operating margins above that point.

In the funeral industry, there are several large public companies such as Service Corporation International (SCI) that own funeral homes, cemeteries, and allied businesses. However, it is a fragmented industry, and the majority of funeral homes are locally-owned and independent operations. Many are family-owned, and have been so through several generations. Death care, as it is commonly called, is a local and personal business. Even the largest company, SCI, claims only 12% market share according to its website, in August 2010. SCI is profiled as a case study at the end of this chapter.

Companies such as SCI have "rolled up" small funeral companies through multiple acquisitions. By doing so, they were able to gain economies of scale by sharing undertakers among funeral homes, using fewer hearses and other vehicles, and consolidating accounting, information technology, and other staff functions within the organization. The result was a reduction of overhead costs. As of December 31, 2010, SCI claimed to operate 1,405 funeral service locations and 381 cemeteries (including 218 combination locations) in North America across 43 states and eight Canadian provinces, the District of Columbia, and Puerto Rico. SCI also had, as of the end of 2010, twelve locations in Germany, which the company has announced its intention to exit when economic conditions become conducive to a sale.[2]

From a supply-chain perspective, the funeral home (and cemetery, crematorium, and other related businesses) is a fixed location that generally attracts its customers from the local area. A person's death usually begins the process, although many if not most funeral homes provide for "pre-need" planning, but that is not the subject of this case. In North America there are two options for disposal of the deceased: burial and cremation. Burial requires that the body be prepared. A casket and other funeral-related merchandise, including memorial products, burial vaults, flowers, and other ancillary products and services usually are sold at funeral service locations. Cemeteries typically provide cemetery property interment rights, lots, lawn crypts, other cemetery-related merchandise and services, including stone and bronze memorials, markers, merchandise installations, and burial openings and closings.

The second option is cremation of the deceased. This requires an urn and (usually) a columbarium, although many people prefer that their remains be scattered at a favorite place such as a farm, a beach, or at sea. Regardless of the means of disposal of the deceased's remains, a funeral service generally is held at a place of worship, the funeral home, or the cemetery.

Death care operations are subject to a wide range of regulations, supervision, and licensing under numerous federal, state, and local laws, ordinances, and regulations, including extensive regulations concerning funeral and cemetery products and services, and various other aspects of the business. Since 1984, the industry has operated in the United States under the Federal Trade Commission (FTC) comprehensive trade regulation rules. The rules contain requirements for funeral industry practices, including price and other disclosures.

Competition in the industry sometimes is bizarre. A few years ago, the Benedictine monks at St. Joseph Abbey in Covington, LA, launched a new business based on the skills they developed from preparing for their own monks' death care.[3] The monks produced a plan to hand-craft and sell caskets. But local funeral directors were trying to stop the monks' activities. The state funeral regulatory board, dominated by industry members, was enforcing a Louisiana law that made it a crime for anyone without a license to sell "funeral merchandise." The morticians were serious. Violators such as the monks could land in jail for up to 180 days and be fined up to $2,500 for each incident. The monks were fighting back, but as of 2010, there was no resolution to the situation. They apparently were arguing that the state law denied them a right to earn an honest living, perhaps as an attempt to stifle competition and block entry to a legitimate business. *The Wall Street Journal* article observed that, "In the past, funeral homes were typically the exclusive purveyors of caskets, a high-margin item. But increasingly, Web marketers and other dealers have been eating into their profits." Now we might have the real reason why the funeral operators are objecting—it's their profits that are at stake!

An Aside: The case of the monks of St. Joseph Abbey was not the only case of a state stifling supply chain entrepreneurialism through regulatory means. The Institute for Justice, an organization that "litigates for liberty," cites numerous other examples.[4] For example, florists, interior designers, and others in regulated states charge higher prices for consumers, as lower-cost competition simply is outlawed by the states' licensing regulations. Black and Hispanic interior designers are nearly 30 percent less likely to have college degrees than white designers; thus, interior designers' regulations with academic requirements disproportionately shut minorities out of the field. I could go on, but you get the point! Supply chains are fertile places to use the power of legislation to stifle competition.

In this chapter, an example business plan for a company that is fictionally called Omega, Inc., is developed.

BACKGROUND OF OMEGA, INC.

Omega, Inc. (not a real company but based on information from real companies) is a rapidly growing casket and urn supplier to the funeral service industry. Omega supplies these items to funeral homes. As mentioned, a supply chain entrepreneurial option is for a company to move forward (downstream) along the supply chain. In this example, Omega anticipates moving forward on a limited scale so that it will own funeral homes as well as supply caskets and urns to those homes and other funeral home companies.

Omega's management has completed its due diligence and decided that it is a good idea to go into the funeral home business. Furthermore, they have the option to start new funeral homes or purchase existing funeral homes. By moving downstream along the supply chain, the company is able to guarantee the sales of its caskets and urns to the funeral homes that it owns, as well as continue with the business it has.

Omega's management recognizes that some of its funeral home customers may change to other casket and urn suppliers if they start owning funeral homes and become, in effect, competitors as well as suppliers. Even though this situation is a concern, they completed their due diligence and decided to go forward on a small scale.

The company hired Robert R. Johnson, who has extensive experience in the funeral home business, as the President and General Manager of the new funeral service company. The decision was made to start one funeral home to determine whether it makes sense to continue the process of expanding in the funeral home business.

Robert was the funeral director for a mid-size funeral home in Dallas, TX, for 10 years and another funeral home in Wesson, TX, since 1998. He has a Bachelor of Business Administration (BBA) degree from the University of Texas and an Associate Degree in Mortuary Science from San Antonio College in San Antonio, TX, which was the first program of its type in Texas.[5] He is a member of various funeral home trade organizations. At this point, he is interested in starting a funeral home and excited about the opportunity to work with Omega. The first funeral home will be named Pinecrest Mortuary and will be located in Wesson.

Experience indicates that when a company decides to enter a new facet of an industry (sometimes referred to as white space), it is best if the new organization is separate from the older company. That way, internal politics and processes do not hamper the development of the new company. Wisely, Pinecrest Mortuary will operate separately from Omega.

OMEGA'S BUSINESS PLAN FOR PINECREST MORTUARY, INC.

The following business plan has been developed for Pinecrest Mortuary.

Pinecrest Mortuary, Inc. Business Plan
Executive Summary

Pinecrest Mortuary, Inc. is being founded by Omega Casket, Inc., to fill the need for an additional funeral service location in Wesson, TX. Presently, Wesson has twelve funeral homes, but there is a demand for another location to serve the increasingly elderly community that lives in the downtown part of the city. (See the Report of Market Analysis, Inc., in the Appendix to this plan.)

The estimated required investment to begin operations is $160,000. Omega will own 100% of the company.

Industry Analysis

Funeral concerns provide two basic services to society: care of the dead and assistance to survivors. The first of these is a necessity in all societies. The second has rather uniquely developed in North America.

The means of caring for the dead depends on the customs, laws, and physical environment of a given culture. In the United States, most families employ the services of a funeral director to take charge of the details of disposition. People generally desire that the remains be transferred from the place of death as soon as possible, and funeral establishments are equipped to accomplish this task quickly and efficiently. The historic custom was to maintain the deceased in the family home during the grieving period (usually from one to several days), but the trend toward urban living with smaller houses and increased apartment dwelling made this impractical. Today, the usual procedure is to have the dead removed to a funeral home where the body is embalmed, prepared, and placed in state, sometimes for viewing or with a closed coffin. After one or more days, a funeral service is held (typically at a place of worship or the funeral home) and the remains are made ready for ultimate disposition. Although all services (removal, embalming, preparation, funeral service, conveyance, and disposition) are not used by every family, virtually all deaths result in the utilization of at least some services offered by a funeral home.

> **KEY IDEA**
>
> Funeral rites are as old as human traditions themselves.

In the process of caring for the dead, the average funeral home will offer a number of merchandise items including caskets, grave liners, vaults, and burial clothing. Some locations also maintain florist shops, and those funeral homes that perform cremation services may offer a selection of cremation urns. Historically, merchandise played a unique role in the development of the funeral industry, and many modern-day funeral homes have their roots in cabinet and carpentry shops that manufactured coffins. Nevertheless, in terms of both importance and cost, the casket is currently only one of the many services and products offered by the funeral industry.

American funeral practice evolved over the years to minimize the inconvenience of the living. Thus, in addition to providing products and services, the typical funeral director can arrange for conveyance of the remains to distant localities, obtain death certificates, provide statistical reports to public health agencies, prepare newspaper notices, aid in the collection of government benefits, secure the services of other professionals (such as clergy, police, and music), and assist in the notification of relatives.

United States Census data from the Department of Commerce indicate that there are over 20,000 funeral home locations in the United States. The majority of these are owned and operated by families, many of whom have been in the funeral business for generations. At present there are a number of multiunit funeral concerns, and a few are publicly held. The largest funeral concern, SCI, owns about 12% of the total number of locations. Despite its fragmentation, the funeral service industry is an important economic market. Consumer expenditures on funerals, burials, and cremations are estimated to be in excess of $10 billion per year.

Market studies have discovered several significant variables that determine funeral receipts. The more significant ones include mortalities in a given market area, median family income, the age distribution of the local population, and proportion of inhabitants of foreign extraction. The first of these is the most significant variable. In fact, demographic factors are of such significance as determinants that a detailed analysis of population trends, life expectancies, and mortality rates must be made in order to appraise the historical performance and future prospects of the industry.

The death rate per thousand of population declined steadily during the twentieth century as people began to live longer. As demographers look forward into the twenty-first century, however, deaths will increase dramatically as the age distribution of the population shifts. On the other hand, a countervailing trend is the longer life spans of that population.

Although most Americans have a traditional funeral service at death, the preferred means of final disposition of the body varies by religion, geography, socioeconomic status of the family of the deceased, and other factors. The details of observance and practice vary according to each community and sometimes even by family.

Ground interment of the remains is still the choice of most people, but garden crypt or mausoleum entombment is also becoming popular. An increasing percentage of deaths in the United States result in cremation. Only a few families elect to have a "direct cremation" without benefit of a funeral ceremony, and the funeral and cemetery industry provides urns, cemetery garden space, and columbarium niches for the ashes of most of those who are cremated.

Most funeral businesses are characterized by the existence of high levels of fixed costs and substantial excess capacity which must be maintained to meet peak-load periods of demand. Salaries, which essentially are a fixed cost for a funeral home, average about 40% of the revenues of American funeral homes. Facilities account for another 15% and vehicles require about 12%. The most important variable cost is merchandise, and this expense item accounts for about 18% of the funeral revenue dollar.

Although the fixed costs for the typical funeral operation are high, this does not necessarily imply that funeral homes are subject to substantial business risk. Actually, the contrary usually is true. Cash flows in the industry are stable due to the nature of the business, and bankruptcy is rare.

The Business

The proposed Pinecrest Mortuary, Inc. plans to take advantage of the demographic trends that will be apparent in Wesson over the next few years. The population of Wesson is aging, and eventually there will be an increase in the demand for the services of funeral homes as a result.

The firm will begin operations with four employees: Mr. Robert Johnson as President and General Manager, a funeral director/embalmer, a clerk/receptionist, and Susan Johnson, wife of Robert Johnson, will be an unpaid assistant to the company. Part-time help, such as drivers, will be required from time to time.

Mr. Johnson is licensed as a funeral director and embalmer in both New Mexico and Texas, and he will have another licensed professional join him in the endeavor. The third employee will be a clerical receptionist who has funeral home experience and can help with family counseling and other matters.

A funeral home location now exists on Second Avenue in Wesson that was closed with the death of its owner last year. The building is owned by the widow of the former owner. She was physically unable to maintain operations of the business. She has agreed to lease the land and building to Pinecrest Mortuary and to provide a purchase option.

A Texas corporation will be established. The firm plans to begin business on or about January 1 of next year. Approximately $160,000 will be required initially. Of this amount, $5,000 will be for inventory; $30,000 for furniture and fixtures; $20,000 for leasehold improvements; $60,000 for vehicles (limousine, hearse, and lead car); and $45,000 for working capital. The firm will be financed with $160,000 of common stock owned by Omega.

Management

Mr. Robert Johnson will be President and General Manager of Pinecrest Mortuary. His resume is given here as are some pro-forma financials:

Robert R. Johnson	Date of Birth: August 21, 1965
	Married, wife Susan, one child.
	Nationality: U.S. citizen
Employment History	
1998–Present:	Funeral Director, Shannon Funeral Home, Wesson, TX.
1989–1998	Funeral Director and Embalmer, Riverdale Mortuaries, various locations in Dallas, TX.
Education	
1987–1989	San Antonio College, Texas, Associate Degree in Mortuary Science
1983–1987	University of Texas, Austin, Bachelor of Business Administration
Memberships	Texas and New Mexico Funeral Directors Associations
Church Affiliation	St. Philip Presbyterian Church, Wesson, TX

Pro Forma Financial Statements:
Opening Pro Forma Balance Sheet as of January 1, 20xx

Assets	
Cash	$45,000
Inventory	5,000
Furniture, fixtures, and equipment	30,000
Leasehold improvements	20,000
Vehicles	60,000
Total Assets	$160,000

Liabilities and Stockholders' Equity

Current liabilities	$0
Long-term liabilities	0
Total Liabilities	$0
Stockholders' equity	$160,000
Total Liabilities and Stockholders' Equity	$160,000

Pro Forma Income Statement: For Year One Ending December 31, 20xx

Net sales	$156,000
Cost of Services	
Merchandise	$28,100
Salaries	62,500
Rent	23,400
Vehicles	18,200
Administration	800
Promotion	2,000
Total Cost of Services	$135,000
Net Income before Taxes	$21,000
Estimated Taxes (30% Assumed Rate)	$6,300
Net Income	$14,700

STRATEGIC PLAN

The Enterprise Mission

To provide the Wesson area community with economical funeral home facilities and services while permitting the owners of the business to achieve personal and financial independence and pride in a sensitive service that is performed well.

Business Definition

The Pinecrest Mortuary will be a limited-service mortuary providing service and merchandise related to the care and disposition of the dead and assistance to their families in the area surrounding Wesson, Texas.

The following products and services will be offered. Others will be offered as demand requires. Not every client will utilize all these products and services.

1. Assistance with acquiring cemetery lot(s) or columbaria and selecting a monument.
2. Assistance with planning funeral service(s).
3. Newspaper notice and posting of obituary on the Pinecrest website.
4. Assistance with selecting clergy.
5. Assistance with selecting musicians and/or singers.

6. Caskets and vaults in all price ranges and urns for cremated remains.
7. Cremation.
8. Use of funeral home facilities including viewing/reception room(s) and chapel.
9. Services of funeral director and staff for funerals in the Pinecrest facility, worship center, and/or cemetery.
10. Flowers.
11. Refrigeration.
12. Dressing, casketing, and preparing the deceased for viewing and burial.
13. Embalming.
14. Transfer of remains from place of death to funeral home, funeral site, and place of burial.
15. Funeral vehicles including hearse, family car(s), flower cars(s), and service vehicle(s).
16. Certified copies of death certificates.

Products and services will be provided either on an a-la-carte basis or in a package. Approximately four packages will be offered, and packages will include price discounts.

Enterprise Goals

1. To provide economical funeral home facilities and services.
2. To be recognized as an honorable and ethical firm.
3. To provide for the major stockholder of the business personal and financial independence and pride in a sensitive service well performed.
4. To earn a fair rate of return for the investors in the business.
5. To be free of debt and eventually to have no minority stockholders.

Enterprise Strategies

1. To provide a dignified and meaningful service to the people of Wesson.
2. To price merchandise and services at a fair, competitive, and profitable level.
3. To achieve long-term profitable growth and to establish a leadership position among Wesson's funeral homes.
4. To hire and train imaginative and competent people, of high character, principles, and sensitivity.
5. To develop and maintain an organization whose conduct at all levels and at all times justifies the trust of the community.
6. To recognize and reward employees according to their abilities and contributions while maintaining a working environment which makes it unnecessary for employees to seek outside representation.

Planning Assumptions

1. We will be able to lease the former Second Avenue Mortuary and will be operating by January 1, 20xx.
2. We will be able to hire two qualified employees by January 1, 20xx.
3. We will have opening ceremonies and an open house at the funeral home in early January 20xx.
4. We will advertise our presence during December, January, and February. A special budget will be prepared for advertising.
5. The mortality rate in Wesson will stabilize in 20xx while the absolute number of mortalities will decrease slightly in subsequent years.
6. Income levels will be rising in Wesson throughout the planning period.
7. Overall inflation will average 3% per year. We will be able to increase the average revenue per service by a somewhat larger percentage through better name recognition and reputation.
8. We will achieve a 3% market share in 20xx and this will increase to 4% by 20xx+2.
9. Marketing activities will focus primarily on contacting religious leaders of the places of worship, through references from other people, and building relationships with various organizations such as the Rotary Club and local hospitals.
10. We expect to handle the following number of services in the first four years.

20xx	93
20xx+1	99
20xx+2	110
20xx+3	128

11. Average revenue per service is expected to be the following in the first four years.

20xx	$1,400	
20xx+1	$1,500	(7.1% increase)
20xx+2	$1,600	(6.7% increase)
20xx+3	$1,700	(6.25% increase)

Some of this increase will come from absolute price increases, but most of it will come from encouraging families to upgrade to higher level services.

Operating Plan

The following budgets will be developed by month for the plan of operations for the company in the first year of business.

1. Types and number of services along with prices.
2. Revenues for services, lots, liners and vaults, clothing, flowers, merchandise, and so forth.

3. Expenses for marketing and sales, promotion, and advertising.
4. Costs for refurbishing the Second Avenue Mortuary, furniture, equipment, fixtures, and other fixed assets.
5. Casket purchases, sales, and inventory by type along with costs.
6. Merchandise purchases, sales, and inventory by type along with costs.
7. Salaries and fringe benefits for president, funeral director/embalmer, clerk/reception person, part-time drivers, and others.
8. Facilities expense for rent, depreciation, utilities, upkeep, and so forth.
9. Vehicles expense for depreciation, fuel, repairs, insurance, and so forth.
10. Administrative expense for office supplies and so forth.
11. Receivables and payables.
12. Debt and interest payments.
13. Cash flow.

Major Strengths and Risks

The major *strengths* for the business include the following.

Location. The Pinecrest Mortuary will be conveniently located on Second Avenue in a building that was formerly a reasonably successful funeral home.

Service. The Pinecrest Mortuary will offer a limited line of funeral merchandise (caskets, grave vaults, clothing, etc.) and will strive to offer the best service available in Wesson.

Price. The Pinecrest Mortuary will price its services and merchandise to offer the best value in Wesson. The principal clientele of the firm will be elderly people with limited wealth. The families of these people should appreciate being able to get good quality for a reasonable price.

Building. The former Second Avenue Mortuary building will be completely remodeled to reflect an image of quality but not opulence.

Employees. The Pinecrest Mortuary will not be unionized. Employees will be personally selected by Mr. Robert Johnson from the most dependable people he has worked with throughout central Texas.

The major *risks* for the business include the following.

Nature of business. A new funeral home typically takes some time to become established in the eyes of the community. Some businesses require months before they handle even a few services, and it may take years for a new location to become profitable. Further, while deaths are statistically predictable, uncertainty always exists as to their exact number and timing, and also as to the amount of money the families will spend on death care. The upward trend of cremations likely will affect our revenues as time goes on.

High fixed-cost business. Any high fixed-cost business has risks. Fixed costs go on regardless of the number of services provided and the revenue generated from each.

Pre-need arrangements. At present, Pinecrest has no agreement to offer pre-need arrangements to prospective clients. However, this service is expected to be offered within a year.

Regulation. The funeral industry is heavily regulated, and the danger always exists that governmental agencies will adopt new or changed regulations that could affect our costs and operations.

Marketing strategy. Marketing funerals is difficult. The nature of the service limits the effectiveness of the usual techniques such as a grand-opening sale or extensive advertising. Price cutting is difficult, since people are not likely to choose a funeral home simply because its products and services have been marked down in price.

Competition. There are currently 12 funeral homes in Wesson. Although it appears that the market could support another one (particularly in the location that has been selected for Pinecrest Mortuary), competition would remain keen. Two competitors have been in business for more than 50 years, and the Wesson Mortuary is clearly thought by almost everyone to be the prestige operation in the city. It is also the fastest growing business. Fortunately, it is located eight miles from the proposed site of the Pinecrest Mortuary.

Market size. The population of Wesson has been decreasing in recent years and the death rate has been declining. As a result, the overall size of the market has been diminishing slightly.

APPENDIX: REPORT OF MARKET ANALYSIS, INC.

The city of Wesson is located in a poorer part of Central Texas. The median income in the city has risen from $15,200 per year five years ago to $20,200 per year in the current year. The recorded population estimates for the city are as follows.

20xx	320,000
20xx+1	318,000
20xx+2	315,000
20xx+5	310,000

The slight decline in population reflects a migration to unincorporated areas outside the city over the past few years. Most of the migration has been to the north and northwest, outside the Wesson city limits, and thus is not reflected in the above statistics. Overall population of the county is approximately 425,000. The northwest area has been growing at a rate exceeding the losses from Wesson. Furthermore, whereas the median income within the city is substantially lower than the national average, these newer unincorporated areas are more affluent.

The survey indicates, however, that the people who proportionately spend the most on funerals, nationally, are not the wealthiest. The distribution for sales of services by income level is skewed below the national income average. Of additional interest is our finding that the death rate within the city of Wesson is higher than the national average; 10 deaths per thousand five years ago, down to 9.8 deaths per thousand in the current year. These figures reflect the same trend, however, as national statistics toward a lower death rate per thousand over the last few years, reflecting longer life spans.

Mortality statistics for the city of Wesson are as follows for the past five years.

5 years ago	3,206 deaths
4 years ago	3,320 deaths
3 years ago	3,092 deaths
2 years ago	3,138 deaths
1 year ago	3,043 deaths

There are no funeral sales figures available for the northern areas of the county as yet, but only two funeral homes are operating there at the moment.

The migrating and new population influxes to the north and northwest are middle class, more affluent families. In contrast, it would seem from the higher-than-average death rates, that the city of Wesson has an older, more established population with slightly lower income base. Wesson currently has a predominantly Christian population with 62% being Protestant, 36% Catholic; and 2% Muslim. Approximately 25% of the city is Hispanic.

Although the central downtown area has deteriorated in recent years, real estate values in the past few years have risen. There are isolated instances of old Victorian houses being rehabilitated within the city. There appears to be little concern by families returning to the downtown area about the condition of the homes or the minority dominance in the neighborhoods. Although no conclusions can be drawn from the tentative evidence, indicators reveal that the average sales price of the older homes has risen 15% in the past 18 months.

The funeral home businesses in Wesson are all locally owned and operated. Two have been in business nearly 50 years; and one (Wesson Mortuary) is the superior location in the city, as supported by both the sales figures among competitors and by several interviews conducted with local civic leaders.

There are currently 12 funeral homes operating in Wesson, down from 13 last year. One of these funeral homes serves primarily the African-American community. Not included in the total are two additional funeral homes opened in the northern part of the county within the past year.

An analysis of the maps supplied to us by Mr. Robert Johnson suggests the possible need for a new funeral location to replace the mortuary that closed last year. That firm was located on Second Avenue, downtown, and served an increasingly elderly market. The business did not fail, but was closed by the widow of the former owner. It is our understanding that the property and physical location can be purchased or leased. In past years, the Second Avenue Mortuary handled about 100 services per year with no marketing effort. Surveys indicate that families selected Second Avenue principally because of its convenient location.

Demographic data on the area surrounding the proposed location of the Pinecrest Mortuary shows approximately 31,000 people with about 20,000 being white Protestants, 6,400 being white Catholics, and the remainder being mostly African-Americans. In this area, approximately 400 deaths occur per year. The old Second Avenue Mortuary handled about 100 to 125 funerals per year for the past few years. We expect that Pinecrest should be able to handle about 80 to 90 funerals the first year rising to 125 to 150 funerals per year within five years.

A CASE NOTE AND AN ARTICLE FOR FURTHER STUDY: Service Corporation International (SCI)

While not intended to be a business plan, a company's 10-K nevertheless can be used as an example of a business plan for the purposes of this book. However, a plan written for internal use obviously will contain more proprietary information than the 10-K, which is a public document. The following plan is presented in a form similar to, but slightly different from, the business plan that was outlined in Chapter 6.

Enterprise Mission

SCI did not have a mission statement on their website in 2010, but it had the following statement called "Our Purpose," which sounds like a mission statement:

> Service Corporation International is dedicated to compassionately serving families at difficult times, celebrating the significance of lives that have been lived, and preserving memories that transcend generations, with dignity and honor.

Executive Summary

SCI is an entrepreneurial company that was incorporated in July 1962. As of December 31, 2010, it continued to act entrepreneurially and was North America's largest provider of death care products and services. Like Hess explained with Best Buy in Appendix A, SCI expanded geographically, expanded its product offerings, added services, focused on operating efficiencies, and created or acquired new concepts, including becoming the first branded death care operation. It grew both organically and by acquisition. It thus fits the definition of an entrepreneurial supply chain company.

As of December 31, 2010, SCI had a network of 1,405 funeral homes and 381 cemeteries (including 218 funeral service/cemetery combination locations) which were geographically diversified across 43 states, eight Canadian provinces, the District of Columbia, and Puerto Rico. Its funeral service and cemetery operations consist of funeral service locations, cemeteries, funeral service/cemetery combination locations, crematoria, and related businesses. SCI sells cemetery property and funeral and cemetery products and services at the time of need and on a pre-need basis.

Business Description

SCI's original business plan was based on efficiencies of scale, specifically reducing overhead costs by sharing resources such as embalming, accounting, transportation, and personnel among funeral homes in a business "cluster." After proving the plan's effectiveness in the early 1960s, SCI applied this operating strategy through the acquisition of death care businesses in other markets. It was the beginning of three decades of expansion that would create a North American network of nearly 1,400 funeral homes and cemeteries by the end of 1992. Beginning in 1993, it expanded beyond North America, acquiring major death care companies in Australia, the United Kingdom, and France, plus smaller holdings in other European countries and South America. By the end of 1999, their global network numbered more than 4,500 funeral service locations, cemeteries, and crematories in more than 20 countries.

During the mid to late 1990s, acquisitions of death care facilities became extremely competitive, resulting in increased prices for acquisitions and substantially reduced returns on invested capital. In 1999, SCI significantly reduced its level of acquisition activity and implemented various initiatives to pay down debt, increase cash flow, reduce overhead costs, and increase efficiency over the next several years. SCI divested its international businesses and many North American funeral homes and cemeteries that were either underperforming or did not fit their long-term strategy. At the same time, SCI began to capitalize on the strength of its network by introducing to North America the first branded death care services and products—Dignity Memorial®.

In 2006, having arrived at a position of significant financial strength and improved operating efficiency, SCI acquired the then second largest company in the North American death care industry, Alderwoods Group. By combining the two leading companies, SCI was able to realize more than $90 million in annual pretax cost synergies, savings, and revenue enhancement opportunities. In 2010, they acquired the fifth largest company in the North American death care industry, Keystone North America.

SCI's funeral service and cemetery operations do not differ significantly from those of other companies. SCI provides all professional services relating to funerals and cremations, including the use of funeral facilities and motor vehicles, and remains preparation and embalming services. A variety of funeral-related merchandise is sold at funeral service locations, including caskets, memorial products, burial vaults, cremation receptacles, cremation memorial products, flowers, and other ancillary products and services. SCI's cemeteries provide cemetery property interment rights, including mausoleum spaces, lots, and lawn crypts. SCI also sells cemetery-related merchandise and services, including stone and bronze memorials, markers, merchandise installations, and burial openings and closings.

SCI sells pre-need funeral and cemetery products and services whereby a customer contractually agrees to the terms of certain products and services to be delivered and performed in the future. SCI defines these sales as pre-need sales.

In 2010, SCI's operations in the United States and Canada were organized into 30 major markets, 45 metro markets, and 70 main street markets. Each market is led by a market director with responsibility for funeral, cemetery operations, and pre-need sales. Within each market, the funeral homes and cemeteries share common resources such as personnel, preparation services, and vehicles. There are four market support centers in North America to assist market directors with financial, administrative, pricing, and human resource needs. These support centers are located in Houston, Miami, New York, and Los Angeles. The primary functions of the support centers are to help facilitate the execution of corporate strategies, coordinate communication between the field and corporate offices, and serve as liaisons for the implementation of policies and procedures.

Competition

Although there are several public companies that own funeral homes and cemeteries, the majority of death care businesses in North America are locally-owned, independent operations. SCI estimates that its funeral and cemetery market share in North America is approximately 12% based on estimated total industry revenues. The position of a single funeral home or cemetery in any community is a function of the name, reputation, and location of that funeral home or cemetery, although competitive pricing, professional service and attention, and well-maintained locations are also important.

SCI believes it has an unparalleled network of funeral service locations and cemeteries that offer high-quality products and services at prices that are competitive with local competing funeral homes, cemeteries, and retail locations. Within this network, the funeral service locations and cemeteries operate under various names as most operations were acquired as existing businesses. SCI has co-branded its funeral operations in North America under the name Dignity Memorial®. It believes its branding strategy gives SCI a strategic advantage and identity in the industry. While this branding process is intended to emphasize SCI's national network of funeral service locations and cemeteries, the original names associated with acquired operations, and their inherent goodwill and heritage, generally remain the same. For example, Geo. H. Lewis & Sons Funeral Directors is now "Geo. H. Lewis & Sons Funeral Directors, a Dignity Memorial® Provider."

Strategic Plans

SCI believes it is well positioned for long-term profitable growth. SCI is the largest company in the North American death care industry; it has unmatched scale on a national and local basis; and it is poised to benefit from the aging population of America. It demonstrated that it can generate significant and consistent cash flow, even in difficult economic times. This, coupled with its financial position and liquidity, allows SCI to deploy capital to enhance the value of the company. SCI's capital deployment focus is centered on strategic acquisitions, share repurchases and dividends, and opportunistic debt repurchases when it believes it can reduce liquidity risk and enhance its near-term maturity profile.

The company has three strategies for growth:

1. *Target the customer* by building on its extensive consumer research as well as testing new products and services including catering services, enhanced floral offerings, a broader cemetery merchandise program, and "green" burial products and services.
2. *Drive operating discipline and leverage the scale of the company*, including standardization of processes and leveraging the company's purchasing spend.
3. *Manage and grow the footprint* by positioning each business location to support the preferences of its local customer base, while monitoring each market for changing demographics.

Risks and Assumptions

SCI makes the obligatory "Cautionary Statement on Forward-Looking Statements" concerning its risks and assumptions, some of which are listed in its Form 10-K, each with an explanation:

- SCI's affiliated funeral and cemetery trust funds own investments in equity securities, fixed-income securities, and mutual funds, which are affected by market conditions that are beyond its control.
- SCI's ability to execute its strategic plan depends on many factors, some of which are beyond its control.
- SCI's credit agreements contain covenants that may prevent it from engaging in certain transactions.
- The funeral home and cemetery industry continues to be increasingly competitive.
- Increasing death benefits related to pre-need funeral contracts funded through life insurance or annuity contracts may not cover future increases in the cost of providing a price-guaranteed funeral service.
- Unfavorable publicity could affect SCI's reputation and business.

- If the number of deaths in its markets declines, SCI's cash flows and revenues may decrease.
- The continuing upward trend in the number of cremations performed in North America could result in lower revenues and gross profit.
- SCI's funeral homes and cemeteries are high fixed-cost businesses.

Company Leadership

The following table sets forth, as of February 14, 2011, the name and age of certain executive officers of the Company, office held, and year first elected an officer. Business plans will contain the names and backgrounds of all the officers and likely the members of the board of directors.

Name	Age	Position	Year
R. L. Waltrip	80	Chairman of the Board	1962
Thomas L. Ryan	45	President and Chief Executive Officer	1999
Michael R. Webb	52	Executive Vice President and Chief Operating Officer	1998

SCI's Form 10-K lists all officers and members of the board of directors.

Concluding Remarks about Service Corporation International

This section is based on both the author's outline of an example business plan as well as information taken from the Form 10-K of SCI. Readers usually do not think of a company such as SCI in entrepreneurial supply chain terms. Nevertheless, you should consider different forms of such companies.

"How to Write a Great Business Plan"

William A. Sahlman wrote a classic article[6] in 1997 entitled, "How to Write a Great Business Plan." This article does a tremendous job of listing what information belongs in a business plan and what information does not.

Sahlman strongly advocates using the same type of business plan for a corporate entrepreneurship venture as for a start-up. The difference between the two essentially is a question of who provides the funding—an established company or perhaps a venture capitalist. However, he observes that corporate entrepreneurship ventures rarely receive the same level of scrutiny as a pure start-up venture. Further, he believes that performance tracking is rarely as rigorous for corporate entrepreneurship ventures—they tend to get lost inside the company's normal operations. The venture's business plans certainly will show returns (substantially) in excess of the company's hurdle rate, but that the actual performance is often (substantially) less than the projections. Sahlman believes that professional venture capitalists are accustomed to tracking the venture's performance closely as a stand-alone endeavor, whereas this is not the normal practice with a company.

Sahlman says the following about business plans: "In my experience with hundreds of entrepreneurial start-ups, business plans rank no higher than 2—on a scale of 1 to 10—as a predictor of a new venture's success. And sometimes, in fact, the more elaborately crafted the document, the more likely the venture is to, well, flop . . ."

Sahlman goes on to assert the reason is because too many numbers are put into the business plan at the expense of the information that really matters to the potential investors. Writers of business plans tend to be wildly optimistic with their financial projections—and sophisticated investors know this, so they discount the estimates. Such inaccuracies tend to weaken the entire presentation.

Sahlman recommends that there are four key pieces of information that should form the framework of a business plan: the people, the opportunity, the context, and the risks and rewards.

The people perhaps are the most important piece of information. Investors want to have confidence in those who will run the business, as well as their advisors such as attorneys and accountants. He suggests asking three questions about the team members: what do they know; whom do they know; and how well they are known. Most venture capitalists invest in people, not ideas. They want to have confidence that the people are capable of carrying out the venture.

The opportunity is focused on two questions, one is the venture itself and the second is the industry. Investors want to have confidence that the venture can grow rapidly enough to reach a critical scale, say, within five years or less. This can happen typically in an industry that is growing; it is easier to gain share in a rapidly growing industry than to fight it out with entrenched competitors in an industry that is not growing.

The context is where the opportunity lies. The context usually includes the economy and the tax rates, interest rates, exchange rates, and inflation. It also includes the governmental context in terms of laws and regulations as well as governmental actions and inactions. Demographics can be an important component of the context of the business. For example, SCI is aware of the role that demographics plays in their business. The context also includes technology and protections for intellectual property, about which has been already discussed, especially in terms of lack of protection in certain countries around the world. Sahlman recommends that entrepreneurs show an awareness of the role of context in their business.

Finally, *the risks and rewards* of the venture, are required to be disclosed in the Form 10-K that is required from every public company by the U.S. Securities and Exchange Commission. While nothing says that risks and rewards *must* be disclosed in an entrepreneurial supply chain business plan, nevertheless, they should be for two reasons. First, it forces the creators of the business plan to think through the risks and rewards. Second, it discloses the risks and rewards to potential investors.

Sahlman says that a business plan must be a call for action. The business plan is vitally important to address the people who will be involved in the venture, describe the opportunity, explain the context of the venture, and portray the risk/reward situation.

A FINAL WORD ON A SAMPLE BUSINESS PLAN FOR AN ENTREPRENEURIAL SUPPLY CHAIN OPPORTUNITY

Business plans are important for entrepreneurial supply chain ventures. Business plans set forth the following components to make the business case for the venture.

1. Enterprise mission
2. Executive summary
3. Business description
4. Industry analysis
5. Competition
6. Strategic plans
7. Marketing and sales plans
8. Product and service development plans
9. Organization structure and management
10. Risks and assumptions
11. Pro-forma financial statements
12. Operating plans
13. Milestone schedule
14. Strengths, weaknesses, opportunities, and threats (SWOT)
15. Legal form
16. Harvest strategy
17. Appendices

Not all of these will be included in any one business plan, and other components may be added as required. An example business plan was provided in this chapter, plus information from SCI based on their Form 10-K.

ASSURANCE OF LEARNING QUESTIONS

The following questions will help you to check yourself on the chapter content:

1. Critique the business plan for Pinecrest Mortuary. What holes do you see? What information should be presented but was not? How would you improve the plan?

2. Visit the corporate website of Service Corporation International (SCI). Analyze the company in terms of its history and long-range prospects. Would you invest in the company? Why or why not?
3. Investigate the death care industry. Is this an attractive industry for a new "roll-up" company?
4. See if you can determine what happened to the casket business of the monks of St. Joseph Abbey, Covington, LA. (As of this writing, the case was still in litigation.) What do you think of state laws that restrict entry into an industry such as casket manufacturing? Why or why not are these good ideas?

REFERENCES

1. Much of this chapter is adapted with permission and assistance from: Williams, Edward E., and H. Albert Napier, *Preparing an Entrepreneurial Business Plan*. Chicago: T&O Book Company, 2006.
2. Service Corporation International, United States Securities and Exchange Commission Form 10-K, December 31, 2009, available at http://www.sci.com
3. Levitz, Jennifer. August 25, 2010. "Coffins Made With Brotherly Love Have Undertakers Throwing Dirt." *The Wall Street Journal*, 1.
4. See the Institute for Justice website for more information.
5. See the San Antonio College website for information on the Mortuary Science program.
6. Sahlman, William A. July–August 1997. "How to Write a Great Business Plan." *Harvard Business Review*.

Web Added Value™

APPENDIX C

SAMPLE EDUCATION AND TRAINING PROGRAMS FOR ENTREPRENEURIAL SUPPLY CHAINS

LEARNING OBJECTIVES

1. Identify the need for education and training programs for entrepreneurial supply chains.
2. Understand how to design an entrepreneurial supply chain academy.
3. Learn the appropriate use of action learning projects.
4. Understand how some companies design and manage their education and training programs.

"If you think education is expensive, try ignorance."
—Derek Bok, President, Harvard University

"I am still learning."
—Michelangelo

"Learning is like rowing upstream; not to advance is to drop back."
—Chinese saying

These quotes illustrate that education and training are expensive; yes, ignorance is even more expensive; and learning should be a lifelong commitment—if you don't keep at it, you are dropping back.

Most people, even in higher echelons of business, have had little or no formal educational exposure to entrepreneurship or to supply chain management. Yet, even Michelangelo admitted that he was still learning after he had created some of his greatest masterpieces. Additionally, rowing upstream illustrates a dilemma in business—we keep doing the same thing expecting that we don't have to learn anything new except perhaps by random efforts. That's a big mistake.

> **KEY IDEA**
>
> If it is done well, adult learning is different from what all of us experienced in school.

Someone once said that the "height of folly" is to continue doing the same things yet expecting different results. Simply wishing to grow the business is not sufficient without commitment and without the awareness, knowledge, and understanding of entrepreneurial supply chains that come with education and training of people in the company.

Unfortunately, some companies continue to do their own informal and uncoordinated education and training on supply chain subjects, if they do anything at all. More than one senior executive has said something like this: "We don't want to spend the time or money to train our people—they can learn it on the job." This is unfortunate. Rarely are these among the best-performing companies.

The author once asked a senior supply chain executive about what his company does to educate and train its supply chain people. He answered that they provide company forums, and people can participate in some interactive online training should they so desire. This same individual did not even know of the existence of APICS, ISM, or other professional societies for supply chains! He was clueless about what makes for qualified supply chain people.

The ideas for an entrepreneurial supply chain academy and action learning projects are discussed in this chapter. Readers should recognize that these are appropriate for most corporate entrepreneurship ventures and for some start-ups.

ENTREPRENEURIAL SUPPLY CHAIN ACADEMY

An "Entrepreneurial Supply Chain Academy" is the terminology for a comprehensive set of educational offerings that companies can provide internally for employees. Academies usually, but not always, are specific to a given company. Sometimes, executive education units of graduate schools of business will offer open-enrollment academies on a given subject.

The idea of an "academy" is to provide a continuing series of integrated programs that can be offered in an iterative manner to successive groups of participants. It is not a single program that is offered once to a selected group of participants. Rather, it is intended to ensure that relatively large numbers of individuals have a consistent exposure to the same education and training content.

Companies have built academies around certain subjects such as a Project Management Academy, an Operations Management Academy, and a Sales Academy. All of these are intended to build a uniform curriculum through which companies can offer education and training programs to help employees gain a consistent level of knowledge, understanding, and terminology in a given field.

Of course, there are university-level executive education programs that are similar to in-house versions. One good example is the University of Tennessee's Integrated Supply Chain Management Program. This consists of "six, 2½-day, non-consecutive courses (offered in pairs) that bring together the supply chain areas of demand planning, customer relationship management, operations, logistics, lean management, and resource/financial management. Certification is available."[i] However, no university to the author's knowledge has specific programs in *entrepreneurial* supply chain management, although universities are usually delighted to discuss customized programs for individual companies.

Today, many companies have a "corporate university." GE and Motorola are two of the most well-known. A relatively old (1994) but well-done and well-known Harvard case study was written about the early stages of Motorola's corporate university.[ii] According to the case, Motorola began its corporate university in the early 1980s when then CEO Bob Galvin made a significant commitment to training and education. He called it the Motorola Training and Education Center (MTEC). In the early days of MTEC, Motorola instituted programs such as the Participative Management Program, Senior Executive Program, Manufacturing Management Institute, Design for Manufacturability course, a course in Utilizing the Six Steps to Six Sigma, and others. Numerous companies followed the lead of Motorola with their own corporate universities.

Those that develop an ". . . academy" (on whatever subject) generally begin with a review of their future directions and needs for customized educational offerings for their personnel. This type of review sometimes has shown that future directions, such as entrepreneurial supply chains, are going to be complex and large in scale, thus increasing the complexity of their management tasks.

In view of this, companies may decide to analyze how they should develop their supply chain and other professionals. They frequently conclude that a more formal and structured approach is necessary to prepare them for the future demands of entrepreneurial supply chains.

There are essentially two ways that a company can develop an "Entrepreneurial Supply Chain Academy":

1. They can do it all themselves, designing the program as well as providing the instruction. On the surface, this may appear to minimize their out-of-pocket expense and be relevant to the needs of their business than other approaches. Also, some companies like the idea of having control of the educational content and using their people as instructors. They feel that insiders can more easily relate the program content to their specific businesses.

   To some extent this may be true, but this is not necessarily the best way. For one thing, the *let's-do-it-all-ourselves* approach risks institutionalizing past practices that are not necessarily the most innovative or best approaches for the company. Those who put together the programs may not understand innovative approaches that are used by other companies. Also, internal personnel are not necessarily good instructors—they may not have the capability or inclination to teach, and they may not understand the subtle nature of teaching. Thus, there is the strong likelihood that participants may leave the programs feeling that "it's the same old stuff that we've been hearing for years" and/or "this is just like other stale company presentations."

Further, there is a difference between *education* and *training*. Education teaches awareness, knowledge, and understanding. Training teaches skills. When companies take a do-it-themselves approach, they are much more likely to be *training* and not *educating* their people. People need both—education and training—and steps should be taken to ensure that the content includes both.

2. The company also can outsource all or part of the Academy (some variation of this approach is recommended). The simplest outsourcing is to use outsiders to provide some of the instruction, while maintaining control of the administrative responsibilities and the content plan. On the other hand, some organizations outsource all of the program(s) after providing a general rationale for and outline of the educational offerings. The executive education units of Rice University, University of Tennessee, Arizona State University, Michigan State University, and others typically have the capability to handle outsourced supply chain programs, and Babson can handle outsourced entrepreneurship programs.

An Aside: When I was Professor of Management Practice and Dean for Executive Education in the Graduate School of Business at Rice University, a number of companies came to talk about custom-designed, company-specific programs on a variety of subjects. Sometimes for these programs we used Rice faculty, faculty from other universities, consulting firms' personnel, or executives from the client company—all to provide variety and appropriate content for the participants. At times, we took on all the program responsibilities; other times, we shared responsibilities with the client company. Some courses were presented in our own executive education facilities at the university and some were presented at company facilities, domestically or globally. We tried to work effectively with the client to make the programs meaningful and cost effective.

Possible Program Development Process

Many companies' academies employ cooperative relationships, as shown in Figure C.1. The company academy consists of five categories of providers for the education and training programs:

1. The core is the primary provider (inside or outside the company), surrounded by four classes of providers.
2. Company subject matter experts can ensure that the subject matter in the programs is appropriate to the company.
3. Universities are often used as providers, because they typically have a cadre of knowledgeable and experienced faculty members as instructors.
4. Other organizations (consulting firms such as McKinsey, Deloitte, Booz Allen, and others) can be used as providers because they often are on the leading edge of entrepreneurial supply chain developments.

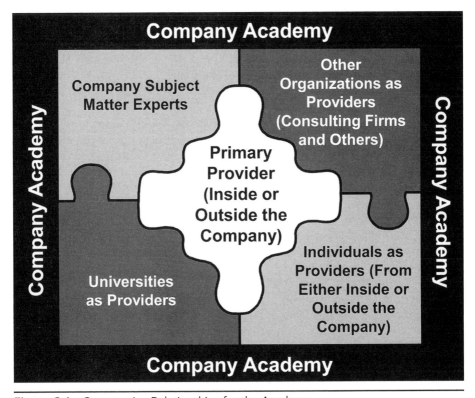

Figure C.1 Cooperative Relationships for the Academy.

5. Individuals (from inside or outside the company) can be providers when they have specialized expertise.

One possible process for proceeding with an academy is outlined in Figure C.2. This step-by-step process is practical and has been shown to be a useful guide to development of an entrepreneurial supply chain academy.

Company-Only Development Efforts

The first four steps as shown in Figure C.2 are for the company to accomplish before they begin working with a provider, whether the provider is internal or external.

Organization and Strategic Plan for Education. Before beginning an academy, the company will need to confirm its commitment to the program and to establish its organizational reporting structure. An important objective is to ensure that the project has support from the affected parts of the organization. As part of this process to set up the academy, the organization also will need to determine how the academy will fit into and support the company's strategic plan.

Needs Analysis and Initial Business Case. Next, the company should conduct an analysis of the detailed learning needs and create a business case along with recommendations for going forward. A needs analysis and business case should assist in gaining organization support. Further, the needs analysis provides a linkage with choosing the target audience.

There are three general elements to a needs analysis: objectives, approaches, and outcomes. The objectives of the needs analysis depend on the answers to a simple question: what is the current or the anticipated future situational gap of the organization between the "as-is" and the "to-be" circumstances? This may seem to be a simple question, but it has a host of difficult possible answers. For example, a company that is embarking on a specific, one-time entrepreneurial supply chain venture is in a much different situation than a company wishing to become culturally more entrepreneurial. The first, obviously, is relatively easier to accomplish and the required needs analysis and resulting education and training plan are simpler than the objectives of becoming culturally more entrepreneurial. Culture change is extremely difficult and usually needs the services of an experienced consultant to accomplish it.

The approaches for the needs analysis can begin with simple analyses of individuals' statements about their needs for education and training. But there also is the possibility of using highly sophisticated quantitative assessments. Such assessments might require, say, a culture diagnostic tool that is available from some consulting firms that specialize in culture change.

The outcomes from the needs analysis likely will vary for different organizational units, job classifications, and individuals, depending on their current versus desired future job requirements. Also, job requirements are multi-dimensional

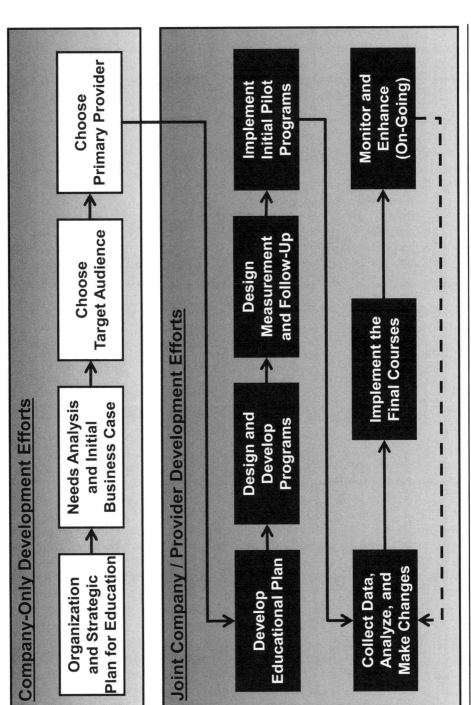

Figure C.2   Outline of a Possible Program Development Process.

metrics, and performance may be superior on some dimensions, satisfactory on others, and deficient on still others. These requirements for different outcomes will have to be ascertained as part of the process. The following possible outcomes have been adapted from several diagnostic tools to illustrate the needs analyses for education and training related to entrepreneurial supply chains:

- Provide a profile of the current entrepreneurial culture and how it impacts current performance of the supply chains.
- Characterize the culture that is required for success with entrepreneurial supply chains.
- Ascertain the differences between current and required cultures to assess the magnitude and types of culture change required.
- Determine the key strengths and opportunities inherent in the current culture that can provide a foundation upon which the culture change can be built.
- Clarify weaknesses and threats within the current culture that will necessitate concentrated efforts to achieve the desired entrepreneurial culture in the future.
- Benchmark current culture so as to measure progress in changing it to what's needed in the entrepreneurial culture.

Once needs analyses are completed, the outcomes can be utilized to put together the initial business case for going forward. This business case, among other things, should provide a sense of the amount of change that is required to achieve effective entrepreneurial supply chains.

Choose a Target Audience. The target audience for an entrepreneurial supply chain academy likely will come from middle management and professionals in the supply chain organization as well as appropriate individuals from sales and marketing, product development, finance and accounting, human resources, and legal. The needs analysis should provide the primary input to choosing the target audience.

Choose a Primary Provider. Choosing a primary provider is a major issue. As noted, the primary provider can come from inside or outside the organization. Inside providers usually are led by the human resources organization or by a training and development organization. Outside providers can be universities, consultancies, or dedicated educational firms. If the primary provider is from inside the organization, perhaps an experienced individual outside consultant might be used to assist the company in the process.

If the primary provider is from outside the organization, there likely will be a company insider named as the director of the academy. This person should have overall decision-making authority,

---

KEY IDEA

Carefully choose a primary provider relatively early in the process and then work with them closely.

working closely with the provider's academy director. When the author was responsible for executive education at Rice University, there was a more-or-less standard way of stating our learning from experience, and thus how it was preferred to work with client organizations in this regard.

An Aside: In one possible academy model, anticipate that the client will name a director of the academy who will have overall responsibility for its success. This person will work closely with a client-chosen faculty director to design and implement the academy. This (client) person will be responsible for recruiting (client) executives and professionals who can assist in program presentations, teaching alongside university faculty. He or she also will be responsible for ensuring that appropriate individuals are selected as participants in the academy. The (client) director will work with the faculty director in managing these relationships.

Preparing a questionnaire to send to potential outsourcing partners is recommended to get consistent responses to a request for information. The following is a possible questionnaire for potential providers of courses:

1. Are you interested in partnering with us to develop and operate, on a long-term basis, an Entrepreneurial Supply Chain Academy? (This question forces both the buyer and supplier of educational programs to consider this as a continuing series of educational opportunities, which is the recommended approach as contrasted with a single program.)
2. We anticipate that the following topics will be included in the academy curriculum.
   a. List key topics likely to be included.
   b. Do you have the capability to provide qualified instructors on these topics?
   c. If you do not have such capability, do you object to us sourcing those individuals or do you source them from elsewhere? Will you work closely with them to ensure a consistent and dependable quality of material and presentation?
3. Do you have programs for entrepreneurial supply chain management or related programs already in place that might be useful for our needs? (NOTE: Count on the fact that potential providers may not have something already in place that will meet your needs, which are likely to be different from those of others.)
4. Are you willing to adapt your own programs to suit our needs? (Note: Be wary of providers who are not willing to adapt to your needs.)

5. Have you worked with other companies on a similar program, and if so, for whom, when, and on what subjects? (Note: Recognize that potential providers may not be willing to disclose the "for whom" part of this question due to confidentiality concerns.)

6. Will you supply references about your work? (Note: Do not count on potential providers to supply any negative references! You will need to do your own due diligence beyond the references that are supplied.)

7. Are you willing to cooperate with other institutions or firms in the development and operation of such a program? (Note: Companies frequently have relationships, say, with consulting firms and universities, and your company may wish to leverage some of those.)

8. Are you willing to run courses at other locations (domestically and/or globally) such as at our company facilities or hotels? (Note: For global firms, it sometimes makes economic sense to take the instructor(s) to the participants rather than vice-versa. However, client companies that prefer to mix U.S. participants with people from around the world may bring non-U.S. participants to the U.S. for the programs. Others prefer to have geographic-centric programs at various locations.)

9. What kind of appropriate accreditations or certifications do you and/or your faculty hold? (Note: Companies may wish to use faculty that hold various certifications in addition to their academic qualifications. Certifications can come from organizations such as APICS: The Association for Operations Management, the Institute for Supply Management (ISM), and others. Further, university business schools should hold accreditation from the Association to Advance Collegiate Schools of Business (AACSB), and their executive education unit should hold membership in UNICON: The International University Consortium for Executive Education. UNICON does not "certify" executive education programs, but a university supplier should hold membership in UNICON as an indication that it is among the best in the world at executive education. For a university to join UNICON, it must demonstrate a high degree of competence in its executive education.)

10. Do you have any existing joint programs or relationships with any other organizations? If so, please specify the organization(s) and the type of programs. (Note: Increasingly, universities have partnership arrangements with other universities around the world. This may be useful for a global company, because it provides local, on-the-ground capabilities in different geographical areas.)

11. We would greatly appreciate you providing us with any additional information about your experience in this area, your reputation, biographical sketches of key people, and so forth. (Note: This open-ended question gives the potential provider an opportunity to suggest other strengths that it may have.)

Joint Company/Provider Development Efforts

Develop an Educational Plan. The next step is to develop an educational plan, such as the one shown in Figure C.3. This framework for an Entrepreneurial Supply Chain Academy is intended to represent an integrated set of educational offerings for entrepreneurial supply chains.

Five general curriculum areas for the entrepreneurial supply chain academy are suggested. The Venn-diagram representation illustrates that some of the material in all modules/courses should be common to provide an integrated framework. Some modules will have materials that integrate with only one or two others, and some material in each module will stand alone.

The heart of the program should be a set of modules generally in each of five areas of the curriculum. However, this framework may not work for every

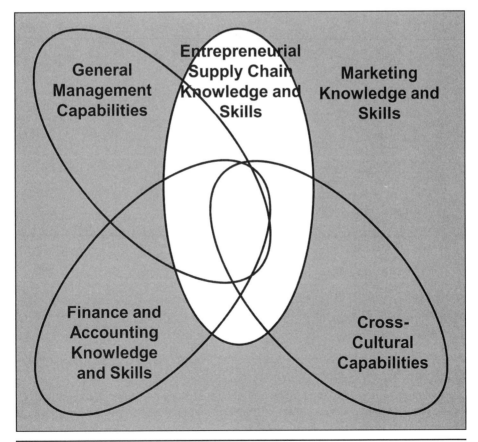

Figure C.3 One Possible Framework for an Entrepreneurial Supply Chain Academy.

company. Some companies may want more subject areas or fewer ones. Also, not every participant in the academy's program necessarily should take all modules, depending on their own expertise and needs, going forward.

Modules typically should include elements of entrepreneurship, supply chain management, general management, marketing, finance and accounting, and cross-cultural and global issues if the entrepreneurial supply chain efforts are going to include foreign components. Modules should be integrated with each other. The following is a brief list of possible topics that could be developed with, say, sections dealing with basic, intermediate, and advanced content:

1. Entrepreneurial Supply Chain Knowledge and Skills
   a. Basic, Intermediate, and Advanced Entrepreneurship
   b. Basic, Intermediate, and Advanced Supply Chain Management
   c. Supply Chain Strategy
   d. Demand Management
   e. Global Supply Chains
   f. Entrepreneurial Supply Chains
2. General Management Capabilities
   a. Business Acumen
   b. Intermediate Program for Managers
   c. Managing for Creativity and Innovation
   d. Practical Negotiating Skills
   e. Leadership Development and Coaching
3. Marketing Knowledge and Skills
   a. Basic, Intermediate, and Advanced Marketing Management
   b. Marketing Strategy
   c. Entrepreneurial Marketing
4. Finance and Accounting Knowledge and Skills
   a. Basic, Intermediate, and Advanced Finance and Accounting
   b. Finance and Accounting for Entrepreneurial Ventures
   c. Financial Statement Analysis
   d. Effective Techniques for Managing Financial Risk
   e. Cross-Border Financial Decision Making
5. Cross-Cultural Capabilities
   a. Cross-Cultural Issues in Business
   b. Managing People Effectively in a Global Context
   c. Leadership Communications with a Global Audience
   d. Leading and Managing High-Performance Global Teams

Design and Develop Programs. Someone once said that, when designing and developing programs, one should "start with last things first"—namely, begin by asking three related questions:

1. "What do you want to be different after the program is over?"
2. "What are the goals of each module?"
3. "What do you want to accomplish with the education or training?"

Extensive interviewing should take place prior to the actual program design. These interviews should be with potential participants as well as with key executives in the company. Some examples of interview questions may include:

- What do you want to be different after the education/training? What should the goals be? What do you want to accomplish with the education/training?
- How should we go about designing the programs?
- What should be the general content of the programs?
- What barriers might exist to achieving the goals?
- If you have participated in any of the company's education or training previously, what were your best and worst experiences with that? If you have not previously participated, why not?
- Please offer any other suggestions that you think might be helpful.

In addition to interviews, surveys are useful in the design phase. A free online software package, such as *Survey Monkey*, is a cost-effective way to survey relatively large numbers of people. However, electronic surveys, while useful, cannot substitute for in-person discussions.

Design Measurement and Follow-Up. How do you propose to follow up to ensure that the education/training programs actually achieve their objectives? What metrics are important to measure the results? Different measurements and follow-up actions should take place over a period of time (say, up to one year) after the program.

A good source for information on measurement and follow up is in a book by Robert L. Craig (Editor), *Training and Development Handbook*, Chapter 16.[iii] This book was sponsored by the American Society for Training and Development, a good source for design and development of education and training programs. Craig lays out a logical four-level evaluation scheme which is adapted below. This scheme has been used by numerous other authors, always somewhat uniquely. It is by and large an accepted approach to *evaluation*:

1. *Reaction.* How well did the participants like the education/training programs?

   Reaction should be measured immediately after the program before anyone has left the room. Most companies use what euphemistically is called a "smile sheet" at the end of the programs to give people an opportunity to provide overall ratings of how much they enjoyed them. A few questions can be asked about how they reacted to the material presented, whether their objectives were achieved, and how effective was the instructor. (However, not much useful new information is usually gleaned from these surveys.) Favorable reactions on the "smile sheets" do not necessarily mean that anything actually was *learned*! The instructor could have been a good entertainer, but whether he or she actually stimulated learning may be another question.

2. *Learning.* What was learned about entrepreneurial supply chains that the participants did not know beforehand?

    During the program is a good time to evaluate if *learning* is happening. Many instructors will use brief quizzes, exercises, or cases to examine how much learning actually is taking place. Plus, it gives the participants an understanding of their own learning process. These also provide the instructor with immediate feedback as to how his or her teaching is being received and processed.

    The real *learning* (that sticks) also should be measured sometime around three months or so after the program in order to give people the opportunity to reflect. Hopefully, they have also had a chance to try to use the learning. Learning is considered to be an increase in the amount of awareness, knowledge, understanding, and/or skills. Learning is an intellectual exercise and not a behavioral exercise—behavior comes up next.

    Usually a test is applied for measuring learning, perhaps a "before or after" test. A test, however, typically does not work for measuring, say, how attitudes have changed; that is a much more subjective measurement that applies to participant behavioral changes.

3. *Behavior.* What changes in behavior resulted from the programs, and how does this behavior manifest itself on the job?

    Behavior changes should be measured about six months after the program so that people can have a chance to practice the new behaviors which they learned. Craig (pp. 312–313) says that five requirements must be met before behavior actually changes (paraphrased here):

    1) The person must have both a desire to change and the capability to change his or her behavior.

    2) The person must know what new behaviors are expected and how they can demonstrate the new behaviors.

    3) The job and organizational climate should be supportive of the new behaviors. Also, the person must feel that failures with the new behaviors will not be punished. Otherwise, they will be reticent to even try the new behaviors.

    4) Advice, guidance, and mentoring should be available to the person who is attempting to apply the classroom learning to his/her behavioral change.

    5) Some form of incentives or rewards should exist to encourage people to change their behaviors.

Ultimately, real payoffs from the academy are the results that it achieves. That is the subject of the next level of evaluation.

4. *Results.* What were the actual and definitive results of the programs in terms of the company's approaches to entrepreneurial supply chains?

   Results should be measured at up to one year after the program, so that the organization has the time to implement changes and see results in action. Most education and training programs ultimately are intended to produce results of some sort, but measuring those results can be easy or difficult depending on the nature of the programs.

   On the one hand, measuring the results of a skills-training program for a new computer software package may be very easy. After the training, people either can or cannot perform their work using the software.

   On the other hand, measuring the results of a complex set of programs on entrepreneurial supply chains may be very difficult. Suppose that an entrepreneurial supply chain venture has been launched within one year of the programs. As a result, one might be tempted to declare victory for the programs. However, could the venture have been *more* successful if participants in the programs had learned more, behaved differently, and/ or implemented change differently? Or, what might have happened with the venture without the programs? Would it still have been implemented successfully? There is no way to know "what if . . ." results, but follow up is still important to assess the learning as best possible.

Implement Initial Pilot Programs. Running one or more pilot programs of the academy is important. Pilots involve a "run-through" with a sample of the target audience plus subject matter experts in attendance. The objectives of pilot programs usually are two-fold.

The first objective of the pilot programs is to ascertain if learning actually takes place with the sample of the target audience. This is the type of measurement that takes place while the program is in process. Failure of the learning reveals that something is wrong with the materials, the instructor, the methods of instruction, or whatever. Also, it could be that the learning objectives were inappropriate. Sometimes, the learning objectives turn out to have been too ambitious, and the participants were unable to keep up or the level of instruction was too advanced for the audience.

The second objective of the pilot programs involves the subject matter experts. They should attend the pilots in order to determine whether the material and the instruction are accurate and acceptable. Subject matter experts should be involved in the course design and development, but frequently they can also offer helpful suggestions during the pilot program.

Collect Data, Analyze, and Make Changes. This involves answering several types of questions from the pilot programs, such as:

- Was the subject matter accurate and at an acceptable level for the participants in the programs?
- Were the participants appropriately chosen for the course objectives, the subject matter, and the level of instruction?
- Were the instructors appropriate in terms of their knowledge of the subject matter and their instructional approaches and styles?
- Was the course design appropriate in terms of a variety of instructional methods, such as a mixture of lectures, exercises, cases, simulations, breakouts, and so forth?

Once the answers to these types of questions have been obtained, appropriate changes can be made.

Implement the Final Courses. All the appropriate changes are then made to the overall design, materials, and methods of instruction, instructors, and target audience. Then the entrepreneurial supply chain academy is ready to be implemented. Usually, this takes place in some form of a roll-out of one course module at a time.

Monitor and Enhance (On-going). There always will be the need for on-going monitoring and enhancement of the programs. Recognize that the programs will change over time; they will not stand still. Most instructors will want to continue to improve the programs. Organizations learn, just as individuals learn. The company's entrepreneurial supply chain efforts will evolve and improve, and the academy must change accordingly.

Instructors should keep in touch with what the company is actually doing with its entrepreneurial supply chain efforts. This likely will involve field trips to observe and interact with those who are leading and performing the effort to get their suggestions for what education and training is appropriate and what needs changing.

It is also suggested that a calendar be established to make formal changes to the programs, say, once a year or every six months. Putting a revision date on each program helps to make it clear just which version of a program is being used currently.

Notice that Figure C.2 has a feedback loop from "Monitor and Enhance (On-Going)" back to "Collect Data, Analyze, and Make Changes." This implies a continuous response to appropriate changes in the programs. Without this response, the programs will become stale and fall out of favor with the organization and the target subject matter of the academy likely also will fall out of favor. The entrepreneurial supply chain academy is ultimately linked with the effectiveness of the organization's entrepreneurial supply chains. Thus, it's imperative that the academy programs continue to be refreshed.

ACTION LEARNING PROJECTS (ALPs)

Action learning projects can be integrated with the entrepreneurial supply chain academies. This section discusses how ALPs can be organized and managed.

An ALP is an effective approach for team building, organizational learning, and beginning an entrepreneurial supply chain project for the company. ALPs frequently begin with an educational program on a particular set of issues that are relevant to the project. After completion of the project, each team studies its actions and experiences in order to learn from them and to go forward with project implementation.

> **KEY IDEA**
>
> ALPs seek to achieve competitive advantage through effective use of the company's strategic resources.

ALPs for entrepreneurial supply chains are intended to build cohesive teams and accomplish important tasks typically at the beginning of the project. They are appropriate because they are focused on getting the project started efficiently and effectively. Plus, they enable each person to enhance his or her own learning by reviewing the actions they have taken and the learning points arising from them. This should then guide future action and improve individual performance as well as overall organizational performance.

ALPs differ from traditional educational methods that concentrate on one-way presentations and lectures to communicate awareness, knowledge, understanding, and skills. Action learning focuses on projects that are undertaken to achieve organizational improvements. Capabilities are developed as a result that should lead to improvement of individual and organizational performance.

An ALP, as its name implies, should result in both *action* and *learning* in the context of a *project*. *Action* should accomplish something meaningful and useful for the organization. *Learning* should include both individual and organizational learning. *Project* implies a series of related activities usually directed toward some major output and usually requiring some period of time to accomplish. An entrepreneurial supply chain ALP frequently will result in an implemented venture. As a result, it is a fantastic way to ensure that such a venture is really put into operation.

Project management of an ALP involves managing the available and required resources to meet the project's technical, cost, and time constraints. Most ALPs are managed by a general, "pure project" type of organization in which a full-time team works on the project. The ALP leader has full authority over the project, but works collaboratively with the team members. Typically, ALPs cross organizational boundaries. Teams thus have a cross-discipline, cross-functional, and cross-geographic nature. The team members come from whatever parts of the organization are affected by the project, so the team leader needs to have the support of the entire organization.

> **An Aside:** One story—although unsubstantiated—is how senior management at Toyota will intentionally choose a project leader whose personality matches with the task of the project. For example, a project dealing with a sports car might be assigned a "fighter-pilot" type of leader; and a project dealing with a luxury car might be assigned an "executive" type of leader. This story presents an interesting idea and makes a good point! Match leader style to project needs.

Some people use the term "ALP coach" to describe the leader of the ALP. This is a good term because it has softer connotations than the term, "project manager."

The theory of action learning usually emphasizes the importance of *reflection* as necessary for learning. Said a little differently, ALPs emphasize the need for participants sometimes to "unlearn what they think they know!" For example, suppose you are asked to "reflect on what you know about supply chains." You may think through notions about the meanings of the words *supply* and *chains*. You may think about a one-way flow of materials from suppliers to customers, using the metaphor of a chain. You may recall the saying, "A chain is only as strong as its weakest link." But unless you reflect deeply, you might miss the notion that both the concepts of *supply* and *chain* are too narrow to represent the real complexity of what supply chains are all about.

As a personal exercise, contemplate the term *entrepreneurial supply chains*. Especially since you (hopefully) read the whole book up to this point, you should have a good idea of the meaning of that term. That contemplation should help with structuring an ALP and associated educational activities to help teach the concepts behind the term.

ALP projects bring theory into practice, providing opportunities for participants to reinforce their learning and for the company to achieve real business impact. ALPs are a version of "learning by doing," but supplemented by an educational component.

A six-step approach to an action learning project is given in Figure C.4. There may be one or multiple teams working simultaneously, each with its own entrepreneurial supply chain project. Teams usually consist of approximately seven to nine individuals, although there may be reasons for the team to be either smaller or larger. Rarely, however, will the team be smaller than five or larger than fifteen. Each step in the process has an example, and the six phases of the ALP should be integrated with the entrepreneurial supply chain academy. In this way, the education and training in the academy is linked in a practical sense with the project in the ALP.

Learning Session 1 usually is an educational session that extends from a couple of days to a week or so. It typically covers topics that will be useful to the team in their entrepreneurial supply chain project. For example, say the project is market

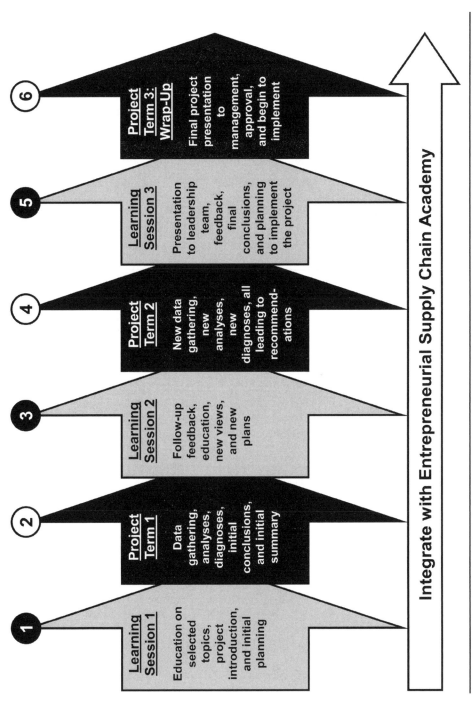

Figure C.4 Action Learning Project.

entry into an emerging market, such as India. The educational topics could be India-specific: introduction to market entry strategies; how to select a market to enter, such as *where* in India; how to analyze likely customers; how to estimate the size and growth rates of the market potential; how to estimate the strengths and weaknesses of possible competitors; and how to determine the extent of and need for knowledge of the local culture and business approaches, such as pricing and other practices, or trade barriers. As each module is presented in Learning Session 1, participants should be mindful of its application to the project and perhaps should write short papers on the subject. In this way, the team is able to relate the content of the education to its practical application on the project.

Also in Learning Session 1 there likely will be an introduction to the project and initial project planning.

Project Term 1 frequently lasts about four to eight weeks. During this time, the teams begin working project plans. Various data gathering and analyses are required. For example, suppose the project involves a modification to an existing product or service. If so, two likely components of the deliverable might be "re-design of the product or service" and "marketing the new or improved product or service." Data requirements might include past demand for the existing product or service. Analyses might include a forecast of demand for the existing plus a forecast for the improved product or service. Data gathering, analyses, diagnoses, initial conclusions, and initial summary are performed during this time period.

Learning Session 2 typically lasts two or three days. It includes follow-up feedback on what happened during Project Term 1 along with additional education, new views, and new plans. Don't forget that each learning session is integrated with the academy.

Project Term 2 usually lasts four to eight weeks and sometimes longer depending on the amount of work to be accomplished. This typically includes new data gathering, analyses, and diagnoses, all leading to new recommendations about going forward.

Learning Session 3 usually lasts two or three days. It typically includes a presentation to the company's leadership team, feedback, final conclusions, and planning to implement the project.

An Aside: I served as an advisor for a large ($20B+) company that was doing an ALP integrated with a supply chain academy. One team did an especially good job with its project, which was to develop a new product with which to enter a new market. After presenting their project to the Chairman/CEO and his staff, the team was asked in a very direct manner, "Do you know the time value of money?" Puzzled by the question, the team leader stammered a bit, and then was interrupted by the CEO questioner. He said, "If you knew the time value of money, you would have recommended that we get going on this project immediately and implement it six months earlier than you recommended. Your delay would cost us $1M in profit, and we might have lost out totally on the opportunity." This was a blunt, but nevertheless effective, way to get the team's attention to an important but overlooked idea.

Project Term 3: Wrap-Up is short, usually lasting two or three days, assuming that everything has gone well up to this point. It includes making the final project presentation to management, gaining approval to begin implementation, and beginning to implement the project.

Action learning projects are team based and directed at real opportunities for learning and innovation in companies. By reinforcing concepts beforehand and applying them to business issues of importance to the company, the projects relate theory to practice and generate fresh insights for individuals and their organizations.

Using ideas, concepts, tools, and techniques learned earlier, teams of participants work together to explore, analyze, and propose solutions to current issues in the company. Some keys to success of ALPs are:

Form Teams. Teams are formed to address an entrepreneurial supply chain issue or opportunity of importance to the company. Teams can be formed with a cross-section of participants such as discipline or functional areas, business units, geographies, and so forth. Teams can be effective in working on issues that cut across the entire company. An example might be a business opportunity that has connections to different parts of the company such as a new market entry strategy perhaps in an emerging market. The business opportunity might be to take selected products and/or services into that market in a coordinated and integrated manner. This requires all affected businesses to be part of the process.

Teams also can be formed with participants from a single business unit. GE prefers this latter approach so as to focus specifically on issues of importance to an individual business. (This is discussed later in this chapter with the article, "How GE Teaches Teams to Lead Change.") This way, they can see measureable results with everyone on the team being held accountable. GE calls this process "workout."

A second approach could work in cases where the entrepreneurial supply chain opportunity is a spin-off from an individual business unit. Continuing in the same vein as the first version of team composition, perhaps the business has the chance to enter a new emerging market with an individual product or product line. This would call for a team composed of individuals from a single business unit.

The objective with the team formation is to recognize that the project presents an issue or opportunity of importance to the company, and the teams should have reasonable opportunities for successfully achieving the objectives.

Plan the Project. The focus of the projects could be a challenge for the future, an opportunity that is currently untapped, or an improvement in a current process—all in the context of entrepreneurial supply chains.

Company management generally develops the initial concepts and presents an overview of each possible project along with its rationale and anticipated benefits from its implementation. Experts usually are identified as resources for the teams. Each team then meets to plan the project, being mindful of keeping the scope narrow and focused enough so the project is "doable" and yet wide enough to provide a significant impact for the company. Project planning should include the following elements.

- Define the deliverable for the project.
- Design the work breakdown structure including components of the deliverable and activities to be performed for each component.
- Define the data requirements and the analyses to be performed.
- Assign responsibilities and agree on milestones and time lines.

Gather Data and Perform Analyses. After the initial education session the teams apply the various subject modules to the project. As each module is presented in the program, teams should be mindful of its application to the project. In this way, teams are able to relate the content of the course to its practical application on the project.

Various data gathering and analyses likely will be required. For example, suppose the project involves a modification to an existing product or service. If so, one likely component of the deliverable will be "marketing the new or improved product or service," which will link into the marketing module of the course. Data requirements might include past demand for the existing product or service. Analyses might include a forecast of demand for the existing plus a forecast for the improved product or service.

Apply Additional Ideas, Concepts, Tools and Techniques. As the ALP unfolds with each new phase, additional ideas, concepts, tools, and techniques will be introduced. These may be incorporated into the project. Teams will continue to manage the project development, get feedback from fellow participants and others, learn about new subject areas, and plan how the teams will generate possible recommendations for the company.

Develop Recommendations and a Proposal for Implementation. Using relevant information from the project and the educational experience, teams generate and evaluate possible recommendations, choose a course of action that would make a difference, and consider what would be required to implement it. In preparation for the final part of the project, teams may develop a presentation that outlines the recommendations, describes the potential benefits, shows the models and frameworks the teams have used, and gives a potential implementation strategy to address the company context and potential roadblocks.

Move Toward Implementation. Teams likely will present their final proposals to fellow participants, company senior management, and others, giving their recommendations and describing how they might be carried forward. The final part of the project provides an opportunity to consider how to proceed with the change that the teams are recommending.

Check-in After Six Months. Teams need to report back to company senior management about which models, frameworks, and tools have proven most useful since the education programs and the project and give their reflections on the education and project as a learning opportunity. Also, and not to be forgotten, they should report on the actual results from the project.

HOW BAKER HUGHES EDUCATES AND TRAINS ITS SUPPLY CHAIN PEOPLE

In discussions with key executives who are responsible for Baker Hughes' education and training for supply chain personnel, the author asked if they provided education or training, and received this reply: "When my children were in middle school, they had sex education. We were not the least bit interested in them having training. There is a difference!"

After a somewhat humorous conversation about the differences between terms, they agreed that both education and training are necessary, but that their in-company emphasis has been on training and skills development. The title of their responsible organization is "Training and Competency Assurance," which is an interesting linkage between training and competency along with the word, *assurance*.

Baker Hughes' supply chain training and competency assurance approach has grown out of the company's strong tradition of technical training. The executives could have claimed that Baker Hughes historically has been a leader in technical training for the industry. As of 2010, the company has two "Education Centers," with the Eastern Hemisphere facility in Dubai and the Western Hemisphere facility in Houston. These facilities are equipped with onsite training rigs, test wells, and well-equipped classrooms staffed by subject matter experts who provide training and continuing education for new and experienced employees. The facilities are used by the entire company, not just by the supply chain organizations. They offer both technical and functional education and training.

The executives were asked about their hiring and development models for the supply chain organization. Their hiring model has the following top three criteria, and they argue that over the long run, leadership will be an individual's most important capability whereas the person's functional expertise will be the least important. They list the hiring criteria in the following order:

1. Leadership capability
2. Business acumen (including an understanding of entrepreneurialism)
3. Functional (supply chain) expertise

Having just done that, however, they argue that functional expertise "obviously is very important to the company's day-to-day operations."

Interestingly, their current people-development model for supply chain is exactly the opposite. As of 2010, they admitted that the supply chain is only in the first level of development. Specifically, for example, they are working to develop functional expertise in sales and operations planning (S&OP) as their top priority because of its importance to the operations of the entire organization. Admittedly, the company is somewhat late to the S&OP party, since other companies have been at it for many years. The result is that current supply chain development priorities are as follows, but they admit that these priorities will change in the future.

1. Functional (supply chain) expertise
2. Business acumen (including an understanding of entrepreneurialism)
3. Leadership capability

The company claims "excellent" capabilities in technical training, but less in these three areas.

When asked about certification, does Baker Hughes encourage or require APICS or ISM certification? The reply was, "No, not generally, but we used to and just let a certification focus lapse." They admit that such an emphasis likely will return in the future.

Organizationally, Baker Hughes has a Director of Supply Chain Training to whom Curriculum Managers report. For example, there are Curriculum Managers for Repair and Maintenance, S&OP, Logistics, and Quality, each of which is attached to a career ladder for personnel in those functional areas. The Director of Training has dual reporting relationships through the Human Resources organization and Supply Chain organization.

A CASE NOTE AND ARTICLES FOR FURTHER STUDY: Goldman Sachs

The cases are available at www.harvardbusinessonline.com. Readers should obtain copies of this case and use it to go beyond discussion in the book. These cases were prepared as the basis for discussion, rather than to illustrate either effective or ineffective handling of any particular situation.

In this chapter, Goldman Sachs' "Leadership Development at Goldman Sachs" is the case.[iv] Two articles from *Harvard Business Review*: "How GE Teaches Teams to Lead Change",[v] and "The Competitive Imperative of Learning"[vi] are also used. In combination, they present a portrait of how to develop an education and training program, adapted to a focus on entrepreneurial supply chains.

Background on Goldman Sachs

Goldman Sachs was founded in New York City in 1869 by Marcus Goldman, who later was joined by his son-in-law Samuel Sachs. The name *Goldman Sachs* was adopted in 1885. In 1906, it managed one of the largest initial public offering at that time, Sears Roebuck & Company. On May 7, 1999, the company converted to a corporation from a partnership through an initial public offering of common stock.

On their website, in 2010, the company stated: "Goldman Sachs is a leading global investment banking, securities and investment management firm that provides a wide range of financial services to a substantial and diversified client base that includes corporations, financial institutions, governments, and high-net-worth individuals." Goldman Sachs' activities are divided into three segments: investment banking, trading and principal investments, and asset management and securities services.

The background for the case begins in 1999 when a Leadership Development Advisory Committee was formed by Goldman's senior management to assess the future leadership development needs of their managing directors (MDs). Heretofore, the firm's development of its people (its "human capital") was, by their own admission, uncoordinated and insufficient for its substantial growth through the 1980s and 1990s. The need for talent development was multi-faceted and required technical skills, business and business development capability, leadership, and the Goldman culture. Historically, Goldman had relied on an apprenticeship model whereby senior leaders mentored junior colleagues through an employee development process. Most formal programs focused on the more junior members of the organization.

There were those in the organization who admired what Jack Welch had been able to do at General Electric with its development approaches such as "work-outs" and other team-based innovations, discussed later in this appendix.

The Leadership Development Advisory Committee decided to be guided by key objectives: developing the firm's key people; winning what they called "the war for talent"; expanding the pool of outstanding leaders; and maintaining quality and cultural strength throughout the organization.

Their research led them in four directions, which other companies could also use as an approach. First, they solicited a broad range of opinion from within the firm. Second, they analyzed the existing development activities and programs within the firm and how effective they were. Third, they benchmarked 14 "best-in-class" firms (listed in the case) to determine how they developed their people. Fourth, they worked with consultants who could bring outside views to Goldman's issues.

Important issues in the design of Goldman's development program were determined to be:

- Where would the programs be physically located? They admired GE's facility at Crotonville, NY, and felt that Goldman's needed to be a location that communicated a special commitment to leadership development. Also, they felt that it should be convenient to Goldman's headquarters in Manhattan.
- Who would teach the programs? They considered several options, including recognized academics, inspirational speakers, content-rich outside speakers, internal staff teaching full time, and practicing line managers teaching part time. Each had advantages and disadvantages.
- Academics would bring outside thinking to Goldman, but would not have the required in-depth understanding of the firm.
- Inspirational speakers would offer little more than entertainment.
- Content-rich outside speakers, while providing outside thinking, likely would be too generic or not sufficiently focused on Goldman.
- Both full-time internal staff and practicing line managers would increase the risk of institutionalizing existing practices.

What topics would be covered, and what would be the format of the instruction? GE had a number of two- and three-week programs at Crotonville, but Goldman felt that these would not work due to the fast-paced nature of their business. The same was true on a lesser scale for multi-day programs. One of the biggest obstacles for the culture-focused type of programs was the necessity for senior leaders to make the time commitment. Also, there was the consideration of how often programs should be run.

In addition to classroom instruction, what other methods of delivery were feasible for Goldman? The company was not enthusiastic about "traditional training" formats. Figure C.5 is a representation of Goldman's thinking about different delivery methods in an array of "company effectiveness" versus "importance to my development."

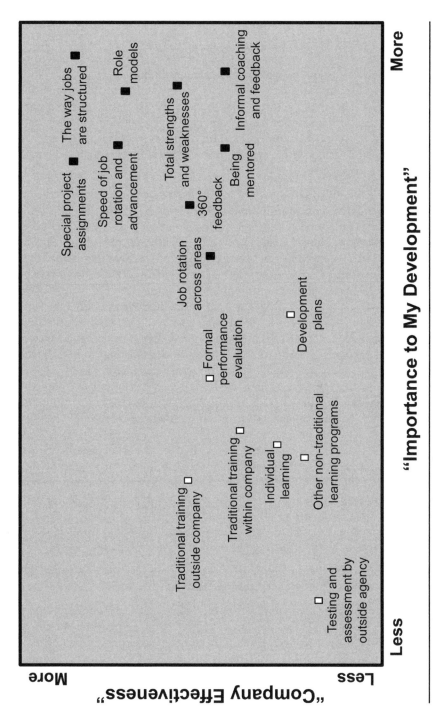

Figure C.5 What Matters Most? Adapted from: Groysberg, Boris and Scott Snook, "Leadership Development at Goldman Sachs," Harvard Business School Case #9-406-002, Rev. March 22, 2007, Exhibit 9, p. 22.

- There was relatively little support within the company for some of the methods. This included traditional training, individual learning, and training and assessment by outside agencies. Interestingly, this also applied to development plans and formal performance evaluation.
- There was much more support for other methods; the top four included the way that jobs are structured, role models, special project assignments, and the speed of job rotation and advancement. These four are all on-the-job type of development approaches and do not require formal education and training programs. There was support for what frequently is called action learning projects.

The target audience is always a subject of much discussion, and Goldman's focus was to be on their MDs, an important and rapidly growing group of senior leaders. As with many companies, Goldman's discussion revolved around whether the MD programs should have broad-based content with attendees from all over the firm. Or, should they be more customized and more deeply focused and thus include attendees from selected parts of the firm? Finally, should programs be offered for participants with varying amounts of experience?

<table>
<tr><td>KEY IDEA</td></tr>
<tr><td>Who should "own"
leadership development?</td></tr>
</table>

Regardless, Goldman had to decide who should "own" leadership development, and how it should be organized. The most obvious answer was to place it within the existing human capital management function. They also discussed creating a Chief Learning Officer position for the firm, which would be organized with appropriate staff support. But Goldman had never had such a position, and the firm rarely filled such a senior post with outsiders.

This case presents many of the same issues that other companies face when trying to decide on how to position leadership development for success within their organization. Like most business school cases, this one does not present firm answers to the issues. As stated, these cases are developed solely as the basis for discussion. Every company is different and may arrive at a different set of answers for the issues presented in the case. It is useful to look at how Goldman identified and wrestled with common education and training issues.

"How GE Teaches Teams to Lead Change"

This is an outstanding article written by Steven Prokesch of the *Harvard Business Review*. Prokesch had attended a four-day program, "Leadership, Innovation, and Growth (LIG)," at GE's Crotonville, NY, management development center. This program was focused on supporting the priority of GE's CEO, Jeffrey R. Immelt, of growing GE through expanding businesses and creating new ones rather than on acquisitions (what might be called "entrepreneurial supply chains."). In effect, the company wanted to concentrate on innovation and entrepreneurship as two of its most important growth engines.

The LIG program was successful for five reasons, all of which have applicability to education and training programs for entrepreneurial supply chains:

1. *Education and training of teams accelerated the rate of change.* The attendees were all from GE and usually only one GE business unit. Like at GE, learning alongside one's peers in the business strengthens both the rapidity with which the results are implemented as well as the quality of the results that are derived from the experience. These are called "custom-designed, company-specific programs" or simply "custom programs."

   This does not say that attending "open-enrollment programs" (say, at a major business school) is not valuable—just that it's different. An open-enrollment program usually has only one or two individuals from each participating company, and each person is there alongside others from other companies. They thus get to listen to and interact with people from entirely different organizational cultures who may have entirely different organizational issues. This has both good and bad aspects. The "good" is that participants get to know something about other organizations, and the "bad" is that what they learn may not be applicable to their own company.

2. *Participants were encouraged to consider the barriers to change, both the* hard *barriers and the* soft *barriers.* Hard barriers to change are those that are inherent in the business, such as an organizational structure that inhibits the sharing of information and experience. Soft barriers are those that are based on the behaviors of individuals and groups.

3. *Balancing the short- versus long-term challenges was explicitly addressed.* Experience over many years with companies is that the short-term frequently overwhelms the long-term. GE recognized this tendency and made explicit the importance of making time for dealing with long-term challenges.

4. *The course created a common vocabulary of change.* The language that is used can be important shorthand for ways to communicate. Referring to use of language, "The urgent crowds out the important." This is a useful saying that communicates better than other, less succinct, ways of speaking. Another example is the quote at the beginning of this appendix: "If you think education is expensive, try ignorance." Your author has often used this quote, or some variation of it, in conversations with executives who want to do executive education without spending the money that is necessary to do it well.

5. *The program was not an academic exercise.* The deliverable from the course was the first draft of an action plan for instituting change in the teams' businesses. Companies have found that adult learning is most effective

when there is some action associated with it. Plus, the whole notion of team-based programming implies that some tangible results are expected from the experience. Otherwise, there is no need to do it in teams—it's the difference between individual learning and organizational learning.

KEY IDEA
Adults usually need to apply their learning in a practical manner.

The following quote from the Prokesch article is very important. Immelt wanted the businesses "to weave innovation and growth into every aspect of their businesses. . . . In short, the purpose of LIG was to make innovation and growth as much of a religion at GE as Six Sigma had been under Jack Welch."

Prior to attending LIG, each business' leadership team had to do three things. First, it had to update its three-year strategy. Second, all members had to undergo a 360° review. Third, the business' success in creating an innovative climate had to have been assessed. The "innovative climate" assessment consisted of nine dimensions:

1. *Challenge and involvement*: team members feel connected and stretched by their work.
2. *Freedom*: team members feel empowered to try new ideas.
3. *Trust and openness*: team members feel safe in sharing ideas with others.
4. *Idea time*: team members have time to think about new ideas.
5. *Playfulness and humor*: team members see their workplace as easygoing and relaxed.
6. *Conflict*: team members experience personal tension at work.
7. *Idea support*: team members encourage others' ideas.
8. *Debate*: team members constructively discuss others' ideas.
9. *Risk taking*: team members can handle uncertainty.

Speakers at the session included external gurus, mostly from leading business schools and internal thought leaders who had demonstrated the value and usefulness of the ideas, concepts, tools, and techniques within GE.

The concluding day of the course was devoted to 20-minute presentations by the teams to Immelt. The presentations included a simplified version of the innovation and growth plans for the businesses in a "spirited give and take" with the CEO. The follow-up from the program included individual letters from executives to Immelt on what they, personally, intended to do as a result of the program.

"The Competitive Imperative of Learning"

The article "The Competitive Imperative of Learning" by Amy Edmondson[vi] is about organizational learning and specifically "execution-as-learning." Early in the article, Edmondson refers to General Motors and its failure to move beyond efficient execution. Her following comments are applied to GM's difficulties: "A focus on getting things done, and done right, crowds out the experimentation and reflection vital to sustainable success."

Experimentation and reflection are two of the core values of education and training for entrepreneurial supply chains. Recall the value of reflection (sometimes the words *introspection* and *reconsideration* are used although they are not, strictly speaking, synonyms) in terms of a psychological process of contemplation after an event, a process, or some activity has occurred—in this case, after the education and training has taken place.

Edmondson observed that companies tend to fall into some or all of the following predictable, self-sabotaging traps and do not learn from their experiences, due to:

An Aside: Some people claim that introspection can be traced to what we know about Socrates and the Socratic method of thinking as applied by an individual to his/her own experience. In this method, a series of questions are asked to stimulate critical thinking, to draw out individual answers, and to provide fundamental understanding of the particular problem under consideration.

- Critical information is kept hidden either by habit or intentionally. There are reports frequently in the press about companies and governmental agencies in which people did not "connect the dots." (For example, it is commonly alleged that warnings existed about the September 11th terror attacks regarding hijacked airplanes, but that law enforcement did not "connect the dots.")
- As mentioned, people do not have time to learn—the urgent crowds out the important. People do not take the time to reflect on their experiences and to learn from them.
- Companies' incentive plans often cause harmful competition to occur between and among organizational units. Thus, one unit will keep information from another when that information could assist in critical improvement programs.
- Many people have said, "If it ain't broke, don't fix it." In other words, companies think they can do no wrong. Companies' success tends to motivate them to keep doing the same things—the GM example is a good one. This can cause companies to lose sight of changes in its business environment.

The bottom line on "execution-as-learning" is that companies following this concept pay a great deal of attention to performing their key activities more efficiently than their competitors. But, they also focus on enhancing their rapid learning from the efficient execution of processes. The essence of this appendix is to assist readers in speeding up the learning process.

A FINAL WORD ON ENTREPRENEURIAL SUPPLY CHAIN EDUCATION AND TRAINING PROGRAMS

Perhaps because of his professorial background, your author is a strong supporter of education and training for both organizations and individuals. For individuals, this should be a lifelong endeavor.

The chapter began with a discussion of Entrepreneurial Supply Chain Academies as a framework for an integrated set of learning opportunities. This approach should be applied to a grouping of programs that are focused on a combination of programs, joined together for a common purpose. Such a framework should include the following groupings.

1. Entrepreneurial Supply Chain Knowledge and Skills
2. General Management Capabilities
3. Finance and Accounting Knowledge and Skills
4. Marketing Knowledge and Skills
5. Cross-Cultural Capabilities

These may or may not be appropriate or useful for all companies. Nevertheless, this is a useful starting point for developing the structure for an academy.

Also, ALPs should be used in conjunction with an entrepreneurial supply chain academy. Many companies successfully use ALPs to supplement the purely educational nature of an academy and provide hands-on learning experiences for the participants. In combination, an academy and ALP is a powerful approach to education and training for entrepreneurial supply chains.

> **KEY IDEA**
>
> Learning is like rowing upstream; not to advance is to drop back.

Finally, we saw how Baker Hughes, Goldman Sachs, and General Electric went about education and training for their employees. Good ideas can come from any of these three outstanding companies.

ASSURANCE OF LEARNING QUESTIONS

The following questions will help you to check yourself on the chapter content:

1. Go to the websites of APICS: The Association for Operations Management (www.apics.org) and the Institute of Supply Management (www.ism.org). Look up their education and certification programs and compare them with the ideas in this chapter.
2. Look up the term "corporate university" using a search engine. If this book is being used in an academic course, your instructor may want you to write a brief paper on the successful (or unsuccessful) use of corporate universities. In any case, given the results of your research, what factors seem to determine whether corporate universities succeed or fail?

3. Go to the website of the Project Management Institute (www.pmi.org). Look up what it says about *The Project Management Body of Knowledge (PMBOK® Guide)*.

REFERENCES

i. For information on universities' executive education offerings, some examples of strong capabilities in supply chain and entrepreneurialism are: Arizona State University, Executive Education, W. P. Carey School of Business; Babson College, Executive Education; Michigan State University, Executive Development, Broad College of Business; Rice University, Executive Education, Jesse H. Jones Graduate School of Business; University of Tennessee, Center for Executive Education, College of Business Administration.

ii. Gogan, Janis L., Handel, Michael L., and Shoshana Zuboff. "Motorola: Institutionalizing Corporate Initiatives." Harvard Business School Case #9-494-139, Rev. October 20, 1994.

iii. Craig, Robert L. (Editor). *Training and Development Handbook: A Guide to Human Resource Development*, 3rd ed. New York: McGraw-Hill Book Company, 1987.

iv. Groysberg, Boris, and Scott Snook. "Leadership Development at Goldman Sachs." Harvard Business School Case #9-406-002, Rev. March 22, 2007.

v. Prokesch, Steven. January 2009. "How GE Teaches Teams to Lead Change." *Harvard Business Review*. 99–106.

vi. Edmondson, Amy C. July/August 2008. "The Competitive Imperative of Learning." *Harvard Business Review*.

APPENDIX D

GLOSSARY OF ENTREPRENEURIAL SUPPLY CHAIN TERMS

"When I use a word," Humpty Dumpty said, in rather a scornful tone, "it means just what I choose it to mean—neither more nor less."
"The question is," said Alice, "whether you can make words mean so many different things."
"The question is," said Humpty Dumpty, "which is to be master—that's all."
— Lewis Carroll, *Through the Looking Glass*

Our words mean what we intend them to mean—nothing more nor less—at least based on the Lewis Carroll quote! However, the meaning of some words will not always be exactly clear to everyone, so a glossary can be useful. Please use it to refer to the meaning of terms within this book.

The glossary is a compilation of definitions adapted from several sources listed in the references at the end of this appendix. The definitions were adapted to focus meaning on the purposes of this book, although original sources were not cited.

ABC Classification: The classification of a group of items in decreasing order of annual dollar volume (price multiplied by annual volume) or other criteria. This array is split into three classes called A, B, and C. The A group usually represents about 15% of the items, and 70% of the dollar volume. The B group usually represents about 35% of the items, and about 20% of the dollar volume. The C group usually contains about 50% of the items, and about 10% of the dollar volume. The *ABC principle* states that effort and money can be saved through applying looser controls to the C-class items than will be applied to

A-class items. However, segmentation will not always occur so neatly; sometimes items are critical to operations and perhaps should be forced into the "A" class even though it should not otherwise be there. Synonyms: ABC analysis, distribution by value, Pareto analysis, Pareto's law, and the 80/20 rule.

Accountability: The outputs that a business endeavor is expected to produce and the performance standards that it is expected to produce.

Acceptance criteria: Those criteria, including performance requirements and essential conditions, which must be met before project deliverables are accepted.

Action-oriented biases: Biases that drive individuals and organizations to take action less thoughtfully than should be the case.

Activity: A component of work performed during the course of a project.

Anchoring and insufficient adjustment bias: A bias that causes one to stay with an initial assumption, leading to insufficient adjustments of subsequent estimates.

Asset impairment risk: The risk that an asset will deteriorate in value.

Assumptions: Assumptions, for planning purposes, are considered to be true, authentic, or certain without proof or demonstration. Assumptions affect all aspects of entrepreneurial supply chains and occur from their conception to their termination. Project teams for new ventures frequently identify, document, and validate assumptions as part of their planning processes. Assumptions and risks are closely related.

Assumptions analysis: A technique that explores the accuracy of assumptions and identifies risks inherent in the assumptions from inaccuracy, inconsistency, or incompleteness of assumptions.

Attribution bias: Pays more attention to easily attributable information, e.g., "Customer X likes that" so it must be good.

Availability bias: Pays more attention to what is available as opposed to what is most important.

Balanced Scorecard: A set of multiple and linked objectives, usually consisting of four objectives: financial, customer, internal, and learning and growth.

Benchmark: A formal representation of process performance expectations based on measurement of "best-in-class" enterprises.

Benefits: Features or attributes of a product or service that have value to a customer. Benefits have a financial equivalent that come in many forms, as services, convenience, experiences, emotions, and identity.

Bill of material, formula, recipe, or ingredients list: The list of components of a product, usually shown in a hierarchical fashion. This is the complete product description, listing not only the materials, parts, and ingredients, but also the sequence in which the product is created.

Business model: The way an enterprise will make money from an innovation.

Capital employed: The assets (capital) that are under the direct control of a business unit. This is often used as a ratio metric, such as "return on net capital employed."

Centralized organization: An organizational design in which business units operate under a hierarchical management and control system. A decentralized organization, on the other hand, allows business units operate semi-autonomously.

Champion: An individual who has the passion, value-creation, and human skills needed to make an important entrepreneurial supply chain venture happen.

Champion bias: The tendency to evaluate a plan or proposal based on the track record of the person presenting it, more than on the facts supporting it.

Change control: Identifying, documenting, approving or rejecting, and controlling changes to the entrepreneurial supply chain's business plan.

Change control board: A formally constituted group of stakeholders responsible for reviewing, evaluating, approving, delaying, or rejecting changes to the entrepreneurial supply chain venture's business plan.

Change control system: A collection of formally documented procedures that define how the venture's deliverables and documentation will be controlled, changed, and approved.

Change management: A structured approach to the transition of individuals, groups, and organizations from a current state to a desired future state. It is an organizational process aimed at empowering employees to accept and embrace changes in their current business environment.

Change request: Requests to expand, reduce, or modify the scope of the business plan; to modify policies, processes, plans, or procedures; to modify costs or budgets; or to revise schedules. Requests for changes can be direct or indirect, externally or internally initiated, legally or contractually mandated, or optional. Many entrepreneurial supply chain ventures only allow formally documented requested changes to be processed and only approved change requests are implemented.

Competitive risk: Changes in the competitive environment that could impair business success.

Competitor neglect: The tendency to plan for an entrepreneurial supply chain venture without factoring in competitive responses, as if one is playing tennis against a wall, not a live opponent.

Confirmation bias: A bias that leads one to over-weigh evidence consistent with a favored belief, to under-weigh evidence against a favored belief, or to fail to search impartially for evidence.

Conformity bias: Going along in order to conform, e.g., "if everyone else thinks so."

Corporate entrepreneurship: Entrepreneurship that occurs within an existing organization, such as building an entrepreneurial business venture as part of an existing business unit of a company. Corporate entrepreneurship usually is contrasted with start-up entrepreneurial ventures.

Cost drivers: Activities that directly cause costs to be incurred.

Disintermediation: The removal of intermediaries in a supply chain, the so-called "cutting out the middleman." Instead of going through traditional distribution channels, which had some type of intermediary (such as a distributor, wholesaler, broker, or agent), companies may deal with every customer directly, for example, via the Internet. Important results may be a drop in the cost of servicing customers and/or an increase in the speed of response.

Dysfunctional competition bias: A belief that one's company is the best at whatever subject is under discussion.

EBITDA: Acronym for "earnings before interest, taxes, depreciation, and amortization" that can be calculated easily from an income statement; a rough calculation of cash-based operating earnings.

Economic value added (EVA): A measure of economic value that is not distorted by accounting conventions. This is trademarked by consultants Stern, Stewart & Co.

Economies of scale: Reductions in unit costs due to more efficient utilization of assets usually through higher throughput.

Economies of scope: Reductions in unit costs due to more efficient utilization of assets usually through a larger number of products.

Elevator pitch: A short, memorable, and convincing presentation with a hook to gain interest and a close to ask for next steps.

Entrepreneur: One who organizes resources productively and bears the risk of the venture.

Entrepreneurship: The act of being entrepreneurial.

Excessive optimism bias: The tendency for people to be over-optimistic about the outcome of planned actions, to overestimate the likelihood of positive events, and to underestimate the likelihood of negative ones. This is prevalent especially in the early stages of an entrepreneurial supply chain venture when people are excited about its prospects.

False analogies: A bias that relies on comparisons with situations that are not directly comparable.

Five forces: An analytical technique developed by Harvard Business School professor Michael Porter. The five forces that impinge on a business unit are: customers, suppliers, substitute products, new markets, and competitive rivalry.

Force field analysis: An analysis that usually is part of a change management program. Force field analysis provides a framework for looking at the factors (*forces*) that influence a situation: forces that either are driving individuals or the organization *toward* a goal (forces *for* the change) or *hindering* movement toward a goal (forces against the change).

Groupthink: A bias that strives for consensus at the cost of a realistic appraisal of alternative courses of action. This is prevalent especially in the early stages of an entrepreneurial supply chain venture when people are excited about its prospects.

Halo bias: These biases occur when a project team assumes that an influential person or organization favors a particular course of action regardless of whether it is appropriate for the situation.

Historical bias: A conviction that history will repeat, e.g., "history has taught us that . . . will happen."

Inappropriate attachments bias: A bias that causes an emotional attachment of individuals to people or elements of the business (such as legacy products or brands), creating a misalignments of interests.

Illusion of control bias: An opinion that one is in control when it may not be true at all.

Innovation: The act or process of inventing or introducing something new; a new idea, invention, or way of doing something; the creation and delivery of new customer value in the marketplace that also provides a sustainable return to the entrepreneurial supply chain venture.

Innovation plan: A written document based on a value proposition for the entrepreneurial supply chain venture. It also includes all the other ingredients necessary for success, such as market positioning, business model, risk analysis, intellectual property, financial plan, product schedule, staffing, and return on investment.

Interest bias: A bias that occurs in the presence of conflicting incentives, including nonmonetary and even purely emotional ones. This is prevalent especially in the early stages of an entrepreneurial supply chain venture when people are excited about its prospects but have different opinions about its incentives.

Internal rate of return (IRR): The discount rate that is applied to any series of cash flows for which the present value of the cash inflows exactly equals the value of the cash outflows.

Intrapreneur: A person acting entrepreneurially within an existing company.

Leverage: A business financing approach that relies on a high percentage of debt.

Loss aversion bias: A bias that causes a tendency to feel losses more acutely than gains of the same amount, making people more risk-averse than a rational calculation would suggest. This bias inhibits individuals and organizations many times from going ahead with an entrepreneurial supply chain opportunity.

Management by example bias: A bias that causes individuals and organizations to generalize based on examples that are particularly recent or memorable. This can cause either over-optimism or excessive pessimism about entrepreneurial supply chain opportunities.

Market positioning: A plan for introducing a product or service into the marketplace, via an entrepreneurial supply chain venture. The plan identifies the specific customers in a market segment, how the product will be sold to them, and how the product will be described and advertised to them.

Misaligned perception of corporate goals: Disagreements (often unspoken) about the hierarchy or relative weight of objectives pursued by the organization and about the trade-offs among them. This is likely to cause a misalignment in the objectives of entrepreneurial supply chain ventures with the parent organization.

Misaligned individual incentives: Incentives for individuals in organizations to adopt views or to seek outcomes favorable to their unit or themselves, at the expense of the overall interests of the company. These self-serving views are often held genuinely, not cynically.

Mission statement: A short statement that communicates the core missions of the business, i.e., what the business is intended to accomplish.

Net present value (NPV): A summation of the current value of a series of cash inflows and outflows after adjusting for the time value of money.

NOPAT: An acronym for "net operating profit after taxes."

Normality bias: When individuals see a major change happening, but attribute it to being "just normal" and do not investigate its causes and effects.

Operations risk: The risk that originates in the core operating (or, frequently, manufacturing) capability.

Organizational development (OD): A planned, organization-wide effort to increase its effectiveness and capability. OD as an approach that is intended to change the behavior of an organization so that it can better adapt to change. OD can involve interventions in the organization's processes as well as organizational reflection, system improvement, planning, and self-analysis.

Overconfidence bias: Overestimating one's skill level relative to others' leading one to overestimate one's ability to affect future outcomes, take credit for past outcomes, and neglect the role of chance. It can apply also to entrepreneurial supply chain ventures in which overconfidence exists as to the prospects of success.

Pattern-recognition biases: These biases lead individuals and organizations to see patterns where none exist.

Payback: The amount of time that it takes cash inflows to pay back an investment.

Power of storytelling: The tendency to remember and to believe more easily a set of information when it is presented as part of a coherent story.

Product mix: The percentage of total sales that is attributable to each product or product line.

Project: Many entrepreneurial supply chain ventures are organized and managed initially as a project. A project usually is considered to be a temporary endeavor that is undertaken to create a unique product, service, result, or business venture.

Return on equity (ROE): A percentage calculated as net income divided by the equity employed in the business unit.

Return on investment (ROI): A percentage calculated as net income divided by the investment employed in the business unit.

Return on net capital employed (RONCE): A percentage calculated as net income divided by net capital employed in the business unit.

Risk: An uncertain event or condition that, if it occurs, has a positive or negative effect on the objectives of an entrepreneurial supply chain venture.

Risk breakdown structure: A hierarchically organized depiction of the identified project risks arranged by risk category and subcategory that identifies the various areas and causes of potential risks. The risk breakdown structure is tailored to specific entrepreneurial supply chain ventures.

Risk category: A group of potential causes of risk. Risk causes may be grouped into categories such as technical, external, organizational, environmental, or project management. A category may include subcategories such as technical maturity, weather, or aggressive estimating.

Risk management plan: This plan document describes how risk management will be structured and performed in an entrepreneurial supply chain venture. It is contained in or is a subsidiary plan of the overall business plan. The risk management plan can be informal and broadly framed, or formal and highly detailed, based on the needs of the venture. Information in the risk management plan varies by application area and venture size. The risk management plan is different from the risk register that contains the list of venture's risks, the results of risk analysis, and the risk responses.

Risk register: This document contains the results of the qualitative risk analysis, quantitative risk analysis, and risk response planning. The risk register details all identified risks, including description, category, cause, probability of occurring, impact(s) on objectives, proposed responses, owners, and current status. The risk register is a component of the business plan.

Saliency bias: These biases occur when the diagnosis of a particular situation is overly influenced by an outstanding success from the past.

Social biases: These biases arise from the preference for harmony over conflict. These can cause distortions of reality and can lead to difficulties with the entrepreneurial supply chain ventures.

Stability biases: These biases create a tendency toward what is known from the past in the presence of uncertainty about the future.

Status quo bias: These biases drive a preference for the status quo in the absence of pressure to change it.

Strategic alliance: A relationship formed by two or more organizations that share proprietary information, participate in joint investments, and develop linked and common processes to increase the performance of both companies. Many organizations form strategic alliances to increase the performance of their common supply chains.

Strategic imperative: A term commonly used in the development of a strategic plan. The strategic imperative is an urgent and obligatory need that the company must achieve for it to achieve its goals.

Strategic risk: An unexpected set of conditions that significantly reduces the ability of a business unit to implement its intended strategy.

Strategic sourcing: A wide-ranging methodology for identifying, qualifying, and utilizing key suppliers, frequently on a global basis.

Strategy: The strategy of an enterprise identifies how a company will function in its environment. The strategy specifies how to satisfy customers, grow the business, compete, manage the organization, develop capabilities, and achieve financial objectives.

Sunflower management bias: These biases cause a tendency for groups to align with the views of their leaders, whether expressed or assumed.

Sunk-cost bias: These biases cause individuals and organizations to pay attention to historical costs that are not recoverable when considering future courses of action.

Strengths, weaknesses, opportunities, and threats (SWOT): A strategic analysis technique that looks at these four components of a business.

Tactical planning: The process of developing a set of tactical plans, usually at the functional and/or business-unit level and usually spanning three years or less. Tactical plans usually are linked to strategic plans.

Value creation: A process that starts when a champion addresses an important customer and/or market need, writes down a value proposition, and then carries it forward to a full business plan and a successful entrepreneurial supply chain venture in the marketplace.

Value propositions: These are the fundamental ingredients of every entrepreneurial supply chain business plan. They are (1) the important customer and market need, (2) the product or service approach, (3) the benefits and costs resulting from the approach, and why these are superior to (4) the competition and alternatives. These ingredients define the value propositions required for every venture: at least one is required for the customer and another for either the enterprise and/or investors. Additional value propositions are required for the other stakeholders—partners, shareholders, employees, and the public. Effective value propositions are quantitative.

REFERENCES

Bias terms adapted from: Lovallo, Dan, and Oliver Sibony. 2010. "A Language to Discuss Biases." *McKinsey Quarterly*, (2), 44–45.

Innovation terms adapted from: Carlson, Curtis R., and William W. Wilmot. *Innovation: The Five Disciplines for Creating What Customers Want*. New York: Crown Business, 2006.

Operations management terms adapted from: Blackstone, John H., Jr. (Ed.). *APICS Dictionary*, 13th ed. APICS: The Association for Operations Management, 2010.

Project management terms adapted from: Project Management Institute (PMI). *A Guide to the Project Management Body of Knowledge (PMBOK® Guide)*, 3rd ed., 2004, pp. 350–380.

INDEX